NEW RUSSIAN DRAMA

RUSSIAN LIBRARY

R

■ □ ■

For a list of books in the series, see page 463

Columbia University Press / New York

Published with the support of Read Russia, Inc.,
and the Institute of Literary Translation, Russia
Columbia University Press
Publishers Since 1893
New York Chichester, West Sussex
cup.columbia.edu

Library of Congress Cataloging-in-Publication Data
Names: Hanukai, Maksim, editor. | Weygandt, Susanna, editor. Title:
New Russian drama : an anthology / edited by Maksim Hanukai
and Susanna Weygandt.
Description: New York : Columbia University Press, 2019. |
Series: Russian library
Identifiers: LCCN 2018052747 (print) | LCCN 2018059157 (e-book) |
ISBN 9780231545846 (electronic) | ISBN 9780231185103 (cloth)
| ISBN 9780231185110 (pbk.)
Subjects: LCSH: Russian drama—20th century—Translations into
English.
Classification: LCC PG3245 (e-book) | LCC PG3245 .N49 2019
(print) | DDC 891.7208—dc23
LC record available at https://lccn.loc.gov/2018052747

Cover design: Roberto de Vicq de Cumptich
Book design: Lisa Hamm

CONTENTS

FOREWORD

What Thomas Hobbes Knows About Today's Russia

RICHARD SCHECHNER

When I was growing up in the theater more than a half-century ago, it was all Russia. Yes, we knew about Brecht, barely, and the drama—plays—was American and international; but the *theater*, that was Russian. Not purely Russian, but doubly filtered. Stanislavski was with us in translation, first *My Life in Art* and then *An Actor Prepares*. But more important, Stanislavski's deputies controlled the "serious" American theater (not the commercial side of Broadway). The Group Theatre people were vitally working—Harold Clurman, Elia Kazan, Stella Adler, Sandford Meisner. And before that, in 1923, defectors from the Moscow Art Theater/USSR, Maria Ouspenskaya and Richard Boleslavsky, started the American Laboratory Theatre, bringing to the New World what they knew of Stanislavski, firsthand. The impact of Stanislavski then—and even now—cannot be overestimated, in the theater and then in the movies and on to television. A kind of realism, softened to be sure (as you will see when you read the book in your hands), but pedestrian enough in the way that postmodern dance featured the way "people really moved." The American Lab and the Group Theatre featured not so much behavior, the outside, but the inside—the way "people really felt." At least that was the guiding principle.

And then came Lee Strasberg, another Group Theatre alumnus, who thought he knew Stanislavski better than the master knew himself. And maybe Strasberg was right. He took Stanislavski's relatively early way of working by means of "affective/emotional memory" and developed it into The Method—mining the "real emotions" of actors and inserting these emotions into the onstage life of the characters. It was not so much building a character that is other as recollecting and abreacting one's own emotions and then applying these to the role. In today's lingo, it was a cut-and-paste job. To put it bluntly: the tears, delights, rages, sexual arousals, jealousies—the whole gamut of human feelings—had once really happened to the actors as people. And now they learned how to make them really happen again, and again. Strasberg taught actors how to access these very powerful personal emotions, repeat them, and skillfully embed them in the behavior of the characters. This kind of "really real" was new for the American stage. It worked even better on film, where editing, camera angle, close-ups, and miking brought movie audiences right into the emotional turmoil and triumph of the characters.

We—I and a bunch of others kind of like me (The Living Theatre, The Open Theatre, Robert Wilson, Richard Foreman, Mabou Mines, postmodern choreographer-dancers, Happeners) rebelled against all this. Who did we look to for guidance? Not Bertolt Brecht, who was in the United States from 1941 to 1947—too early to directly affect us. Somewhat to Brecht's colleague, Erwin Piscator, who emigrated to New York in 1937 and ran his Dramatic Workshop from 1940 to 1951. Judith Malina, cofounder of The Living Theatre with Julian Beck, was one of Piscator's students.

No, we took after Vsevolod Meyerhold, Yevgeny Vakhtangov, and Michael Chekhov—students, then colleagues, then rebels in relation to Stanislavski. Expressionism, biomechanics, and the "psychological gesture" replaced Stanislavski's soft-tinted naturalism. For Meyerhold, the life of the collective mattered most: the emerging epoch of the machine, the factory worker, the utopian side of the Russian Revolution. All that was cut down by Stalin and his murderous regime and overtaken by "Socialist Realism," a grotesque parody of both socialism and realism. Meyerhold was arrested and tortured by Stalin's police in 1939, then murdered in 1940. In 1922, the year of his death, Vakhtangov directed Ansky's *The Dybbuk* in Hebrew at the Moscow Art Theater. Four years later, Habima got away to Palestine where it became, in time, Israel's national theater. Michael Chekhov came to America in 1938 and revitalized acting, offering a powerful alternative to The Method. What the avant-garde of the American '60s took from these Russian émigrés, followers-then-not-followers of Stanislavski, was an intense dedication to both process and experimentation—always searching for the "authentic," the "real," even if these were not "naturalistic" in terms of current style. The range of outflow from Russia/USSR up to the 1930s was extraordinary.

But then came World War II and after that the Cold War. The Iron Curtain descended between Eastern and Western Europe, cutting off the exchange of culture and arts between the Soviet Union and the West. We on our side of the Curtain knew relatively little about what was going on in most Soviet theaters. What came over here before 1989 were productions designed as "cultural exchanges": ersatz, politically optimistic, and designed to make everyone feel (a little) better. Worse, most American theater people didn't care to know what was happening. We had our own Stanislavski canon; we had Michael Chekhov, too; we had the goods. When light came from the East again in the mid-1960s, the supernovae burst from Poland, a restless Soviet satellite. Superstars Jerzy Grotowski and Tadeusz Kantor exploded in Western Europe and America. The glow lasted thirty years. Meanwhile, from farther East, new impulses came from India, Japan, Indonesia, and later China. At about the same time, and continuing to the present, came postmodern dance, performance art, and postdramatic theater. The events of 1989 didn't make much of a difference. Post-Soviet Russia shared the fate of Stalinist USSR: irrelevant to what was happening in the West.

The plays in this book, and the productions of them, will change that. Not, I think, by introducing something new to those who are conversant with Sarah Kane, Annie Sprinkle, or any of the thousands of porn and violence sites available online at the click of a mouse. What's shocking in the plays published here is not the language, the numbingly drab and repetitious dramaturgy, the unappealing characters, or the xenophobia and violence, but the impression they give of contemporary Russian society and outlook, especially the outlook of youth. A subtext of the plays is that both the authors and the texts' inhabitants and speakers (hardly "characters" in the dramaturgical sense) are lost, bitter, and sometimes funny. To these beings, the world beyond Russia exists only via the internet—tantalizing, but as far away and as impossible to reach as Alpha Centauri. Still, there is a resonance with Western European and American nihilism. Where do the speakers in the plays in this book live? In provincial cities, maybe even in Moscow. It hardly matters: wherever their physical bodies reside, the speakers are floating in the never-never land of the internet. Anton Chekhov's three sisters yearned, "To Moscow! Moscow! Moscow!" More than a century later, their successors have arrived in the capital. Now what?

For me, the most scathing work is Teatr.doc's *September.doc*—verbatim transcriptions of blogs, chats, and forum posts after Chechen rebels took about 1,200 people hostage in a school in Beslan, North Ossetia, in 2004. On September 3, Russian troops stormed the school; 334 died, 186 of them children. Killed by whom? The rebels, the liberators? Horrible. The rawness of the not-made-for-the-stage speech acts that is *September.doc* made me wonder how Stanislavski, Meyerhold, or Vakhtangov might stage such . . . documents.

Stanislavski would reject the texts outright. "This is not drama!" he would say. Vakhtangov, also, would condemn the crudity and lack of "imagination." Meyerhold might put *September.doc* onstage. He might distribute some of the texts to spectators. He might form a chorus of *shahids* (martyrs), project footage of the Beslan siege on giant screens, and have a flock of birds (made from paper, Japanese style) fly across the proscenium and out into the auditorium to illustrate the lines, "When our brothers died, Allah placed their souls inside the green birds that fly to the rivers of paradise, eat the fruit of paradise, and rest in the golden lanterns in the shadow of the heavenly canopy." But of course this is not Teatr.doc's intention. This would "elevate" the text, transform it, make theater from it. For Teatr.doc—and I take its values as representative of the plays in this book—the idea is to show as plainly as possible the difference between the fantasy of a *shahid* and the brutal "real words": "Fucking Chechens took a school hostage! Shouldn't have started shit with them! Shoulda just bombed the fuck out of Chechnya and not fucked around, but they dragged their feet. The whole thing is fucked. Completely. . . . Fucking monkeys."

Or like the characters in *Plasticine*, "They are silent, their faces empty." Or again from *Plasticine*, "They should shoot them at birth! Or before birth! Who has kids like that, anyway?" This is Russia today, or at least some of Russia: its anomic intellectuals, its younger artists, its bourgeois-manqué. The Russia of oligarchs is not represented, and the myriad poor barely so. These are plays expressing a postapocalyptic situation without specifying what the apocalypse was. Is it USSR nostalgia? Not on the surface. But maybe underneath, it is a yearning for at least the rituals of forced communist optimism—combined with the realization that post-Soviet society isn't going anywhere. And also, to some degree, it is an indulgence of the coarse, the nihilistic, the pruriently adolescent. Like some quasi-porn comic books and violent video games, or twenty-first-century renditions of Warhol.

Taken as a unit, these playwrights have for the most part surrendered to Putin's grotesque post-Soviet dry rot. They don't advocate, or hope. These plays are short on Brechtian irony, Ibsenian outrage, or Milleresque sentimentality. I think I get it: for these writers, life in Moscow, or life in Chechnya, or Belarus—all over urban Russia and its sphere of influence and hostility, both metropolis and hinterland—is, to quote Thomas Hobbes, "No arts; no letters; no society; and which is worst of all, continual fear, and danger of violent death: and the life of man, solitary, poor, nasty, brutish, and short" (*The Leviathan*, chap. 12).

INTRODUCTION

Drama Against "Theater" and Theater After Drama

MAKSIM HANUKAI AND SUSANNA WEYGANDT

What gives a play, a theater performance, a work of contemporary art that elusive sense of authenticity, the feeling that it can put you in direct, unmediated contact with the real? Recalling the initial inspiration behind the Moscow Art Theater (MAT, founded in 1898), the great Russian director Konstantin Stanislavski observed:

> Our plan for the new enterprise was radical. We rebelled against the old style of acting, "theatricality," spurious emotion, declamation, overacting, against stupid conventions in the staging and the sets, against stardom, which marred ensemble work, against the whole way performances were put together and the triviality of the repertoire of the time.
>
> In our efforts to demolish and rebuild the art of the theatre, we declared war on all conventions, wherever they occurred, in acting, directing, sets, costumes, interpretation, etc.[1]

What the young Stanislavski rejected was not "theatricality" per se—he was no stranger to theatrical artifice and even excess—but those conventions and practices that impeded the portrayal of what he called "the realism of life."[2] For the MAT's inaugural production of Aleksey Tolstoy's *Tsar Fyodor Ioannovich,* Stanislavski led an expedition to the Russian provinces in search of inspiration and remnants of ancient material culture, hired expert costume makers, and commissioned expensive and historically accurate set designs (breaking with the established practice of recycling sets from earlier productions). He also began to strictly enforce the imaginary boundary separating the audience from the stage and, over time, developed a system of techniques and strategies meant to help actors give more psychologically convincing performances. The immediate aim of these innovations was to make audiences forget they were at the theater, to make them respond to the action on stage *as if* it were real. More importantly, it was to make theater responsive to the changing realities of life at the turn of the twentieth century, preventing audiences in an age of great social and scientific transformation from repeating Stanislavski's own favorite phrase: "I don't believe it!" (*Ne veriu!*).

A hundred years after the founding of the MAT, at the turn of another century, Russian theater makers once again "declared war on all conventions." Many of their pronouncements sounded strikingly familiar: "what they call 'theater' today is an entertaining spectacle," "theater is dead, and the one we have . . . is a lie, a great illusion," "what is important is lack of affectation and clarity of expression," "a theater where no one acts."[3] We have, in effect, another attack on "theatricality," one of many that has punctuated the history of Western theater. But certain affinities with Stanislavski and nineteenth-century playwrights such as Chekhov and Strindberg notwithstanding, the playwrights, directors, and actors who came together to form the New Russian Drama movement were operating within a very different cultural and political context and, as a consequence, with a different concept of the real.

Spawned in the minds of largely provincial playwrights who first *read* (rather than staged) their plays at sparsely attended festivals and in cramped, bare-walled basements, the early works of New Drama startled and angered audiences with their hypernaturalistic portrayals of sex and violence, their scathing critique of contemporary Russian mores, and their at times inadvertent flaunting of the norms of "good writing." Traditionalists dismissed these works as *sramaturgy* (from *sram,* "shame") and *chernukha* (from *chernyi,* "black," which is associated in Russian with filth and misery).[4] But like any movement daring enough to offer a fresh vision of reality, New Drama slowly began to attract a growing number of enthusiasts and to expand its reach. In the two decades of its contentious existence, New Drama has helped a new generation of Russian audiences once again believe in the theater. With the movement currently facing another critical juncture, we offer a new English-language anthology of its representative works.

■ □ ■

The rise of New Drama cannot be understood without a glance back at the recent history of Russian theater—a history that closely followed (and at times anticipated) developments in Russian culture and politics.

Theater and politics have long been deeply intertwined in Russia. The theatricalization of life was one of the rallying cries of the Russian avant-garde, which embraced the 1917 revolution in part because it promised to transform everyday life into living theater. The performative turn enacted by artists in this period radically expanded the very notion of theater: no longer confined to the scenic realization of dramatic texts, revolutionary performances drew on popular forms such as the variety show and the circus, often spreading beyond the physical confines of traditional theaters to occupy public squares, factories, and even trains. Soviet citizens in the late 1910s and 1920s were treated to a kaleidoscope of theatrical styles and genres—from Vsevolod Meyerhold's experiments in biomechanics and the absurdist theater of the OBERIU group to traveling agitprop performances and participatory mass spectacles. This period of intense experimentation lasted until Stalin's consolidation of power in the late 1920s. In 1932 the Central Committee of the Communist Party disbanded all existing literary and artistic groups and organizations, replacing them with centralized professional artist unions; and at the First Soviet Writers' Congress in 1934 Socialist Realism was declared to be the official method for artistic production. Defined by Andrei Zhdanov as a combination of realism and revolutionary romanticism—"the most stern and sober practical work with a supreme spirit of heroic deeds and magnificent future prospects"[5]—Socialist Realism proved to be utterly divorced from any authentic experience of Soviet reality. Showing the triumphs of positive heroes over forces hostile to the communist project, theater now had to glorify Soviet achievements in ways that were comprehensible to the uncultivated masses. Avant-garde experimentation was attacked on the grounds of "formalism." At the same time, a superficial form of Stanislavski's "system" was officially canonized as part of Stalin's campaign against nonrepresentational art—in effect, entrenching psychological realism in Russian theater for decades to come.

Restrictions on cultural production were relaxed, however, after Stalin's death in 1953, bringing a new generation of artists and audiences to the theater. Soviet society in the period of late socialism was fervently theatrical. Although censorship was never eliminated and many Western authors remained taboo, theater makers began to test the boundaries of artistic speech through the camouflaging techniques of Aesopian language. Ordinary citizens went to great lengths for the chance to attend Yuri Lyubimov's Taganka and Oleg

Efremov's Sovremennik (Contemporary) theaters in Moscow, contributing to the virtual sacralization of theater in Soviet culture. The playbills of select theaters now included daring adaptations of the classics, such as Lyubimov's legendary staging of *Hamlet* starring the singer-songwriter Vladimir Vysotsky, and, increasingly into the 1980s, works by contemporary playwrights that went against the dictates of Socialist Realism. Alexander Vampilov, Mikhail Roshchin, and Ludmila Petrushevskaya painted a darker, more sinister picture of reality than had been previously possible in Soviet theater. Their works paved the way for the brutal realism of New Drama. The 1980s also saw the proliferation of small theater studios and amateur theater circles in both the capitals and the provinces. In a country with few independent civic institutions and officially without religion, theater became a substitute for the church, the parliament, and the free press.

All of that changed after the collapse of the Soviet Union in 1991, which plunged Russian theater into what some have described as a decade of stagnation.[6] Historians cite various reasons for theater's decline in this period: the rate of emigration among educated Russians was high; the economy was in free fall; new social and civic institutions, however imperfect, had begun to emerge; and theater now had greater competition from other media, such as commercial film and television. The institutional organization of Russian theater also underwent radical change: whereas the state held a total monopoly on theater in the Soviet Union, censoring its contents but also guaranteeing its livelihood, the post-Soviet period gave rise to a more complicated network of state-, municipally, and privately funded theaters, many of which struggled to survive in Russia's new economic reality. The American theater critic John Freedman, who has done perhaps more than anyone to promote contemporary Russian playwriting in the United States, observes that the collapse of the former administrative system left gaping holes in theaters' budgets: "Subsidies for production, salaries, and infrastructure were slashed or wiped out, and nothing was instituted to remedy the situation. Inflation hit so hard that even theaters with money at the beginning of the month were not sure it would be worth anything the next." He also recalls that the unprecedented rate of social and political change had a "stunning" effect on the Russian public, that "historical disclosures made daily, even hourly, on live television in the early 1990s were so grippingly dramatic that theater attendance plummeted."[7] Those who did attend theater wanted to escape, rather than relive, the hardships of post-Soviet life. As a result, Russian theater completely lost touch with contemporary reality.

This is not to say that Russia lacked groundbreaking experimental theater in those years. In fact, as Birgit Beumers and Mark Lipovetsky point out in a seminal study of New Drama, Russian theater in the early 1990s was changing, absorbing the artistic energy of the theater studios that emerged in the previous decade, many of which were transformed into larger theaters with charismatic directors at their helm.[8] In their search for new playwriting, however, these auteur directors rarely strayed further than well-known Perestroika authors such as Petrushevskaya and Nina Sadur. The repertoires of their theaters consisted largely of new interpretations of Russian and foreign classics, as well as plays by authors who had been forbidden in the Soviet Union: Samuel Beckett, Eugène Ionescu, Russian avant-gardists such as Velimir Khlebnikov and Daniil Kharms. Reflecting a growing international trend to reach beyond the dramatic text (more on this later), many directors also turned to adapting short stories and novels. Kama Ginkas, for example, created a whole series out of the works of Dostoevsky, and Pyotr Fomenko adapted Pushkin's *The Queen of Spades* and Gogol's *Dead Souls*. These directors had little interest in the work of young playwrights, who were shut out of their experimental theaters no less than from the booming entertainment industry. With few possibilities to see their works on stage, the playwrights who came of age in this period came to be known as Russian theater's "lost generation."

The movement that eventually came to be known as New Drama has its roots in the private initiatives of veteran playwrights such as Viktor Slavkin, Mikhail Roshchin, Alexei Kazantsev, and Nikolai Kolyada, who sought to nurture young talent by founding new journals of dramaturgy, festivals, playwriting schools, and theaters (see the chronology for details). The annual festival of young playwriting Lyubimovka—initially held at Stanislavski's family estate on the outskirts of Moscow—became an especially important forum for the alternative theater crowd, providing an opportunity for young playwrights to share their work and come into contact with potential collaborators. A reading of Olga Mukhina's *Tanya-Tanya* at this festival in 1995 led to its staging at the Fomenko Workshop Theater the following year, and after creating a sensation with his rowdy staging of Vassily Sigarev's *Plasticine* at the 2000 festival, the now world famous theater director Kirill Serebrennikov was invited to stage two other influential works of New Drama at the MAT: the Presnyakov Brothers' *Terrorism* (2002) and *Playing the Victim* (2004).

Among the best-known works of New Drama thanks to a film Serebrennikov made of it in 2006, *Playing the Victim* exhibits many features that characterized the early phase of the movement: e.g., aimless and socially alienated heroes, the use of obscene language (traditionally taboo and, as of 2014, again subjected to censorship in Russia), matter-of-fact portrayal of sex and violence. Estranged from his parents and unable to form meaningful relationships with anyone around him, the play's hero Valya makes a living reenacting the final movements of murder victims for a homicide investigation team, pretending, at different moments in the play, to be stabbed, drowned, poisoned, and shot. His strange job offers him "inoculation" against death, we are told, but it may also be a way of muffling the sense of meaninglessness that pervades his life. Valya's behavior brings to mind the nihilistic heroes of British "in-yer-face" playwrights Mark Ravenhill and Sarah Kane, both of whom came of age under the neoliberal leadership of Margaret Thatcher. But the play is also deeply rooted in the Russian experience of the post-Soviet period, when the loss of an earlier value system, combined with poorly executed market reforms, resulted in the erosion of the social fabric. Valya's case becomes symptomatic of a society caught in a vicious cycle of (self-)victimization and violence. The legitimizing myth of the Putin regime has been that it put an end to the rampant violence of the "wild 1990s" (a term popularized by Putin's United Russia party in the run-up to the 2007 parliamentary elections). Written in 2002, three years after Putin first came to power, *Playing the Victim* suggests that violence had simply become routine.

While the success of Mukhina and the Presnyakovs showed that contemporary playwrights were finally breaking into the mainstream, the majority of their colleagues continued to be shunned by the establishment. At the turn of the century, several new theaters appeared to help remedy this problem: The Playwriting and Directing Center (f. 1998), Teatr.doc (f. 2002) and Praktika (f. 2005) in Moscow, and Kolyada-Theater (f. 2001) in Ekaterinburg.

One of Russia's few truly independent theaters, and the host of Lyubimovka from 2004, Teatr.doc has in many ways become the spiritual home of New Drama. The ".doc" in the title stands for "documentary," signaling the most important new tendency popularized by this theater. In fact, documentary theater is native to Russia: it was one of several forms of "literature of fact" (*literatura fakta*) that sprung up in the immediate aftermath of the 1917 revolution. However, along with other avant-garde trends, it largely disappeared from the Soviet Union in the 1930s only to be rediscovered again at the turn of the twenty-first century thanks to a series of seminars and workshops conducted in Moscow by delegates from London's Royal Court Theatre. Trained in the "verbatim" technique—a method for constructing plays on the basis of interview transcripts and other primary documents—Teatr.doc's artists introduced audiences at their small basement theater to heroes never before seen on the Russian stage: migrant workers from Central Asia, prison inmates, prostitutes, sexual minorities, etc. From the start, Teatr.doc also used theater to respond critically to social and political crises. It was only at Teatr.doc, for example, that one could see plays about the 2004 terrorist school siege in Beslan or about the prison murder of whistleblower Sergei Magnitsky. There have also been shows about the 2011–2012 protest movement in Russia, Russian political prisoners, and the war in Ukraine.

Written by Teatr.doc's founders, the husband and wife team of Mikhail Ugarov and Elena Gremina, *September.doc* helps us understand why documentary theater has become such an important, if controversial, trend. The play centers on the September 1, 2004, terrorist school siege in the North Ossetian town of Beslan, which, after what many consider to have been a botched rescue operation on the part of Russian security forces, resulted in the deaths of 334 hostages (186 of whom were children). Given the extremely sensitive nature of this event—often called the Russian 9/11—the authors had to think carefully about how to approach it, in the end choosing to focus less on the event itself than on the public reaction to it from different groups within Russia. Although Teatr.doc's usual method entails conducting interviews with real human subjects, this time the authors decided to construct their play entirely out of messages culled from Russian, North Ossetian, and Chechen internet blogs and forums. The resulting play exposed aggression to be the one trait shared by *all* segments of Russian society, as largely anonymous internet users trade insults, peddle in conspiracy theories, and even call for genocide. These voices are presented verbatim and in keeping with Teatr.doc's principle of the "zero position" (*nol' pozitsiia*), which requires that the author refrain from taking sides. The task of judging is left to the individual audience member who is confronted with a difficult moral choice. The reception of *September.doc* testifies to the provocative nature of this approach: Ugarov and Gremina were accused of anti-Muslim bias when they presented their play at a theater festival in France, while many who saw the play in Moscow thought it was pro-Islamist and anti-Russian.

The rise of documentary theater in Russia not only helped remind artists and audiences of theater's social mission but also had a profound effect on the language of Russian theater. Exposing stories of trauma and giving voice to those living on the margins of society entails striving to render these stories and voices as accurately and ethically as possible, without manipulation, judgment, or heavy-handed editorial intervention on the part of the artistic team. For this reason, stagings of documentary plays in Russia have usually privileged oral speech over physical acting—a practice reinforced by the central role that *chitki* ("readings") have played in the development of New Drama.[9] Moreover, scarcity of funding has led small theaters like Teatr.doc to embrace a minimalist, "poor theater" aesthetic. While the resulting shows can often seem unprofessional—and stand in stark contrast to the many well-funded productions of documentary plays in some European countries—the lack of expensive stage and costume design, supporters argue, has the positive effect of ensuring that the audience's full attention is given over to the performer's words. Actors deliver their lines in a manner that preserves all the quirks and flaws of the original testimony, with even the hemming and hawing intact. As a result, the language of Russian theater has been enriched through the assimilation of different sociolects and speech registers, enraging traditionalists but more accurately documenting the linguistic range of contemporary Russian society.

The rise of documentary theater has also sparked a wave of formal experimentation by nondocumentary playwrights, who were forced to reevaluate not only their roles as producers of texts for the theater but also the changing relationship between theater and the real. The works of both Ivan Vyrypaev and the Belarus Pavel Pryazhko may be called "postdocumentary" for the way they assimilate or ironically respond to contemporary documentary trends.[10] Pryazhko, who writes in Russian,[11] has developed a pseudo-documentary approach to storytelling, placing his audiences in the position of a camera lens that records whatever is happening in front of it. Here's a typical passage from his play *The Locked Door*:

> An apartment. Valery is visiting a friend. Not thinking about anything, Valery waits for his friend to make coffee. Valery's friend walks in with a tray holding two cups of coffee, sets down the tray, and offers a cup to Valery. Valery takes the cup. Drinks. The friend sits down on the couch holding a cup of coffee and also drinks. This does not produce any tension. Each one is preoccupied with his coffee and is not thinking about anything. A cell phone beeps. Valery's friend gets up from the couch, walks over to the phone, reads the new text message. Valery finishes his coffee and gets up from the couch.
>
> VALERY'S FRIEND (*without taking his eyes off the phone*):
> Taking off?
>
> Valery doesn't respond, he waits for his friend to see him out. Without taking his eyes off the phone, the friend is first to make toward the exit in order to see Valery out. Valery follows him.

Pryazhko himself prefers to call his works "texts" rather than "plays," and indeed *The Locked Door* follows none of the conventional rules of dramatic writing. There are no fateful conflicts, peripeteia, or climaxes; the "action" is limited to mundane events such as watching television and boiling the kettle. None of the characters are psychologically fleshed out; despite the overabundance of stage directions—the artistic function of which Pryazhko radically reinvents—the characters' interiority is "locked" to outside viewers and maybe even to themselves. One of Pryazhko's most frequent stage directions is "he [or she] is not thinking about anything," and indeed the meager cerebral activity of his heroes is shocking in the context of Russian drama after Stanislavski and Chekhov. The texts are constructed according to paratactic, rather than syntactic, principles of composition, forcing us to give equal weight to all aspects of the text. As theater critic Pavel Rudnev observes: "Into the 'lens' of the playwright [Pryazhko] falls what would have previously been considered dramaturgical refuse: small motions, small movements, fragments of phrases, interjections, etc. Not only does all of this comprise a curious documentary method of observing reality, but also an ordeal for the school of Russian psychological theater, which is prepared to 'run' the life of a character through the mill of events, but not of uneventfulness."[12]

If Pryazhko's heroes speak little and not very well, the heroes of Ivan Vyrypaev suffer from veritable logorrhea. One of New Drama's most internationally acclaimed playwrights, Vyrypaev rose to fame with his "modern gospel" play *Oxygen,* which premiered at Teatr.doc in 2002. Since then, he has written more than a dozen plays, all of which deal, in one way or another, with problems of an essentially spiritual nature (Vyrypaev's outlook has been informed by Russian Orthodoxy and Buddhism). Vyrypaev's 2012 play *Summer Wasps Sting in November, Too* centers on a seemingly trivial argument among three friends over whose house their friend Marcus visited the previous Monday. Each character's account is contradicted not only by those of their friends but also by later accounts given by the same character. But what at first feels like an Abbott and Costello comedy routine quickly turns into a drama of existential suffering as the heroes grow increasingly exasperated by their inability to arrive at the truth. Speaking in repetitive sentences whose rhythm is reminiscent of scripture, the heroes can't help but call to mind the biblical Job: "Oh, why is this world such a monster? A monster that devours its own children? Why is this hideous world so bloodthirsty, why does it bite off the heads of its own children? What have we done to deserve this, how have we sinned? What is it all for? What is it all for? What for?" The only reply comes in the form of the nonsensical phrase that gives the play its title, leaving the characters (and Vyrypaev's audiences) in a state of aporia. Moreover, in *Summer Wasps*, Vyrypaev continues his baroque reflection on the illusory nature of modern life, begun in plays like *July* and *Illusions*. Modifying an alienation device first employed in *July*—in which the gruesome monologue of a sixty-three-year-old cannibal named Pyotr was to be performed by a female actor—Vyrypaev has the heroes refer to each other by the names Donald, Sarah, and Robert, even though the names given in the stage directions are, inexplicably, Joseph, Elena, and Mark. The play's emotional rhetoric is thus ironically undercut as audience members are led to question the authenticity of the characters' suffering.[13] Whereas the heroes of verbatim theater functioned as vehicles of sincerity, promising to put audiences in touch with the real, in Vyrypaev's postdocumentary plays, all reality claims are to be accepted with caution.

What we have begun to outline, therefore, are the contours of an evolving, multifaceted artistic movement in which new dramatic texts coexist with experiments in documentary, postdocumentary, and even postdramatic theater,[14] and which, in the last two decades, has moved from the peripheries to become an influential force that has impacted a wide range of media.[15] But what, if anything, can possibly give unity to such a motley phenomenon? What does Vassily Sigarev's *Plasticine*, a play about the violent upbringing of a teenager from the provinces, have in common with Andrey Rodionov and Ekaterina Troepolskaya's slam poetry play *Project "Swan,"* in which migrants must pass a poetic test in order to acquire Russian citizenship? Or Pryazhko's *The Soldier*, a two-sentence "text" about a deserting soldier (it ran for five minutes in Dmitry Volkostrelov's staging at Teatr.doc), and Gremina's *The Brothers Ch.*, a family docudrama based on the life and works of Anton Chekhov? Or finally, to round off the list of plays included in our anthology, Yaroslava Pulinovich's *Somnambulism*, which explores disillusionment with post-Soviet reforms, and Mikhail Durnenkov's *The Blue Machinist*, a modern production play in which machine workers pass the time by composing *haiku*?

It is possible to approach the question of unity from several angles. The first centers on the network of institutions and associations that has served to promote the emergence of New Drama. Rudnev, for example, defines New Drama as "a series of events, actions, festivals, competitions and private initiatives, which are concerned with elevating the prestige of the playwright in the context of contemporary theater."[16] In this respect, New Drama has been fantastically successful. The name itself stems from the New Drama Festival that was first held at the MAT in 2002; although this particular festival no longer exists, other theaters, such as the Meyerhold Center and the Russian Academic Youth Theater, now regularly hold their own. Works by contemporary Russian playwrights made for 22 percent of new dramatic productions in Russia in 2014—still falling behind the classics and works by foreign authors, but a significant improvement over the 1990s.[17] There has also been an upsurge in young writers wanting to write for the theater, prompting Durnenkov to once ironically observe, upon entering a well-attended playwriting workshop, that Russia has so many playwrights now that they can't all fit into one room.[18] At the same time, despite its expanded influence and ranks, the movement has largely managed to preserve its "coterie" spirit. Many of the playwriting festivals held in Russia today are run by writers, directors, and critics who began their careers in the late 1990s and early 2000s, and who represent the first generation of New Drama. Teatr.doc continues to attract young talent through its myriad workshops and laboratories. Finally, there is constant dialogue and movement between companies and theaters—both in the capitals and the provinces—contributing to an atmosphere of exchange and collaboration rather than competition.

Another approach to the question of unity is to consider New Drama as a distinct aesthetic project. Critics point out that works of New Drama often exhibit some combination of the following: hypernaturalistic portrayal of sex and violence; the use of profane language and other forms of "nonnormative" speech; fragmentary (often "filmic") plot structures with little character development or action; a preference for monologic discourse over true dialogue. The heroes of New Drama also tend to fall into one of several categories: the "little man/woman," be it an orphan or a member of a socially marginalized group, who is usually portrayed as a victim or martyr (for this reason, many New Drama texts function as secular hagiographies); the "adultescent" or "kidalt" who is unable or unwilling to grow up; the "migrant" or "wanderer" who finds him- or herself far from home (this could be either an actual place, such as Central Asia, or a metaphorical home, such as "childhood" or "the Soviet Union"). Finally, typical New Drama themes include social anxiety and alienation; disillusionment and the search for truth; the problem of survival in a hostile and violent world; and dream, imitation, and cosplay as means of escape. Of course, this list is not meant to be exhaustive, and some Russian playwrights have begun to explore new themes in response to a changing social and political context. Still, the model set during the early years of New Drama has been surprisingly stable and it may take a more radical embrace of new forms and themes to keep Russian theater from falling into another malaise.

Fortunately, this has already begun to happen thanks to New Drama's most important unifying trait: its pursuit of the real. "If you cannot change reality, you have the duty, at the very least, to document [*fiksirovat'*] it," Mikhail Ugarov liked to proclaim, repeating a phrase that he attributed to the German filmmaker Rainer Werner Fassbinder. Although the early phase of New Drama privileged the verbal representation of reality by means of written or oral speech, documenting or "fixating" the real today requires finding new forms of communication and new performance practices that critically respond to our increasingly digitized and mediatized world. It is no longer uncommon to see performances without dramatic dialogue or professional actors, experiments with participatory and immersive theater, and site-specific performances that take place in nontraditional spaces. The emergence of new technologies, from the iPhone to VR, has also led theater makers to explore new ways of telling stories, bringing theater into contact with such media as computer gaming and digital art. This does not mean that theater no longer needs provocative, intelligent writing, only that the role of the playwright—as well as that of the actor, the director, the spectator, etc.—has begun to change. Some worry that these transformations pose a direct threat to New Drama—a movement that sought to elevate the prestige of the contemporary playwright. But the fact that many of the boldest theatrical experiments in recent years have come from New Drama artists testifies to the latter's prevailing concern with the real. Thus, when Teatr.doc announced a spinoff company called Transformator.doc, whose stated mission was "to do what runs counter to economic, physical, theatrical, and artistic laws, and to the laws of common sense," and whose projects have included a partly improvised show that takes place on the streets of Moscow and an adaptation of *The Bacchae* in which naked female actors slap their male counterparts for more than an hour, no one was much surprised (its latest project is a new "School of Aesthetic Extremism"). After all, documentary theater is itself a product of that radical revolution in literature and art that gave us found poetry and the readymade. The adoption of practices from performance art (and other art forms) is thus part of a longstanding tradition that is at present sparking a new wave of interdisciplinary experimentation in Russia.

A more immediate threat facing Russian theater comes from the current political climate in Russia. In fact, the history of New Drama roughly coincides with Vladimir Putin's hold on power, making it one of the most important documents that we have of this period. On the one hand, the recent resurgence of Russian theater was made possible by the 2000s petroleum boom, which greatly improved economic conditions in Russia and resulted in increased funding for the arts. It was also facilitated by the presidency of Dmitry Medvedev (2008–2012), which, despite its largely cosmetic character, appeared willing to support cultural modernization projects, leading to the construction of innovative theater spaces and the promotion of experimental artists to several important posts. However, much of this support was redirected or withdrawn in the wake of the Russian protest movement (2011–2012) and Russian military intervention in Ukraine (2014–), and Vladimir Putin's third and fourth presidential terms have been marked by numerous repressive actions directed against theater makers, including instances of public shaming, police raids, forced closures, and criminal prosecution. Teatr.doc was forced to relocate twice in six months between January and May 2015—the first time coinciding with its screening of a documentary film about the war in Ukraine and the second with its premiere of a show about men and women arrested during the "March of Millions" on May 6, 2012. And at the time of writing, Kirill Serebrennikov, who had been appointed artistic director of the new Gogol Center (formerly, Gogol Theater) in 2012, is awaiting trial with several former colleagues on what most objective observers consider to be patently fabricated embezzlement charges. Provocative new works continue to be written and staged, but there is an air of uncertainty about the future of Russian theater that was not there only a few years ago.

If these obstacles don't thwart the progress of Russian theater makers, they may lead them to once again reflect on theater's relationship to the real. The historian Kirill Kobrin has recently observed that the defining feature of contemporary Russian society is its inability to comprehend its own economic, cultural, and political reality, thereby enabling the government to manipulate it for its own ends and keep it from imagining a different future: "Any serious image of the future . . . is grounded in the present and in the ability to perceive it. . . . If the reality of the present is not perceived by the Russian citizen on any level except the everyday one, then there's simply nothing on which such an image may be grounded."[19] Kobrin also notes that this state of affairs is partly the result of diminished trust in institutions, suggesting unflattering parallels to the contemporary situation in a number of Western countries, including the United States. With traditional institutions currently in crisis, other organizations have a chance to step in. Comprehending the present in order to imagine alternative futures—this is the mission that theater must embrace today. More than ever, theater must become not only a site of memory but also a public laboratory of the future—a place of collective dreams, discussions, and actions that help build a new social and political consensus. There are encouraging signs that theater makers are accepting the challenge. Only time will tell whether the rest of us will follow suit.

■ □ ■

No single anthology can do justice to an artistic movement that is still evolving and that has produced many dozens of texts that deserve serious attention. In the course of our selection process, we strove to balance three main objectives: to highlight those texts that have been instrumental in defining New Drama; to capture New Drama's formal and thematic diversity; and to give some sense of how New Drama has evolved and where it may be heading. We also strove to select works that would appeal not only to students and scholars but also to theater makers who could give them a new life outside of Russia—either on stage or as inspiration for their own quests and dreams. As a result of this process, we have chosen ten texts written between 2000 and 2013 (the year that saw the suppression of the Russian protest movement and the beginning of the Maidan protests in Ukraine). The two translations by Sasha Dugdale had been earlier commissioned by London's Royal Court Theatre and published by Nick Hern Books; we include them here in new versions that have been adapted for American audiences. The rest of the translations were made for the present volume.

We would like to thank several individuals and groups for making this anthology possible: the editorial staff at Columbia University Press, and especially Christine Dunbar and Christian Winting; the board members for the Russian Library series; our dedicated team of translators; and the inspiring playwrights who have generously agreed to entrust us with their works. We would also like to pay special tribute to Mikhail Ugarov and Elena Gremina, both of whom passed away, less than six weeks apart, as we were preparing this anthology. With their untimely deaths the New Drama community has lost its two strongest pillars. We hope that the inclusion of not only their works but also works by playwrights whose talents they helped discover and nurture will play a small part in spreading their already growing legacy.

A CHRONOLOGY OF NEW RUSSIAN DRAMA

1991 The annual playwriting festival Lyubimovka is first held at the old family estate of Konstantin Stanislavski.

1996 The Debut Center at Moscow's Central House of Actors becomes the first theater to open its doors to young playwrights.

1998 The Playwriting and Directing Theater is founded in Moscow by Alexei Kazantsev and Mikhail Roshchin.

1999 Vadim Levanov takes over as art director of the May Readings, an annual literary festival held in Tolyatti that thereafter shifts its focus from poetry to drama.

1999 As a result of a joint initiative by the Golden Mask Festival and the British Council in Russia, Graham Whybrow of London's Royal Court Theatre gives a series of lectures in Moscow on contemporary dramaturgy, soon followed by professional workshops on documentary theater led by Elyse Dodgson and Stephen Daldry.

2001 Nikolai Kolyada founds his Kolyada Theater in Yekaterinburg. On its basis he will go on to establish a theater school and the international drama competition Eurasia.

2001 The New Drama Festival is instituted by Eduard Boyakov and Elena Gremina. Giving the growing movement its name, it will be held annually from 2002 to 2009 as a joint venture between the Moscow Art Theater, the Golden Mask Festival, and Teatr.doc.

2002 The Moscow documentary theater Teatr.doc is founded by Elena Gremina, Mikhail Ugarov, and Alexei Rodionov.

2005 The Praktika Theater is founded in Moscow by Eduard Boyakov.

2011 St. Petersburg director Dmitry Volkostrelov founds Teatr Post, a theater company that specializes in blending theater with practices borrowed from contemporary art, which will become especially known for its many collaborations with Pavel Pryazhko.

2013 The independent theater for new dramaturgy Teatr18+ is founded in Rostov-on-Don with Yuri Muravitsky as artistic director.

2014 Teatr.doc is forced out of its basement theater in Patriarch Ponds after police raid it during a film screening about the war in Ukraine. Less than six months later, it will be forced to relocate once again after staging a documentary play about the so-called Bolotnaya Square Case.

2016 Teatr.doc's "commissar" Vsevolod Lisovsky founds Transformator.doc, a company devoted to doing "what runs counter to economic, physical, theatrical, artistic laws, and to the laws of common sense." Many of the company's performances are situated on the boundary between traditional theater and contemporary art.

2017 Moscow's Meyerhold Theater holds its inaugural New Drama Festival, which includes readings and new productions of plays by Olga Mukhina, Ivan Vyrypaev, and Pavel Pryazhko.

2017 Kirill Serebrennikov, the artistic director of the Gogol-Center, is placed under house arrest on embezzlement charges that most objective observers believe to have been fabricated.

2018 The deaths of Mikhail Ugarov and Elena Gremina mark a new turning point in the history of Teatr.doc.

NEW RUSSIAN DRAMA

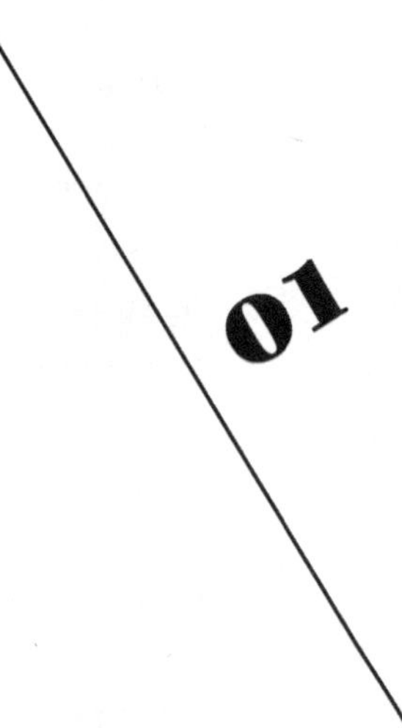

PLASTICINE

VASSILY SIGAREV

TRANSLATED BY SASHA DUGDALE[1]

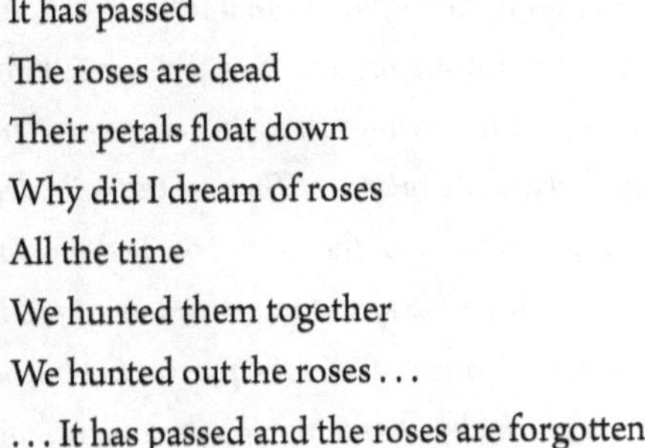

It has passed
The roses are dead
Their petals float down
Why did I dream of roses
All the time
We hunted them together
We hunted out the roses . . .
. . . It has passed and the roses are forgotten.

▸ *Dino Campana*

CHARACTERS

MAKSIM

LYOKHA (ALEXEI VASSILIEV)

GROOM (SLAVA)

BRIDE

SCHOOLTEACHER (LUDMILA IVANOVNA)

LYOKHA'S MOTHER

HEADMASTER (OLEG PETROVICH)

MAKSIM'S GRANDMOTHER (OLGA IVANOVNA)

SPIRA

NEIGHBOR

NATASHA

MAN IN T-SHIRT (CADET)

BARE-CHESTED MAN (SEDOY)[2]

SHE, HER (TANYA)

VARIOUS MEN, WOMEN, AND CHILDREN

1

He sits on the floor in a room that is bare apart from a table, a bed, and a carpet hanging on the wall. His fingers are working plasticine into a strange shape. He finishes and puts the strange thing he has created in a bowl containing a glutinous, dirty white mixture. Then he takes the lead plates out of a car battery and bangs them on the edge of the bed to knock the residue off them, breaks them into pieces, and puts them in a pan. He fetches a small burner with a bare element, places the pan on the burner, and turns the burner on. He takes the bowl and touches its contents with his hand: it is as hard as stone. He scrapes out the plasticine. He looks into the pan—a small lead-colored pool of liquid reflects his face and a white pin of light from the lampshade on the ceiling. He takes the pan and pours the lead into the bowl. The remains of the plasticine hiss, catch light, and flare up. Smoke rises to the ceiling and goes in his eyes. The tears well up. He turns away, but the tears continue to roll down his nose and then down to the corners of his mouth. Now he is actually crying. He is sobbing.

Crying as if he knew something . . .

The bowl cracks . . .

2

The entrance hall of a shabby five-story apartment building. MAKSIM *climbs up the stairs to the fourth floor. People pass him on the way up. They are silent, their faces empty. The stairway comes to an end. There is a door in front of* MAKSIM. *It is open; a felt boot stuffed in the crack keeps it ajar. There is a mirror hanging inside opposite the door. A red plush tablecloth with a fringe hangs over it, covering it.* MAKSIM *stops by the mirror and looks at it. The tablecloth suddenly falls to the floor and* MAKSIM *sees his own reflection in the mirror. He looks at it in amazement as if looking at it for the first time.*

Someone touches him on the shoulder. MAKSIM *turns around and sees a* WOMAN *in a black shawl.*

WOMAN: What you do that for? You shouldn't have. Are you a schoolmate of his?

MAKSIM *nods.*

Go on through . . .

MAKSIM *goes into the main room. It is full of people. In the middle of the room there is a coffin with its lid on.* MAKSIM *stands behind* TWO OLD WOMEN. *He stands on tiptoe, trying to look at the coffin.*

FIRST OLD WOMAN: Hey—don't push!

MAKSIM: Say what?

FIRST OLD WOMAN: Beat it!

MAKSIM *looks at her in bewilderment.*

I said beat it!

MAKSIM: But I . . .

SECOND OLD WOMAN: Go on then.

MAKSIM *moves away.*

FIRST OLD WOMAN: There was one like him on the bus. He got right behind me and started to rub himself up and down on me.

Got a hard-on straight away. I took hold of him and pulled his hair. The things that bleepin' go on. I mean, you'd think he was only a kid—but he was already getting it up . . .

VOICE FROM THE ENTRANCE HALL: The crane is here.

The WOMAN *in the black shawl goes over to the window and looks out. A* LITTLE MAN *in an overlarge jacket goes up to her.*

MAN: Where do you want the logs?

WOMAN: What? Oh . . . (*She was caught up in her own thoughts.*) Put them over there and here. It's all the same, isn't it . . .

The MAN *goes out and the* WOMAN *begins to open up the French windows onto the balcony. The windows are sealed for the winter and the doorframe is stuffed with rags. She rips the rags out, getting angry.*

WOMAN (*It isn't clear to whom she is talking.*): Couldn't they have opened them up before now? The bastards . . .

She tugs at the balcony door and it flies open with a crash. Cotton wool scatters from the doorframe.

VOICE: It won't go through there. It'll have to go through the window.

WOMAN: You're a lot of help. Why am I killing myself. . . . You do it yourselves then—I've had about all I can take.

She goes out. A man stands on the window frame and opens up the windows. People begin to leave the apartment together, as if by agreement. MAKSIM *leaves with everyone else. The* SECOND OLD WOMAN *catches up with him; she stops and whispers something in his ear.* MAKSIM *pales and runs off down the stairs. The* SECOND OLD WOMAN *smiles strangely.*

3

On the street outside. A truck with a crane stands under an apartment window, surrounded by a crowd of people. Everyone is looking up, watching the coffin being fixed to the jib of the crane. MAKSIM *stands next to a* YOUNG MAN *and a* YOUNG WOMAN.

YOUNG WOMAN: What's that for?

YOUNG MAN: The hallway is too narrow for the coffin. It won't fit through. My aunt had an apartment like that. They unloaded her though, and just carried her out. She was fat, so they had a rough time with her.

YOUNG WOMAN: Oooh.

YOUNG MAN: Hey, what if it fell?

YOUNG WOMAN: What?

YOUNG MAN: Just imagine. Right on his head . . .

YOUNG WOMAN: C'mon, let's go.

YOUNG MAN: It won't fall. They're pros. Their stuff is all tested.

VOICE FROM ABOVE: Take it away!

The jib of the crane begins to lower, swaying like a tall slender tree. A funeral march pipes up, although from where it is not clear. MAKSIM *looks around for the source of the music. He sees the* LITTLE MAN *in his baggy jacket with a tape recorder hanging around his neck on a shoulder strap. The* MAN *is stroking the black plastic body of the tape recorder lovingly as if it were his only child.*

YOUNG WOMAN: Who are they burying anyway?

YOUNG MAN: Don't know. Some pansy, I think. Hanged himself over a girl. Or so I've heard.

YOUNG WOMAN: What, really?

YOUNG MAN: Like I said. I don't know. (*To* MAKSIM.) Hey, buddy, any idea who they're burying?

MAKSIM: Spira.

YOUNG MAN: Who?

MAKSIM: This . . . boy.

YOUNG MAN: What sort of a boy? Who was he?

MAKSIM: Just a boy.

YOUNG MAN: So what happened to him?

MAKSIM: He died.

YOUNG MAN: I get it. You don't fucking know anything either. (*He turns away.*)

By now the coffin has been lowered, taken off the jib, and carried to a car with a stainless steel plaque on it. On the plaque there is a photograph of a little boy smiling. The crowd moves after the coffin. Two WOMEN *in black dresses are left. One is an old woman, the other is younger, but they look almost identical. They are both drunk.*

MAKSIM *stops and looks at them.*

FIRST: Don't I even get to keep the clothes?

SECOND: What, to sell for booze? Not likely! I still have grandsons, you know. They'll get them.

FIRST: Oh right. So I don't exist anymore, huh?

SECOND: That's right!

FIRST: I was his mother, you know!

SECOND: You're no mother—you're just a slut! They should cut the wombs out of mothers like you an' all.

FIRST: You're not giving us nothing, then?

SECOND: I should think not. Come on, get out of here. Don't make a scene. It's disgraceful.

FIRST: I'm still going to the cemetery.

SECOND: Oh you are, are you? You think you're going to the wake an' all?

FIRST: And the wake. It's my right.

SECOND: For the free booze?

FIRST: No. To mourn.

SECOND: Off you go then. Mourn! (*She walks away.*)

FIRST (*Catches up to her*): So you're really not going to give me his stuff, then?

SECOND: No, I'm not.

FIRST: Oh you're not, huh?

SECOND: Get out of it, you good for nothing idiot!

FIRST: I'll sue you! (*Suddenly shouting.*) You sent him to his grave, you fucking witch! It was you! I knew it! You old bitch! You fucking evil witch! You sent my only child to his grave! It was you! (*She falls down crying.*)

The SECOND WOMAN *walks away quickly.*

FIRST (*To* MAKSIM): Come over here.

MAKSIM: Fuck you, you slut! (*Walks off quickly in the opposite direction.*)

FIRST: What? Hey. . . . C'mon, help me up . . .

MAKSIM: Fuck off and die!

FIRST: Say what? I know you, you little shit! I'll come to your parents! They'll . . .

MAKSIM: Suck—my—dick!

He runs off. The WOMAN *shouts something after him. The funeral march starts up again but suddenly slows down and finally cuts out altogether. The* LITTLE MAN *in his overlarge jacket takes the cassette out of the tape recorder. The tape has unraveled and caught on the head of the recorder, and the* MAN *attempts to free the tape without success. He rips the tape out of the recorder, stuffs it into his pocket, and runs over to the bus. The* FIRST WOMAN *runs toward the bus too, but the doors of the bus close right in her face and it drives off. She shouts after it for a while, then she spits on the ground and swears.*

Finally she calms down and walks off down the road in the same direction that the bus took. A BARE-CHESTED MAN *hangs over a first-floor balcony of the next block.*

MAN: Not having a good day?

WOMAN: Shut your mouth!

MAN: Come on. Want a drink?

WOMAN: Have you got one?

MAN: Yeah.

WOMAN: Alright.

MAN: Apartment number ten. (*He disappears.*)

The WOMAN *gets a broken piece of mirror out of her pocket and makes an attempt to pretty herself up. Then she goes in the door of the building, smiling and contented.*

MAKSIM *has been watching all this and he turns and walks down the road. Suddenly he sees* HER. SHE *is walking toward him, carefully avoiding the puddles on the pavement.* SHE *doesn't walk, she floats—all light, ethereal, and otherworldly.* MAKSIM *freezes as if under a spell. He watches her. She turns the corner and disappears.*

4

In the men's bathroom at school. MAKSIM *and* LYOKHA *are smoking, hiding behind a partition wall. The cisterns are hissing loudly.* LYOKHA *blows a smoke ring up to the ceiling and smiles.*

MAKSIM: Didn't you go and see Spira off?

LYOKHA: Bet I didn't miss much.

MAKSIM: They didn't open the coffin.

LYOKHA: Bet he was already rotting.

MAKSIM: Did you know her?

LYOKHA: She's rich and pretty hot, but I wouldn't turn my nose up at her. (*Throws the cigarette away.*) Finish your smoke or you-know-who will be sticking her nose in here again.

MAKSIM: Let her.

LYOKHA: Doesn't mean anything at all to you, does it? My mom'll kill me though.

The door opens. MAKSIM *drops the cigarette into the toilet bowl.* LUDMILA IVANOVNA, *the Russian teacher, comes in. She is wearing a long, drab brown dress.*

LUDMILA: Aha. I have you now. (*She comes over.*) Who do we have here?

MAKSIM *and* LYOKHA *turn to face the toilets and pretend to piss.*

Turn around then.

LYOKHA: In a sec.

LUDMILA: Come on, quickly.

LYOKHA: Just a sec.

LUDMILA: I said quickly!

LYOKHA *turns around, doing up his fly.*

Now you.

MAKSIM: I haven't finished.

LUDMILA: What haven't you finished?!

MAKSIM: Pissing.

LUDMILA: What did I hear you say? You say that again . . . (*Turns him around by force.*)

MAKSIM: Get your hands off me!

LUDMILA (*She is stunned for a second. Then she grabs* MAKSIM *by the hair and shakes him.*): You little wretch! Are you raising your voice to me?

MAKSIM: Get your hands off!

LUDMILA: You . . . right. So that's how you want it . . .

MAKSIM: Take your hands off me, you cow!

LUDMILA: What?!

MAKSIM: Hands off! (*He wrenches himself free and walks to the door.*)

LUDMILA: Stop right there!

MAKSIM (*Quietly*): Go fuck yourself.

LUDMILA: I told you to stop!

MAKSIM: You've got no right to come into the men's bathroom . . .

LUDMILA: What did you say? Stop there!

MAKSIM *goes out.*

I don't know why you go around with that good-for-nothing. His number was up a long time ago. But you—what are you doing? Can't you find yourself a nice normal friend? What are you doing with him?

LYOKHA: I'm not his friend . . .

LUDMILA: Oh, don't start.

LYOKHA: I'm not his friend.

LUDMILA: He'll be thrown out before too long. Do you want to be thrown out with him?

LYOKHA: No.

LUDMILA: If I catch you with him again we'll be thinking about you as well. Do I make myself clear?

LYOKHA: Yes

LUDMILA: Move it.

LYOKHA *goes.*

(*Looking into the toilet bowl and sniffing.*) I've got you, you little viper. We're going to have a good talk.

5

MAKSIM *and* LYOKHA *are sitting in the playground.* LYOKHA *is eating an ice cream cone.* MAKSIM *sits with his head lowered and is spitting on the ground. There is a large pool of saliva under his legs.*

LYOKHA: She says you're finished—they're going to chuck you out, Maxie.

MAKSIM: Like I mind.

LYOKHA: Really.

MAKSIM: So what?

LYOKHA: Don't you get it . . .

MAKSIM: . . . Why does that cunt have it in for me? What have I ever done to her?

LYOKHA: Don't you get it? It's all 'cause of that . . . what's his name? Y'know, you punched his head in, in the locker room . . .

MAKSIM: So? The asshole was going through everyone's pockets. They'd have thought it was me.

LYOKHA: Well he was her nephew or something.

MAKSIM: So? I know who he was.

LYOKHA: Well that's it.

MAKSIM: Well, she can. . . . She comes into the bathroom again I'll give her something to look at . . .

LYOKHA: Are you going to piss on her or something?

MAKSIM: Like I give a shit about the old cow. . . . I'll make a plasticine cock that comes down to my knees and she can get off on that.

LYOKHA (*Laughing*): Sure you will!

MAKSIM: I'm not joking. You'll see.

LYOKHA: What? Right to your knees?

MAKSIM: We'll see.

LYOKHA: I can see it now. Want some ice cream?

MAKSIM (*Looks at the ice cream*): No.

LYOKHA: Come to the movie theater tonight. Guess what's on? Remember Bogatka was going on about watching *Caligula* on video. Porno movie.

MAKSIM: And?

LYOKHA: It's on at the movie theater.

MAKSIM: They'll cut out all the good bits.

LYOKHA: No way! My mom and dad went. Springs on their bed were squeaking all night. Means they didn't cut out the good bits.

MAKSIM: Let's go then.

LYOKHA (*Looks at his watch*): Meet you 'round seven then. I'm fucking starving. We've got dumplings for dinner. See you!

MAKSIM: See you.

LYOKHA *runs off.* MAKSIM *looks down into the pool of saliva. A drop of blood drips from his nose. He touches his nose with his hand and it comes away bloody. He looks up into the sky, craning his neck. Swifts are circling in the sky like black dots. They fuss and rush through the air, filled with some horror to which only birds are prey.* MAKSIM *closes his eyes.*

6

It is evening. MAKSIM *and* LYOKHA *approach the back of the movie theater. They stop and look around.*

LYOKHA: Give it a whack, so it opens straight off.

They creep over to the theater's exit door. MAKSIM, *without saying a word, breaks into a run and hits the door with his shoulder. Something falls with a bang and there is a clanking sound.*

Got it?

MAKSIM: Hasn't budged.

LYOKHA: Try again. I'll stand guard.

MAKSIM *hits the door again. There is a bang and the sound of a metal padlock coming loose and falling off.* MAKSIM *bends double and clutches at his head.*

What's wrong, Maxie?

MAKSIM: My fucking head again . . .

LYOKHA: Did you get it open then?

MAKSIM: I guess so.

LYOKHA: Let's go off and have a quick cigarette then.

MAKSIM: Let's go in.

LYOKHA: What, like—straight away?

MAKSIM: No point in wasting time.

LYOKHA: What if they heard us?

MAKSIM: Fuck them. (*He pulls at the door and it opens. The sound of music by Prokofiev pours out through the door.*) In you go.

LYOKHA: Alright. Shhh!

They enter and shut the door.

Darkness.

MAKSIM'S VOICE: Sit down on the floor.

LYOKHA'S VOICE: They're having a screw, can't you hear? Open it up quickly.

MAKSIM'S VOICE: Wait a minute.

LYOKHA'S VOICE: Quick, Maxie. We've already missed it all anyway.

The inner door opens slightly and they can see a screen with two naked women caressing each other on it.

Phwoar! Get a look at that!

MAKSIM'S VOICE (*His voice is shaking.*): Shhh!

LYOKHA'S VOICE: Shit! (*There is a long pause.*) Maxie.

MAKSIM *doesn't answer.*

Maxie . . .

MAKSIM'S VOICE: What?

LYOKHA'S VOICE: Maxie . . .

The sound of clothes rustling and unzipping.

MAKSIM'S VOICE: What are you doing?

LYOKHA'S VOICE: Come on, Maxie. Don't be like that . . .

MAKSIM'S VOICE: Watch it . . .

LYOKHA'S VOICE: Just once, Maxie . . .

MAKSIM'S VOICE: Later . . .

LYOKHA'S VOICE: Just once, Max . . .

A scuffling noise, the sound of LYOKHA *breathing deeply. He groans. On the screen two women urinate on the corpse of a man who has just been murdered.*

7

In front of the movie theater. MAKSIM *and* LYOKHA *stand in front of a board with "Caligula" painted on it in large red letters.*

MAKSIM: We could go cruising on Broadway.

LYOKHA: Pick someone up?

MAKSIM: We'll see.

LYOKHA: No. I'm going home. Mom'll get mad. And I'm starving. I'll see you later.

MAKSIM: See you.

LYOKHA *walks off.* MAKSIM *goes in the opposite direction. A black cat runs across the path in front of him. A woman holding several bags and walking toward him stops dead, as if rooted to the spot. She looks at* MAKSIM. *Only when* MAKSIM *has reached the point where the cat crossed does she start walking again.* MAKSIM *looks around and smiles. The woman also turns and smiles. The cat watches from the darkness with unblinking, burning eyes, and does not smile.*

8

MAKSIM *walks past a café with blaring music and the shouting of loud drunken voices coming from within. Inside he can see tables laid with food and people dancing. By the entrance a* GROOM *in a bowtie is sitting on a bin with his bride on his lap. The* BRIDE *is smoking and talking very loudly. Then she notices* MAKSIM *and throws her cigarette away. She whispers something in the ear of the* GROOM *and jumps down from his lap.*

BRIDE: Hey . . .

MAKSIM *doesn't turn around.*

Hey, you!

MAKSIM *stops and waits.*

(*Walking toward him, holding her skirt up and smiling.*) Give us a cigarette, gorgeous!

MAKSIM: I've only got a packet of Prima.

BRIDE (*Smiling*): Prima'll do fine.

MAKSIM *gets out the packet and gives her a cigarette. He puts a cigarette in his own mouth. He pulls out a lighter and holds it out to the* BRIDE.

Hang on. What's your name?

MAKSIM (*Lights his own cigarette*): What's it to you?

BRIDE: Don't be like that.

MAKSIM: Alright. Max.

BRIDE: Maxie?

MAKSIM: Mm.

BRIDE: You know what, Maxie—take me away from here . . .

MAKSIM: Say what?

BRIDE: Come on, Maxie, let's get out of it, just you and me. I'll be your lover, Maxie. You should see my tits. (*She laughs.*) Go on, have a feel . . . (*She grabs* MAKSIM*'s hand and pulls it against her breasts.*) I want you, Maxie—I'm all wet between the legs for you, Maxie.

MAKSIM (*Pulls back his hand and walks away*): You can go to . . .

BRIDE (*Laughs*): You asked for it! (*Shouts to the* GROOM.) Slava, the pervert grabbed my tits! Stop there, you sneaky rascal!

The GROOM *jumps up and runs toward* MAKSIM.

You stay there, you bastard!

MAKSIM *keeps walking, without turning around.*

GROOM: Stop, you prick!

MAKSIM *stops.*

(*Runs up to him.*) What are we going to do with you, you little fucker? (*He lifts his hand threateningly.*)

MAKSIM *trembles.*

BRIDE: Rough him up, Slava! Aren't you fucking man enough?! Do him over! The bastard!

The GROOM *wavers for a few seconds and then punches* MAKSIM *in the face.* MAKSIM*'s cigarette flies in a different direction from his body.*

Finish him, Slav! Kick the pervert bastard's ass!

The GROOM *kicks* MAKSIM.

BRIDE (*Brays with laughter, takes off her shoe, and starts to hit* MAKSIM *with it*): Beat him senseless! Not man enough? Do him over!

GROOM: Alright. That's enough! (*He pulls away the* BRIDE.)

The BRIDE *bends over and spits on* MAKSIM*'s head. They roar with laughter and run away.* MAKSIM *lies there for some time without moving. Then he sits up, holding his head. His breath rattles. A car drives past and someone throws an empty beer bottle out of the car window. It lands next to* MAKSIM *but doesn't break. He stands up and walks back the way he came. Then he goes back, picks up the bottle, and walks over to the café window. Right by the window the* BRIDE *is hugging a* WOMAN. *The* WOMAN *kisses her and is saying something animatedly. The* BRIDE *laughs. She is radiant.*

MAKSIM *knocks against the window with the bottle. The* BRIDE *stops the* WOMAN *with a gesture and presses against the window to look out.*

MAKSIM (*Lifts the bottle threateningly*): Die, bitch!

The BRIDE *doesn't react. She probably doesn't even see him.* MAKSIM *doesn't move. There is a long pause and then the* BRIDE *turns back to the* WOMAN, *shrugging her shoulders.*

Fuck off, all of you!

He runs off, throwing the bottle through an apartment window on his way. There is the sound of breaking glass.

9

MAKSIM *is walking toward the entrance hall of his apartment building. He stubs his cigarette out on the doorframe.*

VOICE BEHIND HIS BACK: Max . . .

MAKSIM *turns around. A boy is standing in the gate of the children's playground.*

BOY: Let's go.

He moves back. The light falls on his face and it becomes clear that he is the BOY *whose face was pictured on the stainless steel plaque.*

Let's go, MAX.

MAKSIM *takes a few steps toward him, then stops.*

Come on. (*He moves away.*)

MAKSIM: Later, Spira . . .

BOY: Let's go . . .

MAKSIM: I'll be along . . .

He turns and runs into the entrance hall. The BOY *vanishes into the darkness.*

10

It is nighttime and dark in MAKSIM*'s room.* MAKSIM *is lying in bed and holding his head. He stares at the ceiling. Suddenly he starts to whisper.*

MAKSIM: Don't . . . don't . . . it hurts . . . it hurts, Jesus, it hurts. Don't . . . don't . . . I can't take any more. Jesus, please. Please. Don't . . . (*He whimpers and clenches his teeth.*) Fucking stop it! I said stop! Stop!!! (*He bangs his head with the palm of his hand.*)

Silence. MAKSIM *climbs out of bed and turns on the light. He gets a box out from under the bed. There is a large ball of plasticine in the box.* MAKSIM *sits on the ground and starts shaping it. He has light blue bruises on his back from the* BRIDE*'s white shoes.*

11

The school bathroom. MAKSIM *is smoking.* LYOKHA *is crouching next to him.*

LYOKHA: Hey, so guess what. . . . I didn't go home last night, right. I'm walking along and I see this hottie purring toward me. Fucking wasted. . . . I go up to her all smooth, like, you know, and go "want to grab a beer, darling?" and she's fucking all over me. I get the beers and the Marlboro. We did some stuff on the stairs, I can tell you. Anyway, she's not from around here. And a bit of a nut job. (*He puts his finger to his temple to illustrate.*)

MAKSIM: So what happened?

LYOKHA: What happened. . . . I stuck it to her. She's all coy at first. . . . All "it's my first time" and all that crap. Then she comes onto me herself. It was tight as fuck on the stairs, I can tell you. It's the third time I've done it there. You should have come with me. Her aunt lives in that tower block the size of the Wall of China. . . . She can. . . . Hey, who beat you up?

MAKSIM: It's nothing. Forget it.

LYOKHA: We could go after them. I'll bring some friends along. Who were they?

MAKSIM: I don't know.

LYOKHA: Be like that then.

MAKSIM: It's nothing. Forget it.

The door opens.

LYOKHA: Watch out! (*He stands up in front of the urinals.*)

MAKSIM *goes over to the toilets and gets something out from underneath his jumper.* LUDMILA IVANOVNA *appears, wearing the same brown dress.*

LUDMILA: So it's you two again, is it? I warned you, Vassiliev, didn't I?

LYOKHA: I wasn't smoking. You can smell my breath if you like.

LUDMILA: That won't be necessary.

LYOKHA: I wasn't smoking, I said.

LUDMILA: I really don't care.

LYOKHA: I get it. . . . Going to the toilet is against the law now, is it?

LUDMILA: You are getting yourself in deeper and deeper. And you, my sunshine, are you just going to stand there?

MAKSIM: Any law against it?

LUDMILA: Yes.

MAKSIM: Who says?

LUDMILA: I say. Now turn around.

MAKSIM: I haven't finished.

LUDMILA: Do my ears deceive me?

She turns him around by force and then pales. LYOKHA *also pales.* MAKSIM *smiles. He is holding a long plasticine penis against his fly. It is shiny and very real looking. There is silence.*

12

The Russian language and literature classroom. There are portraits of great writers along the walls. LUDMILA IVANOVNA *sits behind the teacher's desk, and opposite her across the desk sits* LYOKHA'S MOTHER, *a formidable looking woman with short hair.*

LYOKHA'S MOTHER: He was such a lovely boy. Used to spend all his time at home. As soon as he started mixing with that . . . he was like another person. Don't be hard on him, Ludmila Ivanovna. Do you know what he says? He says he's scared of that Maksim. Apparently Maksim said he would turn the others against him if he didn't . . . go 'round with him. He says he hits him all the time.

LUDMILA: He's quite capable of it.

LYOKHA'S MOTHER: Lyokha's promised to confirm this . . . your . . . incident at the board meeting.

LUDMILA: They'll throw him out anyway. Before you can say the word . . .

LYOKHA'S MOTHER: Then, if it isn't a big deal, I'd like you to leave Lyokha out of this. I'm sure I can, you know, sort you out a pass at the swimming pool. I'm in charge there.

LUDMILA: I understand. No need to ruin the boy's life. Not a bad boy. Never a bad word . . .

LYOKHA'S MOTHER: The other one you can throw to the dogs as far as I'm concerned. Make life easier for everyone. Turns up here with his hard luck stories. . . . Only takes one of them to get a hold and the rest live in terror.

LUDMILA: Well he's finished as far as I'm concerned.

LYOKHA'S MOTHER: And quite right too.

LUDMILA: He'll probably wind up in a street brawl and that'll be that. As I see it, one less scoundrel in the world to worry about.

LYOKHA'S MOTHER: My thoughts exactly . . .

LUDMILA: So can I rely on you to sort my nephew out a pass, too? We'd be down at the pool together.

LYOKHA'S MOTHER: It would be a pleasure, Ludmila Ivanovna. Do a good person a good turn, I say.

13

The HEADMASTER*'s office. The* HEADMASTER*, a man of about forty, wearing a three-piece suit, sits behind the desk.* LUDMILA IVANOVNA *sits on his right-hand side. Opposite them sits* MAKSIM'S GRANDMOTHER*, and* MAKSIM *stands behind her.*

HEADMASTER: So you see, Olga Ivanovna . . . that is your name, isn't it, Olga Ivanovna?

GRANDMOTHER: Yes.

HEADMASTER: Well, Olga Ivanovna, do you understand that we are excluding your grandson from this educational establishment?

GRANDMOTHER: But . . . how?

LUDMILA: It's simple.

HEADMASTER: Ludmila Ivanovna, please. Maksim, surely you told your grandmother?

MAKSIM: What difference does it make? I told you to give me the papers and leave it at that.

HEADMASTER: What do you mean—give them to you? According to the law it is the parents or guardians . . .

MAKSIM: Fine. Give them to her then.

HEADMASTER: No, it is not fine! You see, Olga Ivanovna . . . do I have your name right, Olga Ivanovna?

MAKSIM: Yes.

LUDMILA: Speak when you're spoken to.

HEADMASTER: You see, Olga Ivanovna, we were forced to turn to the extreme measure of expulsion.

GRANDMOTHER: But what for?

LUDMILA: His glorious deeds . . .

GRANDMOTHER: What did he do?

MAKSIM: Smacked her pickpocket nephew's face.

LUDMILA: That's enough you little wretch! Oleg Petrovich, I am utterly astounded. This woman, whoever she is, has the nerve to sit here and defend the total delinquent she dragged up. Do you, whatever-your-name-is, not even understand the situation?

GRANDMOTHER: What's that?

LUDMILA: I can't take any more of this, I really can't, Oleg Petrovich! You, do you understand that you've brought up a delinquent?

GRANDMOTHER: Oh he's not a de, er, linquent. He's a good boy. Brings me bedpans and all such when I'm bedridden and takes them away again. Does lovely plasticine models.

HEADMASTER: Not the ones he should be making.

LUDMILA: So he's a good boy is he?

GRANDMOTHER: Oh yes.

LUDMILA: Then I give up, Oleg Petrovich. I have no idea how to communicate with this woman. When did you last set foot on school premises, dear?

GRANDMOTHER: Well it's my legs, see . . .

LUDMILA: What about them?

GRANDMOTHER: I barely made it here.

LUDMILA: If you've got something wrong with your legs, then maybe you shouldn't have taken on the boy's welfare. I am astounded, Oleg Petrovich, that she was allowed to at all. What on earth were they thinking? It's a huge responsibility, dear.

GRANDMOTHER: Where else could he have gone?

LUDMILA: Don't give me any of that. The state, thank heavens, provides all the right conditions. You people haven't yet worked it out, have you? You attempt your home-grown welfare and the results are like this—(*She points to* MAKSIM.)

Look—the result: drug addicts, delinquents, and the dregs of society.

GRANDMOTHER: Why, you . . .

LUDMILA: Don't you get familiar with me . . . two can play at that game . . .

HEADMASTER: Ludmila Ivanovna, please—a little restraint.

LUDMILA: What use is restraint with these people? He should have been put away long ago—and her to boot.

MAKSIM: Shut up, you old cow!

LUDMILA: What?

MAKSIM: Shut up, you bitch!

HEADMASTER: Maksim, Maksim.

MAKSIM: Maksim what, you fucking . . .

GRANDMOTHER: Maksim.

MAKSIM: Come on, Nana. Let's go. What's the point of staying around to listen to the cow. Or she can get out.

LUDMILA: Did you hear that? Now you see what you've brought up!

MAKSIM: Shut up, you bitch! (*He grabs a vase from the table.*) Or I'll knock your brains out.

LUDMILA (*Jumping up from her chair in terror and hiding behind the headmaster*): Get rid of him, Oleg Petrovich! He's a psychopath! What next! We should call the police!

HEADMASTER: Maksim, calm down.

MAKSIM: I'll tell you where you all can go. Come on, Nana.

The GRANDMOTHER *gets up.* MAKSIM *puts the vase back in its place.*

HEADMASTER: I haven't finished yet.

MAKSIM: I have.

They leave.

LUDMILA: What a nightmare! They should shoot them at birth! Or before birth! Who has kids like that, anyway?

HEADMASTER: Go back to your class, Ludmila Ivanovna.

LUDMILA: What?

HEADMASTER: Go back to your class.

14

MAKSIM and his GRANDMOTHER come out of the school. LYOKHA is standing by the gates with a group of boys.

MAKSIM: You go on, Nana. I'll catch you up. (*He stops and shouts.*) Hey, Lyokha, Lyokh!

LYOKHA doesn't react.

MAKSIM goes up to him.

Lyokha, are you deaf or something?

All the boys look at MAKSIM and smile nastily.

A BIG BOY WITH FLUFF ON HIS CHIN: Hey. The fag's turned up.

MAKSIM: Who's a fag? You want to get your facts straight, buddy.

BOY: You're a fag.

MAKSIM: Had enough of life, have you?

BOY: Oh yeah. Had enough. You fag.

SECOND BOY IN A RED JACKET: Lyosha told us all about how you were up for it in the movie theater . . .

MAKSIM: What are you talking about? (*Throws himself at the boy.*)

The BIG BOY tries to punch him in the face but misses and hits his forehead. He grabs his own hand and howls in pain. MAKSIM runs at the BIG BOYbut someone grabs his collar and pulls him down onto his back.

LYOKHA: Get him—the fucking gay boy!

The BOYS all start kicking MAKSIM.

(*Jeering.*) Finish him! In the face! Kick his ass!

LUDMILA IVANOVNA comes out of the school and watches, smiling.

15

MAKSIM is washing in a fountain. His face is swollen and bruises are already appearing. The buttons on his denim jacket have been ripped off.

He hears voices behind him.

FIRST: Mom, we're going to be late.

SECOND: We've still got time.

FIRST: How long?

SECOND: I don't know, I don't have a watch. Ask that boy over there.

A pause.

FIRST (*Close up*): Excuse me . . .

MAKSIM looks up from under his arm. A GIRL is walking toward him. But not just any girl: SHE is walking toward him.

MAKSIM looks at his face in the water.

SHE: Could you tell me the time?

MAKSIM takes to his heels and runs. He runs and runs and runs.

16

It is night again. Once more it is dark and MAKSIM is lying in bed. He is holding his head as before and whimpering with his teeth clenched. Suddenly he shudders, listening to something. He shudders again. He gets out of bed and goes over to the window. He jerks the blind back and looks down. The same BOY is standing by the gate to the children's playground. He is saying something—his lips are moving, but he can't be heard.

MAKSIM: I'll come later, Spira . . .

The BOY's lips are moving and he recedes into the children's playground.

Not yet.

The BOY *shakes his head and speaks. He recedes further.*

Not yet . . .

Darkness swallows the BOY. MAKSIM *pulls the blind shut. He gets the box of plasticine out from under the bed and starts kneading it.*

17

MAKSIM *is going down the stairs. His* NEIGHBOR, *a man in glasses, comes up to him.* MAKSIM *tries to pass him, but the neighbor bars his way.*

NEIGHBOR: Got a light?

MAKSIM *gets out his lighter and stretches it out toward him.*

(*Takes the lighter.*) I've got you, you little shit. You set light to my fucking box?

MAKSIM: Say what?

NEIGHBOR: I said, you set light to my fucking box?

MAKSIM: What box?

NEIGHBOR: My fucking mailbox. I'll twist your ear. (*He takes* MAKSIM *by the ear and twists it, sticking his tongue out with the effort.*)

MAKSIM *doesn't defend himself.*

I'll punch your fucking face in next time. D'you hear?

MAKSIM: Now give back my lighter.

NEIGHBOR: What do you want it for, you little. . . . Go on, beat it.

MAKSIM: Give me back my lighter.

NEIGHBOR: So you can go 'round setting light to mailboxes?

MAKSIM: I didn't set light to it.

NEIGHBOR: Beat it!

MAKSIM: Give back the lighter.

NEIGHBOR: Got a problem, you little shit?

MAKSIM: My lighter . . .

NEIGHBOR: I'll show you! (*Grabs* MAKSIM *by the scruff of the neck and shoves him.*)

MAKSIM *runs down the stairs, barely able to keep upright.*

Breeding like fucking rabbits and then the kids run wild and ruin all our lives too. (*He goes up the stairs.*)

MAKSIM *stands on the landing, listening with his neck craned. A door slams.* MAKSIM *goes downstairs and collects up some papers from the mailboxes and climbs back up the stairs. He gets to the door where the* NEIGHBOR *went in and pushes the newspaper behind the door handle. He feels for a match in his pocket and strikes it against the floor. The match breaks.* MAKSIM *gets out another and strikes again. The match lights.* MAKSIM *gives it time to take and then lights the paper with it. He goes down the stairs.*

CHILD'S VOICE BEHIND THE DOOR: Dad, smoke . . .

MAKSIM *races back to the door, rips the newspaper out from behind the handle, throws it on the floor, and stamps on it. The door opens and the* NEIGHBOR *sticks his head out.*

NEIGHBOR: So it's you, you little nit!

MAKSIM *runs downstairs.*

I'll kill you, you bastard! Trying to burn us to the ground, you little shit! I'll see you behind bars!

MAKSIM *runs out of the building.*

18

It is evening. MAKSIM *is sitting in the stand of a small stadium. He is eating a hunk of bread, breaking the pieces off with his fingers. There is no one around. Frogs are croaking their dirty mating songs in the park faintly, as if from a long, long way off.* MAKSIM *is listening. He is deep in thought and stares in front of him, eating mechanically. Two indistinct figures appear below: a man and a woman. They approach and it becomes clear that it is not a man, but an eighteen-year-old* BOY. *The* WOMAN *looks around thirty and she's slightly drunk. The boy has an unsealed bottle of vodka in his hand. They walk over to the stand at the bottom. They don't notice* MAKSIM. *The* BOY *puts the bottle down on the bench and begins touching the woman.*

WOMAN: Not so fast, hey. . . . Let's have a drink first.

BOY (*Speaks with difficulty—he has a lump in his throat.*): Later.

WOMAN: What's the rush?

BOY (*He is trembling.*): I want you.

WOMAN: Give me a kiss.

The BOY *kisses her, groping her ineptly.*

Cold hands.

BOY: I want you.

WOMAN: Am I beautiful?

BOY: Beautiful . . .

WOMAN: Do you love me?

BOY: I love you . . .

WOMAN: I love you too. What's your name?

BOY: Dima . . . Please . . .

WOMAN: Will you marry me?

BOY: I'll marry you. Please . . .

WOMAN: Well, go on then. (*She bends over and lifts up her skirt.*)

The BOY *unbuttons his fly and positions himself behind her. He is trembling all over.*

Not in there. . . . What, is it your first time? . . . Not in there! What you doing now? Have you finished?

The BOY *moves away, buttoning up his fly.*

That was fast. You never even put it in.

The BOY *picks up the bottle of vodka from the bench and walks off.*

Hey! Where are you off to?

BOY: Piss off, you slut.

WOMAN: Stop!

BOY: What do you want?

WOMAN: Give me the bottle, you impotent shit.

BOY: What did you say? (*Advances on her.*)

WOMAN (*Backing off*): No need to get nasty . . . I'm off now. My dad's in the police . . . hey, don't be like that . . .

The BOY *kicks her in the stomach. She totters back and falls over.*

BOY: You fat cunt! I see you 'round here again, I'll finish you! Slut! (*He goes.*)

The WOMAN *waits until he has disappeared from sight. Then she gets up and brushes herself down, grumbling to herself.*

WOMAN: Impotent shit. Came in my panties. . . . And he was so young. Couldn't even pour me a drink, the miserable bastard. (*She sees* MAKSIM.) Hey! Who's that?

MAKSIM *doesn't answer. The* WOMAN *climbs up the steps.* MAKSIM *gets out a cigarette and lights it.*

Hello . . .

MAKSIM *nods.*

Give me a smoke?

MAKSIM *gives her a cigarette and lights it. His hands are shaking. The* WOMAN *takes a drag and sits down next to him.*

Out for a walk?

MAKSIM: Mm.

WOMAN: My dog ran away. I'm out looking for it.

MAKSIM: What sort of dog would that be?

WOMAN: Oh, you know . . . with a pedigree.

MAKSIM: Right.

WOMAN: Not seen it then?

MAKSIM: Uh huh.

WOMAN: You cold sitting there?

MAKSIM: No.

WOMAN: Let me warm you up. (*She hugs him.*)

MAKSIM *doesn't resist.*

(*Stroking him.*) I'm beautiful, aren't I?

MAKSIM: I don't know.

WOMAN: Will you marry me? My dad owns a factory. He'll give you a car as a present. A Mercedes. And a five bedroom apartment. Marry me?

MAKSIM *doesn't answer.*

You love me . . . (*She touches his fly.*) There. You love me and I love you too. Do you know how I love you? (*She kisses his face and whispers.*) My lover . . . my one and only. . . . Do you love me? Prove your love to me. Prove it.

MAKSIM: How?

WOMAN: Kiss me there . . .

MAKSIM: What?

WOMAN: Kiss me there.

MAKSIM: Where?

WOMAN: There. (*She pulls up her skirt.*)

MAKSIM: What for?

WOMAN: I want you to.

MAKSIM: Why?

WOMAN: Kiss it. (*She bends him over.*)

MAKSIM (*Pulling away*): Don't!

WOMAN: Kiss me, bastard! (*She pushes his face in her torn panties.*) Kiss me, bastard! Kiss me if you love me!

MAKSIM *vomits on her. The* WOMAN *pushes him away.* MAKSIM *staggers back, blood dripping from his nose.*

Why?

MAKSIM: It's just . . .

WOMAN: What was that for? You fool. That hurt. You fool.

MAKSIM *makes his way down the stand climbing from row to row.*

Fool . . . it hurt . . . fool. It hurt. Fool . . . it hurt . . .

MAKSIM *breaks into a run.*

Fool . . . (*She picks up a half-digested piece of bread and stuffs it in her mouth.*) Fool . . .

19

It is night. MAKSIM *is in bed, holding his head and quietly wailing. He looks at the ceiling with glassy eyes. The walls begin to pulse and the room presses in on him. The ceiling comes down on him. Everything is alive and moving. Everything is breathing, whispering to him, living. Everything is moving and pulsing and laughing at him. The room gets smaller and smaller. Now it is no longer a room but a little box, the walls covered in black material. It is no longer a room, it is a coffin.* MAKSIM *cries out . . .*

20

It is day. MAKSIM *is sitting at the table and modeling the figure of a girl out of plasticine. The doorbell rings.* MAKSIM *goes to open the door.*

GRANDMOTHER'S VOICE: Maksim, get the door.

MAKSIM: I've got it. (*He opens the door.*)

LYOKHA *stands on the doorstep. He is holding a plastic bag filled with beer bottles.*

LYOKHA: Help me out, Maksim.

MAKSIM: What do you want?

LYOKHA: Well I picked up this hottie . . . with a place of her own. . . . You know, the works. . . . She goes to me, "bring a friend" . . . she's got some other girl there or something.

So I went round to Bogatka's house and he wasn't there, so I tried Dlinny and he's at home painting something with his mom. So he couldn't go. So . . . I'm up shit's creek. . . . Help me out, Maxie.

MAKSIM: What sort of a girl?

LYOKHA: Phwoar! She's tight. I've just spent all my money on beer. She says her friend'll be a total babe too. Help out will you, Maxie? Let's go.

MAKSIM: Come in.

LYOKHA (*Enters*): Get a move on, Maxie. She's waiting downstairs.

MAKSIM: I'll just get dressed.

LYOKHA: Get a move on.

MAKSIM *goes into his bedroom and gets dressed.*

(*Standing in the doorway.*) I've been up to some unreal stuff without you around. Do you know Bulka?

MAKSIM: Mm.

LYOKHA: I gave her a good one. We went to some girl's dacha with Bogatka and . . . phwoar . . . what we got up to! I drank so much I fucking pissed myself. Guess what I did down at my mom's swimming pool?

MAKSIM: What?

LYOKHA: I made a hole in the wall of the women's shower room. Well, in the door. Now I can get an eyeful whenever. The bodies in there. Wow! Like, all different women. Some of them have got gray hair, y'know down there . . . (*He roars with laughter.*) And you know what's-his-name? The one you punched a while back? The nephew . . .

MAKSIM: Well?

LYOKHA: Well, he's croaked . . .

MAKSIM: What?

LYOKHA: Fucking drowned.

MAKSIM: How?

LYOKHA: How d'you think? Mom got them both a free pass and he couldn't swim to save his life. The end.

MAKSIM: Fuck me.

LYOKHA: Serves him right. Worthless prick. I went in the showers with him once and he hasn't got a hair on his body. And a little kiddy dick. Although he's a big fucker to look at. I mean, think about it—he was already in fifth grade. Why couldn't he croak earlier. . . . Then you'd still be at school. Should have told my mom to get a pass for them ages ago. And that old cow has joined the God squad. She's all butter wouldn't melt now. . . . Stopped hanging around the bathrooms anyway. You ready?

MAKSIM: Mm.

LYOKHA: Hit the road, man!

MAKSIM: Let's go.

They go out onto the landing. MAKSIM *closes the door and they go down the stairs.*

LYOKHA: Maxie. . . . I wanted to say . . . y'know . . . don't be pissed off about all that . . . stuff. It was like this. . . . I was telling them about *Caligula*. Like what those men were doing. . . . Anyway, Dlinny starts talking smack about how we must have done it too. Fucking asshole. And then you come up and that's it—they're off. I tried to pull them off you . . .

MAKSIM: Forget it. It's okay.

LYOKHA: No, I mean it, Max.

MAKSIM: It's history.

LYOKHA: Need a cigarette?

MAKSIM: I've got some.

LYOKHA (*Gets out a pack*): There you go. Pack of Camels. (*He thrusts the pack at* MAKSIM.) Take them all. You'll be breaking open your local crap in front of the babes otherwise. My mom's been topping me up with cash recently.

21

By the entrance to the apartment building, LYOKHA *looks around and* MAKSIM *squats, waiting.*

LYOKHA: She was here. Did that slut take off? I told you to get a fucking move on. What a mess. That bitch. Now what?

A GIRL *of about twenty comes out from around the corner and waves at* LYOKHA.

(*Smiles.*) There she is! Come on, Maxie!

They walk toward the GIRL.

What do you think of her?

MAKSIM: Alright.

LYOKHA: Oh, right. Got to be a supermodel for you, huh?

MAKSIM: The beer'll improve her.

LYOKHA (*Laughing*): Out of order . . .

They reach the GIRL.

Where were you, Natasha?

NATASHA: One of my old boyfriends lives here . . .

LYOKHA: Aha.

MAKSIM: And who's that?

NATASHA: You won't know him. They've left anyway.

LYOKHA: This is Max.

NATASHA: Right. Let's go.

She walks off. MAKSIM *and* LYOKHA *follow her.*

LYOKHA: Where are we off to?

NATASHA: You know the barracks?

LYOKHA: Mm.

NATASHA: There's a tower block there.

LYOKHA: And?

NATASHA: That's where we're going.

LYOKHA: Your friend's not some dog is she? She won't frighten Maksim off?

NATASHA: She's cool. (*Smiles strangely.*)

LYOKHA: Hear that? Hold the bag for me.

He hands MAKSIM *the bag and catches up with* NATASHA. *He puts his hand around her waist.*

NATASHA: You crazy or something?

LYOKHA: What?

NATASHA: Not here. Half the town knows me. You'll have your chance later. (*She removes his hand.*)

LYOKHA: But I'm with you, right?

NATASHA: Yeah, that's right. Get moving. (*She starts walking faster.*)

22

MAKSIM, LYOKHA, *and* NATASHA *walk toward the entrance of a four-story apartment building that rises above the low wooden roofs of the barracks. The door hangs on one hinge.*

NATASHA: Through here.

LYOKHA: Fuck, it stinks in there. (*He touches the door.*) Concentration camp you got yourselves here.

NATASHA: Let's go, then.

They go in through the door and climb up the stairs. On the landing between the ground floor and the first floor, they pass a row of twisted, broken metal mailboxes.

LYOKHA: Nice place.

NATASHA: So?

LYOKHA (*Holds onto* MAKSIM*'s arm and whispers*): She's not really going for me, is she? . . . Maybe she's into you. If her friend isn't too rough then you can take this one.

MAKSIM: Let's see.

NATASHA: What are you doing?

LYOKHA: Coming. Which floor are we going to?

NATASHA: Fourth floor.

They climb the stairs. On the fourth floor, NATASHA *is waiting for them by a derelict old wooden door. She puts a key in the lock.*

LYOKHA: So where's your friend?

NATASHA: I locked her in.

LYOKHA: Oh, right. What's her name?

NATASHA: Ask her yourself.

LYOKHA: I get it.

NATASHA (*Opening the door*): Come in.

MAKSIM *and* LYOKHA *enter and take off their shoes.* NATASHA *locks the door and puts the key in her jeans pocket.*

LYOKHA: Where's your friend then?

NATASHA: In the main room.

LYOKHA (*Walks into the room*): Nice . . . (*He stops dead.*)

NATASHA (*Nudging* MAKSIM): Come on now.

MAKSIM *goes into the main room. Two* MEN *of about thirty are sitting there. One is bare to the waist. His body is covered with tattoos. The second is wearing a t-shirt. He is also tattooed.*

NATASHA (*To* LYOKHA, *smiling*): What are you staring at? Go on, ask.

LYOKHA (*In a different voice*): What?

NATASHA: What you wanted to ask.

LYOKHA: I didn't want to ask nothing.

BARE-CHESTED MAN: Have the courage of your convictions, my friend. Sit down on the sofa and we'll have a heart to heart.

LYOKHA *sits down on the sofa. He is shaking.*

NATASHA: Scared? Shitting yourself, huh? (*Takes the plastic bag of bottles from* MAKSIM.) You sit down too.

MAKSIM *sits next to* Lyokha.

(*Puts the bag on the table.*) To think he was so tough back there . . . Going, "I'll give you one you won't forget" and groping my ass an' all. (*She laughs.*)

BARE-CHESTED MAN (*Opening the bottle with his eye muscles*): Is that true, friend?

MAN IN T-SHIRT: Just beer?

NATASHA: He even went and got them himself . . . (*She sits down on the* BARE-CHESTED MAN*'s knees and takes the open bottle. She drinks. To the man in the t-shirt.*) You not drinking then, cadet?

CADET: Gives me the shits.

NATASHA: Lovely turn of phrase.

CADET: Gets my meaning across though.

NATASHA: Then why don't you make a vodka run?

CADET: Plenty of time for that.

BARE-CHESTED MAN: Do they have names?

NATASHA: That one's called Lyokha or something. Don't remember that one's.

BARE-CHESTED MAN: Hey, mongrel, what's your name?

MAKSIM: What's it to you?

NATASHA: One's got a name and the other's a tease.

CADET: Got honor, doesn't he?

NATASHA: As long as he doesn't have gonorrhea . . .

CADET: I love 'em like that.

NATASHA: You made your choice, then? (*She laughs.*)

BARE-CHESTED MAN: So what's your name then, scumbag?

MAKSIM: How about Maksim?

NATASHA: Come for a pee, Max-y! (*Laughs.*)

BARE-CHESTED MAN (*Opening another bottle of beer*): So Maksim, fancy a game of cards?

MAKSIM: I don't know how to play.

BARE-CHESTED MAN: Let me teach you. How about it, Alexei? Game of Strip-Jack? (*He smiles.*)

LYOKHA *shrugs his shoulders automatically.*

What's that?

LYOKHA: What?

NATASHA: Learn to speak properly and stop fucking around like some retard.

LYOKHA: If you like.

NATASHA: He's on board. Let's go.

BARE-CHESTED MAN: What about you, Maksim?

MAKSIM: I don't want to.

BARE-CHESTED MAN: Why not? Don't you like my face?

MAKSIM *doesn't answer.*

Well?

MAKSIM: I just don't want to . . .

CADET: I didn't neither, but my mom still went and had me. What a bitch, huh?

BARE-CHESTED MAN: What have you got against it, Maksim?

MAKSIM: I just don't want to.

BARE-CHESTED MAN: But we've already told you—that's no reason.

Pause.

Go on then, Maksim—one game and you're off . . .

LYOKHA: Go on Maksim—what's wrong with you?

NATASHA: Max-y . . .

MAKSIM: What?

NATASHA: Come for a pee! (*Laughs.*)

BARE-CHESTED MAN: What about it, Maksim?

MAKSIM: Alright then.

NATASHA: He's on board.

BARE-CHESTED MAN: Get the cards out, Tash. The boys want a game.

NATASHA (*Gets up*): Where are they?

BARE-CHESTED MAN: In the kitchen.

NATASHA (*Goes over to the kitchen. On the way she bends over* LYOKHA *and tweaks his cheek.*): So what was it you were going to do to me?

LYOKHA: I can't remember.

NATASHA: Touch my ass. Go on. (*She turns her back to him.*) I said you could and I keep my word.

LYOKHA *doesn't move.*

Forgotten how to? Or don't you find it attractive no more?

BARE-CHESTED MAN: You pull your pants down, Tash. You're just sticking your jeans in his face and he could touch up his own jeans, if he wanted.

NATASHA: He's getting worried.

BARE-CHESTED MAN: No, you get them down. You said you keep your word, didn't you? Or don't you?

NATASHA *bares her buttocks.*

Now touch her. Go on, my friend. Look at the fucking fine ass on her.

LYOKHA *touches her buttocks gingerly.*

CADET: Don't just stroke them, like some girl. Give her a fucking pinch.

LYOKHA: How?

CADET: Like she's a tart.

NATASHA: Watch yourself!

CADET: Give her a pinch!

LYOKHA: How?

CADET: Do I have to show you how?

LYOKHA *pinches her.*

NATASHA: That's enough. It hurts!

BARE-CHESTED MAN: Now kiss her where you hurt her.

LYOKHA *kisses her.*

CADET: Bite her!

NATASHA: Don't you dare.

CADET: Bite her or you'll fucking get it!

LYOKHA *bites her.*

NATASHA (*Jumps away from him, pulling up her jeans*): Bastard! Shit! (*She kicks* LYOKHA *on the leg.*) Fuckhead. (*She pulls her jeans down again.*) Can you see anything?

CADET: Cellulite.

NATASHA: You can just fuck off. I'm going to bite you an' all. (*She goes over to the* CADET *and grabs his cheek in her mouth and bites as hard as she can.*)

The CADET *doesn't react.*

(*Pushes him away.*) Got it? (*She rubs her teeth.*) That fucking hurt.

The CADET *smiles. He has white teeth marks in his cheek.*

BARE-CHESTED MAN: Now go and get the cards, Tash. We wouldn't want to bore the boys.

NATASHA *goes out to the kitchen.*

Was that the first time you've pinched a woman then, Alexei?

LYOKHA *nods.*

Was it nice?

LYOKHA *shrugs his shoulders.*

Was it?

LYOKHA *nods.*

Was it?

LYOKHA: Yes.

CADET: You still a virgin then?

LYOKHA: What?

CADET: Still a little boy?

LYOKHA *nods.*

And not a little girl?

LYOKHA: No.

CADET: Sure?

LYOKHA: No.

CADET: You're not sure? Perhaps we should check?

LYOKHA: I'm not a little girl.

CADET: How come you're still a virgin? A big grown-up boy like you?

LYOKHA: I don't know.

CADET: What d'you mean? No luck with the ladies?

LYOKHA: S'pose.

CADET: And why's that?

LYOKHA: Don't know.

CADET: You not asking nicely?

LYOKHA: Don't know.

CADET: Try Natasha. If you ask nicely . . .

NATASHA (*Coming back with the cards*): What is it this time?

CADET: Lyokha here wants to have a go with you.

NATASHA (*Turns to* LYOKHA): You can fucking . . .

LYOKHA: No I don't!

CADET: There's an offer now. You want to make use of the popular demand, Natash.

NATASHA (*To* LYOKHA): Watch yourself, you moron—just who d'you think you're turning down?

BARE-CHESTED MAN: That's enough, now. We're getting to you, aren't we, my friend?

LYOKHA *nods.*

Sit down then, you two. Let the game begin.

MAKSIM *and* LYOKHA *sit at the table.*

(*Shuffling the deck.*) What are we going to play for?

LYOKHA: I don't know.

CADET: For flicks 'round the ear?

LYOKHA: No.

CADET: What then?

LYOKHA: You'll make it hurt.

BARE-CHESTED MAN: Are we just playing, then?

LYOKHA: Alright.

NATASHA (*Laughing*): He's on board, then.

BARE-CHESTED MAN (*Deals*): Two sides: two against two.

NATASHA: "Just playing" to lose. (*She laughs.*)

BARE-CHESTED MAN: There you go.

They all take their cards and look at them.

Who's got the lowest card?

MAKSIM: Me.

BARE-CHESTED MAN: Take it away.

They play. NATASHA *stands next to the table, smiling.*

He's taken the forfeit.

CADET: No luck, bud?

NATASHA: Max-y . . .

MAKSIM: What?

NATASHA: Come for a pee. (*She laughs.*)

They play. There is silence.

BARE-CHESTED MAN: There. In the bag. (*He balances two cards on* LYOKHA*'s shoulders like epaulettes.*)

LYOKHA *smiles sourly. A pause.*

NATASHA: Nailed you, did they, snotface?

LYOKHA: And?

NATASHA: You want to watch who you play cards with. (*She collects the cards.*)

LYOKHA (*Stands up*): Right. We're off then.

BARE-CHESTED MAN: Off where?

LYOKHA: But you said a game and then we could go.

CADET: What about your gambling debts? We should settle them now, shouldn't we?

LYOKHA: I thought we were just playing . . .

NATASHA: Don't you know what "just playing" means?

LYOKHA: No.

BARE-CHESTED MAN: Let me shed a little light for you. . . . Tash, are you going to watch?

NATASHA: Don't think so. Hand me a beer.

The BARE-CHESTED MAN *gets two bottles out of the plastic bag and opens them. He gives one to* NATASHA *and gulps the second one down himself.*

Go on then. Amuse yourselves.

She goes out to the kitchen and sits by the window on a stool. She picks idly at the paint on the windowsill and drinks beer.

BARE-CHESTED MAN'S VOICE: Take off her pants then, Aleksei.

LYOKHA'S VOICE: Please . . .

BARE-CHESTED MAN'S VOICE: Pants down.

LYOKHA'S VOICE: Please, don't . . . please! Jesus! Help!

There is a scuffle.

BARE-CHESTED MAN'S VOICE: Keep still, fuck it!

LYOKHA'S VOICE: Please, don't . . . please don't. . . . Please . . . I'll get my mom to give you money. . . . She runs the swimming pool. . . . Please. . . . Don't! Help me! Christ!

NATASHA: Will you fucking shut him up!?

BARE-CHESTED MAN'S VOICE: Fuck off! And you . . . I told you to keep still! You have your go then, Cadet!

CADET'S VOICE: He's grabbed hold of the chair!

BARE-CHESTED MAN'S VOICE: Whack him!

MAKSIM'S VOICE: Hands off, bastard!

The sound of a blow and a body falling to the ground.

BARE-CHESTED MAN'S VOICE: Get your hands 'round his neck! And you . . . keep still, I said! Keep fucking still!

LYOKHA'S VOICE: PLEASE!!! (*He is screaming and crying.*)

The BARE-CHESTED MAN *groans and pants.* NATASHA *smiles.*

CADET'S VOICE: Sedoy, this one's foaming at the mouth.

BARE-CHESTED MAN'S VOICE: Don't interrupt me.

CADET'S VOICE: What are we going to do?

NATASHA: Grow up!

CADET'S VOICE: You give me that one—you can have a try with him.

SEDOY'S VOICE: Had enough? Go on then, take him!

More scuffling.

LYOKHA'S VOICE (*Hoarsely*): Please . . .

SEDOY'S VOICE: Nice and easy.

NATASHA *laughs hysterically and beats the windowsill with the palm of her hand.*

23

It is night. Rain is pouring down. MAKSIM *and* LYOKHA *are walking along a deserted street.* LYOKHA *is walking slightly ahead. They are silent.*

LYOKHA (*Stops and turns around*): Stop following me.

MAKSIM: We have to go to the cops.

LYOKHA: Never. Understand?

MAKSIM: They'll catch 'em . . .

LYOKHA: I said never! Understand?

MAKSIM: Okay, okay.

LYOKHA: Anyway, you can fuck off, you prick! This is all because of you! (*He walks away.*)

MAKSIM *follows him.*

Stop following me, you bastard! I said stop it! (*He walks off.*)

MAKSIM *stays standing there.* LYOKHA *goes another few yards and then turns around.*

If you so much as fucking breathe a word of this to anyone, I'll kill you. You understand? My mates will finish you! You and your Nana. Is that clear? Bastard! Bastard! (*He starts crying.*) It's all because of you. . . . My mom told me to steer clear of you. . . . Fuck it. . . . Jesus . . . you bastard! Fuck off! Fuck off, I said! Why are you standing there? Fuck off!!!

MAKSIM *walks off down the road.*

LYOKHA *stands there. He is shouting, almost screaming.*

But suddenly . . .

Max! Shit. Max! Stop, Max! Maxie!

MAKSIM *starts running.*

LYOKHA: Maxie, please! Stop! (*He runs after him and falls. He lies there.*) Maxie! Max! Max! Max! Maaaaaax . . .

24

MAKSIM *goes into his room and turns on the light. He goes over to the table, sits down, and takes the plasticine figure and kneads it frenziedly. He looks down at the shapeless ball of plasticine he is holding and wants to throw it back in the box. But instead he starts to model. The ball takes on features: arms, legs, a head, hair, a face . . .* MAKSIM *looks at it and smiles.*

A drop of blood falls from his nose and lands on the figure's forehead. MAKSIM *wipes it away neatly. He stands up, undresses, and turns off the light.*

25

GRANDMOTHER'S VOICE: Maksim . . . Maksim . . .

MAKSIM *opens his eyes and shudders. It is morning and the room is light.*

GRANDMOTHER: Maksim, go down to the elections and buy me some ground beef.

MAKSIM: Where?

GRANDMOTHER: The town hall. They're holding the elections there and giving meat away cheap. Will you go?

MAKSIM: What, right away?

GRANDMOTHER: It would be better. It'll all be gone soon.

MAKSIM: Alright.

GRANDMOTHER: Are you going?

MAKSIM: Yes.

GRANDMOTHER: Here's some money. (*She puts it on the table.*) The shopping bag is in the hall. Where were you yesterday?

MAKSIM: What?

GRANDMOTHER: Where were you, I asked?

MAKSIM: Oh that . . .

GRANDMOTHER: Nevermind. Just get a move on, will you? . . . They'll be sold out otherwise.

MAKSIM: I'm going.

His GRANDMOTHER *goes out and* MAKSIM *gets up and dresses. He sees the flattened plasticine figure in his bed.*

26

MAKSIM, *holding a cloth shopping bag, walks through a large hall filled with stalls. The crowds are buzzing around the stalls. Some people are buying things, others just looking.* MAKSIM *goes up to the long queue in front of the meat stall.*

MAKSIM (*To* WOMAN *at the end of the line*): Is this where the ground beef is?

WOMAN: This is it, son. Get in line behind me.

MAKSIM *stands behind the* WOMAN.

Did your mom send you?

MAKSIM: What? Oh.

WOMAN: Good for you! Helping out your mom like that. They've got good sausage here as well—very cheap. You could get some of that too.

MAKSIM: I've only got enough for the ground beef.

WOMAN: You get the ground beef then, love. That's good, an' all. Would you like a biscuit?

MAKSIM: Who, me?

WOMAN (*Takes a biscuit out of her bag*): There you are.

MAKSIM: What for?

WOMAN: What do you mean? To eat.

MAKSIM: Don't want it.

WOMAN: Take it, take it. (*She puts it in his hand and turns away.*)

MAKSIM *holds the biscuit, not knowing quite what to do with it. He puts it into his bag.*

FAMILIAR VOICE: Mom, come over here!

MAKSIM *stiffens and turns around.* SHE *is standing by a shoe stall. She is holding some white high-heeled sandals. A beautiful woman,* HER MOTHER, *goes across to* HER. MAKSIM *watches.*

SHE: Look at these beauties.

MOTHER: I can see them. (*She turns to leave.*)

SHE: Buy them, mom.

MOTHER: Haven't you got enough sandals?

SHE: Not like these.

MOTHER: You've got others.

SHE: But mom . . .

MOTHER: No.

SHE: But mom . . .

MOTHER: I said no. (*She walks away.*)

SHE (*Walks off behind her still holding the sandals*): But mom!

STALLHOLDER: Hey! Where you going with those?

MOTHER: Put them back, Tanya. (*She tries to take the shoes away.*)

TANYA: But mom . . .

MOTHER: Put them back! (*She grabs the shoes.*)

TANYA: Stupid cow! You'd have bought them for Galka but you don't want to buy them for me. Stupid cow! I hate you! I'm going to live with dad! And you can go and live with your Galka! Two stupid cows together! (*She starts crying.*)

The MOTHER *puts the shoes back and drags* TANYA *away by the arm. Her face is distorted with crying.*Don't touch me, you stupid cow! You're not my mom anymore! Let go of me! Let go! Stupid, stupid cow! I wish you'd die!

STALLHOLDER: What a silly nag, eh?

MAKSIM *looks at the sandals. He is pale. A* WOMAN *comes up behind him with a bag that is bulging and straining at the seams.*

WOMAN WITH BAG: You in line?

MAKSIM: What?

WOMAN WITH BAG: Are you in line?

MAKSIM: No . . .

WOMAN WITH BAG: Out of the way then.

MAKSIM *moves to one side, but then staggers and drops to the floor.*

WOMAN (*Runs over to him and lifts his head*): What's wrong, son? Are you sick? Sick, huh?

WOMAN WITH BAG: He's probably some druggie . . .

WOMAN: I've got to get him outside into the fresh air. Mind my bag, will you?

WOMAN WITH BAG: Anything else? Seen the size of mine?

OTHERS IN THE LINE: Go on—we'll watch it.

The WOMAN *lifts* MAKSIM *and carries him out onto the street. She puts him down on a bench and fans him with her hand.* MAKSIM *opens his eyes and looks at her.*

WOMAN: Feeling a bit better?MAKSIM *nods.*

Not enough air. It was a bit stuffy in there. All those people. Now you've got your breath back you'll be feeling better.

MAKSIM *gets up.*

You stay there and I'll buy you everything and then take you home.

MAKSIM: No. Don't do that.

WOMAN: What do you mean, don't do that? Got to help your mom.

MAKSIM: I don't have one.

WOMAN: What don't you have?

MAKSIM (*Grinning*): A mom.

WOMAN: What do you mean? Where is she?

MAKSIM: Flown away. (*He walks off.*)

WOMAN (*Following him*): Oh, what a shame. . . . Hey, where are you going? You wanted some ground beef, didn't you . . .

MAKSIM: Leave me alone!

The WOMAN *is stunned.*

(*Shouting.*) Get off my back, I said! What d'you want?! Your biscuit back? Take it! (*He gets it out of his bag and throws it at the woman.*) You're all getting to me, you bitches. . . . You know where you can all go!

He runs off.

The WOMAN *watches him go. She looks utterly bewildered.*

27

MAKSIM *runs into the block and up the stairs. He goes past his own door and up to the top floor. He climbs into the attic space. Startled pigeons move out of the way and take off, flying down to the street.* MAKSIM *climbs through the window onto the gray slate roof and goes to the edge. He looks down. People are scurrying around like ants down there. Running about their business and always running late; saying hello and goodbye to each other in the same breath; throwing cigarette butts at bins and missing them; telling jokes and then laughing at them themselves.*

Tripping on their left side and spitting over their left shoulder, tripping on their right and smiling; blowing their noses onto the ground and then treading on the phlegm themselves, finding kopecks and losing roubles, running after buses they can't catch, meeting and parting, feeling joy and grief, love and hate. But none of them look up into the air. Up to where the pigeons are darting in the sky, where the rain is born, and where MAKSIM *is standing on the edge.*

MAKSIM (*Closing his eyes*): Fuck all of you.

28

MAKSIM *goes into the apartment holding a bag with something in it. He goes toward his* GRANDMOTHER*'s room, opens the door, and looks in.*

MAKSIM: Nana, where do you want the meat?

Silence.

Nana . . .

*No answer.*Nana . . . (*He goes into the room.*)

29

In MAKSIM*'s room.* MAKSIM *is sitting on the floor, modeling brass knuckles out of plasticine. He has a plate of diluted alabaster in front of him. When he has finished modeling, he presses the plasticine into the alabaster. He takes out the lead battery plates and knocks the residue off them on the edge of the bed. He goes out and comes back with a burner and a pan. He turns on the burner and puts the pan on it. He breaks the lead plates and puts the pieces in the pan. He takes the plate of alabaster and cleans the plasticine out of it. Then he pours the molten lead into the cast. Smoke pours from the plate and makes his eyes fill with tears.*

MAKSIM *turns away. But then he starts to cry in earnest, sobbing violently, anguished. The plate snaps.*

30

MAKSIM *leaves the apartment, closing the door quietly and locking it. Then he unlocks it again and leaves the key in the lock. He goes over to the neighboring apartment and rings the doorbell. He waits, but no one answers. He tries another apartment. There is a pause.*

CHILD'S VOICE: Who's there?
MAKSIM: Your neighbor.
VOICE: There's no one home.
MAKSIM: My Nana . . . she's . . . tell someone, will you . . .
VOICE: There's no one home.
MAKSIM: My Nana . . . she's . . . tell someone, alright?
VOICE: There's no one home.
MAKSIM: Tell someone, will you . . .

He runs downstairs.

VOICE: I'm not allowed to open the door . . .

31

MAKSIM *runs out of the block and bumps into the* NEIGHBOR *with the burned mailbox.*

NEIGHBOR: Hey! Stop, you! I've got you now, you bastard!
MAKSIM: Just keep walking . . .
NEIGHBOR: What? Into the block with you. (*He goes up to* MAKSIM.)
MAKSIM: Just keep walking . . . (*He puts his hand in his pocket.*)

NEIGHBOR: What? What have you got there?

MAKSIM: Just keep walking!

NEIGHBOR (*Retreating*): Eh! You got a knife?

MAKSIM (*Going toward him*): I said, keep walking . . .

NEIGHBOR: Help! Someone help! He's trying to kill me! Call the police! (*He runs off.*)

MAKSIM *runs in the other direction.*

32

MAKSIM *approaches the four-story building among the wooden barracks. He goes through the door hanging on one hinge and climbs up the stairs, past the warped and broken mailboxes, to the fourth floor. He stands in front of that same derelict old door. He stands in front of it for a long time, holding his breath. Then he walks away and starts to go back down the stairs. He stops, as if remembering something. He climbs back up the stairs and puts his ear to the door and listens.*

He knocks . . .

The sound of footsteps on the other side. MAKSIM *stiffens and adopts a belligerent pose. He looks at his hand. The sound of bolts being drawn back . . .* MAKSIM *puts his hand into the pocket of his denim jacket and tries to pull out the brass knuckles. They won't come out. The door opens slightly and the* CADET*'s head appears in the opening.* MAKSIM *lashes out with his bare hand and hits the doorframe. He punches again. The* CADET *moves his face away and pulls at the handle, trying to shut the door. The door hits* MAKSIM*'s hand. The wood splits and bends. The lock breaks off and flies across the landing.* MAKSIM *drops to the ground as if felled.*

CADET'S VOICE: Sedoy, give me a hand!

SEDOY'S VOICE: What's going on?

CADET'S VOICE: Some fucker just tried to kill me!

SEDOY *runs out onto the landing in his underwear. The* CADET *stands behind him holding the door handle in his hand.*

SEDOY: Did you knock him out?

CADET: Don't know.

SEDOY: Get him into the apartment.

The CADET *grabs* MAKSIM *by the collar and drags him into the apartment.*

33

Darkness.

NATASHA'S VOICE: You gone out of your fucking mind?

SEDOY'S VOICE: Cadet broke his arm in the door.

NATASHA'S VOICE: Like I care. Get him out of here.

CADET'S VOICE: Alright.

NATASHA'S VOICE: Get him out!

SEDOY'S VOICE: What's your problem, you slut?

NATASHA'S VOICE: Fucking me off!

SEDOY'S VOICE: Who's fucking you off?

NATASHA'S VOICE: You are!

MAKSIM *opens his eyes.*

CADET: He's coming 'round.

SEDOY (*Goes over and squats next to* MAKSIM): Hello, my lovely.

NATASHA: Get rid of him, Sedoy.

CADET: Yeah, what are we going to do with him, Sedoy?

SEDOY: I'm thinking. (*To* MAKSIM.) What are we going to do with you then, my lovely?

MAKSIM *puts his left hand in his pocket.*

What have you got there? (*He puts his hand in* MAKSIM'*s pocket and pulls out the brass knuckles.*) Oh, I see. . . . These were for me, right? (*He tries them on, but they don't fit his hand, so he just holds them in his fist and punches* MAKSIM *in the face.*)

NATASHA: What the fuck are you doing?

CADET: Stop that, Sedoy.

SEDOY: I'm finished now. (*He punches* MAKSIM *once again.*)

NATASHA: What are you fucking doing? (*She pushes* SEDOY *away from* MAKSIM.)

SEDOY (*Standing up*): What's wrong with you, you cunt? I'll fucking finish you off while I'm at it.

CADET: Don't, Sedoy . . .

SEDOY: What, I'm done! (*He kicks* MAKSIM *in the head.*)

NATASHA: You're fucking out of your mind. (*She goes into the kitchen.*)

SEDOY: Can't let him go like that, anyway. When they put the plaster on his arm they'll want to know what happened . . . and he'll squeal. . . . Pick him up.

CADET: Where are we taking him?

SEDOY: The landing.

CADET: Why?

SEDOY: Pick him up!

They pick MAKSIM *up, carry him out onto the landing, and go down one flight of stairs.*Open the window.

CADET: Why?

SEDOY: Just do it!

MAKSIM: My Nana . . . she's . . .

SEDOY: Yeah, yeah. . . . Get a fucking move on, cadet.

The CADET *opens the window.*

MAKSIM: I won't do it again.

SEDOY: You won't.

The window is open.

Lift him up.

They lift MAKSIM *up and push him out of the window.*

MAKSIM: Please . . .

SEDOY: Fuck it, cadet!

CADET: He's grabbed hold of my shirt!

SEDOY *beats* MAKSIM*'s hand. Again and again and again.*

He's pissed himself, Sedoy!

MAKSIM *looks down. By the entrance to the block,* SHE *is standing, looking up with* HER *neck craned.* She *is wearing high-heeled white sandals and showing them off to* MAKSIM*, smiling and laughing noiselessly.* SHE *sticks out her tongue at him and then lifts her skirt and strokes her legs.* SHE *runs her hand between her legs and over her breasts.* SHE *wriggles in delight and laughs again. Then suddenly* SHE *turns and runs away.*

There is no one down there. It is deserted.

MAKSIM *closes his eyes.*

Darkness.

THE END

PLAYING THE VICTIM

THE PRESNYAKOV BROTHERS

TRANSLATED BY SASHA DUGDALE[1]

CHARACTERS

VALYA/YOUNG MAN IN SOUTH PARK BASEBALL CAP

FATHER

MOTHER

POLICE INSPECTOR

DOLZHANSKY

POLICE SERGEANT/SEVA

FEMALE POLICE OFFICER/LYUDA

WAITRESS IN THE CAFE

SWIMMING POOL OFFICIAL

TAKHIR ZAKIROV/HAIRY MAN

WAITRESS/JAPANESE WOMAN WITH A MYSTERIOUS PAST

SOMEONE FROM MANAGEMENT

VERKHUSHKIN

SECOND POLICE INSPECTOR

VASSYA THE CHEF

BEARDED MAN

SECOND MAN

In scenes with the MOTHER *and* FATHER, *Valya's part is indicated by* VOICE. *In the original Russian, these speeches are not attributed to a character.*

A room in an apartment.

VOICE: Man has invented many wonderful things. For example . . . for example, seafood salad with crabsticks, or cornflake crunch cake . . . if you ate just the crabsticks without the rest, then that wouldn't taste as good . . . the same if you ate the dry cornflakes without the melted chocolate. But if you put them together, then that's quite another thing. . . . Although one of my friends told me not to eat crabsticks because they make them in the Baltics and according to him those Balts jerk off over the crabsticks because they hate the Russians. . . . Especially the Latvians. . . . They definitely jerk off, and they piss all over the crabsticks, which they export to our country. . . . We really upset them. . . . I remember doing the history . . . we conquered them and they wanted the Fascists to conquer them, so we never really hit it off. . . . Imagine, I mean, could you ever be so upset with someone that you wanted to piss on their food . . . you'd have to have done something really bad to get someone down like that, wouldn't you? They've even got special workers at these factories where they make crabsticks. They load them up with beer and then they piss in the containers of fish flesh, and if they want, they can jerk off in there too. . . . And they export Klondike bars to us as well. . . . I wonder what they do with them . . .

I don't believe everything I hear. . . . I mean, I don't even trust what I see . . . but the smell, there's no getting away from it—those crabsticks have the same smell as urine. I know what urine smells like because I never quite flush it out of my toilet,

I mean the toilet at home, at my parents' home, where I live. I live with my parents and never quite flush the toilet properly. As soon as I hear the water gurgling a little bit I stop pressing the handle down . . . so our toilet, the toilet at home, where I live, the toilet in my parents' home, always smells of urine. The fact that you can send your urine, and all the other stuff that comes out of you, out of the house you live in to a different place—that's another one of man's clever inventions. I like crabstick salad, I like cornflake crunch cake, I use the toilet. I am a happy exploiter of man's achievements. . . . That's why I am a One Hundred Per Cent Person . . . although I never flush the toilet properly . . .

FATHER: There's a fish called the false spadenose! So which is false—the spade or the nose?

MOTHER: Why does the toilet always smell of urine? I clean it every day . . .

VOICE: My father and mother have different levels of "cultural involvement," but they haven't worked it out yet, just as they haven't worked out why the toilet always smells of urine. . . . Every day they argue about something. Mom proves she's right, dad proves he is. . . . Then they wonder why they're living together, how on earth it could have happened . . . and then they make up and wonder why they're always unhappy with one another. But I know—they've got different levels of "cultural involvement." . . . Great phrase, that—I heard it doing exams in the winter, at a revision session for one of the exams, don't remember which one. I failed them all. . . . Different levels of cultural involvement . . . great phrase . . . it means that, for example, if you've got syphilis it's not worth your while living with a healthy person who's going to comment on your illness every day and get at you for being a syphilitic and it rubbing off on everyone else.

MOTHER (*To* FATHER): You're an idiot and it's rubbing off on everyone else.

VOICE: I know why they can't live together and why the toilet always smells of urine . . .

MOTHER: Why do you do it?

VOICE: What are you talking about?

MOTHER: How many times have I asked you and your father not to put paper down the toilet after you've wiped yourself. There's a bucket for it! The pipes block and everything you flush away drips into the kitchen. I wash the dishes with the same water that's in the toilet bowl. How do you like that. How many times have I told both of you. It's an old building, the pipes are rusty, and you can't just throw paper down the toilet.

VOICE: I don't throw paper down the toilet . . .

MOTHER: Don't start that one, how many times have I had a look in the toilet bowl after you, you don't even flush it properly . . .

VOICE: There's a huge gulf between us. All our complaints, interests, everything that brings us together . . . it's all centered on the toilet bowl . . . someone has forced all of us to center our lives on the toilet bowl. . . . Talk about dropping us in it.

An avenue on an urban riverbank with a small outdoor café. There is a pay toilet. Near the toilet there is a police sergeant, a police inspector, a FEMALE POLICE OFFICER *with a video camera, a waitress from the café, a young man in handcuffs, and another young man in a South Park baseball cap.*

INSPECTOR (*To the* FEMALE POLICE OFFICER): Turn on the camera, Lyuda.

LYUDA: It's on already.

INSPECTOR: Right, let's begin the reconstruction. So, Dolzhansky, where were you sitting?

DOLZHANSKY: At this table here. (*He points to the café table nearest him.*)

INSPECTOR: And then what?

DOLZHANSKY: Then she got up, said she needed a tinkle . . . went over to that . . . (*Points at the* WAITRESS.)

INSPECTOR: So she went off as soon as you arrived.

DOLZHANSKY: No . . .

INSPECTOR: So what happened before that?

DOLZHANSKY: We talked . . .

INSPECTOR: Right, and what were you talking about?

DOLZHANSKY: We talked . . . I asked her . . .

INSPECTOR: What about?

DOLZHANSKY: About Igor's birthday party.

FEMALE POLICE OFFICER: He's muttering—can't hear anything!

INSPECTOR: What about? Speak up!

DOLZHANSKY: About Igor's birthday party.

INSPECTOR: Right. So let's hear exactly what you asked her.

DOLZHANSKY: I've just told you!

INSPECTOR: Listen. This is a reconstruction and we're recording everything, so once again speak up for the camera! Or am I not making myself clear?

The SERGEANT *punches* DOLZHANSKY *in the stomach, the young man falls down and rolls around on the ground for a long time, making a pathetic noise and swallowing air—it appears that the* SERGEANT *has winded him with his punch. The* FEMALE POLICE OFFICER, *in order to maintain the purity of the reconstruction, turns the camera away at the exact second when the* SERGEANT *reminds the young man in exactly which reality he has been dropped. She starts filming the view.*

INSPECTOR (*To the* WAITRESS): Have you got any ice cream?

WAITRESS: No.

INSPECTOR: What about beer?

WAITRESS: I've got beer.

INSPECTOR: Is it fresh?

WAITRESS: It's cold.

INSPECTOR: Let's have it then. How much is a glass?

WAITRESS: Eighteen . . .

INSPECTOR: Phew. . . . Bit steep, isn't it?

WAITRESS: Town center . . . what d'you expect? We make all our money when it's hot.

INSPECTOR: Alright. (*Goes into his pocket and gets out two ten ruble notes.*) Does anyone have eight rubles? 'Cause I don't really want to change a ten.

YOUNG MAN: I do . . . (*He passes some coins to the* INSPECTOR.)

INSPECTOR: Give them to her—(*He points at the* WAITRESS.) Thanks. . . . I didn't really want to change a ten . . .

The WAITRESS *goes to get the beer for the* INSPECTOR. DOLZHANSKY *comes around, gets up, and brushes himself down. The* FEMALE POLICE OFFICER *trains the camera on him.*

So, then, what was it you asked the victim about?

DOLZHANSKY: Why she stayed the night at Igor's . . . after the birthday party.

INSPECTOR: Come on, keep going, what did she say?

DOLZHANSKY: She said that everyone stayed and so she didn't go home either, because it was already dark.

INSPECTOR: Right. Keep going. (*The* WAITRESS *brings over the beer and holds it out to the* INSPECTOR.) Aha. Thank you. One minute. (*He signals to the* FEMALE POLICE OFFICER *and she points the camera away. The* INSPECTOR *drinks the beer in one gulp and screws up his face.*) Right, carry on . . .

DOLZHANSKY: I said to her that I rang her friend that night, she went home, and she said that only Anya had stayed with Igor. Anya said that her friend had got mixed up and then she said she wanted a tinkle and she went over to that . . . (*He points at the* WAITRESS.) and asked her for the key to the toilet.

INSPECTOR: Right. So you were sitting at this table? (*He points to the table nearest him.*)

DOLZHANSKY: Yes.

INSPECTOR: Let's sit down then.

The YOUNG MAN *in the baseball cap sits down at the table.*

DOLZHANSKY: No—he didn't sit down right, I was sitting in his place . . .

INSPECTOR: Right—change seats.

The YOUNG MAN *in the baseball cap and* DOLZHANSKY *sit down at the table.*

So then she said she wanted a tinkle and went off?

DOLZHANSKY: Yes . . .

INSPECTOR: Go on then, Valya.

The YOUNG MAN *in the baseball cap gets up and goes over to the* WAITRESS.

INSPECTOR (*To the* WAITRESS): You were standing here?

WAITRESS: Yeah, I gave her the key and she paid me. . . . I asked her to pay straight away, before, because afterward when they come out I don't like it, I've got to handle the food as well and sell stuff, so I always take the money upfront.

INSPECTOR: Right, carry on, Dolzhansky.

DOLZHANSKY: Then I got up and went . . . no—first I sat there for a while, first, I thought for a bit, thought she's lying to me . . . and, also, it was with Igor—she knew that I'd be upset, I asked her not to go to his birthday party, let alone sleep over on her own. . . . I got really angry and went over to the toilet, knocked—

INSPECTOR: Right, get up, go on.

DOLZHANSKY *goes over to the toilet.*

How many times did you knock?

DOLZHANSKY: Twice, and then twice again.

INSPECTOR: Right, let's have this knock then!

DOLZHANSKY *knocks on the toilet door.*

Go on!

DOLZHANSKY: She . . . she said it was engaged and I told her that it was me, she opened the door . . .

INSPECTOR (*TO THE* WAITRESS): Right, open it up for us please.

The WAITRESS *opens the toilet door.*

WAITRESS: There you are.

INSPECTOR: Right. What next?

DOLZHANSKY: Then . . . Anya opened the door and this woman here starts shouting to me to pay, 'cause it isn't allowed for two to pee for the price of one . . .

WAITRESS: Well, not like that, I mean, I said that, if two people go together, even if they're related, you have to pay for two people, if two people go in together, I just reminded him of the rules . . .

INSPECTOR: I see.

DOLZHANSKY: I paid, went in, and shut the door.

INSPECTOR: Right, go in, only don't shut the door, so we can see, like that. Where was she? Was she sitting down?

DOLZHANSKY: Yeah. On the toilet.

INSPECTOR: Right, Valya, sit down.

The YOUNG MAN *sits down on the toilet, smiles, and looks into* DOLZHANSKY*'s eyes.*

DOLZHANSKY: I shut myself in and then I got out a knife and stabbed her in the neck.

INSPECTOR: Right. Where did you get the knife from?

DOLZHANSKY: From my pocket. In my pants . . .

INSPECTOR: Right, give him the . . . (*To the* SERGEANT.) Take off his handcuffs and give him the pencil . . .

The SERGEANT *carries out the* INSPECTOR*'s commands and moves to the side, out of the way of the video camera but not so far that he couldn't react if* DOLZHANSKY *started behaving in a less than perfect manner.*

Right, show us how you stabbed her.

DOLZHANSKY: Like this. (*He touches* VALYA*'s neck carefully with the pencil.*) No, like that! (*He jabs more confidently at* VALYA*'s Adam's apple with the pencil.*) Yes, that's it.

INSPECTOR: Right. Keep going. So how did the victim behave?

DOLZHANSKY: How?

INSPECTOR: I mean, what did she do?

DOLZHANSKY: She farted . . . then she started wheezing and then . . . I don't remember . . . I don't remember that bit . . .

INSPECTOR: How many times did you stab her?

DOLZHANSKY: Once. Just that once in the throat . . . I thought that would be enough.

INSPECTOR: Right, go on. After you thought that would be enough, what did you do then?

DOLZHANSKY: Then I thought that I had to get rid of her somehow, so I wasn't arrested here, so they wouldn't find her . . .

INSPECTOR: Right.

DOLZHANSKY: I decided to cut her up into bits.

INSPECTOR: Right.

DOLZHANSKY: I started cutting across the hand . . . across her hand . . .

INSPECTOR: Right, show us.

DOLZHANSKY: Well, like this . . . (*He draws the pencil across* VALYA*'s wrist.*) Only she was lying down by then.

INSPECTOR: How?

DOLZHANSKY: Head forward. . . . Legs, like, sticking out . . .

INSPECTOR: Go on then, Valya.

VALYA lies down as DOLZHANSKY indicated.

Right. Then what?

DOLZHANSKY: Then I got to the bones and I realized that she had bones and I couldn't saw through them . . .

INSPECTOR: Right, and why on earth did you start sawing? What would you have done with the bits? Did you have a plastic bag with you?

DOLZHANSKY: A small one. I was going to flush away the stuff that didn't fit in—

WAITRESS: Flush it away—you moron! It would have blocked up the drains!

INSPECTOR: Quiet, please. No interfering! Right. Carry on then.

DOLZHANSKY: Well, then . . . I just couldn't get my head 'round it straightaway. I . . . er, felt a bit off . . . I decided to unscrew the toilet bowl and stuff her in there.

INSPECTOR: In where?

DOLZHANSKY: Well, I didn't exactly know how it was built—I thought there was a cesspit down there and I decided to stuff her in there.

WAITRESS: You idiot! A cesspit, indeed! If there had been a cesspit we would hardly have put a toilet over it!

INSPECTOR: Quiet please now! I've already told you once!

WAITRESS: Yeah, yeah . . .

INSPECTOR: Enough, I said! No more butting in! Right, Dolzhansky, where did we stop?

DOLZHANSKY: I was deciding to unscrew the toilet bowl . . .

INSPECTOR: That's right! Okay then, show us.

DOLZHANSKY: There's nothing to see. It wouldn't unscrew. I gave it a pull here and then I decided to call it a day, resigned myself to it. . . . I went out and went home . . .

INSPECTOR: Right. (*To the* WAITRESS.) So when did you discover the victim?

WAITRESS: When? When she crawled out, that's when we discovered her.

INSPECTOR: And why not straightaway—you saw that there were two of them in there together and only one came out?

WAITRESS: Well, who knows? I just thought that he'd had his turn and she was still sitting there. After all, they'd paid . . . you never know. My husband, he can sit there for an hour and a half sometimes, squeezing it out. That's if he doesn't have soup or salad at dinner for a while—

INSPECTOR (*Interrupting the* WAITRESS): Right then! Well, that's all, then . . . (*To the* FEMALE POLICE OFFICER.) Did you get it all down?

FEMALE POLICE OFFICER: Yes. Is that it?

INSPECTOR: Yeah, turn it off! Right . . .

WAITRESS: Can I go then?

INSPECTOR: Oh—yes, yes. How much is a glass of beer?

WAITRESS: Eighteen rubles—you've already paid for one.

INSPECTOR: Oh yes. (*To the* FEMALE POLICE OFFICER.) Do you have twenty-six rubles?

FEMALE POLICE OFFICER: Yes I do. (*Roots around in her pocket.*)

INSPECTOR: Let's have a beer then?

FEMALE POLICE OFFICER: Why not?

SERGEANT: Inspector, Sir, can I have one too?

INSPECTOR: And what about him?

SERGEANT: Him? He can just stand near us.

INSPECTOR: Yeah, right—not likely. Take him off to the car and wait for us there.

VALYA: What about if you lock him in the toilet for the moment? And we'll have a beer. He can sit there a bit, think things over—

where the crime was committed. An educational measure, if you like.

INSPECTOR (*Considers it*): Okay then, but quickly.

The joyful SERGEANT *locks* DOLZHANSKY *in the toilet. The* INSPECTOR *and* FEMALE POLICE OFFICER *sit down at one table, the* SERGEANT *and* VALYA *sit down at another. A waitress brings them the beer.*

VALYA: Is he on drugs?

SERGEANT: Him? No . . .

VALYA: Strange. With logic like that. Cuts her up without realizing she's got bones in her arms, I mean, not like she hasn't got them in her legs too . . .

SERGEANT: No—he's not on drugs.

VALYA: Strange . . .

SERGEANT: Yeah . . . he lost his head. . . . I mean, cutting her up was the right idea, because you never find them, then—any documentary about criminal life tells you that. . . . Just not in situations like this. They were seen together . . . he just lost it . . . jealousy . . . fit of pash . . . passion, fit of passion, yeah . . .

VALYA: Jealousy?

SERGEANT: And?

VALYA: Maybe it was curiosity? After all he did try chopping her up.

SERGEANT: No, jealousy.

VALYA: And what about her?

SERGEANT: Who?

VALYA: His girl, the one he wanted to flush away . . .

SERGEANT: Anya?

VALYA: Yeah, Anya—I mean, did she really sleep with his friend?

SERGEANT: Well, yeah, that's what he thought.

VALYA: What he thought, huh? If I attacked people with a knife every time "I thought" something, they'd be calling it genocide by now . . .

SERGEANT: Well he was going on about how he'd been jealous of him for quite a while, and when they were on their own together it was just too much for him.

VALYA: Who was he jealous of?

SERGEANT: Well, her, doing it with him.

VALYA: Hang on, her with who, I mean who did he love?

SERGEANT: Him, of course. Igor! He's not going to kill the one he loves . . . do you think he's completely nuts . . .

VALYA: Then he's a queer?

SERGEANT: Well, looks like it, seeing as he loves Igor.

VALYA: How did they catch him?

SERGEANT: Well Anya survived, didn't she, as he only gave her a little. . . . I mean, she collapsed more from fear than anything else, and he decided she was finished, blood loss and that, her hand hanging on a thread, they say, but she survived . . .

VALYA: Lucky for him.

SERGEANT: Yeah! Igor's hardly going to look at her now. She's got a scar on her neck and on her wrist too, probably, so yeah, lucky for him.

VALYA *looks hard at the* SERGEANT, *obviously wanting to object and explain what he meant when he said that* DOLZHANSKY *had been lucky. But after thinking for a while,* VALYA *smiles at the* SERGEANT, *who is drinking down his beer in a gulp.*

INSPECTOR: Right, let's go then. (*To the* SERGEANT.) Get him out! (*To* VALYA.) Are you coming with us?

VALYA: No, it's easier for me to walk from here.

INSPECTOR: Right, off you go then.

VALYA: Goodbye, Inspector, Sir. (*To the* SERGEANT.) Bye then, Sevik!

SERGEANT: Bye!

A room in an apartment.

MOTHER: Go out and get some bread for me. Your father will be home from work soon and we're out of bread.

VOICE: What kind?

MOTHER: Rye bread.

VOICE: And if there isn't any?

MOTHER: Get some flatbread then.

VOICE: Flatbread? Isn't that dangerous?

MOTHER: What's dangerous?

VOICE: Isn't buying flatbread dangerous?

MOTHER: What are you talking about? Flatbread is still bread! It even tastes better!

VOICE: Tastes better, but we're at war with them.

MOTHER: With whom?

VOICE: The ones who make the flatbread.

MOTHER: Well, so what? They're the ones who live here.

VOICE: Who?

MOTHER: The ones who make this flatbread, they live here.

VOICE: Still, they're all the same.

MOTHER: Well, they're not all bad, after all.

VOICE: Not all of them. Definitely not all of them, over there the majority aren't bad, but they all want one thing, and that's why they're not bad, in theory, and why we can't beat them.

MOTHER: So now what? We can't buy flatbread?

VOICE: Well, I don't know . . . we could risk it, of course. Although what happens if they get a secret message to poison all the flatbread? And flatbread tastes better than our bread, even better than rye bread, yeah?

MOTHER: Yes . . .

VOICE: So there you are, they'll sell all the flatbread and then that'll be it, if they've had their orders. . . .

MOTHER: But they'll work out straightaway who did it.

VOICE: Of course they'll work it out. Everyone will work it out after the event. Afterward. . . . But I can work it all out and warn you beforehand. Afterward working it all out won't make any difference to us, after we've eaten their flatbread . . .

MOTHER: I think we'll probably manage without bread today. . . . I've cooked some noodles and that's a carbohydrate, and tomorrow I'll buy some myself.

VOICE: Whatever you say.

MOTHER: I'll go out and buy it myself.

VOICE: I was always good at thinking up ways to get out of things. From when I was a kid, I never did anything I didn't want to. And not because I was lazy. . . . That's not the reason, or at least that's a reason, but there's something else deeper that makes me lazy. I think it's fear. Sometimes I'm afraid just to go out in the street. I'm afraid to go for bread or take a walk. And then comes the laziness. . . . Maybe, if you could find out, you might find that there's a reason for fear as well. . . . Still, I've stopped being scared of everything that used to scare me because I can think of ways to get out of everything. Even in school, in junior high, when they started taking us to the swimming pool and I was scared of water—my mom almost drowned when she was young, that was before I was born, so it must have been passed on to me. . . . I mean, her fear of drowning was passed on to me, although she was a good swimmer actually, and even after she almost drowned she didn't stop swimming—but I can't stand water, deep rivers, seas . . . I never go in—not even to my knees . . . I don't like crossing bridges either. And in school, when they started taking us to the swimming pool for P.E., I just didn't take my swimming trunks with me and they wouldn't let me into the swimming pool, because according to the rules you couldn't go swimming in the same pants you were wearing for hygiene reasons, although I suppose you could have been walking around in clean pants anyway. . . . But they didn't take into account that people could be walking around during the day in clean pants. Or I guess you could take swimming trunks, but dirty ones, and give everyone a nasty little dose of something. Anyway, I never took my trunks, I used to pretend I'd forgotten. They told me off but never put me in detention, and I pretended I really wanted to go swimming and I begged them to let me in in the pants I was wearing. . . . But they didn't let me and they thought they were punishing me like that. By the way, if people think you're being punished as it is, they never punish you anymore. . . . Yeah . . .

The swimming pool. At the edge of the swimming pool are the SERGEANT, *the* INSPECTOR, *the* FEMALE POLICE OFFICER *with the video camera, the female* SWIMMING POOL OFFICIAL, *a* MAN *covered in an exceptional amount of body and facial hair in swimming trunks and handcuffs, and a* YOUNG MAN *in a South Park baseball cap and pants. The* SWIMMING POOL OFFICIAL *is arguing with the* INSPECTOR, *the* HAIRY MAN *is cold, and the* YOUNG MAN *has a wide smile on his face.*

SWIMMING POOL OFFICIAL: No, I said no, and that's it. He has to have swimming trunks or he's not getting in the water.

INSPECTOR: Well, how about that. (*To the* YOUNG MAN.) Valya, well you fucked up! I warned you we'd be in the swimming pool, didn't I!

VALYA: I didn't know, Inspector, Sir, that you needed trunks to go in. I mean, what for? (*To the* SWIMMING POOL OFFICIAL.) My pants are clean, honest they are. I put them on today.

SWIMMING POOL OFFICIAL: No!

VALYA: Honest! I haven't even had a tinkle, I mean pissed in them today.

SWIMMING POOL OFFICIAL: So what?

VALYA: Have a look—not a stain!

SWIMMING POOL OFFICIAL: Well it doesn't matter—there are still germs!

VALYA: And there aren't any germs in trunks?

SWIMMING POOL OFFICIAL: No—because they're trunks and you don't walk around in them all day.

VALYA: But they're clean.

SWIMMING POOL OFFICIAL: How can they be if you're wearing them? How many germs are there in them by now? And we add chlorine to the pool! Everyone follows the rules here.

INSPECTOR: Alright, that's enough. In that case we'll do it all here on the bank, I mean poolside. Right, Lyuda, turn the camera on!

FEMALE POLICE OFFICER: It's already on.

INSPECTOR: Right. Let's begin the reconstruction of the Takhirov case.

HAIRY MAN: Zakirov.

INSPECTOR: Right, that's it, Zakirov Takhir.

SWIMMING POOL OFFICIAL: Just make sure they don't get in the water!

INSPECTOR: We got the message.

SWIMMING POOL OFFICIAL: I'm watching you—I'll see if you do!

INSPECTOR: We get the message! Right . . .

The SWIMMING POOL OFFICIAL *goes and the* INSPECTOR *mutters something rude as she leaves.*

Right then, Zakirov, how did you get into the pool?

ZAKIROV (*He has a strong Caucasian/Middle Eastern accent.*): Swim pass.

INSPECTOR: And the victim?

ZAKIROV: She had a swim pass here.

INSPECTOR: Right, so that is, you knew that she would be here at the time when your pass was valid.

ZAKIROV: Yeah . . . I knew.

INSPECTOR: Right. So you came in, and where was the victim?

ZAKIROV: Right here, in the second lane, here . . .

INSPECTOR: Right, and did she notice you?

ZAKIROV: No. I didn't want her to notice me.

INSPECTOR: Right. Carry on, your actions after that.

ZAKIROV: I am jumping into the pool.

INSPECTOR: Right then, show us how you jumped. Only stay right here, no going into the water.

ZAKIROV (*Jumping on the spot*): Something like that.

INSPECTOR: Well, this is a complete mess. . . . Valya, you fucked up big time. I did warn you we'd be going to the swimming pool, didn't I? Now what are we going to do? I've got to get this case finished and a report on the desk by tomorrow.

VALYA: Well, Inspector, Sir, well I mean. . . . I really didn't know, I put on clean pants especially, I didn't know that you had to bring trunks with you, did I?

SERGEANT: Maybe he should just get in, what's she going to do to us?

INSPECTOR: No. . . . Getting involved with all that shit . . . she'd make such a fuss . . . alright . . . right, Taki . . . Zakirov, what happened after that, you're in the water . . .

ZAKIROV: I am in the water, looking at her. She is having a grin, her friends are here, she is shouting to them. I dived straight-away so she didn't notice me.

INSPECTOR: Right, you dived. Sit down like that.

ZAKIROV takes a big breath, as if he was really diving for a long time under water, and sits down.

INSPECTOR: Right. Then what?

ZAKIROV (*Breathing out*): I swam over to her . . .

INSPECTOR: Right, and what distance did you swim?

ZAKIROV: Well, maybe ten, fifteen . . . no more than seven meters . . .

INSPECTOR: Right, Valya. Stand about ten meters away from him. Right, Zakirov, imagine that he is the victim and swim across to her, I mean, to him, and do what you did to the victim.

ZAKIROV: No problem! (*He crawls across to* VALYA, *paddling at the air with his hands.*)

INSPECTOR: O fuck fuck fuck Valya . . . I mean we've even found spare trunks for Takhir here, but you . . . you came straight from home and not from prison—surely you could have guessed.

VALYA *moves the correct ten meters away and guiltily looks away from the* INSPECTOR. ZAKIROV *swims up to* VALYA *and sits by his feet.*

INSPECTOR (*To the* FEMALE POLICE OFFICER): Nice pool, eh, Lyuda?

FEMALE POLICE OFFICER: Not bad.

INSPECTOR: Do you go swimming? Look after yourself, your figure, I mean?

FEMALE POLICE OFFICER: When? We have shooting practice once a month, but I don't have time for much else . . .

INSPECTOR: No, it's not a bad little pool. Once or twice, say, twice a week you could come up here for a swim.

FEMALE POLICE OFFICER: What's wrong with the crazy boy, is he tired or something?

INSPECTOR: Come on then, Zakirov, how long are you going to sit there? Show us then!

ZAKIROV: I don't really remember. . . . I think I swam up to her, she was splashing around, moving her legs . . .

INSPECTOR: Come on then, think, try to remember.

ZAKIROV: Well, I started to search for her legs because the others were moving their legs . . . she had green on her toes . . . green nail polish, I found her. . . . She was. . . . (*To* VALYA.) Wave your legs around, eh—it'll be easier for me to remember.

INSPECTOR: C'mon, Valya, make an effort and do something at least today . . . what are you grinning for? Go on!

VALYA *begins to wave his legs around as if he were trying to do a pirouette.*

ZAKIROV: Then I grabbed her like that and pulled her toward me like she was diving. She. . . . Hang on . . . (*He strokes* VALYA*'s legs and grabs his own head as if he was just about to remember some detail of the drowning.*)

INSPECTOR: Well, go on then—grab him, grab him, pull him toward you as if you were underwater . . .

ZAKIROV: Hang on . . . right . . . (*He grabs hold of* VALYA*'s legs,* VALYA *sits down, and* ZAKIROV *lies down on the tiles, squeezing* VALYA*'s legs tightly.*) She was splashing around, splashing . . . and then she stopped—I let her go and swam underwater to the other side of the pool, climbed out, and left. She came to the surface and, well, everyone thought she was swimming . . . and I left.

FEMALE POLICE OFFICER: So how much time did he spend underwater?

INSPECTOR: Six minutes, minimum, because he swam about ten meters over to her, held her under, and then swam off. . . . Is that right, Zakirov? Did you show us everything exactly as it was?

ZAKIROV: That is how it was . . . more or less. . . . I loved her, Inspector, Sir, I loved her, but she didn't . . . she didn't love me, she was only pretending. I did everything for her and she went to live with my brother. . . . "Why did you do that?" I asked her, and I asked him. . . . I said to him, "You are my brother, why do you act like this?" But he is older than me—in our culture, you must not argue with elders. That's how it was at first, I mean, I could only talk to her about it. . . . I gave her many presents, everything, everything I could. . . . If she wanted new stockings, she got 'em, everything I had, everything I traded, she had it all, one or two of everything, I always said to her, "Come and choose something," if you want stockings. Take some chocolate, only the imported sort, "Carly-Varly" chocolate from England, the very best, I gave her three bars of everything, gave some to her friends . . .

INSPECTOR: Alright, that's enough of the sob story, Zakirov. Keep quiet for a bit. Right, so how long . . . tell me, Zakirov, were you wearing diving equipment?

ZAKIROV: I was wearing what I came in . . . no diving equipment . . . just pants.

FEMALE POLICE OFFICER: We should check. It doesn't make sense. He'd have to be like a fish, like one of those pearl divers, and even they can't go that long without air.

INSPECTOR: Right, Zakirov, I'm going to time you, I'll give you a signal and you hold your breath, hold your breath for as long as you can, because we need to test this. Do you understand?

ZAKIROV: Yes!

INSPECTOR (*Looking at his watch*): Right, let's go!

A minute passes.

ZAKIROV: So shall I hold my breath?

INSPECTOR: Are you breathing?!

ZAKIROV: I'm waiting for the signal . . .

INSPECTOR: Oh fuck. . . . Right, try again. (*He looks at his watch.*) Right, hold your breath! (*He gives a signal.*)

ZAKIROV: Got it! I'm holding my breath! (*He breathes in and holds his breath.*)

A minute passes.

How long do I hold my breath?

INSPECTOR: What a day. Takirov, I'll give a signal and you hold your breath for as long as you can. As long as you can manage to hold it. Do you understand?

ZAKIROV: No!

INSPECTOR: What don't you understand?

ZAKIROV: I'm not Takirov. I am Zakirov.

INSPECTOR: Listen, Zakirov, if you don't get the message right now, then we'll tape over your nose and mouth and untape you in half an hour. Then we'll see what a diver you'll fucking make!

ZAKIROV: Explain what to do—I'll do it. I'll do it all myself. I'm not resisting.

INSPECTOR: Shut your mouth and hold your breath and when you run out of air, tell us.

ZAKIROV: Right. I got it. I'm shutting my mouth.

The INSPECTOR *looks at his watch, timing him. Thirty seconds pass.*

ZAKIROV: That's it! I've run out of air.

INSPECTOR: We should beat him fucking senseless right here in the swimming pool . . . he didn't even last a minute.

FEMALE POLICE OFFICER: Maybe it wasn't him that drowned her?

INSPECTOR: Who was it then?

FEMALE POLICE OFFICER: Well how could he have drowned her, if he can't even hold his breath for a minute?

INSPECTOR: Something's not right here. He probably did her in some other way . . . and he's just spinning us a line. . . . Right, Zakirov, have you shown us exactly what happened?

ZAKIROV: Exactly . . . well, I don't remember . . . what I remember I showed you . . .

INSPECTOR: Bastard. . . . Well, screw him. We did the reconstruction and his fingerprints were found on her legs, right? Her friends in the pool didn't see him because he dove underwater, right? That's it! Some things fit, and that's enough!

FEMALE POLICE OFFICER: Well, yeah, in theory . . . and anyway he could have been in such a state that he didn't notice he wasn't breathing. 'Cause he wanted to kill her. . . . Everything depends on state of mind, I mean, what your intention is. . . . If you ask him now, without the urgency, he has to breathe, plus he's thinking about it now and then he wasn't. It's like one of those feats people achieve, racing around without thinking about it. Like, you know . . . driving a burning car out of a fire, saving people . . . there was a case when this man pulled two women out of the water, and he couldn't even swim himself. Just jumped into the water, grabbed onto them, and dragged them out, and couldn't remember himself how he did it. . . . And our Colonel, Filipov, when he came to our housewarming, he drank a bit and played the guitar all evening. Really well too—Spanish Flamenco. The next morning we woke him up and we're sitting having breakfast and we say to him, "Play us a tune, Colonel, Sir" and he told us all to fuck off . . . saying he's never in his life even held a guitar in his hand.

INSPECTOR: Right, okay, we get it. . . . (*He thinks of something and looks around.*) Nice pool. Zakirov, how much did your swim pass cost you?

ZAKIROV: I don't remember. I bought it for one session. If you get it for several then it's cheaper, you get a discount. You can get a monthly pass, then it works out almost for free. I got a day pass. I didn't need very much.

INSPECTOR (*To the* FEMALE POLICE OFFICER): We could get a monthly pass? Come swimming. . . . It'd be more fun for the two of us. I wouldn't make it here on my own.

FEMALE POLICE OFFICER: You could get a family pass . . .

INSPECTOR: Yeah, but I get to swim in the bath with my family. . . . Would you join me? Just for the company?

FEMALE POLICE OFFICER: Why not? (*She points to the camera.*) Should I turn it off?

INSPECTOR: What? Was it on?

FEMALE POLICE OFFICER: Yeah, I'm just turning it off now.

INSPECTOR: Get rid of the last bit—about the colonel, and the swimming pool . . .

FEMALE POLICE OFFICER (*Laughing*): Compromising material, huh?

INSPECTOR (*Laughs too and then stops suddenly*): Right. Now we're here, let's go and find out how much it costs . . .

FEMALE POLICE OFFICER: Let's go.

INSPECTOR: Where's the office? Through this door? Where did the old cow appear from?

FEMALE POLICE OFFICER: Yeah, I think so.

INSPECTOR (*To the* SERGEANT): Right, Seva, wait for us, we won't be a minute. Valya, honestly . . .

The INSPECTOR *and* FEMALE POLICE OFFICER *leave.* VALYA *sits on the side of the pool and smiles.*

VALYA: Hey, Zakirov, how did you hold your breath underwater then?

ZAKIROV: What's it to you? None of your business.

VALYA: I'm just interested . . . c'mon, tell me.

ZAKIROV: Asshole! (*He turns away.*)

VALYA: Hey, that's what I thought! You hiding that, then? Why didn't you show them on camera how you breathe through your asshole? Because you don't want us to learn? It's your secret weapon, huh?

ZAKIROV *suddenly starts singing a very beautiful song with a soft, Eastern melody, paying no attention to* VALYA, *although the insults woven into his song are obviously meant for him.*

ZAKIROV: Kyzlyari, queerlyari, cumquickly, shitty-shitty . . .

VALYA (*TO* ZAKIROV): Oh, lovely. . . . Hey, do you know anything from "Ali Baba"? That would be just about your thing . . .

ZAKIROV (*Continues to chant*): Sing it, sing it, queers all around . . .

SERGEANT: Hey, I want to start an evening course this year . . .

VALYA: Where?

SERGEANT: University.

VALYA: Go for it.

SERGEANT: You were there, weren't you?

VALYA: Not for long.

SERGEANT: Listen, give me some advice. I want to study history.

VALYA: So what's the big rush to start studying?

SERGEANT: Well, you can't get anywhere without higher education these days. What should I do? Spend my time rounding up lowlifes?

VALYA: Right—let's dig deeper—let's work out your real motives for wanting to study.

SERGEANT: Alright, let's dig deeper. After all I need to sort it out myself.

VALYA: Like, you obviously want to get an education without any effort . . .

SERGEANT: Well, I suppose . . .

VALYA: So if that's what you want, go for journalism or philosophy. You don't need to do a thing there and you'll still get a degree, I'm telling you . . .

SERGEANT: Yeah, and what do I do with it?

VALYA: Right, let's go back to basics—what you want is a well-paid job, a bit of prestige, yeah?

SERGEANT: Well, and what's wrong with that . . .

VALYA: Nothing at all, Seva, but why take such a roundabout path to something you could do in half a minute.

SERGEANT: What do you mean?

VALYA: Look, all this study stuff, all the misery, hard work, I mean, after all it's just so you can make a lot of money, yeah?

SERGEANT: Well, that's if you don't take friends and conversation into account . . .

VALYA: Come on. What are you being so touchy about? I'm talking to you as a grown-up person . . .

SERGEANT: Alright, alright . . .

VALYA: So here he is—right here—your loyal genie Takhirov, ready to grant your every wish if you only set him free. He is the captive of the lamp, and you, Seva, you could be his Aladdin!

SERGEANT: What are you . . . no, I don't . . .

ZAKIROV *stops singing and moves closer to* SEVA *and* VALYA.

VALYA: What are you scared of? We'll tell the Inspector he escaped. The worst that can happen is that you'll lose your job.

SERGEANT: Come on, Valya, stop it . . .

VALYA: Look it's simple, very simple. He'll disappear straightaway, before you can say the word, back to his own country, you'll get a reward . . . think of it like Gorky wrote: "He didn't go to university, but life itself became his university . . ."

ZAKIROV: Hey, how much do you want, we've got a car, a white Lada, money, I'll give you as much as you need . . . all above board . . . before they get back, let me go friend. . . . Listen, eh, honest to God, anything you want, I'll do it, in thanks . . .

SERGEANT: Come on, now . . .

VALYA: Hey, taking your time, aren't you? Look, it would only take a minute and his hairy ass would be out of here faster than the speed of light and you'd be sitting in your white car with a pile of money.

SERGEANT: Yeah, not bad. I could go for that.

VALYA: Oh, and you'd lose your job, like that would be a hardship . . . how embarrassing, eh . . .

SERGEANT: And you? You'd want something too, wouldn't you? A share?

VALYA: Come off it, I just want to help you out. My reward would be if one person, (*Looks at* ZAKIROV.) no, two whole people found happiness on this earth . . . complete happiness . . .

VALYA looks into SEVA's eyes and gives him a wide, fatherly smile. SEVA chews everything over in his mind for a long time, doubtingly for a while. Then all at once he makes a sudden movement and reaches into his pocket, gets out the keys for the handcuffs, and goes over to ZAKIROV, who is delighted. He puts his two hands out toward SEVA in the hope that his hairy arms are about to be freed, and in a short while his whole hairy body will be free. But at the last moment VALYA knocks the keys out of SEVA's hands with a violent movement.

SERGEANT: What did you do that for?

VALYA: I was joking, Sevik—we'd get in such shit for this, for this friend of yours. And even if he had agreed, d'you think he'd come searching us out to give us our due? He'll sooner snitch on us . . .

ZAKIROV: No, honestly, friend . . . honestly, don't listen to him!

SERGEANT: So why did you tell me all this crap then?

VALYA: Well, so that . . . so that you'd grasp what morality is.

SERGEANT: What?

VALYA: Morality, Sevik, resides in the way you satisfy your desires. . . . When you really want something, you have to count on other people, society, its codes, you have to study history, work, so that the reward you get from society, many, many years later is earned. . . . Takhirov didn't realize that and that's why he's in handcuffs as a result. And now you're warned, and because you're warned you're on guard against it. . . . It's so easy to go wrong, Seva, and I don't want it to happen to you . . .

SERGEANT (*He is upset and hasn't completely come to his senses.*): Fuck you . . .

ZAKIROV: Hey friend, Seva, come on, eh . . .

The INSPECTOR *and the* FEMALE POLICE OFFICER *come over to the swimming pool.* ZAKIROV *starts to howl, realizing that now there definitely won't be any chance of escape. The* FEMALE POLICE OFFICER *is straightening her uniform; the* INSPECTOR *is checking his fly.*

INSPECTOR: Well, that's it then. Why's he howling? What's got into him?

VALYA: He's repenting . . .

INSPECTOR: Yeah?

VALYA: Yeah, he's just opened up his soul to us, told us that he'd thought too much of himself . . . he said that he'd tried the murder as a way of testing if he could do it, or if he'd be too scared.

INSPECTOR: Yes?

VALYA: And when he could do it he understood that even for the highest goal you couldn't treat someone else like that, not even the most worthless person.

INSPECTOR: Kind of late for these ideas, Takhirov.

ZAKIROV, *grinding his teeth, mutters something very indecent in his native tongue.*

VALYA: He wants you to send him as far as possible, to Siberia, so that he can be spiritually cleansed. He got quite hysterical while you weren't here.

INSPECTOR: Never mind Zakirov, you're not the first and you won't be the last. . . . And as for Siberia, well that's for the court to decide—where they send you, that's where you'll have to get spiritually cleansed, and it doesn't have to be Siberia . . . we've got lots of places which are good for that. . . . Right then, let's go. (*They leave.*)

A room in an apartment. Dinnertime. FATHER *watches his son spending a long time attempting to pick up a piece of food. His son drops the food on the floor and* FATHER *winces.*

FATHER: Why can't you eat like everyone else? Where did you find those chopsticks? Why are you eating with them?

VOICE: So life doesn't get too easy.

FATHER: I mean, I would understand if you were eating what you're supposed to eat with them.

VOICE: And what are you supposed to eat?

FATHER: Well, what's it called? Raw fish, rice balls . . . whatever the slant-eyed people eat . . .

VOICE: Dad, it's not just the "slant-eyed people" who eat with chopsticks. Half the world uses them. And you can eat anything you like with them, except soup, although if you put your mind to it you could probably get good enough to gulp down soup with them.

FATHER: Well, I've noticed that it's a whole hour . . . your mother and I eat and a whole hour later you leave the table. . . . It's enough to drive anyone mad! Eat with a spoon, like a normal human being!

VOICE: Do you know when the brain sends you a signal that you're full?

FATHER: When?

VOICE: Half an hour after you start eating. So you and mom overeat because while you're eating you don't get a signal that it's time to stop stuffing your belly . . . this way you eat little by little and keep everything under control.

FATHER: But it's not our culture—what's the point in associating yourself with something you'll never have?

VOICE: Well really, dad—not our culture?

FATHER: Son, in Russia, if you want to live you need this! (*He stands the spoon up.*) This is what you eat with, you shovel up as much as possible and you eat—you don't pick around with those chopsticks. Look, right—we Russians put a ladle on the end of the stick, because you can't do anything at the table with just a stick. . . . I mean look at you reaching out for morsels with your chopsticks and never managing to eat them. . . . Let them keep their sticks to themselves in the East!

VOICE: But dad, after Genghis Khan was here all the borders between East and West disappeared!

FATHER: Maybe for you they did, for your university, if that's what they teach you there . . . but they didn't disappear for me—or for your mother.

VOICE: Right, and in the village where you were born, didn't the Germans invade? Wasn't it occupied? So why do you like European culture so much? Is it your German blood calling?

FATHER: Leave the fucking table! Bastard! Look how you've brought him up!

MOTHER: Me?! You're the one who brought him up like that! Look at him! He's the living image of you!

VOICE: Actually I use chopsticks so I don't have to do the washing up. They do it all while I'm still eating. No one's got the patience to see the dirty dishes and me still chewing calmly. Chopsticks are really annoying to eat with—even when you get good at it. . . . There's never any guarantee that some small bit won't drop off. I also find chopsticks really revolting. In fact, anything connected with Japan and China fills me with distrust. I mean it's clear that there's something wrong . . . in their relationship with reality, and that's one hundred percent clear in Japan, especially after the atom bomb. I heard that the idea of "The Great Revenge" is very popular over there—"great revenge" on America for the atom bombs dropped in 1945. They make cars, computers, all of it just to get their revenge . . . and then they'll make a load of robots and send them to America and every robot will be filled with small atomic devices. The whole country is working on it—every day, no weekends, and a week's holiday a year. Anyway, I eat with chopsticks so I don't have to wash the dishes, I'm not stupid. I realized a long time ago that in order to get out of doing something, you have to do something else. If you want to avoid doing something nasty, you have to do something else you don't like, and that helps you get out of the thing that's worse. It isn't an easy concept, especially to have explained to you. . . . It sounds complicated, but if you don't think too much about it and don't even talk about it, you don't mention it, you just do it, just do it without thinking, then it'll work out . . .

A half-empty Japanese restaurant. In the middle of the hall stand the SERGEANT, INSPECTOR, FEMALE POLICE OFFICER *with a video camera, a tipsy, gray-haired* WAITRESS *in a kimono, a* MAN *in handcuffs, and the* YOUNG MAN *in a South Park baseball cap.*

INSPECTOR: So you prepare live fish here?

WAITRESS: Yes.

INSPECTOR: And people order it?

WAITRESS: Yes.

INSPECTOR: And eat it?

WAITRESS: Yes.

INSPECTOR: Well fu . . . amazing. So how much does it cost?

WAITRESS: Depends. We have fifteen different types of sushi alone—a single portion costs from sixty rubles . . .

INSPECTOR: Oh . . . I see . . . well. . . . No. I'm scared of getting worms! Once you've got them they live in you. Someone I knew once had a big worm living in his stomach. . . . He was quite friendly with him—when he drank kefir he used to joke that he was feeding his worm.

WAITRESS: Worms come from live fish if you don't freeze it.

INSPECTOR: But it says here that the sushi is made from fresh—

WAITRESS: Fresh, but frozen.

VALYA: But in Japan the fish is no sooner out of the river than it's in the restaurants.

WAITRESS: When there are salmon in the Moscow River, that's when you'll have to worry about worms, but the fish we get doesn't have anything in it, let alone worms—it's completely sterile.

INSPECTOR: Right. Let's get started. You're in a kimono . . . are you Japanese?

WAITRESS: 'Course not. The manager dreamed this up. There's thousands of these restaurants in Moscow. 'Til someone gets food poisoning, people will be raking it in from these exotic theme restaurants. 'Til the first accident, if you get me. (*Lowering her voice.*) Because if I'm honest, it's a dangerous business, you have to spend a long time learning how to cook all this crap, even the fish—'cause if you don't cut it right it could be poisonous . . .

INSPECTOR: Really?

WAITRESS: The most expensive fish—we've got it on our menu, too—our cook Vassya prepared it recently. Took a lot of courage. He cut this enormous fish up, put salad round it, brought it out to the table and all the staff watched to see what would happen . . .

INSPECTOR: And?

WAITRESS: Got away with it, looks like. We were probably saved by the fact that we didn't have any sake left, so we gave them normal vodka . . . that might be the reason we got away with it. . . . We were all very worked up though. . . . It was unbelievably stressful.

INSPECTOR: Right. And what about wearing the kimono then?

WAITRESS: I told you. Our manager said that there had to be a samurai in every corner of the restaurant . . . he meant like the ones you have in restaurants . . . samurai . . . that's it . . . and he says to me, "You can be an elderly Japanese woman with a mysterious past . . . do you get me? Grabs their attention."

Suddenly she wrinkles up her face as if she were about to cry and narrows her eyes. She pulls up her lower lip to the end of her nose and sings.

An English sailor, straight from a gunship,
Came to a teahouse, sunk like a boat
Beneath the waves of blossoming roses,
To meet with sailors, there he sought
To meet with the sailors known on the sea,
And he called for some wine and a cup of tea.

She hesitates, unable to remember the words, and then continues.

. . . And then he said nothing more.
And in the corner a Japanese beauty
Sang a song of longing and love
And he remembered his own dear country
And in him stirred his own sea blood.
Still the next morning the ship sets sail
The orders are given: "set course," "ahoy!"
And she weeps hard, and he feels joy.
Ten years pass quickly, like in a story,
And the Japanese girl has a little son.

He asks wide-eyed, "What's my story?
Who's my Daddy? Tell me the one."
And the Japanese beauty presses his hand
And says, "A sailor from England."
So pour me some wine, the strongest you can
The roses are blooming. Pour me some more!
The wine makes it better and easier to bear,
I still love him now as I did before.

SOMEONE FROM MANAGEMENT *comes into the restaurant.*

SOMEONE FROM MANAGEMENT: Excuse me, but we open in fifteen minutes and could I ask you, if possible, not to sing, or get carried away . . .

INSPECTOR: Alright . . .

SOMEONE FROM MANAGEMENT: Vassilina Rikhardovna, I shouldn't be seeing you here by now . . .

WAITRESS: I'm giving evidence, I'm a witness.

INSPECTOR: We still need her.

SOMEONE FROM MANAGEMENT: Vassilina Rikhardovna, come and find me when you're finished . . . fifteen minutes alright?

INSPECTOR: We'll see how it goes. You know . . .

SOMEONE FROM MANAGEMENT: Right. Fine . . .

INSPECTOR: Indeed. Right, Lyuda, have you turned it on?

FEMALE POLICE OFFICER: Yes.

SOMEONE FROM MANAGEMENT *goes out, continuing to argue with him- or herself about the impossibility of opening a restaurant late.*

INSPECTOR: So, right, Verkhushkin, once again . . . why were you at the restaurant?

VERKHUSHKIN: Ten years . . . anniversary of our graduation . . .

INSPECTOR: Right, let's be more precise, which graduation? Graduation from space academy? Where exactly?

VERKHUSHKIN: Ten years since we finished school. We had a party . . .

INSPECTOR: Right, and who are "we" exactly?

VERKHUSHKIN: Our class . . . our old class . . .

INSPECTOR: I see. And was the victim from your class as well?

VERKHUSHKIN: Yeah . . . me and the Horse used to sit together at one desk.

INSPECTOR: The Horse?

VERKHUSHKIN: Well, that was his nickname . . . y'know . . . the Horse . . . er . . . we were friends.

INSPECTOR: Right. So you were friends.

The INSPECTOR *winks at the* JAPANESE WOMAN WITH A MYSTERIOUS PAST. *She bows to the* INSPECTOR.

Could you bring over the—(*Coughs.*)—menu and make sure you come back.

The JAPANESE WOMAN WITH A MYSTERIOUS PAST *rushes off for the menu.*

Right, so you two sat together at school. So where were you sitting here?

VERKHUSHKIN: Together as well.

INSPECTOR: Right, Valya, sit down with him . . .

The INSPECTOR *gets up and lets* VALYA *take the seat.*

You can be the Horse today.

The FEMALE POLICE OFFICER *and the* SERGEANT *roar with laughter.*

Right, so you were sitting there . . . what were you talking about . . . and let's have it all straightaway: how, why, where, and from what did you shoot the Horse . . . I mean the victim?

The JAPANESE WOMAN WITH A MYSTERIOUS PAST *brings across the menu and the* INSPECTOR *runs his eyes across it, amazed, but still without losing his attention to the matter at hand.*

VERKHUSHKIN: Well . . . like . . . he started getting at me, right, when we'd all had a drink and all, in front of everyone . . . see, I've got my own car wash, "Montana" it's called, and he started going on about how I should eat up quicker, 'cause he wanted to go and get his car washed and he wanted me to do it . . . like, I mean, he was in prison after school and . . . see, it all worked out for him after that, 'cause he had contacts and that, met the right people . . . it wasn't like that for the rest of us! Yeah, but I'm clean—I pay my taxes, pay all the right people, don't break any laws . . . but your victim, see . . . you check it out . . . he had a firm! Yeah! And I know how they worked. They send all these Caucasus types up to the North, take five hundred off each of them for sorting them out work! Eh! I saw it once, bunch of idiots, about a hundred of them standing around with rucksacks and thermos flasks—waiting for the group leader to turn up and take them to the work site up in the North, for the big money! All the wives and kids were saying goodbye to daddy. It only gets through to them about three hours later that they've been fucked.

INSPECTOR: What's the difference between the rolls and the sushi?

JAPANESE WOMAN WITH A MYSTERIOUS PAST: Same crap, just a little sprinkling of caviar on the rolls.

VALYA *looks at the* INSPECTOR *and realizes that he is completely indifferent to what* VERKHUSHKIN *is saying.*

VALYA: So come on then, show us what happened.

VERKHUSHKIN: Well, right . . . anyway he started going on at me again, about the car and that . . . I mean, even my Olga doesn't stick her nose in . . . and see, she's got a salon, she does the deputies' hairstyles before the election, gives them a, what's it called, an image . . . so it's not just the hairstyle, but it even goes as far as the color of their ties she advises them . . . and the Horse even started going on at her . . . going . . . yeah? . . . going on about the pants she could tell them to wear . . .

The INSPECTOR *tears himself away from the menu.*

INSPECTOR: Right, so how did it all happen?

VERKHUSHKIN: Well I went "stop laughing" to him and he kept on laughing, so I went "stop laughing" and he's laughing—

INSPECTOR: Come on, spit it out.

VERKHUSHKIN: So I said to him "let's step outside" . . .

INSPECTOR: Right . . .

VERKHUSHKIN: We got up . . .

INSPECTOR: Right, get up.

VERKHUSHKIN *gets up.*

Did the victim stand up too?

VERKHUSHKIN: Yes.

INSPECTOR: Valya, get up!

VALYA *stands up.*

So you went out. Who was first?

VERKHUSHKIN: Well, him to start with, then me . . . he went over to the bar toward this . . .

VERKHUSHKIN *nods at the* JAPANESE WOMAN WITH A MYSTERIOUS PAST.

JAPANESE WOMAN WITH A MYSTERIOUS PAST: . . . Yes, he'd just got to me, when this one here shot at him!

INSPECTOR: Right, hang on please . . . so he came over . . . Valya, go over to her.

JAPANESE WOMAN WITH A MYSTERIOUS PAST: Oh God, do I really have to . . .

The JAPANESE WOMAN WITH A MYSTERIOUS PAST *runs over to the bar, Valya runs after her, and the* FEMALE POLICE OFFICER *films it all, twitching strangely as if she were filming an overactive pop video.*

VERKHUSHKIN: He went over to her, said something, and I got out my gun, pointed it at the back of his head, and popped a few bullets at—

INSPECTOR: Popped them! Popped them! They aren't corks, bullets. . . . Like children, they are, this fucking lot. . . . Fuck. . . . These bastards buy themselves the fucking works, and then we have to sort out the mess. . . . Fucking hell. . . . I mean, where did you get the gun from? Where did you get all of it from, in fact? What fucking planet did you fall from, huh? I swear, as long as I've lived, I never thought I'd see the likes of this effing mess! Where did you all spring from? I mean, I dunno, you went to the same schools, had the same teachers, your parents are almost the same fucking age as me, so how come you turned out like this, I don't know. . . . All of you! This cunt here forgets his swimming trunks when he's going swimming, this one fucking well pops a few bullets into his school friend. . . . What the fucking hell do you want out of life? How you going to get on? That cunt over there is the same . . .

The agitated INSPECTOR *points unexpectedly at the* SERGEANT.

What were you up to yesterday?

SERGEANT: But, Sir . . .

INSPECTOR: I mean, for fuck's sake, I just don't understand you, although I mean, I'm hardly an old man. . . . I just don't understand you. . . . I mean, your jokes, what sort of effing jokes are they? Huh? I mean, what was it . . . getting that private drunk, what's his name . . .

SERGEANT: Zavarov.

INSPECTOR: Getting him trashed, then dressing him up in women's clothes, so he looks like a prostitute, and then throwing the poor drunken wretch into a remand cell! I just don't get it. I mean, you're hardly little kids anymore. You're almost thirty, all of you! At your age I already had a child, by my wife. . . . So where did you get the women's clothing? Those slutty stockings?

SERGEANT: I went and got my mom's.

INSPECTOR: You went all the way to your mom's?

SERGEANT: We live opposite the station.

INSPECTOR: I mean, well, I mean, I'll go as far as, well, First of April, April Fools, I'll stick a bit of mustard in the wife's toothpaste. . . . I mean, that's a normal sort of thing to do . . . but you people! And the main thing is you don't give a shit! Don't give a flying fuck about fucking anything! And worse still, it's your generation who are driving trains, planes, you're lawyers, you're working in nuclear reactors! And worse than that, you go to work without giving a shit! No one gives a shit and you're off to work doing these responsible jobs and that's when everything starts to get fucked up, in society . . .

FEMALE POLICE OFFICER: Calm down, Stasik.

INSPECTOR: I mean . . . honestly . . . popped some bullets, fucking hell. . . . Let's have some of your fish over here, and sake . . . if I don't try it now I probably never will.

JAPANESE WOMAN WITH A MYSTERIOUS PAST: You mean this one?

The INSPECTOR *pokes at the menu.*

INSPECTOR: That one!

JAPANESE WOMAN WITH A MYSTERIOUS PAST: One moment . . .

The JAPANESE WOMAN WITH A MYSTERIOUS PAST *runs off and the others stand there, uncertain how to react to the* INSPECTOR*'s hysterics.*

INSPECTOR: Fuck off and find yourselves another table where I can't see you.

The INSPECTOR *sits down, takes off his cap, and lays it on the table. The others move further away and watch the* INSPECTOR *nervously.*

Right, while I'm sitting here eating why don't you show me what happened. Only quickly and without wasting time on memories of your school days and who did what.... Answer questions when they're put to you, otherwise get on with it.... Get a move on or I'll fucking well give you something to think about.

VERKHUSHKIN: Well, he stood up and went over to the bar...

VALYA *runs over to the* INSPECTOR'*s table and the frightened* VERKHUSHKIN *follows him. They get ready to take the fateful steps toward the bar.*

I got the gun out while he was walking over there. I've got a license, I'm the legal owner... so he went over to the bar, said no more than a couple of words to this, er, lady here in the kimono, and then I pop... er, gave... er shot him... twice in the back of the head.

VERKHUSHKIN *finishes his account and everyone looks at the* INSPECTOR. *The* INSPECTOR *is staring into the middle distance and it looks like he wasn't paying any attention to what* VERKHUSHKIN *was telling and showing him. No one can make out whether to interrupt the* INSPECTOR'*s reverie, so they all stand there silently, waiting for the* INSPECTOR.

INSPECTOR: How long has it been now... four, eight... I started going to matches at fourteen... twenty-six years! Twenty-six years this football team has been fucking me around! Well, alright, it was better a few years back—they had their successes, got through to the finals... but now... it's hardly the big leagues, more like fucking around.... I've waited four years now, and what for? And that's because it's a bunch of fuckheads playing, just like all of you, useless fuckheads.... And they can pretend, that's the main thing, oh yes! Like, before, people used to riot, but that was more a social position—like "we don't give a fuck about it" and we're protesting—but now it's all on the quiet, no protests, people pretend to be something else, get where they need to be, any sort of work, and then they don't fucking do anything, just play around. You play around in life and the people who attach importance to life, they're made miserable, it drives them mad. . . . In football you've got to fucking play! But these fuckheads, they take their image makers with them, their stylists, and as a result they fuck it all up. You've got to fucking concentrate on scoring goals, and they're standing there backcombing their pubes so they stand up in the rain! The stylist is in there at half-time doing their hair—and they're not listening to the coach—they're having their hair reset!

The JAPANESE WOMAN WITH A MYSTERIOUS PAST *brings in a small bottle of sake and places it on the table, together with a plate of exotic half-cooked fish. The restaurant staff come out of the kitchen and observe from a distance.*

INSPECTOR: Oh . . . right . . . pour it for us then, little lady.

The JAPANESE WOMAN WITH A MYSTERIOUS PAST *pours some sake for the* INSPECTOR, *and he drinks and wants to chase it down with some fish but isn't sure how to eat it—instead of a fork a neatly packed pair of bamboo chopsticks lie next to his plate. His mouth burning, the* INSPECTOR *panics and rips the packet open and eats with the chopsticks in the way that seems right at that moment. That is, by skewering a piece of fish on one chopstick and using the other one to help bring it to his mouth.*

INSPECTOR: Shit, this isn't food . . . this is an effing perversion. . . . Yeah, and worst of all, worst of all is it's all on the quiet, and they use their own childish expressions—"popping bullets," "getting off on stuff" . . . 'cause they realize that if they want everyone off their backs, they've got to have a cover. . . . Total not giving a fuck, total, on every level of society . . .

JAPANESE WOMAN WITH A MYSTERIOUS PAST: I mean, what do you expect? . . . Yesterday I was on the twenty-six, the tram, and I asked the driver if the tram went down Malyshev Street, and he says "Fuck knows." I mean, imagine—that was the driver and he didn't even know which streets he was driving down . . .

The INSPECTOR *stops chewing, reflects, then pours himself another glass and drinks.*

INSPECTOR: What did he say to you?

JAPANESE WOMAN WITH A MYSTERIOUS PAST: Who?

INSPECTOR: The one he popped at?

JAPANESE WOMAN WITH A MYSTERIOUS PAST: Well, you see, he looked at me and I didn't see what he had behind his back, and he looked at me and said "to he . . ." and then this one here shot at him, so "to he" and then he dropped.

INSPECTOR: To he . . .

JAPANESE WOMAN WITH A MYSTERIOUS PAST: So that's the mystery, what he was about to say . . . to he . . .

INSPECTOR: No mystery there . . . he meant to he . . .

At this point the INSPECTOR *unexpectedly throws his head back and turns blue. Yellow foam starts trickling from his mouth and then his head falls forward onto the table. The* FEMALE POLICE OFFICER *kneels down and starts filming from the ground, still apparently not realizing what has happened, possibly because some completely professional instinct has taken over and she is just filming from below for a future crime reconstruction.*

A room in an apartment.

FATHER: Are you asleep?

MOTHER: No.

FATHER: The wallpaper is coming off. It needs repasting.

MOTHER: Be my guest . . .

FATHER: Why are you issuing orders—if the wallpaper is coming off then it needs repasting . . . what's the point in issuing orders if you can even hear it unsticking itself . . . we could take action, choose a day to paste it back up.

MOTHER: I did tell you . . . that wallpaper is stuck on vinyl and it'll never stay up.

FATHER: You told me when I'd already stuck it up. You're a great one for telling me afterward and not before, like, even yesterday I'd drunk the milk and you only mentioned afterward that it had gone bad and I shouldn't drink it.

MOTHER: Honestly! I mean, why can't you just use your eyes, work it out for yourself, take a sniff . . .

FATHER: But surely you could have warned me, I mean after all if you see someone doing something—

MOTHER: What on earth do you want from me now? The only peace I get is when I'm asleep! I only get to have my own life when I'm asleep! Let me live my life! Let me get a little sleep! You've got a grown-up thirty-year-old son—ask him to help, put the wallpaper up with him!

FATHER: Yeah, right—ask him! Like I'm going to humiliate myself in front of him, I'd be better off doing it all myself . . . he doesn't want to do anything, I'll be asking him for a year and on top of that he'll try to convince me that it's better to live with the wallpaper falling off. . . . He never wants to do anything. . . . I never thought we'd have a child like that . . .

MOTHER: Well I knew—like father, like son.

FATHER: There you are! You knew before and didn't say!

MOTHER: You speak to him, father to son . . .

FATHER: What are you talking about? I spoke to him not so long ago. . . . I asked if he planned to get married and he told me he's already burnt out. So I said, what do you mean? There won't be anything left to make the babies if you leave it, you're getting on, and he says "I'm hardly having a great time. So why would I want to get someone else born so they can suffer, too"—

MOTHER: What does he mean "hardly having a great time"? We've given him everything, we do everything for him, he doesn't even know how to make food or wash clothes, I do it all for him—and he's having a bad time!

FATHER: And it's not like he even drinks or smokes . . .

MOTHER: Yeah, well, exactly, I mean if he was a . . . what do you call it . . . if he was taking drugs, we'd know what to do and how to help, but what do you do for this?

FATHER: I don't know what to do with him.

MOTHER: You can't do anything with him. It's too late—we just need to come 'round to the fact, stop asking for things. . . . We'll buy it all ourselves, the paper sort. I've seen some good wallpaper for sale, embossed and double thickness . . . the paper sort won't fall down and the walls will be able to breathe—because that film stuff has glued up the walls and the walls are crumbling too.

FATHER: Yes.

MOTHER: Yesterday we were having a cup of tea in the kitchen and he got up and came over to me and, joking, tensed his muscles and starts boasting about how strong he is. He says, "Punch me in the stomach mom, I've got a six pack," and I thought, well, I'll punch him as he asked me to and he said he'd got this six pack . . . so he looked like he'd tensed his stomach muscles and I hit him, not hard though. . . . And he fell over and started rolling around on the ground and he hasn't got any six pack—just a soft tummy like a girl's . . . and he's lying there on the ground and rolling around, breathless, and I'm sitting there and thinking, why on earth did he ask me to punch him if he hasn't got this six pack . . .

The half-empty Japanese restaurant. In the middle of the restaurant stand the SERGEANT, *a different* INSPECTOR, *the* FEMALE POLICE OFFICER *with video camera, the* JAPANESE WOMAN WITH A MYSTERIOUS PAST, *a* MAN *in handcuffs,* SOMEONE FROM MANAGEMENT, *the* CHEF, *and a* YOUNG MAN *in a South Park baseball cap.*

INSPECTOR: Right, let's switch the camera on and get down to work. Sit down at the table where they were sitting. Is the camera working?

FEMALE POLICE OFFICER: Yes.

The new INSPECTOR *stands in front of the lens and recites:*

INSPECTOR: Commencing the crime reconstruction of the case concerning the crime reconstruction by Inspector C. D. Shnurov of the case concerning A. V. Verkhushkin, charged with the murder of C. V. Korsov in the Japanese Food Restaurant "Japanese Food" . . .

VALYA: Inspector, Sir!

INSPECTOR: Yes!

VALYA: Who should I be? Korsov or the Inspector?

INSPECTOR: Right. . . . Is that important at this stage?

VALYA: Well, yes. If I'm Korsov I should sit here and if I'm the Inspector I should stand up and after they've killed Korsov sit down and die at the table.

The new INSPECTOR *sits down, takes off his cap, and wipes the sweat off his brow. He's sweating under his arms and two small stains have appeared on his shirt that keep spreading and spreading.*

INSPECTOR: Right, and who died first?

EVERYONE: Korsov!

INSPECTOR: Right, then, sit down to start with, that is, die in the right order, as it all happened.

VALYA: But in order to recreate the chronological sequence, I mean, in order to get to the circumstances in which the Inspector died, don't we need to take him into account in the Korsov crime reconstruction?

INSPECTOR: Yes . . . we have to keep him in mind too.

SOMEONE FROM MANAGEMENT: Why don't I be someone?

INSPECTOR: You can't be anyone, so keep quiet. We'll come to you in a minute.

SOMEONE FROM MANAGEMENT: But we've been standing around for ages and we still have to do—

INSPECTOR: What do you "still have to do"? I could have you shut down today! I mean, after all, you gave someone food poisoning!

SOMEONE FROM MANAGEMENT: Well, for starters, we have an arrangement with your bosses, and second, it hasn't yet been proved whether the food killed him or he—

INSPECTOR: We'll get to the bottom of it all! And actually, let me tell you a little secret, all of you, there are a lot of bosses and no matter who you had your arrangement with, you may have to rearrange it with someone else! Right. For the moment I'll be the other Inspector and you, Valya, can be the one who was shot.

VALYA: So who's going to be you?

INSPECTOR: Me, in what sense?

VALYA: Well, in the sense of the Inspector leading the crime reconstruction, because if you're going to be the Inspector who led the other crime reconstruction, then someone has to lead this crime reconstruction . . .

INSPECTOR: First of all, Valya, I was warned about you and your unhealthy sense of humor, and second, let's move on from this hairsplitting of yours, it's not relevant.

VALYA: I didn't mean anything by it. . . . I just wanted to make sure we got it right . . .

INSPECTOR: Come on then, let's just calm down . . . doing two cases at once is hard on everyone . . . alright? Calm down and everyone will be who I say. I'll be in two of the hypostases . . .

JAPANESE WOMAN WITH A MYSTERIOUS PAST: You mean, you'll be sort of like two inspectors?

INSPECTOR: Well, in a manner of speaking . . . right . . . how did it all start?

JAPANESE WOMAN WITH A MYSTERIOUS PAST: With a song . . .

INSPECTOR: Which song, precisely? I need everything to be as it was then!

The JAPANESE WOMAN WITH A MYSTERIOUS PAST *suddenly wrinkles up her face as if she were about to cry, narrows her eyes, pulls her lower lip up as far as the tip of her nose, and sings.*

JAPANESE WOMAN WITH A MYSTERIOUS PAST:

An English sailor, straight from a gunship,
Came to a teahouse, sunk like a boat
Beneath the waves of blossoming roses,
To meet with sailors, there he sought
To meet with the sailors known on the sea,
And he called for some wine and a cup of tea.

She hesitates, unable to remember the words, and then continues.

. . . And then he said nothing more.
And in the corner a Japanese beauty
Sang a song of longing and love
And he remembered his own dear country
And in him stirred his own sea blood.
Still the next morning the ship sets sail
The orders are given: "set course," "ahoy!"

And she weeps hard, and he feels joy.
Ten years pass quickly, like in a story,
And the Japanese girl has a little son.
He asks wide-eyed, "What's my story?
Who's my Daddy? Tell me the one."

The INSPECTOR *grinds his teeth but doesn't interrupt the* JAPANESE WOMAN WITH A MYSTERIOUS PAST. *He wipes the sweat from his brow. The stains under his arms have now reached right around his chest.*

And the Japanese beauty presses his hand
And says, "A sailor from England."
So pour me some wine, the strongest you can
The roses are blooming. Pour me some more!
The wine makes it better and easier to bear,
I still love him now as I did before.

The JAPANESE WOMAN WITH A MYSTERIOUS PAST *stops singing. Everyone is silent, waiting to hear what the* INSPECTOR *will say.*

INSPECTOR: Right. Have you finished?

JAPANESE WOMAN WITH A MYSTERIOUS PAST: Yes.

INSPECTOR: So what happened then?

JAPANESE WOMAN WITH A MYSTERIOUS PAST: That's when Gennady Anan'ich came in . . .

The WAITRESS *nods at* SOMEONE FROM MANAGEMENT.

SOMEONE FROM MANAGEMENT: I came in and said—

INSPECTOR: Right, and where did you come from?

SOMEONE FROM MANAGEMENT: I came in from the kitchen and said—

INSPECTOR: Right then, you go to the kitchen and come back out from there, come over here and speak—I've already said that I want everything as it was then.

SOMEONE FROM MANAGEMENT: Surely it doesn't have to be that formal?

INSPECTOR: We're all waiting for you!

SOMEONE FROM MANAGEMENT *goes out to the kitchen and comes back immediately.*

SOMEONE FROM MANAGEMENT: I came in and said that it was time to open and, if at all possible, please hurry up. . . .

INSPECTOR: Go on.

SOMEONE FROM MANAGEMENT: Then I went out. Should I go out?

INSPECTOR: No, no need. Stand here as if you'd gone out . . . right, and you went out and started cooking the fish?

SOMEONE FROM MANAGEMENT: I went out and started writing. I don't cook. The chefs cook, the waiters take the food out, and I'm the manager . . .

INSPECTOR: Right—let's not have any funny stuff, alright? I asked a question. When did they start cooking the poisoned fish?

There is a long silence. Everyone is scared of answering the new strict INSPECTOR, *because if they answer then they will seem to agree with him that the fish was poisoned and was offered especially to the* INSPECTOR *in order to poison him.*

INSPECTOR: I'll ask once more—who started cooking the poisoned fish and when did they start?

JAPANESE WOMAN WITH A MYSTERIOUS PAST: They started cooking when they got the order. That's the way here. Nothing is prepared in advance. So it doesn't have to be reheated. This isn't McDonald's, you know. Customers arrive and they order when they want to eat. Your Inspector ordered and Vassya began to cook it.

VASSYA THE CHEF: I didn't cook it, I mean, I did cook it, but I have to, I cook everything—here's my hygiene certificate, I'm in the top category and no one has ever died on me! I even cook at home, I do stuffed marrow with meat and mayonnaise, I've got two daughters and they need their dad, whichever way you look at it, and they eat it and they're alive and well . . . the youngest one's got gastritis, but that's not from my cooking—she swallowed a badge when she was at junior school, a round badge with writing on it . . . from a packet of those cheesy Cheetos crisps, a round badge, number 33 from the Lego Bionicle series. She swallowed it with the crisps, we've got a medical certificate—

INSPECTOR: Right, that's enough—Silence, Vassya! Chef Vassya . . . cooked. . . . Right, so we don't get confused, this means that the fish wasn't ready at that point? The song was sung and you went off to write . . . what were you writing?

VALYA: Haiku.

INSPECTOR: Valya! I've already told you to shut up! What were you writing?

SOMEONE FROM MANAGEMENT: Well, accounts and so on.

INSPECTOR: And you didn't come back into the restaurant?

SOMEONE FROM MANAGEMENT: No. Not into the restaurant.

INSPECTOR: Right, and how did things move onto the food order?

VERKHUSHKIN: The food order was after me . . .

INSPECTOR: Right. And what happened with you?

VERKHUSHKIN: I killed my school friend, Korsov Slavka, and I was just beginning to talk about it, at the last crime reconstruction, right after the song . . . or actually immediately after the Inspector told us to hurry up and we started . . .

INSPECTOR: I see.

VERKHUSHKIN: . . . to proceed with the crime reconstruction. I started talking and showing how I killed the Horse . . .

INSPECTOR: I see . . .

VERKHUSHKIN: Oh, that's it! I was saying that the Horse is his nickname—the other Inspector asked me what horse I was talking about, and I explained it was a nickname for him. . . . It was when we had new teachers for lessons they used to take roll and get confused and say, "Today we'll have a homework report from . . ."

VERKHUSHKIN *puts on a strict look and clearly attempts to imitate a teacher's intonation and delivery.*

And everyone used to sit up and tense up and the teacher—especially the biology teacher—used to drag it out and then suddenly " . . . Horsov!" And everyone howled with laughter and we started calling him the Horse . . . there . . .

INSPECTOR: Right, and why on earth did you just tell us all of that?

VERKHUSHKIN: But you asked for everything to be exact and that . . .

INSPECTOR: Right, everything exact—but please keep to the point, alright—that is, if you don't want me to pass sentence before you reach the courtroom! This is no joke. Am I making myself clear?

VERKHUSHKIN: Yes . . . clear . . .

INSPECTOR: Right, you killed him, and you were telling everyone how you killed him. Right, let's have it.

VERKHUSHKIN: Should I tell you?

INSPECTOR: Yes!

VERKHUSHKIN: Well, I was saying that the Horse started getting at me about the carwash . . . and I—

VALYA: Don't forget Olga was in it as well!

VERKHUSHKIN: Oh yeah! There was Olga . . .

INSPECTOR: Olga? What Olga?

VERKHUSHKIN: Our school friend. Now she does hair styling for the deputies. When we were just kids, me and Slava—

INSPECTOR: You and Slava who?

VERKHUSHKIN: I mean, me and the one I just killed!!

INSPECTOR: Go on, then.

VERKHUSHKIN: Well he and I used to run around after Olga and look after her. We played at pretending that she was the beautiful princess the wicked wizard wanted to lock up in a tree. There was a tree in our playground, an enormous one, an oak, probably, and our teacher Svetlana Yurievna, we pretended that she was Gertrude, the evil fairy Gertrude, and she wanted to lock Olga up in this tree, and we ran around everywhere after Olga when we were out and defended her against everyone, especially Svetlana Yurievna, that is, Gertrude in our game! And then later we even fought over her, well that was when we were a bit older. Actually I was pretend fighting and they started beating me up for real and then Slava stepped in and gave these other ones such a run for their money . . . he always helped me out in situations like that . . .

INSPECTOR: Right, stick to the point, if you don't mind: how did you kill him, what was it you were telling or showing them? Let's keep to the matter at hand, if it's not too difficult. How did you kill him?

VERKHUSHKIN: Right, well, Slavka went over to the bar . . . go on then . . .

VALYA *jumps up and goes over to the bar. The* JAPANESE WOMAN WITH A MYSTERIOUS PAST *catches up with him and goes to stand behind the bar.*

He went over to her, said something to her, and I got out my gun—

INSPECTOR: So he went over with his back to you and you—

VERKHUSHKIN: Not like that. We'd been arguing before that, he'd been having a go at me and even at Olga—

INSPECTOR: That's enough! I get it, you'd been arguing and he went off, and you . . . ?

VERKHUSHKIN: I told him to go out, right. I said let's go out and sort this out. He'd only just started going and I got the gun and popped him in the back of the head a few times . . .

INSPECTOR: Show us at what distance.

VERKHUSHKIN: Well, from about here-ish.

VERKHUSHKIN gets up from the table and stands the same distance as at the moment of those fateful shots on the night of the anniversary. The INSPECTOR points at VALYA.

INSPECTOR: Is he standing correctly?

VERKHUSHKIN: Yeah, we already went through this with him last time . . .

INSPECTOR: Keep to the point!

VERKHUSHKIN: Yes. The Horse was standing there, and after the shots he fell onto the bar and then rolled on the floor . . . but we never got to that bit last time . . .

INSPECTOR: Where did you get to last time then?

JAPANESE WOMAN WITH A MYSTERIOUS PAST: We got to "to he"!

INSPECTOR: To what "to he" was that?

JAPANESE WOMAN WITH A MYSTERIOUS PAST: That was my "to he," because he, I mean the one who was shot, said "to he" and he was shot . . . "to he" and he died and your Inspector, that last one, said "to he" and he died too . . .

INSPECTOR: Right, and where was the Inspector, before the "to he"?

EVERYONE: At the table!

INSPECTOR: Right.

The INSPECTOR sits at the table.

And what was he doing?

JAPANESE WOMAN WITH A MYSTERIOUS PAST: Eating fish . . .

VERKHUSHKIN: . . . and shouting.

INSPECTOR: Who was he shouting at?

SERGEANT: Um, actually he was displeased with the civic and social situation and expressed his displeasure . . .

INSPECTOR: You mean he was criticizing the government?

SERGEANT: Not that . . . although . . . it was more aimed at contemporary law practitioners, football . . .

JAPANESE WOMAN WITH A MYSTERIOUS PAST: The public transport system . . .

FEMALE POLICE OFFICER: He was just fed up and so he was attacking everything . . .

VALYA: Mainly about generational differences . . . he was eating fish and polemicizing.

VASSYA THE CHEF: I was cooking it as normal, that is, of course it's an unusual fish, it's only caught in Japan once a year on a certain special day and they prepare it and eat it—it's a delicacy and I know exactly how it's prepared and we've had it ordered here before and everything was going very well indeed! I didn't know at all who we were cooking for and how it was all going to turn out . . . if I'd known I'd have done boiled cod with eggplant and he'd never have noticed the difference!

The INSPECTOR*'s right eye starts twitching and he turns away to the wall, incapable of even shouting at the* CHEF *to shut him up.* VASSYA *takes off his chef's hat, flushes, and cries, his stout belly wobbling.* VASSYA *knows that at the very least he will lose his job and he may even be put in prison, because that's how it is, even if the restaurant buys itself off, someone will have to be punished. The* FEMALE POLICE OFFICER *is also crying, remembering her innocent fun with the departed Inspector. She knows that* *she is unlikely to succeed with the new young* INSPECTOR*—the* FEMALE POLICE OFFICER *is no longer young and Inspector Shnurov had had a bit of imagination and liked older women with a good figure. Actually in her heart of hearts she hopes that in six months at least, when they all get used to each other and the new* INSPECTOR *grows tired, he'll even get to the point where he'll agree to her. Thanks to this knowledge the* FEMALE POLICE OFFICER *is not sobbing with grief but hiding her tears, crying in a maternal way. The* JAPANESE WOMAN WITH A MYSTERIOUS PAST *is also sobbing slightly as she's playing the part of a Japanese woman with a mysterious past and she can't let an opportunity to practice pass her by.* SOMEONE FROM MANAGEMENT *is not crying but is very agitated. He's working out how much extra he'll have to pay so that the police leave his establishment in peace and whom to employ in* VASSYA*'s position as he will probably soon be sacrificed. Only* VALYA *and the* SERGEANT *are completely calm and dry eyed. They are waiting for everything to finish so they can leave and go about their own business, although in fact neither of them have anything else to do.*

VALYA: They say that the "Japanese," the "Oriental," that is, relaxes you . . .

JAPANESE WOMAN WITH A MYSTERIOUS PAST: Well, that's a fact. The number of people relaxing in here after a busy day in the evening, I mean, it's not that easy to get a table in here! Only by reservation—you need to book a table! The thing is, everyone's so good at the chopsticks, they use them like they were spoons! No one asks for forks!

The INSPECTOR *frowns at the words of the* JAPANESE WOMAN WITH A MYSTERIOUS PAST *and nods at her kimono.*

INSPECTOR: It'll come as no surprise when they let people walk around in a sheet like that out on the streets! What is the world coming to! What about our own country, huh? Have we just slung it all out? Where are all the pancake stalls, the pie shops? What about if I want to relax in my own national way? Forcing all these foreign customs on us! And then they're amazed when crime rates rises and the kids are on drugs! I mean, if only they'd allow us to get on with it like it used to be: guilty—then you'd be lined up and flogged . . . that's it, flogged! We've let go of all our national traditions, our culture . . . ! And what have we got? Japan on every corner!

JAPANESE WOMAN WITH A MYSTERIOUS PAST: What do you have against the Japanese? I dunno, I mean have they ever stopped you from relaxing? You go ahead and relax! I mean after all everything still comes out our way, like that fish of theirs . . . it's all like that! Like them, how they understand "relaxing" is relaxing . . . and look at us! Got our own way of doing it . . . "relaxing our way" means you can be in a kimono and eating with chopsticks, but if someone starts teasing you, you put a bullet in the back of their head or a chopstick in the eye. We've got our own ideas about having a good time and no one's going to force anything different on us—you might as well not worry about it, let it all in! Any old culture! You're getting worked up for nothing, national culture won't suffer at all!

INSPECTOR: Well, to hell with it all. . . . Right, I think we've done what we needed to—

JAPANESE WOMAN WITH A MYSTERIOUS PAST: To hell, that's it! He probably wanted to say "to hell"—that's what "to he" was, he wanted to tell him to go to hell!

INSPECTOR: That's right . . .

JAPANESE WOMAN WITH A MYSTERIOUS PAST: Only he didn't manage to tell him—he died. His schoolmate there was too busy "relaxing."

The Japanese restaurant. A BEARDED MAN *sitting at one of the tables is drinking juice and looking through some papers.* A SECOND MAN *comes across to the table.*

SECOND MAN: Hello!

BEARDED MAN: Hello there!

The SECOND MAN *sits down and calls over the* WAITER.

BEARDED MAN: Hang on, I'll just finish reading it. You order something in the meantime.

SECOND MAN: Don't want anything really—are you going to have something?

BEARDED MAN: Something sweet.

SECOND MAN: And to drink?

BEARDED MAN: I've got something.

SECOND MAN: That's all you're having?

BEARDED MAN: Yes.

The SECOND MAN *turns to the* WAITER.

SECOND MAN: I'll have a freshly squeezed grapefruit and orange juice and a dessert. What do you have? I don't feel like reading, just tell me.

WAITER: We have Japanese, Chinese, and European desserts, which sort would you like?

SECOND MAN: And what European desserts have you got?

WAITER: Poppyseed cake.

SECOND MAN: Is that it?

WAITER: That's it.

SECOND MAN: Then I'll have poppyseed cake and that's it. . . . And bring us the check straightaway please.

WAITER: Right.

The WAITER *goes and the* BEARDED MAN *puts the papers into a file.*

SECOND MAN: Well, what do you think?

BEARDED MAN: Not bad . . . not bad. We can shoot it now, only if you don't mind, in the scene where the father is crying beside the body of his daughter—that's a monologue for a musical, you've written there . . .

SECOND MAN: What makes you think that?

BEARDED MAN: Hang on, hear me out. . . . I didn't say it was a bad thing. Yes, you've written a musical-style monologue, but it's not a bad one. It's a good musical monologue, keep it in, but it needs some work on it. . . . Leave it in. . . . And where is he sitting with the body in your version?

SECOND MAN: At the edge of the highway.

BEARDED MAN: And what is there at the edge? Forest? Or what?

SECOND MAN: Well, yes . . . forest, meadows, and so on. . . . She runs out of the forest and gets run over . . .

BEARDED MAN: But look, when the father finds the run-over body and speaks his monologue and cries. . . . I mean, we could put something else in here to develop the drama. . . . So who squashes her, then?

SECOND MAN: You mean, who runs her over?

BEARDED MAN: Well, yes—who is it?

SECOND MAN: Well that's not important for the plot, you read it—it's just a passing car driver who hits her. What's important for us is that she dies . . . her father finds her, forgives her, and everything should have been fine, but then she dies in this cruelly absurd way . . .

BEARDED MAN: That's all clear, I'm talking about something different. . . . Hey! The way you did it, this absurd accident . . . I mean this driver. . . . He could be involved. . . . Why don't we make him, say . . . the host of a popular TV show?

SECOND MAN: The host? But what does that have to do with—

BEARDED MAN: Well, look, this host of a popular TV show, "Wheel of Fortune" say, he runs over the girl, you see, and while the father is doing his monologue beside the body, we could make this guy say something too, I mean, something like . . . "Well, what a mess, I was going out to my garden at my dacha, and my wife's been getting at me, because all the berries are out ripe on the branch." . . . Yes that's it! He's off to collect berries at the dacha, and bang! Straight into this.

He laughs, drinks down his juice; the WAITER *comes over to the table with the order and the bill.*

. . . Or you could have it that they're both there, groaning—one about his daughter, the other about his berries, and suddenly all the cars going past are stopping and the police arrive and begin sorting everything out and then all the people who were going past recognize this TV show host and start asking for his autograph. . . . See, look how it works out—the father is going mad with grief, the TV show host is giving a statement to the police and giving out autographs to his fans on the motorway at the same time! Hey, what do you think? It's starting to take shape!

SECOND MAN: Well, I don't know, I'd have to think about it.

BEARDED MAN: Have a think about it, alright?

SECOND MAN: Alright then.

BEARDED MAN: But do it, please, do it. It's vital—I mean, after all, as a director I can judge better, if you get me. . . . Because when he's crying there all on his own, it's not about anything in particular, is it, so what am I going to film? I mean, do I just train the camera on the body, if you see what I mean . . .

SECOND MAN: Alright then.

BEARDED MAN: Well I'm glad we've got that sorted out.

SECOND MAN: Listen, I had an idea myself . . . I even started drafting it . . .

BEARDED MAN: Well?

SECOND MAN: It's a film really, but you could drag it out to a TV series . . . whatever works best . . .

BEARDED MAN: Well, what's it about?

SECOND MAN: Well, it's about a young idiot, well not so young, really—about thirty, so already you're dealing with midlife problems . . .

BEARDED MAN: Well?

SECOND MAN: Well, this young man is at the center of it, and the great thing about it is that he's got this really unusual job—he plays a victim! I mean, what d'you make of that! He gets a job with the police—I mean, it's obvious he doesn't want a serious job, so he chooses this line of work for himself, basic but weird . . . he plays the victim during crime reconstructions. So if, like, for example, someone's murdered, then they hold a crime reconstruction and take the criminal to the scene of the crime and ask him to show them how it happened, how he killed or raped, and then they film it all on a video camera so they can compare it with his statement, so as to find out exactly who did what, because he could be innocent, or hiding something, and during the crime reconstruction things fall into place.

BEARDED MAN: By the way, not long ago someone was killed in here, maybe even at this table . . .

SECOND MAN: Really?

BEARDED MAN: Never mind . . . anyway, you were saying, this young man?

SECOND MAN: So this guy is the victim during crime reconstructions, I mean, he plays the victim. Sometimes he even plays a corpse.

BEARDED MAN: Hang on . . . that's interesting . . . is there really a job like that?

SECOND MAN: Who knows, it makes no difference, I was told there was, and I heard a story about it . . . well I'll write it up. . . .

If they have these crime reconstructions, then it means they must have people like that. But I thought this guy up myself, and he's, well, like he dropped out of university, so I mean, he's clever, but he doesn't give a damn, and he doesn't even give a damn about giving a damn . . .

BEARDED MAN: Hang on, hang on—that's not bad, it's catchy—but I need something else—to begin with there's got to be someone else in there . . .

SECOND MAN: Well, he's got his mother and father and the situations themselves, see. . . . Then there's the crime, murder, and then there's his thoughts and, like, then there's the fact that it's not completely pointless work because after all the crime is being reconstructed. He's misunderstood . . .

BEARDED MAN: No, no! That's crap! Everyone understands him, who isn't understood nowadays—that's all in the past, now everyone understands everyone else perfectly. It needs something special, if you catch my drift. The fact that he's a fuckhead, but smart and funny—all that won't shock anyone, every second person is like that nowadays—I mean think about it—producers, actors—they're all like that, they've all dreamed up their own jobs, no one gives a fuck about reality. They're not going to want to make films about people like themselves—you need something special, we need to romanticize this weirdo.

SECOND MAN: Alright. But what if he's scared . . .

BEARDED MAN: Of what?

SECOND MAN: Scared of really becoming a victim, scared of dying, and that's why . . . that's why he decides to. . . . Hey! It's like an inoculation—he's inoculating himself with a little bit of what he wants to avoid catching. . . . That's why he chose this job for himself. He plays the victim in crime reconstructions, he plays to inoculate himself with a little bit of what he is trying to avoid . . .

BEARDED MAN: Death!

SECOND MAN: Brilliant!

BEARDED MAN: Hang on, hang on! Wait a moment . . . I see it . . .

The BEARDED MAN *grabs his head and tries to gather his thoughts. The* SECOND MAN *takes a bite out of the poppyseed cake.*

BEARDED MAN: Stop! I've got it! It'll be a film, a feature-length film, two hours long, and this is what we'll add in—a young gynecologist. He's working and he hates it all, gets no enjoyment from it, but he keeps working. And it's right at the end of the working day . . . it's summer, hot, really hot, and they're burning turf, so a smog is hanging over the town . . . and right at the end of the working day a woman tramp is brought in, she's off her face, completely out of it, and while she was asleep her drunken friends stuck a cone up her vagina—a pine cone! Only, imagine, they got it in, but they couldn't get it out—once a pine cone goes in it won't come out—it's like a lightbulb in your hole. Anyway, they put her in the chair, all dirty and drunk, and he's young and handsome and he has to go in and get out that pine cone. And then, once he gets this pine cone out, she farts! Like think about it, he moves his head back suddenly to avoid smelling her fart and he hits his head on the frame of an open window, the glass smashes and falls on his head, and he gets cut . . . I mean, imagine it! What a story, huh? We'll have to put it in!

SECOND MAN: Where?

BEARDED MAN: Into your script. I mean, our script . . . well, we can write "with my participation" or something . . .

SECOND MAN: So how do these stories fit together?

BEARDED MAN: That comes later . . . in the film everything will fit together. For now you just get on with it and write it. The quicker you write it, the quicker we can shoot it.

SECOND MAN: But will they pass it? Won't they make a fuss about scenes like that? Woman tramp . . . vagina . . .

BEARDED MAN: They won't make a fuss! I'll see to that! See, that story—I made it up a while back! I was just waiting for the right moment! It's a good one, isn't it? Directors, see, directors have to think up stuff as well, you know, not just make films. . . . Otherwise they're hardly directors! Otherwise they're just cowards and have no right to do anything! I heard that story a while ago and then I thought up . . . no, it's a good'un—we'll have to put it in!

SECOND MAN: Alright. Whatever you say.

BEARDED MAN: Right then, I'm off. I've got casting today. I'm stuck with another commitment—we're filming a historical serial in a month's time, about the Decembrists. It's crap for the masses of course, they've asked for the homosexual theme to be strengthened . . . put in a young tart. . . . Well, so what? Pays well, so why not? Are you staying?

SECOND MAN: No—I'm heading out too.

BEARDED MAN: Right then. By the way, think about it, this victim character has to have some love interest, he definitely has to fall in love with someone! Hey! It would be even better if he could fall in love with a criminal or a victim! A real victim, who survives!

The SECOND MAN *puts some money on the table and the* BEARDED MAN *collects his papers and briefcase.*

BEARDED MAN: And he definitely has to die, at the end he should die, otherwise they might not pass the script. They won't understand it if we leave him alive at the end. I mean, a great finale would be if there was another crime reconstruction, but it was already another man playing the victim, another man in his place.

SECOND MAN: Bit sick.

BEARDED MAN: Do you think so? I think it would be good. And the main thing is it's a symbol of the fact that nothing dies with him and someone else will go on with it all . . .

SECOND MAN: No, I was talking about the cake, actually . . .

BEARDED MAN: What do you expect? It's only a "restaurant" on the sign—underneath it's a normal little café making itself out to be something really special—and the prices are pretty steep. But I suppose there's no choice, they're all the same . . .

The men leave the restaurant.

THE END

03

SEPTEMBER.DOC[1]

ELENA GREMINA AND MIKHAIL UGAROV
TRANSLATED BY ANIA AIZMAN

PART I: THE SCENT OF MUSK

1. Musleem

As-Salaam alaykum, my Muslim brothers and sisters, I would like to tell you about our brother, whose name is Musleem. This is a story about him and me, and about how he became a shahid.[2] And about how I didn't.

We met in Sernovodsk in agriculture school, where we studied together. We saw each other every day, discussed many issues, argued about various topics, played pool, and ate barbecue.

And then one day we decided to take the path of Jihad and go into the mountains. Everything was excellent, but Shaitan[3] (curse him!) made us quarrel because of one person. I don't want to say who, but there was a wedge in our relationship. I felt that I would never forgive him, but on the second day I went to his house to become friends again and forget what happened between us, but it turned out that he had already left.

While crossing Pankisi Gorge to Chechnya he became a shahid in the Itum-Kalinsky district. I'll just say that when his mother went to retrieve his body from the feds, the kafir colonel saluted upon realizing that this woman is the mother of the Chechen who sacrificed his soul to his religion and his land.

I hope that says everything.

And I trust that he forgave me, as I did him.

2. Mairbek

I want to tell you about Mairbek, my cousin thrice removed.

There was a brutal struggle on the Minutka.[4] And when there was a command to retreat, he said that he was staying to cover the retreating soldiers and remained in one of the houses on Shahumyan Alley. He kept on for two hours, and when he ran out of bullets, he was cornered. The Russians couldn't make up their minds about entering that house and waited for about an hour, and then, not seeing any activity from the side of the "separatist squad," they overcame their fear and entered the house. Mairbek came forward to meet them, wounded, with a dagger in his hand. And before he was laid low by a round of machine gun fire, he slayed three (!!!!) people.

All this was told by a Russian general who raised a white flag and came with a squad of his subordinates to bring Mairbek to the Jihadists. He returned his dagger and spoke the following words: "If in every platoon you have one such man, then you will win this war."

To this day, his mother keeps the dagger, with dried blood on the handle and the blade.

3. Khamzat

There was a battle in the mountains of Dagestan. Khamzat, who was defending himself with a light machine gun, had his arm torn off.

Khamzat leaned on the ledge and continued to fight until he died from loss of blood. The occupiers shot at the dead commander for several hours. When the enemies approached the shahid, they saw that Khamzat's uninjured hand was clutching a grenade with the ring half pulled out.

After his death, the Russian media concocted a story about how this Chechen commander died standing on all fours.

But unbeknownst to these fools, they themselves recorded that Khamzat died in sujud.[5] In this pose of prayer the believer is closer to his Creator. That's how Allah forces the enemies of Islam to communicate the truth with their own tongues to Muslims, truth that is hidden from the unbelievers.

4. Abdul the Prankster

Abdul was my neighbor across the courtyard. What a guy! He was the greatest "prankster" and just a good brother! In those days, when Abdul became a shahid, we had a battle in one of the courtyards of the five-story houses. There were just 25 of us left, and there were many more Russians. They were taking building after building, stone after stone. We were sleeping 2–3 hours a night, at most 4. We were in different buildings. I hadn't seen Abdullah in almost three weeks even though there were only 30 meters between us. And one afternoon I decided to call him on the radio, and he answered. I asked him how he was. I said I missed him a lot, him and his pranks, and would like to see him. He said, "Wait, you'll see me now." And I saw that he had climbed up to his waist out of the window and emptied a magazine on the Russians. That was another one of his "pranks."

Half an hour passed. I heard a message on the radio: "Vadud—Abdullah became a shahid! . . ." I can't tell you how bad I felt. This was my friend. I got used to him since childhood, since school, and now he's gone. Before Allah took him to Himself, for a half a minute before that, he struck a Russian tank and became (Inshah Allah[6]) a shahid.

5. Alkhazur

When the OMON[7] came to take Alkhazur, who was 19 years old, he and his mother were in the apartment. The OMON officers restrained him and started putting handcuffs on him. He said: "Please don't put them on in front of my mother, I will come out by myself and you can put them on me outside." The mother managed to shout, "Alkhazur, don't do it, I know what you're about to do, you are my only son, I don't have another."

At that moment he drew the ring on one of the OMON officer's grenades and pulled it to himself. At that moment his soul flew to heaven, where he will be happy, taking with him—but to the opposite side—the souls of three Russians.

6. Green Birds

"When our brothers died, Allah placed their souls inside the green birds that fly to the rivers of paradise, eat the fruit of paradise, and rest in the golden lanterns in the shadow of the heavenly canopy.

Allah asks them, 'My slaves, what do you want?' And they say, 'Oh, our Lord! We want our souls to return to our bodies, so that we could once more lead Jihad and fight for You, until we are killed once more . . .'"

7. Our Ambulance

One of my brothers, Ali, became a shahid. This was during Ramadan, at the very beginning of the war. Driving up to the base one day I saw my brothers; they were standing by an ambulance. I saw Ali there. He was the best among us. A happy person and, by Allah, a very good person, a kind soul, in a word. Now he was lying in the ambulance. . . . He was the first among us who became a shahid.

We stood around the ambulance and looked at him. Not three minutes passed before I smelled a slight scent, the scent of musk. Waves of this scent started spreading wider and wider and, by Allah, I get goosebumps to this day remembering it.

I was silent, I was afraid to say a word out loud about the scent. If no one smelled it except me, they wouldn't understand me. But I knew that it was coming from Ali. He was the one who deserved it. He was on Jihad, it was the month of Ramadan.

Abdul-Nasr was with us. He came from Moscow, where he was studying in college. He abandoned everything, bought the full gear with his own money, and came out to Jihad!

So this Abdul-Nasr was the first to say out loud: "Allahu akbar, brothers, do you not smell the scent of musk that is coming from Ali?" Subhan Allah,[8] every one of us felt it, but, like me, they were afraid to say it out loud!

You won't believe it, but our ambulance smelled of musk for 3–4 days after that. People even visited us, people we didn't know, just to smell the scent.

8. The Scent of Musk

During battle, when a shell hit, one commander who had powerful Iman[9] was thrown against the wall of a building. Mortally wounded, he got on his knees and recited the Shahada.[10] He died with his index finger pointing up—a symbol of God's Oneness.

Two fighters from his platoon buried the commander, and when they returned, their fellows started asking, "Did you spray yourself with perfume?" That's how strong the scent of musk was that emanated from those who took part in the shahid's burial.

Another Mujahid[11] had his eyes knocked out by shards. Dying, he smiled joyfully and exclaimed: "What I see is so beautiful!"

There were instances when, for a long time, the relatives of the dead couldn't retrieve their bodies for burial from the Russians and, finally retrieving them, found that the bodies were completely unspoiled by decay, as if the shahids endured martyrdom just yesterday. They seemed asleep . . .

Bodies untouched by decay, the scent of musk, faces radiant with smiles—these are signs that identify a shahid.

9. Firdous—Door of Heaven

"Firdous" was written on the rusty doors of our headquarters in very beautiful letters, followed by an explanation in regular font: "Firdous—one of the best doors to Heaven."

And you know what's so interesting? Near that inscription there was a plaque. A regular plaque, like in a business office or a factory, with the words "Trespassing prohibited."

10. White Envy

SubhanaLlah. . . . How I envy those brothers. . . . Allahu akbar, how lucky they are. . . . Allahu akbar!!!! I have no words. . . . I also knew several brothers, one of them was called Saihan. . . . Oh God, how I loved him, how I love him even now . . . he was shot when they were attempting to assassinate Baraev[12] (they confused the cars) . . . when our neighbor Lida came running to tell me what happened, I cried for a moment, but without hysteria, I cried because I envied him. . . . I envy all of them with a white envy. . . . Allahu akbar, how lucky they are!!!

11. Like Saffron

That's how brothers depart from this world, to fly as green birds above the rivers of paradise. . . . Their wounds will shine and, like saffron, give off the scent of musk.

That same scent has permeated the Chechen soil for the past 10 years.

12. A List of Shahids

Shahids of the neighborhood jamaat:[13]

Umar Mulia, "Ibn." Became a shahid in Dagestan (Inshah Allah!).
Mukhammad (lived by Dudaev's credo). Became a shahid in Dagestan.
Khamzat (blue-eyed, wore a shirt in observance of the sunnah). Became a shahid in Dagestan.
Adlan (Abdul-Adil').
Ibrahim (it's after Adil's death that he ran at the Russian side and became a shahid there).
Artur (Abdul-Jaleel).
Zurab (Abdullah, code name "Darar"). Became a shahid while in sujud.
Abdul-Khamid (who among us didn't know him?!).
Saipi (already an older man, born in 1963).
Musleem (lived across from the mosque, on the first floor, 12 Dyakova St.).
Ruslan (Rasul; code name "The Sixteenth").
Alikhan.
Abdul-Malik.
Musa.
Timur.

Khasan.

Abdul-Wahhab.

Khamzat.

Rashid.

Mamed.

Zelim.

Said.

Rustam.

Zelim.

PART II: SEPTEMBER 1

13. On the Phone

On the phone. Men:

- Fucking Chechens took a school hostage!
- Shouldn't have started shit with them! Shoulda just bombed the fuck out of Chechnya and not fucked around, but they dragged their feet.
- The whole thing is fucked. Completely. . . . Fucking monkeys.

On the phone. Women:

- First the downed planes, then the Rizhskaya metro, and today—Beslan . . .
- It's scary to live in Moscow nowadays . . .
- No words for all this. No words but swearwords.
- Fear, and anger, and helplessness . . .
- And relief, that it's not here.

On the phone. A joke:

Question: What should you give a dead child for his birthday?

Answer: A dead puppy.

14. Five Condoms

- Chechens and the rest of those khachi bitches[14] need to die! I fucked your mothers and sisters and daughters.
- You fucked them? I can't even look at those monkeys, never mind fuck them.
- You can fuck a Chechen girl only after she soaks in a bath for three days and you gotta wear five condoms so you don't catch a disease. And, of course, you have to cover her face with a black bag. Like, only then can you fuck her.
- Death to towelheads, kikes, and niggers!
- Chechens? The ones, like, in the hills, grazing with the sheep? Aaaaa!

15. Pink Floyd

We're peaceful people, BUT. . . . We've killed and will continue to kill! We'll line up those Chechen towelheads and goatfuckers in two rows and blast them at random. We'll cut them up slowly and gracefully to the sounds of Pink Floyd, Queen, and Russian balalaikas. We'll level the whole area two yards below where it was. We'll curse it with our Christian Orthodox faith, fill it up with chlorine, make a nuclear dump site there so that for 500 years people won't come near that cursed place. Amen!

16. Short Dick? Stay home

- A BLOODY RUSSIAN SPECTACLE. EXECUTION OF CHILDREN IN OSSETIA. Playwright, director, and producer: V. V. Putin. Allahu akbar!
- You're not one of those bastards from Beslan who was trying to get away by running through the crowd in a tracksuit, are you? Where's the insider knowledge from?

– “Oink” is what the ugly pig said. As for insider knowledge, yeah, I know for sure, and not from some rumors. FSB specialists executed even more people, turns out. The latest news gives a figure of around 400 children. That’s why Vlad was getting close and personal with Gerhard Schröder, probably doing an exchange with the fascists via his KGB ties! Though Mother Russia has plenty of experience with cannibalism.
– I don’t understand, are you, like, the clown on here, or something? Peddling drivel to entertain the masses? I see through you, in short.
– What do you see? You know the phrase, “Short dick? Stay home.”

17. A Russian Probably Wrote That

– If you think all Chechens are the enemy, then you should go ahead and say that!
– I think:

1. All Chechens have always hated Russians.
2. All Chechens will always hate Russians.
3. Every Chechen would rather enrich himself by dishonest means than honest ones because that would be easier and more admirable.
4. Most Chechens don’t see the killing of a Russian as a crime, regardless of his gender and age.

Note that I am not calling for Chechens to be killed. I just don’t want to live in the same country as them. I’m for granting Chechnya independence with strong border control: if you approach the border, you’ll be executed on the spot.

For any display of disloyalty among Chechens living in Russia: deportation to independent Chechnya within 24 hours.

– A Russian probably wrote that.

18. Sheep on the Square

Ahahaaaa I just can't. . . . I was laughing my ass off, just, like, movies and Nazis! This herd of sheep, 150 million strong, came out on the square to beg for protection from a bunch of Chechens. . . . Holy moly! People, have you seen the sheep that gathered by the Kremlin for a protest! These sheep can be killed, shot, run over with tanks, they won't resist!

Putin, you promised to "kill the Chechens, even in the toilet," but you kill our people in the theater, in the school. You bomb sleeping people in Russian homes!

That's right, that's what they deserve!!! Brainless sheep, they don't see anything beyond their vodka bottle!

19. This Is Just Bullshit

THIS IS JUST BULLSHIT, GUYS. GOT THIS EMAIL. In the name of life on earth! Spreading like spam mail. I'm posting the letter:

"Moscow Echo Radio Station, Moscow News, MK, The New Times, Pravda, Izvestiia, RusBusiness Consulting ask you to participate in a solidarity action.

"Our children died in Beslan. It turned out that we are powerless to protect them from death. We are all guilty. On this ninth day after the first death in Beslan, please, don't begrudge ten seconds of your time.

"On Thursday, September 9, 2004, at 9 p.m. If you are walking outside, stop. Be silent. Think about those who died. If you are driving, honk. Don't turn off your headlights today, as a symbol of mourning. In the name of the dead and the living."

THIS IS JUST BULLSHIT. I'M SORRY I POSTED IT, BUT I CAN'T LIVE THROUGH THIS HELL BY MYSELF.

20. I'm a Dagestani Girl

Hey you people! Why is this hard to understand? . . . The Jewish mob in the Kremlin is trying to ignite hatred between us. I'm a Dagestani girl, obviously neutral. Didn't you see how because of a dozen criminals sent by the FSB, calling themselves Chechens, these pathetic animals in the Russian army shot up a school full of children in front of their parents and all humanity!

People of the Caucasus, in the eyes of Moscow we are niggers, apes. Haven't you seen the apartment ads? Caucasians, Chinese, and Vietnamese need not apply. We Russian people are being compared to the Chinese and Vietnamese! But we're Russian citizens. WAKE UP!!!

Chechens are getting ready to sue Russia in international courts, demanding revenge for the death of their loved ones, that's millions of dollars per person. What is this going to come to for Russia? This is the only way to strangle the gang in the Kremlin!!!

21. What Do Jews Have to Do With It?

– What do Jews have to do with it? You're probably a Wahhabi that wants to fan the flames. What do Jews have to do with it at all, I don't understand! Jews, like Ossetians, suffer from terrorist attacks every day, but then of course they demolish them with rockets, planes, and tanks, killing your terrorists just like that haha! Then all of sell-out Europe yaps that the

Jews are clobbering Palestine to death. And I suggest to you Ossetians that you also clobber those Islamist terrorists, no mercy for them!

– Ughhhh I just can't. . . . I'm guessing you're a Jew? I don't have anything against the Jewish people, but I'm against that greedy mob sitting in the Kremlin with that idiot Putin! I hope you're not in the Kremlin, even if you're a Jew? If you're not there, then I'm sorry for the Jews! If you are, then, you know . . .

22. Flowers for Israel

– Israel sent 500 flower bouquets to Beslan to honor the dead.
– Israel sent 500 flower bouquets to Beslan to honor the dead. Why don't we all grow flowers for Israel!
– Why don't you go fuck yourself!!

PART III: VENGEANCE

23. Malgobek, Vladikavkaz

Among the subhumans that killed our children in Beslan was one Mussa Tsechoev from the Ingush village Sagopsha. That's not far from here. I want and am entitled to want for as many people as possible to go look into the eyes of the subhumans that reared this animal and into the eyes of the woman who bred with him and reared this animal's brood. And may their eyes grow dark; they won't be able to bear the people's gaze. In Sagopsha: Marem Umatgireevna, who conceived that creature, Mussa Tsechoev; Issa Soslanbekovich, a hyena in human clothing who sired that creature; Zareta Lechaevna, a creature that produced the creature's brood, Alina and Khalis. Look at them, people. *Malgobek, Vladikavkaz.*

24. Go and Take Revenge

- Since you know the family SO WELL—go and kill them, clean up the garbage in your own hut, don't foist it on others.
- If you want to take revenge, go ahead. Are you disabled or infirm? I'll wheel your wheelchair all the way to his parents' house. If there is a desire for revenge.

25. Chechen Mothers for Peace

Announcement from the Chechen Mothers for Peace:

> There is a message going around the internet, signed by Malgobek from Vladikavkaz, calling for vengeance on a family that lives in the Ingush village Sagopsha for their relative Mussa Tsechoev (a participant in the Beslan events). We are extremely surprised by the call to violence against people who were not directly involved in the events in Beslan. We will keep track of their well-being and take action against anyone who threatens those whose guilt has not been established. *Madina Madomagova, on behalf of Chechen Mothers for Peace.*

26. Look at Them

He didn't say anything about death. . . . He just wanted to shame the killer's family. He didn't say, "kill them, people," he said, "look at them, people" . . .

And this universal judgment will be more terrible than death.

For example, the mother of that bastard Soslanbek doesn't live in El'khotovo any longer, and probably won't return there. . . . She understands that she has nothing to do there anymore.

27. You're Not the Only One Who Waits for the Fortieth Day

Peace unto you, Malgobek from Vladikavkaz. We say to you, Malgobek, and everyone else, that in the Sagopsha village, cursed forever by God, live not only the creature Tsechoev and his brood; other creatures live there too. The sister of the bastard Asiat lives in Malgobek on Pliev Street, we're not sure about the house number—10 or 12. And you're right, Malgobek, that Beial Tsechoev from Sagoshpa was with Tsokiev in Beslan. His dishonorable father Bashir croaked a long time ago. Tsechoev's brothers live somewhere in Russia, we will find them and tell everyone where. Let this be important to everyone. Look at them, people. *Malgobek's brothers from Beslan.*

28. Bobby

Fellow citizens, ladies and gentlemen, and comrades! Wondrous news came to me by way of wireless telephone connection. My buddy Dima called me from I kid you not Ossetia—Northern, naturally—where he journeyed in search of vast quantities of *spiritus vini*. But the point is not in the *spiritus*, of course.

So this buddy of mine told me that word was Beial Tsechoev and his family should be publicly shamed. I'm not exactly ready to fight for justice worldwide, but what they did there was obviously over the top. So about Tsechoev. Beial I don't know, obviously. But the fact that his father is called Bashir, that riled me up. Because that dirtbag has brothers who stroll about our land freely and openly. We're used to anything around here, but these guys have nothing to lose; if bad times come, God forbid something might happen here too.

So notifying anyone interested (even if that doesn't make me look good): Tsechoev the terrorist, who killed children in Ossetia, has brothers who are doing quite well and prospering in the pleasant town of Langepas, in the Tiumen' district. They have a business where they are all directors. The business is called Slava and Co., LLC. Issa is a director, Musa is a marketing director, Ismail is a project manager. They have another brother there too, Movsar. Musa and Ismail definitely have a crib on Parkovaya Street in Langepas. Let them all repent for their brother.

Bobby.

29. Where Is Gapur?

Thanks, Bobby. I knew that I wouldn't be abandoned in this difficult task. Found Tsechoev's brothers. They have another brother, Gapur from Sagopsha. Is he over there too, by any chance?

30. Tsk-Tsk-Tsk, Shame on You!

Muslim brothers, why do you cast stones? Do you seriously think that someone from Ossetia is going to drive to Ingushetia and go to the terrorists' families and say to them, "Tsk-tsk-tsk, shame on you for your brother, husband, son, or father!"

31. Ossetians Themselves

Don't forget that the people killing children were Ossetians themselves. So it starts from them. But you should back off, you're not going to do anything about it anyway.

32. I Shit on Your World!

Listen to me! I shit on your world, if you're trying to gloat about what happened in my country. Listen to me! Not a single one of these animals, the people who came up with this sick idea, should be left alive. And they won't be. I'm going to do everything I can, even if it's only a little bit.

And about Ossetians shooting at children—there was one son of a bitch with an Ossetian last name. And he was a bastard. An Ossetian would never do this!

33. Wake Up!

Ossetians, wake up! Shame on us if we think we can forgive. These hyenas came here because they thought Ossetians "are not going to do anything." We can't forgive this! Or we will be ashamed to meet each other's eyes tomorrow!

34. Beat the Cops

Ossetian brothers, who should we punish? How could this happen, who is to blame? Why do our cops do nothing but take bribes? Why don't they want to catch these bastards, why do they let criminals go free? They're guilty too.

Maybe, as a start, we need to organize to beat up the cops? Take care of it ourselves, since the government doesn't train them? So they'll be afraid to take bribes.

35. Mussa

- Who started the hostage situation? And who started shooting at the children running out? Look at the gun wounds on the children—the bullets came from the front, not from the back. Remember the interview with the first freed hostages who insisted that the terrorists were speaking in Ossetian.
- If the terrorists turn out to be Ossetian, then the issue will look quite different. *Mussa.*

- Mussa! Ah, hero of many a dad joke! You saw the gun wounds with your own eyes, I take it?
- Well if there was one among you that didn't cry like a woman, then you could have seen it for yourselves. But you wouldn't know the size of the wounds formed by bullet entry and exit. You're experts only at sniveling and sucking up.
- Tell me what kind of dad jokes there are? Probably Ossetians started telling them about their bearded women?
- And about bearded women, you better just shut up. You're the ones capable of using women for war, your own women, moreover.

36. Pig Hide

There is a simple way to thwart the endeavors of madmen: after a terrorist attack, the body of the shaitan should be wrapped in pig hide. That's the practical way to make sure you know what happens to heroes like these after death.

37. Flesh Strewn About

I just don't get it. When one of the members of your race wants to end their life by committing suicide, why do they take hundreds of other lives with them? A shot in the head and that's it, not human flesh strewn about for miles.

PART IV: HIJAB

38. Which Girl Here

- Could I ask, which girl here is ready to become the wife of a Mujahid wounded in battle? That is, of an invalid?

Because right now in Chechnya there are a lot of crippled people—hands or legs torn out. Are you ready to marry them?

– Salam Aleikum, brothers and sisters, I have a request. . . . I really need photos (as soon as possible) of the female jihadists that took part in the events of Nord-Ost, this is vitally important to one sister, she asked me. For now my search has been unsuccessful, everything is in the hands of God. . . . Help me, bismillah, if you have some info about them or photos, email me: *Dzhazak.*

39. Hijab

– I've been temporarily dislocated to Almaty.[15] I don't wear a hijab because my Iman is not so lofty yet. Some day I will get there . . . not because of peer pressure, because everyone is wearing them, but by myself. . . . But society has influence here too. I can't imagine how I would go out on the street in it. I have one friend, also an Ingush woman, who wears a hijab, and I am very jealous of her. But she gets called a Wahhabi and gets stared at. Of course if I were ready for it myself, I would defend my right in front of my relatives. It's all up to me. But it's just that this process is gradual, and eventually we will all get there. Happiness will knock one day, knock knock knock . . .

– I didn't take to the hijab at first, I thought it was "ugly." Then I signed up for a Muslim women's club, where there were lots of photos of models or just young women in hijab—Such beauty! That made me want to wear a hijab . . . *Queen Margo.*

40. If a Woman Starts to Question

Recommended for married couples!

Brothers, if a woman starts to question her husband's love, then she loses her confidence in herself, in her beauty, in her behavior and way of life. And then the devil goes after the wife. She starts to think that he has another wife or that he wants to marry someone else. Then she starts to question all of his actions, when he comes home, when he leaves, who he's talking to, etc.

It is possible to be happily married without love as long as there is fairness between the husband and wife. Make her wishes come true. But how can a husband understand what his wife wants if she doesn't know what she wants herself? There is one simple question: "What are your wishes?" Ask it. She might not answer at first, thinking that it is a cruel joke. Be patient and repeat the question, continue to smile. Ask it until she starts to flirt with you. You will be pleasantly surprised by the results.

Don't yell at her. Compliment her from time to time in front of her relatives and yours. The best way is when she hears a compliment after being absent. For example, when your relatives are visiting, ask your wife to get you some water, and when she returns, compliment her with the words, Praise be to Allah, who gave me such a wonderful woman for a wife. Protect me, Allah, from the loss of her, etc. Do this and you won't regret it.

Listen to her when she speaks. Some husbands, out of love for their wives, are quick to anger. Of course, your mind can scarcely bear the boring details of her conversation, but nevertheless be patient. That is her nature, accept her as she is.

From time to time take care of your appearance and dress up for your wife. This way you will protect your wife from the temptations of other men who have become much worse tempters than women.

Praise Allah, sins do not smell and do not distort one's looks. . . . For every Muslim man and woman, I ask Allah to strengthen love and family feeling among us!

Ahmad Ikhia AbuAbdurrakhman, address: Under the gaze of the Almighty.

Ahmad Ikhia AbuAbdurrakmhan.

View profile!

Add Ahmad Ikhia AbuAbdurrakhman to friends!

—Ahmad Ikhia AbuAbdurrakhman! I will come to you. . . . Well said!

BRIDE, address: Sparrow Hills.

View profile!

Add BRIDE, address: Sparrow Hills to friends!

—No wayyy that's not for our people!!! That's for some low-down Arabs, Tatars, etc., not for us! I heard that if you want to do something, you have to ask your wife and then do the exact opposite! They say that always works!! No, Ahmad Ikhia AbuAbdurrakhman, don't put this on your neighbors! *Firstperson, address: Saint Helena Island*

Firstperson, address: Saint Helena Island

View profile!

Add Firstperson, address: Saint Helena Island to friends!

41. You're Alive and I Am Dead

You live in a cozy house,
Recite Pushkin by rote.
I mix joy and sorrow,
And choose both.
You give gifts to girlfriends,
Drown in love.
I walk around bombed-out parks,

Drown in blood.
You hurry to the party
I hurry from the shots.
You'll probably thrive,
I just hope to reach the truth.
Your dreams came true—like in a fairytale.
My dream is smashed to bits.
Choosing everything for happiness,
All I get is: nix.
You find what you look for,
I look for distant light.
You say, "quiet!"—it'll be quiet,
If I say it, there'll be riot
Your castles rise—crystal and gold,
My city's smashed to bits.
Everyone parades about
I am dead; you live.

PART V: IT'S EEASY TO SIT AT THE COMPUTER

42. Guess

I was meeting someone at the airport today and got searched top to bottom! They did everything short of looking between my legs with a flashlight . . . and I'm not even flying.

Guess who I was cursing in my mind?!

44. Well, Putin Isn't Going to Negotiate!

He attacks. So what if 500 people died? What's it to a big politician like him? And what then? He's always going to attack? And people will die again, and children? Where is the limit that determines how many ordinary people can be sacrificed for the sake of Putin's career and for him to save face?

44. My Girls Cry A Lot

The government gives those chichens everything, gives those "refugees" entire homes! Look at their children going to our schools! Those snotty kids in first or second grade tell our children that they're gonna kill them! My girls are afraid to go to school, they're afraid of the Chechen girls. They cry a lot.

45. The Rest of the Scum

If someone is thinking of waiting it out in England, that's bullshit. They'll wipe Russia off the map, and they won't even glance at England (that goes to the rest of the scum—Belgians, etc.)

[Alternate 45.] I'm Tatar

It's painful to read these words. So I'm Tatar—do you think I'm happy with this? You think I'm not scared for my relatives? Or maybe you think that people like me aren't glued to the TV to find out if there's been any news?

46. No Nationality?

They say these subhumans don't have a nationality.

How's that, they don't have a nationality? Did they come from Mars or something?

Let's assume they really don't have a nationality. Just a handful of bastards without nationality digging graves for slaves, trafficking people, cutting off heads, blowing up houses, sending their wives to blow up planes, and killing children. This handful of bastards doesn't have relatives or ties. No one helps them hide, feeds them, lodges them, gives them information or money . . .

Then I have a question for Chechens and Ingush people:

Why is it that you haven't gotten rid of this handful of bastards by YOURSELVES, when they've cast shame on your peoples?

Because this is the easiest way to stop this war.

47. I Took Pity on a Woodlouse

Yesterday I took pity on a woodlouse. A woodlouse was crawling on the wall, and mom said that spring is their mating season. And that they are nice. My mom thinks everything and everybody is nice. I felt so bad for the woodlouse—it was probably crawling to its husband, so I didn't kill it.

48. Two Rams

I saw a flyer listing rates:

IED downtown: $20.
Bomb: $50.
Landmine: $300–500.
Murder of a general: $15K (three cows or twenty rams).
A senior officer (from major to colonel): $7K (one cow and five rams).
A junior officer (lieutenant to captain): $3K (three rams).
Commissioned officer or mercenary: $1.5K (two rams).
If the explosion has many casualties: $10K. Advance paid first, the rest follows when the media begins to talk about the number of casualties.
Taking hostages: either you're paid or your relatives (in case of death). Rate: $10K per hostage. To the relatives of the dead: $30K per hostage.

49. F***!

F***! Since the government can't or doesn't want to do anything about the Chechens, then the people have only one solution! If people are getting on a plane and they see someone from the Caucasus, get together and kick them off the plane with their luggage and tell them, "We don't need people from the Caucasus on our fucking plane!" And do that everywhere—on the street, in the stores, in the subway! Only this way will we be able to curb these animals. F***!

50. Bro, You're Wrong

– Disgusting, shameless, cynical trash, your Maskhadov and everyone like him. . . . Let him burn in hell!
Moscow girl.

– Whatcha piping up for, ho? Who let you talk about our president that way? Blinded by the truth, huh? Yeah? You bitch?
Chechen.

– Bro, you're wrong. Your president is a criminal. Basaev admitted to taking hostages in the school. Say what you want, but only shaitans can hide behind children's bodies (Auzubillah[16]). They should burn in hell together with the murderers of the innocent Chechen as well as Ossetian children.
Also a Chechen.

51. Whose Father Is He?

– Listen, you Russian DOORMAT! Neither you nor anyone else can laugh at the president of the Chechen Republic of Ichkeria. He's a pure-blooded Chechen, and he knows his roots, and precisely determined Chechen blood courses through his veins.

- What's in your veins? What's in the veins of POO-TIN? Name the names of your seven ancestors, or at least your great-grandfather. You don't even know who your father is. You might be struggling but POO-TIN knows who his father is, and how he left his mother because of her loose character. And he knows how his stepfather hated him and his mother hated him.
- You're all bastard cattle. Aslan Maskhadov worked in Russia for many years, like other Chechens. Who knows whose father he is. Maybe yours too?

52. A Fountain of Oil

What prevents you from living peacefully, working, studying, raising children peacefully? I can tell you: THE DESIRE FOR POWER AND MONEY, and also—Chechen oil. You don't even have anyone left to fight anymore, and you don't pity your wives, sisters, or mothers. You destroy the Caucasus with your ambition. Your stupid desire for money. Maybe you want us to help you with that? What do you want—a castle with a fountain of oil? A cocaine tree in the garden? And a bunch of monkeys, so you can rule over them.

53. Fuker

Salam 2aleikum! This SHAMIL BASAYEV's a total idiot! With htis declaration he shit on everthing that was don before this! Evan if he did htis, he should not have admitted he did htis. Our people all overthe world are persuading that we didn't do htis, it's provocateurs, htis fuker ruined everthing! He should be a janitor not a leader. And also I AM a CHECHIN, I have a right to write htis, caus I know, what I write! Bex ma bilash, he should be hospitalized in a psych word.

54. Daughter of the Mountains, Silent in Anticipation

I think we shouldn't even pay attention to this disgusting mob pouring all this dirt on Islam. We have to put the question otherwise: "How do you feel about the FSB after the events of Beslan?"

Daughter of the mountains, silent in anticipation

55. Ivanov Russian Federation

– Russia will raise these orphans! They will be rightful citizens of Russia and the world! And you guys are in the dustbin of history!!!
  IVANOV, Russian citizen
– You're way wrong. Russia will raise them to be alcoholics, like all other Russians, who had an alcoholic for a president! What else can we expect from Russia? Huh, Ivan?

56. Chechens, Georgians, Muscovites

– Most Chechens should be killed. There are some good people there, but they are very, very few.
– Personally I also dislike Georgians and their president for their arrogance and self-confidence.
– Let's add Muscovites to this list. . . . Very self-involved peeps. . . . All the problems come out of there. Moscow is "an empire of evil." And soon it will collapse!

57. Gofukyaself

Fuck you, punkin! Wanna hear someth funnee? Gofuckyaself. More than 5 percent of the population of Siberia is chinks. And according to our fucken laws more than 5 percent of the population can call up some shit like a referendum to the tune of joining our territory to another country. In that case everything is decided by a majority of VOYces. You think drunken, burned-out Russians will always cum out to elekshans? Fuck off. Only the chinks will cum. And then Siberia will belong to China, no dicking around!

ACHTUNG, RUSHIANS! Fukk them and don give up! Fuck up the non-Russians without prior warning!!

A Siberian.

58. It's Eeasy to Sit at Your Computer

—Its eeasy to sit at your computer and debate all htis! When Basaev was able to make the Russians sit at the negotiation table by taking hostages in the maternity hospital in Budenovsk he was a hero! But htis time he failed. Should we blame him for htis? We have to stand as one to defend our Heroes.

59. What Kinda People Are They?

Lots of Dagis would spit in Basaev's face. He has a lot of blood enemies here, and now the whole people of Ossetia is a blood enemy too. . . . There's a lot you don't know! Or know but don't tell.

Here are the facts.

1. Shamil is a junkie and don't even argue with me. (I know this for a fact!!) There is evidence . . .
2. One of the oldest mosquesin the Caucasus, in the Tondo settlement, Botlikh region. . . . We made a toilet out of that mosque!! And wiped ourselves (not washed, wiped!!!) with paper from the holy Koran!
3. I personally cut people's hands off!! . . . I saw. . . . Don't argue. Dagis' heads. It was hard for me to write this!

4. He says he is the great Imam of Dagestan and Chechnya (Imam Shamil), that he is actively liberating people from Russian ideology from the plague. . . . Then liberate, DON'T KILL CHILDREN—Chechen, Dagestani, Ingush, Ossetian!!!

I'm a highlander and I won't lie, and I don't want to argue with you. . . . I saw what kinda people they are . . . MONEY! *That's* their life's work!

60. The Best Time for Jihad

Jihad will remain sweet and green as long as rain falls from the sky, and there will come a time upon the people in which the scholars from them will say, This is not the time for Jihad. So whoever lives to see that time, then this is the best time for Jihad.[17]

61. Russians Are in Their Own Country

I would understand the Chechens if they were blowing up the Duma, the bureaucrats, the army bases. . . . That would be normal guerrilla warfare. Instead it's a defenseless crowd walking on the street. And then BAM . . . WHAT FOR? WHY ATTACK REGULAR PEOPLE?! So if Russians can still think for themselves, they'll start a genocide, because in Russia Russians are in their own country! Just get it started! Before it's too late, or it will be like Paris, where there are Arab nationals instead of French people . . .

62. You Eat Shawarma, You Help Basaev

I'm not a nationalist, generally. The size of your nose, the color of your eyebrows, the shape of your lips are inconsequential to me.

But yesterday I realized: EVERY market, kiosk, and store has a brown-haired person looking out of it. And looking out in an unfriendly manner, angrily, arrogantly, bossily. You eat Big Macs, you help Bush. You eat shawarma, you help Basaev.

63. An Evolutionary Dead-End in Civilization

Chechens are an evolutionary dead-end in civilization. They appear to be rational, but they are not people. Stone Age, basically. Having a savage next door, it's best to get rid of him by destroying him.

64. Russofucker

You wanna fuck with your Russian weenies? You have a historical jealousy of men from the Caucasus! We fucked all of Russia. God gave us courage and huge humpbacked Cocks. And he shortchanged you, alcoholics. Your weenies are only good for fucking kittens. You filthy cowards. You sow division. When the USA surrenders Putin, we'll have a mass rape on Red Square. Your pink asses will be blood red. Greetings to all the anti-Chechens. *Russofucker.*

65. I'm Fucking Sick of the Churkas[18]

Fuck, I'm fucking sick of the Churkas! Churkas, you're like animals, you don't abide to any behavioral norms. You huddle together in packs, and when you're facing each other one on one, you tuck in your tails! Fuck, when you walk past the Lomonosov monument, it feels like the university campus is somewhere in the mountains.

The pigs oink: the Jihad is on.

66. I Still Have to Walk Lidka Home

You can't feel bad for everybody. I didn't fall into depression, I didn't cry. And didn't watch TV. I just didn't let it get to me. Because I have to walk Lidka home, because my ma has to go to the doctor, because I have to work nights and go to class in the morning.

PART VI: HOSTAGE

67. Say Goodbye to Life

When someone makes a hostage out of you, a sheep in the slaughterhouse.

When we encounter hoodlums trying to steal a wallet, do we fight until our last breath? When we encounter bastards tying bombs to our wife or children, we help tie them and keep mum. Will the police save us? This is what I'd like to take issue with.

The men who were among the NORD-OST hostages in large numbers and, in smaller numbers, in the school helped build the barricades and tie explosives to backboards. And the women bandaged the bastards and administered first aid. These shitheads have a simple strategy: chase everyone into a place where they will all be trapped within walls, kill three-quarters of them in a comfortable, safe space, then run out with the rest to the streets, breaking the police cordon, and escape.

They didn't have demands, but they had toothbrushes. I haven't heard of suicide bombers who were real men.

In light of this, I suggest a different approach.

First. Say goodbye to life.

Your life has ended. Lose your human face immediately; go nuts. Let all your emotions out. Whatever you do, don't do what you're told. Kill, maim those bastards. Create chaos. Think about dying.

Sink your teeth into a nose, an ear, a throat—if you can reach it. First, jump on their women—maybe she'll blow herself up in fear and then you'll get the brunt of their death balls.

Second. If you are in the middle of the crowd being penned in, don't let yourself get penned in. Yell, "there's gas there, they're gassing people!" Push people so that there is a stampede.

Third. If there's something heavy you can throw, throw it until it runs out. And yell so others will join.

Fourth. If someone else is already attacking one of the shitheads, grab the gun and twist.

Fifth. If you managed to capture a firearm, throw yourself on his back and pull the trigger. Or just shoot. You're dead meat regardless. Might as well take at least one of them with you.

Sixth. Yell more—you'll feel braver.

Seventh. Inconspicuously, take out pens from your pockets or remove your belt. God willing, you'll stab someone in the eye or neck.

Eighth. Pretend you're ill or disabled and let them come close. Once you see their legs near you, grab them and drag over yourself and sink your teeth in their face, tear their eyes with your hands . . .

Ninth. If someone's already started a commotion, run to the nearest bastard. And seize him. and break his neck, twist it like a wheel to one side.

What you should not do.

Don't try to remain human.

Don't obey, even indirectly. Don't start fist fights, you won't have time to do anything, and they'll survive a black eye. It's important to disable them for a maximum amount of time, even if you are killed right away—at least they won't pry open your jaws.

Even in bloated America: one of the planes fell where it wasn't supposed to, because some computer programmers started a fight.

And the fact that you're already dead—that's been the case since the beginning. The only thing that depends solely on you is whether you'll kneel to make it easier for them to slit your throat or you'll die in a fight.

If you're too piss scared to do all of the above, then *just don't help*. Sabotage. They give you a bomb, throw it out the window. Ruin everything that helps those shitheads. Throw a fit like cut me up or shoot me, I'm not gonna hang up this filth and I'm not gonna help you!

Please understand me, I don't want to outlive my wife or child and get my chance at life that way. Every shithead that's bleeding to death is a weakened line of defense. Don't let yourself be penned in in a herd, don't let yourself be beaten without biting back. Die with dignity, because if we start to behave this way, they'll fear us.

After Nord-Ost I gave my wife strict instructions: when the shit hits the fan, vomit, piss, and shit; from the moment go—you don't know me anymore. I no longer exist!

PART VII: I'M OUT

68. The Whole Rationale

The whole rationale is in the one phrase from our general: "If we take our troops out of Chechnya, we will betray the memory of the twenty thousand of our troops that died there. Then their death would be meaningless."

So if we want to give meaning to all this, we need to have another twenty thousand people killed.

69. The Price

There's so much money trading hands, and you keep going on and on about some people. . . . So much cash invested into absolute chaos. And so much money made on this. . . . People are our raw material—in their monetary equivalent, of course. Every one of us is either in on the deal or a commodity being bought and sold. I'm telling you as a lawyer. The role of politics here is establishing the appropriate price. So don't worry! And I suspect that's how it is everywhere, so stop blaming our country.

70. They Went for It Withope

If what happened in Beslan happened every week, then they would get out of Chechnya right away. And screw the opinions of other countries htat supported the Russian murderers even before.

I dontsee anything forbidden by Allah in the school seizure, since their goal was not to kill children, if they wanneta do it, they woulda done it withouta loss on our side. Justa BOOM and thas it. They went for it withope . . . that's all.

They were to blame only for one thing . . . they naively thought that Russia would go for concessions forthe sake of kids . . .

71. I'm Out

Have you walked in our shoes?

There, I said it!

I'M OUT!

72. Muslim Face

Why do your martyrs cry out Allah Akbar when they kill? I don't know the Koran, but is there a religion where death is justified? Why can't anyone admit that terrorism has a Muslim face?

73. Ballet and Ceramics

The media is shit when it thinks only about the value of the material, the ratings, the salaries. I personally would not be able to shove a camera into the faces of children just freed after those 3 days. But the channels are competing with each other to give the "hottest" facts.

Fuck. All these terrorist attacks are done FOR the media!

The organizer is sitting there, thinking, the terrorist attack is, like, carried out, but he turns on the idiot box and there's nothing there, just ballet and ceramics.

How's that? He's switching channels, flipping through newspapers—nothing, no hysterical announcements, no videos of the work he's accomplished, no striking photos of corpses . . . nothing! And then the sponsors call: where's the account of the work accomplished, the money spent, bitch?

Ballet and ceramics!

74. Not the Main Thing I've Got Going

- For me, a Russian person, I'm sick of feeling sorry for negroes in Africa! I don't want to and I won't! Yeah! I consider Ossetians negroes. I felt a lot worse observing the effects of the terrorist attack in Rizhskaia metro, where Russian people died . . .
- Ossetians are definitely not the main thing I've got going on.
- To honor them I propose we don't flush the toilet. For a week.

75. That Was Our Vega Group![19]

On December 9 last year people in camouflage and automatic rifles seized the Passage Mall in Yoshkar-Ola. The employees (almost all of them women) were forbidden from leaving the premises.

They were not allowed to eat or drink. They called their families and screamed on the phone that they were taken hostage. But that was . . . our Vega Group!

76. Cherenkova in Exchange

Personally, if that's how it is, then I would like to give a shit at least about what I can't change.

Because what I *can* change I've ceased to give a shit about a long time ago and absolutely hopelessly.

Just that other people seem affected by all these explosions and hostage crises, and I am surprised because I see that and don't feel anything. So sometimes, when someone is yet again weeping on TV about corpses, I think to myself: would you look at that, how it's all turned out like shit. I, a person no one needs, not even I myself, continue to live, while people who were necessary to others up and die on them. I would rather offer myself in exchange for someone who really made life beautiful and bearable for others.

But that's probably just speculation. When they really come for me, like, "Alright, Cherenkova, you were offering yourself in exchange—come on," I'd start hedging, "Ah, well that one I wouldn't change for, even if his wife adores him and his three kids, but I don't like him, give me someone more wonderful, a Nobel laureate and a beauty queen in one."

77. When I Have Kids

So after the Beslan events there's a whole wave of this. People are changing their profile photos for black ones, candles in the windows . . .

But I thought to myself. I don't feel sorry for any of those kids. I just don't feel anything. I didn't know any of the dead. They are strangers to me. And I don't give a damn about their grief.

The only thing I feel is . . . maybe just the beginning of fear . . . and the relief that it didn't happen to me or anyone close to me. And outrage that this is even possible. But not sympathy. I cannot sympathize with strangers.

So I think I won't light a candle. Or change my profile photo. Or even pretend like I'm in mourning. Because everything is going great for me! I don't want to dissemble and simulate grieving because that's "how it's done"—I don't want to.

When I have kids, I will be even happier after a terrorist attack that my kids weren't there.

And if they were there . . . then the sympathies of those around me will not mean shit to me, to put it mildly.

THE END

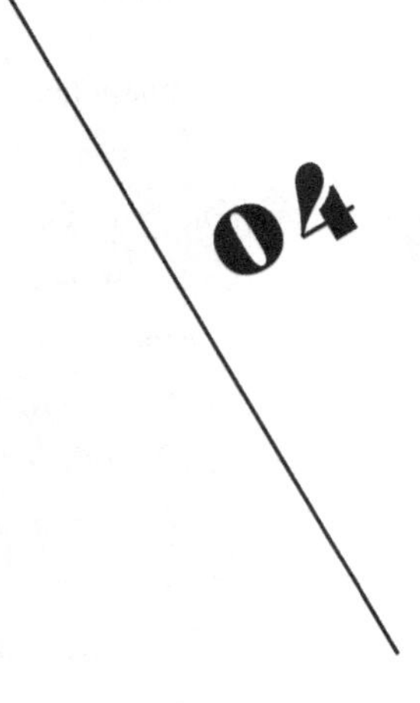

THE BROTHERS CH.[1]

ELENA GREMINA
TRANSLATED BY MAKSIM HANUKAI

CHARACTERS

ANTON
NIKOLAI—Anton's older brother
ALEXANDER—Anton's older brother
FATHER (PAVEL EGOROVICH)
DUNYA (EVDOKIA ISAAKOVNA EFROS)
NATASHA (NATALIA ALEXANDROVNA GOLDEN)

ABOUT THE HEROES

FATHER *is approximately sixty years old—hardly an old man. Smart and neat in his choice of dress. Always content with himself, almost comically self-righteous—this is the reverse side of that faith in himself that has allowed him to "socially transform himself."* PAVEL EGOROVICH *was born a serf but became a merchant of the second guild; he was able to provide a good education for his sons.* FATHER*'s folksy manner and little catchphrases are paired with the manufactured, polite, somewhat* *sanctimonious conduct of the "positive man." In contrast to his sons,* FATHER *has nerves of steel. He always keeps his cool. He sincerely loves and cares for his children but lacks the words to express his feelings. Outburst of cruelty, the desire to demean his sons are in reality pedagogically mandated maneuvers. "What other choice do I have?" And* ALEXANDER, *with whom he constantly quarrels, is his favorite.*

All of the other characters are between twenty-five and thirty years old. ANTON *and* ALEXANDER *are real dreamboats. True,* ALEXANDER*'s looks are spoiled by his nervousness—in the course of the entire play he is trying to quit drinking and is therefore experiencing symptoms of withdrawal.*

NIKOLAI *is a true "bohemian." Uncomely, shabbily dressed, slovenly. But this does him no harm—his charm is great. He is the only truly kind protagonist in the play. He is constantly tipsy and "a bit high." But this isn't the only thing that "estranges" him from what's taking place. He is an artist and is always busy "sizing up" the best way to capture what he sees on canvas. These mental images are enough for lazy and disorderly* NIKOLAI. *As a rule, things always stop short of actual painting.*

ANTON *resembles* FATHER *more than anyone else—he is also "a positive man of character," yet the goal he has set for himself is to become not a merchant of the second guild but "an intelligent man," a man with a special code of honor that he himself has thought up.*

DUNYA *is an elegant young woman from a wealthy Jewish family who has received a brilliant modern education. A mischievous, hot-tempered "shrew," as* ANTON *called her in his letters, her passion is kept somewhat under a lid by the "solid, normative education" that her wealthy father provided for his favorite daughter but that is somewhat alien to her nature.*

NATASHA *is hardly a beauty, but she's one of those women whom men always value: a friend with whom they don't need to put on airs, a woman whose potential availability involuntarily excites them.*

NATASHA *is dressed a bit slovenly, in poor taste. She must earn her own living, and her life, the life of an emancipated working woman of the end of the nineteenth century, isn't easy.*

The set conforms to our vision of a corner of a Russian gentry estate at the end of the nineteenth century.

At the beginning and end of the action the stage may be empty.

1. BEGINNING

The sound of a squeaking swing. ANTON *is on stage.*

ANTON: How sadly this swing squeaks . . .

(*Remembering something.*) People, lions, eagles, quail . . . alleys in blossom, a wooden annex with a mezzanine . . . officers in snow-white tunics . . . ladies in tight corsets, insolent lackeys and servants faithful unto death, wasteful and weak-willed landowners, bingo on summer evenings at the estate, superfluous men, crises of conscience, merchants in dark shops, gymnasium students with penknives, duels, bishops, eternal students, proud maidens in love with losers, questions and answers—and if one only knew . . .

All these Russian lives have withered, having completed their dismal cycle. . . . The white cherry orchards have crumbled. Silent are the sounds of the breaking string. The highways roar. Everyone I loved has died. Father, mother, younger and older brothers, sister . . . beautiful women who loved me. . . . Their bodies have grown old, returned unto dust, and eternal matter has reduced them to stone, to water, to cloud, and all their souls have melded into one. Only I remember them.

It's cold, cold, cold. Empty, empty, empty.

Pause.

But I'm a writer. And I can bring everything back with one flourish of the quill, one stroke of the pencil. Bring back that summer day. That river, that muddy pond where carp once dwelled, and now only frogs croak, that wooden annex for which I paid a hundred rubles that summer. A hundred rubles—that's four summer months in a wooden annex for the whole family, or twelve stories for *Fragments*.[2] Twelve stories, one hundred lines each, 8 kopecks per line. (*Calculating.*) Or if it's 6 kopecks per line . . . fourteen short stories. And then this wooden annex, this shaded orchard, this vegetable garden with its henhouse will be ours.

With one thought. One flourish of the quill, one stroke of the pencil.

2. ARTIST AND MODEL

NATASHA *poses, standing.* NIKOLAI *draws. One drawing, another. It doesn't do. Crumples the paper. Throws it away.*

NIKOLAI: He wants me to draw a painting.

NATASHA: He always wants something that doesn't exist.

NIKOLAI: An oil painting, not a sketch for the newspapers.

NATASHA: And you don't want to.

NIKOLAI (*Irresolutely*): I do. (*Having thought it over.*) I do! He's right. He wants me to draw a large painting *in oil.*

NATASHA: Of course, just like Levitan. That's his hobbyhorse.

NIKOLAI: I can draw it better than Levitan. My brother knows that. A real painting. And not some sketch for the journals. Schechtel has come to an agreement with Tretyakov[3] and . . .

NATASHA: Antosha's always right.

NIKOLAI: Are you angry with him?

NATASHA: Aren't you?

NIKOLAI: He's concerned about me, about all of us.

NATASHA: He calls Anyuta "the Sledgehammer." He doesn't allow you see her.

NIKOLAI: Sledgehammer. (*Chuckles.*) Anton's constantly giving out nicknames. He calls our brother Childbearing Bureaucrat. Customs House Ass. Fire Station Swine.[4]
He calls me Crosseye, Slantface, Slantmug. Because I squint with one eye . . .

NATASHA: It's so rude. It's inelegant.

NIKOLAI (*Explains*): I squint with one eye in order to better distinguish colors.

NATASHA: It's because he despises all of you. That's why he gives you nicknames.

NIKOLAI: He loves us. He gives us nicknames because he's cheerful.

NATASHA: Antosha's cheerful?

NIKOLAI: And he calls your sister the Sledgehammer because . . . because . . . Sledgehammer boom tara boom.

NATASHA *can't help laughing. They make indecent gestures.*

Sledgehammer—tara boom boom. I miss her! Anyutochka.

NATASHA: Sledgehammer. Let's even suppose it suits her. It suits my sister's conduct. But what does it say about the way he treats *you*?

NIKOLAI: My brother says that women drain us of our creative juices. That I must pour everything into this (*Points to the canvas.*), and not into . . .

NATASHA: Really? Poor man. Then Mlle Efros hasn't yet . . . ?

NIKOLAI: He says that Levitan has worn himself out and that's why his landscapes have become gray.

NATASHA *laughs. He watches her and also begins to laugh. They are co-conspirators.*

NIKOLAI (*Lowering his voice*): What have you brought me?

NATASHA (*Laughing*): Antosha will be mad. Nothing.

NIKOLAI: Stop it. Anyuta gave you. . . . For me.

NATASHA *pulls up her skirt.* NIKOLAI *watches greedily.*

NIKOLAI (*Licking his lips*): A remote place. Perfect for a landscape painter. But I'm not a landscape painter. I need people, movement . . .

NATASHA: And women.

NIKOLAI: I miss Anyuta.

NATASHA *pulls out a bottle from under her skirt, and we realize what* NIKOLAI *was lusting after. He grabs the bottle. Drinks greedily. Hands it to* NATASHA. *They drink.*

NATASHA: It's funny. Just because Levitan makes oil paintings and Tretyakov buys them up, you too have to paint landscapes in oil.

NIKOLAI *shuts his eyes. He feels better from the wine.*

NIKOLAI: I can paint better than Levitan. I'm not afraid of painting people. He is. Anton has faith in me. After all, he's my brother.

NATASHA: If you're so obedient to him, why haven't you finished your painting?

NIKOLAI (*Quietly, in-between sips*): If he asks why you've come, tell him I wanted you to pose for me. I'm not a landscape painter. I need life.

NATASHA: A woman? He needs one too. He's just like you at heart. All of you brothers Ch. are the same.

NIKOLAI: How do you know? Are you with Sasha too?

NATASHA: Alexander isn't my type. He's too serious.

The long figure of ALEXANDER *may be seen in the distance. He walks nervously, mumbling to himself.*

NIKOLAI (*Pensively*): Sasha has quit drinking to please Anton.

NATASHA: And what about you?

NIKOLAI: Things will get better once I finish the painting. It's just that . . . I can't when I feel so sad. Like I said, I'm not a landscape painter.

NATASHA: My little worm.

Comes up to him. Unbuttons her blouse, takes out a vial. Hands it to NIKOLAI.

NIKOLAI: Oh!

NATASHA: Opium. You said you were in pain. Terrible pain. What hurts? Where? Where does it hurt? (*Touches him all over, laughs.*) Will Antosha be angry?

NIKOLAI (*Pours a few drops from the vial into his mouth*): Seems you couldn't care less.

NATASHA: Antosha dumped me for a long nose. (*After a moment of silence.*) And for a large dowry. Ugh. (*Takes a swill from the bottle in front of* NIKOLAI.) So I've made up my mind: I'll rip this love out from my heart, I'll rip it out by the roots. To love hopelessly, to spend years waiting for something. . . . One more?

NIKOLAI (*Sincerely, persuading*): That's what I'll say. Brother. Thank you, but . . . I need life. I'm not Levitan, I'm not a landscape painter.

ANTON *appears. They're alarmed.* NIKOLAI *can't decide what he should do first: cover the blank canvas or hide the bottle.*

NATASHA (*Distracting* ANTON *by drawing attention to herself, loudly*): . . . But once I get married, there won't be any time for love. New cares will drown out everything from the past. . . . (*Goes to meet* ANTON.) The villain Anto-chez-vous! How's life without your little skeleton? Do you remember how you once traced the ilium bone on my body for your exam?

ANTON (*Coughing*): You've come? Good. Fine weather today. It'll stop raining soon.

NATASHA: Aha! You're talking about the weather. Then you do have a conscience! Hmm? (*Tries to catch his glance.*) You don't visit, you don't write. . . . I must really be in your way! Admit it, Anto-chez-vous, it's Mlle Efros that holds you back.

ANTON *is not happy to see her.*

ANTON: Natalia Alexandrovna.

NATASHA: But I'm still alone. Because I love you. Can't forget you. This wonderful smile. You voice. Your hands. See, I said it and I immediately feel better. But you don't even respect me. (*With a ringing voice.*) Just don't start talking about nature and fishing. I know your manner. Why can't I forget you? (*Chuckles.*) What you deserve is for me to find a suitable playmate. You're a terrible person. What's so great about you?

ANTON *feels bad for her, he makes a wry face.*

But how can you marry? You neither love nor respect women. What? Is the dowry really so large?

By the way, is it true that Efros's nose has grown by two centimeters? That's a terrible pity. How do the two of you kiss? And she's hysterical. Does she suffocate you with her embraces?

ANTON *tries to approach the painting.* NATASHA *uses her body to hide the painting—or rather the empty canvas.*

How will she ever kiss you? Big-nose Efros. After all, you can't live without all that.

NIKOLAI (*To* ANTON): What is it? What is it?

ANTON: I want to look at your painting.

NIKOLAI (*Shields the painting*): It's not time yet.

ANTON: Why not? You've been leaving the house for two weeks to work on this painting. It's time. Levitan . . .

NIKOLAI: Enough already with your Levitan.

ANTON: First of all, he's your friend. . . . Brother. Slantface. You've been blessed from on high with something that others don't have: you have talent. This is an important commission. Schechtel could have given it to another artist, but he gave it to you. This painting will catapult you into the forefront, it will make your name. *Nikolai* Chekhov. Tretyakov might purchase your painting, but how will he purchase it if you can't finish it? You have talent, you're one out of thousands. This talent places you higher than millions of people. Even if you were a toad or a tarantula, even then you'd be respected, because people forgive everything for the sake of talent. What's more, you'll be able to demand a higher price for your newspaper sketches. Isn't it high time that you became an honest man?

NATASHA: Anto-chez-vous. Isn't it impolite not to notice me?

ANTON: When a man has talent, for its sake he has to sacrifice women, revelry, trivial matters. Sacrifice peace, women, wine, trivial matters. . . . Slantface. Is it true that you got drunk with police officers? You shouldn't do that. Men with talent are proud of it. Instead of boozing with police officers, they should exert a moral influence on them.

NATASHA: Another rule from your rule book, Anto-chez-vous? Aren't you tired of making it all up?

NIKOLAI (*Weakly*): You know, I can't stand this.

ANTON: Can't stand what?

NIKOLAI: . . . Someone looking over my shoulder. And when you speak this way. . . . My ass starts to burn! (*Explains.*) I begin to think that you're not you . . . but our father . . . and that someone's about to give me a whipping.

ANTON *looks at* NIKOLAI. *Approaches him. Decisively pushes away* NATASHA, *who tries to hide the canvas.*

The canvas is empty. ANTON *immediately understands everything. Dry and businesslike. Looks at* NATASHA*, then at* NIKOLAI. *They're completely innocent. And they pretend not to understand what's wrong.*

ANTON: Where is it?

NIKOLAI *and* NATASHA *sincerely shrug their shoulders.*

ANTON: Nikolka. You're not allowed to drink.

NIKOLAI: I know. The doctors have forbidden me. You're a doctor yourself, brother, so you must also know that I'm very sick, you must treat me more—

ANTON: The hell with your doctors! You're as healthy as a shoemaker! Where's the stuff that she's brought?

NIKOLAI: Are you going to search me? You know, this is funny.

ANTON: . . . It's not funny—what you're doing to yourself.

NATASHA (*Chuckles*): And I thought that Nikolai Pavlovich was your *older* brother, Anto-chez-vous!

ANTON: Where did you hide the bottle? Where did you hide what she brought you? Miss Golden, what you're doing isn't nice . . .

NATASHA: "Miss"! "Miss"! You speak to me this way. . . .
Is it because I don't have a long nose and a large dowry?
Is it because I love you, when one should really treat you differently?

NIKOLAI: Alright. I'm going . . . to work on my studies. Before the sun sets.

ANTON: There's no sun. Fine. You won't give me what you're hiding. . . . The vodka. . . . In that case . . .

Pushes NIKOLAI, *who falls.* NIKOLAI *has a coughing fit.* ANTON *pulls on his leg.*

ANTON: Give me your boots.

NIKOLAI: Are you out of your mind? It's my only pair. . . .
What am I supposed to do without them?

ANTON: You won't go far without them. You'll work instead of fooling around and getting up to silly tricks. That's settled then. I'm taking your boots and locking them up. Until you've finished the painting.

NATASHA: This is simply . . . unheard of! I'll tell Anyuta.

ANTON: . . . and I have forbidden Nikolai to associate with the Sledgehammer.

NIKOLAI (*Coughs*): This is simply ridiculous. You're ridiculous.

ANTON: She's trying to get you drunk. She's doing it so you'll come back to her. You screw the Sledgehammer until your groin's torn up and then you return depleted. And this is the result! (*Points to the canvas.*) Empty! Empty!

NIKOLAI *hesitates but can't resist* ANTON*'s will. He takes off his boots.* ANTON *pulls the vodka out of the boot leg. Pours it out on the ground.*

ANTON (*Weary*): What are you doing to yourself? Why?

They notice a foul smell coming from the boots. ANTON *and* NATASHA *make wry faces.* NIKOLAI *blithely wiggles his fingers.*

NIKOLAI (*With delight*): I had a blister.

ANTON: You still don't wash your feet?

NATASHA *laughs.*

Natalia Alexandrovna, I ask you not to visit us.

NATASHA: Why not?

ANTON: Because who does Nikolai drink with? Every time you come, he gets drunk out of his mind. A fine Russian talent is dying. If you want to attract my attention so much . . .

NATASHA: It's because you're getting married to those Jewish bones. I know what I'm saying. I'm also a woman, and also Jewish. And it's unbearable. Does she smell like garlic when you kiss her? You always laughed at it, why aren't you laughing now? Out of respect for her money? Admit it, you would've married me too if I had money! (*Pause.*) Do you think it's fair? You don't love her. Admit that much, at least.

Meanwhile, seeing that ANTON *is distracted,* NIKOLAI *takes out another stash that was hidden in his easel. Drinks.*

NATASHA: Anto-chez-vous. How big is her dowry? Tell me.

ANTON: An intelligent man values a woman not for her body, not for her horse sweat, not for her bed . . .

NATASHA: Another entry for the rule book? Just tell me that it's all over between us.

ANTON: An intelligent man requires femininity, elegance, the chance to be with her not who he is but who he can become if he tried for her sake.

NATASHA: Innocence! Say also that you need innocence. You!

ANTON (*Flings in her face*): I love Dunya.

NATASHA hides her face in her hands. FATHER *appears.*

FATHER: Kolya and Antosha, you've waited until the last day. It's no good to behave this way. I've told you several times that we need to pay the rent on the tenth. You know that we can't delay and that I like punctuality. You've put me in a tight spot. To turn red before the landlord at my age. I'm a man of character, a positive man. It's better to deny oneself but always pay one's debts on time. Antosha, one must also pay for one's brothers. Why do I need to remind you? Misha needs five rubles for a table and for the apartment, and Vanya needs new linen. And new boots. He's got to walk and walk to get to school. He has a hard life, he's a serious man. He doesn't fool around like some others do. Why did I provide you with an education?

Looks at his children, sighs. He pities them, wants all to be well. But he doesn't know how to say this. Chews his lips.

FATHER: Good weather, by the way. The rye's shining. Thank God, the field crop's cheered up after the rain, now we can really place our hopes on the harvest. Very good!

3. FISHING

ANTON *is fishing.* ALEXANDER *appears.*

ALEXANDER *isn't feeling well. The effects of abstaining from alcohol are making themselves known. He's licking his lips.*

ANTON *is upset that someone has interrupted his fishing.*

ALEXANDER *notices this and also sours.*

ANTON *recognizes this too and tries to start up a friendly conversation with his brother. As always happens to him in difficult situations, the only thing he can think of is to praise the landscape.*

ANTON: Look how beautiful it is all around. It's as if each branch is begging Levitan to paint it.

ALEXANDER: I don't see anything good in any of it, Antosha. To constantly go into raptures over nature is to admit the poverty of your imagination. All these cliffs and brooks are nothing but trash compared to what my imagination can give me.

ANTON *doesn't want to argue and remains silent.*

ALEXANDER: Why are you silent? Don't you believe in the power of your brother's imagination? Oh! You're working. Creating. Forgive me. I forgot. You're our family's benefactor! (*Sarcastically.*) Forgive me, I forgot!

ANTON: Anyone can write for *Fragments*. As long as they don't hold back their manuscripts. You could easily make a living. Six kopecks per line, not counting the humorous captions for the illustrations. You get paid for those separately. Only you can't miss deadlines.

ALEXANDER: I can't make jokes on order! Not when I'm so sad.

Silence.

ANTON: What news do you have?

ALEXANDER: I don't have any news. I'm a man without news. Are you also angry that Anna and I have come here, that we're crowding you? (ANTON *shrugs his shoulders. After a pause.*) Picture this: it's after dinner, and I'm boring into the mother of my children with the entire breadth of my equine penis. Meanwhile, father's reading his canon and suddenly takes it into his head to come in and check if the windows are locked. One picture like this is worth ten painted by your Levitan. But *Vater* isn't rattled. He approaches the window gravely, locks it, as if not noticing anything, gathers that he should put out the candle, and leaves the room in total darkness. I think he even paused to pray before the icon, but I don't dare vouch for this last part with any certainty.

The brothers laugh.

ANTON (*Suddenly*): Sasha. Customs House Cattle. Childbearing Ass. How I love you when you're not pitying yourself.

ALEXANDER: Pitying myself? I've got Anna on my neck. And two little pups.

ANTON *turns away.*

ALEXANDER (*Defiantly*): Why don't you ask me about how they're feeling? (*Mockingly adopts different voices.*) "Hey brother, how are Kolya and Antosha feeling?" "How do you think, brother?" "As for me, brother, I think your children are inadequate."

ANTON *wriggles the fishing rod.*

What is it? Not biting. Not biting. Does it upset you? Let me guess: I'm keeping you from your work?

ANTON: What difference does it make what others think of you? The main thing is to be satisfied with your own life.

ALEXANDER *pulls out a gun and shoots it in the air.*

ALEXANER: Almost killed that seagull. Not enough luck even for that.

ANTON: You can go hunting with Levitan.

ALEXANDER: Hunting? Don't make me laugh. I don't have time for such amusements. I'm not a bachelor, unlike Levitan. Unlike you. I have a family.

ANTON (*Lightly reprimanding*): *We* have a family. Misha's still in the gymnasium. Vanya's salary is too small. Masha's in a boarding house. One must keep constant watch on our artist . . .

ALEXANDER: Enough of your prose! Think I have time for it? Father hates my little ones, thinks they're illegitimate. So does Masha. I thought I could get some sympathy from her, at least, but no way. Our sister is ambitious as hell. She thinks my children are pulling our family down. Like Nikolai's tattered boots. That's why you're the only one she loves. She's hoping you'll turn the Chekhovs into a solid, respectable family.

In a nearby hammock, NIKOLAI *mumbles in his sleep, drunk.*

ANTON: Stop weeping, wailing, and speaking in manifestos like Uncle Mitrofan! You say you don't understand the essence of the comical. Well, right now you're making me laugh.

Silence.

ALEXANDER: I wrote a poem:

Arrived in Tula in trepidation
My gray-haired love had dragged me there
Not being aware that I didn't care
That much for Tula. What vexation
I suffered in this situation.

(*Watches for his brother's reaction, but the latter is busy following the bob.*) You didn't like my poem. "Suffered" again? You don't like it when I suffer. You never suffer yourself, and that's why. . . . Listen. You have to give it to me. I haven't touched alcohol in a week. Eight days.

ANTON: You counted the exact number of days? That's a bad sign.

ALEXANDER: You don't understand me. I need your understanding so much right now. But how can you understand me? I live badly, but I do live. And you? (*Swallows.*) You don't know how dry it is in my mouth. My hands are dancing.

ANTON: Only no adjectives, I beg you! You'll never become a writer until you rid yourself of adjectives.

ALEXANDER: But you've already become one. (*Gradually begins to speak more passionately, excitedly.*) Don't believe any of them. Don't pay attention to the critics. Don't write any novels for them. Don't spread the plot thin as if it were porridge—just because they think that writers have to write novels. You're great even without a novel. You're a genius, Antosha. (*Cries.*) You're a real genius. You're the sun of Russian literature. You're that new Gogol, the one they've been waiting for but who hasn't appeared. It's you who'll be remembered—not Grigorievich, not Korolenko. Your Suvorin will also been completely forgotten. But you won't be.

Suddenly falls to his knees before ANTON.

ALEXANDER: Brother. Speak to mom. Tell mom to take in my little ones. Until Anna Ivanovna's finished suffering, at least until then. My poor children. They cry for the potty all night, until they finally burst right in their beds—there's no one to look after them. I beg you. Anna's dying. I'm not angry with you for ignoring my requests. (*With a bitter sneer.*) Dr. Anton Chekhov never deigned to examine my illegitimate bride. But now. (*Sobbing.*) The children, help my little children. Antosha, brother.

A long pause. ANTON *attentively watches the fishing line in order to avoid looking at his brother. The bob jumps.*

ANTON (*With quiet disgust*): How can you be well fed, clothed, go out boozing every day . . . and say that you spend everything on your children? (*Trying to make another joke.*) Stop being such a pair of slacks, Mr. Customhouse!

ALEXANDER *slowly gets up from his knees.*

ALEXANDER: You got one.

ANTON *looks at the fishing line. The bob stops jumping.*

ALEXANDER: Forgive me for this little scene. Again manifestos, weeping . . . it's funny! (*Crying.*)

ANTON (*Quietly*): I know you held back part of the proceeds from my stories. From *Fragments* and *The Petersburg Gazette.*

ALEXANDER *wasn't expecting to hear this. These words strike him like a gunshot. His heart begins to beat fast, he rubs his chest with unconscious motion.*

ALEXANDER (*In a flat voice*): How long have you known?

ANTON: What difference does it make?

ALEXANDER (*Loudly*): HOW LONG HAVE YOU KNOWN?

ANTON: You're scaring away the fish. Bullhead is a terribly nervous fish.

ALEXANDER: Don't you dare speak to me about the weather and fishing! (*Guesses.*) From the very beginning. You knew from the very beginning. Or no. You knew in advance that I would take that damned money, that a part of your money would stick to my palms. And you still . . . you still . . . wrote to me. Trusted me to. . . . Trusted *me*?

ANTON: It's just so natural. Buddy, I'm a doctor. Nothing natural is . . .

ALEXANDER (*Yelling*): "Shameful?" One brother stealing from another . . . from a brother who's honest, who works to the point of exhaustion . . . sweating . . . to feed their elderly father, their ailing mother, sister and brothers . . . stealing his hard-earned kopeck. Not shameful?

ANTON (*Coldly*): Again with the adjectives. More florid phrases? How long can you remain Agapofod Yedinitsyn?[5] When will you finally become . . .

ALEXANDER (*Bitterly*): Who? Who can I become? Chekhov?

The brothers look at each other. ANTON *turns away first.*

ALEXANDER: I can never become Chekhov. There already is a Chekhov.

ANTON *doesn't respond. He's dead tired from this scene. And he's very attentively watching the fishing line and bob.*

ANTON (*Mechanically, without taking his eyes off the fishing line*): It's entirely up to you. When will you finally come to your senses and become a human being?

ALEXANDER (*With hatred*): And you? Are you really a human being?

As if not hearing anything, ANTON *pulls on the fishing line. Pulls out a fish. It's jumping, trying to free itself from the hook.* ANTON *laughs with joy.*

ANTON: Bullhead! It's a bullhead!

ALEXANDER *looks in astonishment at the fish struggling on the hook. He grabs himself by the throat—there's clearly not enough air for him.*

ANTON: And I don't want to hear any monologues about how, right now, you're just like this fish, caught on a hook. There is no hook, everything's fine, just wonderful! You only have to stop drinking and boasting and get to work.

ALEXANDER *wants to say something else, but he quickly walks away, swinging his arms awkwardly.*

ANTON (*Quietly, confidentially*): I have a little family club. I always travel with it, as if it were a piece of luggage, so it won't bother me. I've gotten as used to it as to a bump on my forehead. It's much easier and cheaper to take it with me than to leave it at home. . . . An ordinary man has a wife who'll forgive her husband's poverty, but what I have is order that will be destroyed if I don't make a certain number of rubles every month. In the winter my little club consists of eight people: father, mother, brothers—two older brothers, Sasha and Nikolka, and two younger ones, Ivan and Misha. My sister Masha. And five in the summer—not including two servants. (*Persuading himself.*) That said, my little club is a benign rather than a malignant growth. In any case, I'm more often happy than sad, even though, if you think about it, I'm tied hand and foot . . .

ANTON *hooks a new worm and casts his fishing rod.*

4. THE BRIDE

DUNYA *appears. Looks around. Walks up to* NIKOLAI*'s easel. Looks at the easel. The canvas is empty. Strewn about are* NIKOLAI*'s crumpled drawings. She picks up and smooths out one of the drawings—a grotesque female nude in a provocative pose.*

NATASHA *approaches* DUNYA*, looking her over critically.* DUNYA *notices* NATASHA.

NATASHA (*Referring to the drawing*): That's me. Expressive, isn't it? The artist has a remarkably true hand. When Nikolai will finish the painting, it will be simply . . .

DUNYA (*Shocked, looks at the drawing, then at saucily smiling* NATASHA): Oh!

NATASHA (*Shaking* DUNYA*'s hand*): I have long wanted to meet you. My name is Golden. I'm a friend of the family.

DUNYA: Oh, you must be the one they call the Sledgehammer! You're especially close to (*Looks at the portrait.*) Nikolai Pavlovich, am I right?

NATASHA (*Peeved*): My sister's the Sledgehammer. I'm a friend of the *whole* family. Incidentally, there's a portrait of me hanging over Anton's bed. . . . It is entitled "Poverty."

Turns around, notices ANTON, *whom* DUNYA *doesn't notice, walks away.* DUNYA *squints; she's near-sighted. Looks around. Calls out : "ANTON." Settles down on the swing.*

ANTON (*Whispering, behind her*): I love you, Dunya.

DUNYA *frowns in distress—she must have misheard it. Looks around. Did she imagine it? Jumps off the swing.*

ANTON (*As before*): We'll be happy.

DUNYA (*Looks around*): What? What?

ANTON (*Hiding from her like before*): I love you, I love . . .

DUNYA *looks around. Where's the voice coming from? Or is she merely imagining these sounds? This is no longer fun, it's painful, she's on the verge of tears. But suddenly* ANTON *appears in front of her.* DUNYA *screams.*

DUNYA: I didn't notice you. Were you here long? I couldn't hear, did you say something to me?

ANTON *is calm.*

ANTON: I'm so glad you've come. It's nice here. The air's so thick that you can grab it and cut it with a knife.

DUNYA: I thought I heard you say something to me?

ANTON *looks directly at her. She lowers her eyes.*

ANTON: I said the air is pleasant here.

DUNYA: No. Something else. I . . . thought I heard . . .

ANTON: What?

DUNYA: It must have been the wind. It doesn't matter.

ANTON: Where would the wind have come from?

DUNYA: Oh, there's a swing here. Shall we?

ANTON: What for?

But DUNYA *settles down on the swing. He begins swinging her. She waits for him to say something.*

ANTON (*From behind*): I love you, Dunya.

DUNYA (*Jumps off*): This is awful! Are you laughing at me? Masha told me, "Don't trust my brother."

ANTON: Masha's jealous.

DUNYA: I just can't understand you.

FATHER *appears.*

FATHER: I've heard a lot about. . . . Oh . . . (*Bows.*) Evdokia Isaakovna.

DUNYA: I'm not used to people calling me by my Russian name.

FATHER: How will you marry then, Miss?

DUNYA (*Looking at* ANTON): Nothing has been decided yet.

FATHER: That is to say, my mistake . . . that is to say. . . . And how about this weather! There's dew in the morning. The manure's brought in. No rain, just wind.

Pulls ANTON *aside.*

FATHER: Antosha, listen to what your father's heart tells you. You're counting on mommy and daddy to give you mountains of gold for marrying her. And what if mommy and daddy won't even want to know her after she changes her faith? You won't get a kopeck.

ANTON: Why are you so sure that I'm getting married because of her dowry?

FATHER: Antosha. You won't fool me. You're a positive man, a practical man, you take after me. Remember how I'd leave you to watch over the shop? You were only eleven, but you managed. Why else would you marry a Jewess if not for her dowry? Aren't there enough Russian women around?

DUNYA *is sitting on the swing.* ANTON *speaks with his father and brothers in a hushed voice.*

ANTON (*Addressing his father*): What's with the sour face? Everything will be fine. I'm still with you! I'm not going anywhere. We'll get the dowry. (*Winks.*) What's with the moping?

(*To* NIKOLAI.) Hey, Slantface, you'll go to Italy. You'll paint the blue sky in oil there. Bright colors, the sun, bright swarthy faces. . . . You'll leave that little Yid Levitan in the dust. Old man, we'll buy an estate for you, a real house in Lopasna or outside Moscow, in Lyubimovka or Melikhovo. . . . With a garden and a henhouse. . . . Well?

ALEXANDER: What about me? Have you forgotten about me again? Am I a band apart, on my own?

ANTON *approaches* DUNYA.

DUNYA: I regret . . . that I've come.

ANTON: That's because you're a shrew.

Offers her flowers. She tears them up, breaks them into pieces.

DUNYA: Who gave you these flowers? What woman? I despise these flowers! I despise you.

DUNYA *approaches* ANTON *as if enchanted. Closer.*

ANTON: A shrew. Instead of a long-nosed Jewess, a bluestocking, I should marry a merchant's daughter. With a large dowry. I'll take her, that anathema, to the cleaners.

DUNYA: I know a girl like that, she's just your type. She's very plump, just as you like them, and has lots of money, that's the main thing, isn't it? Very stupid—just what you want.

ANTON: Well, if there'll be lots of money then I'll stop writing for magazines and will write a novel better than Turgenev.

They look at each other. DUNYA *is pulled toward him.*

ALEXANDER (*Quietly to* NIKOLAI, *about* DUNYA, *in rapture*): A hysteric! I know the type. Just look at her ankles. One has to keep ploughing them. Antosha's no match for her.

ANTON (*Introduces* DUNYA*to his family*): Dunya. These are my brothers. This is my father. Well, then. I could have some tea.

FATHER (*Puffs up his chest, speaks with feeling—this young woman worries him, she's a wealthy bride.*): A merchant of the second guild. Pavel Egorov Chekhov. I devoted myself to my children, provided them with an education. Alexander studied at the university. Nikolai in art school. Anton studied medicine. Misha is still at the gymnasium. Ivan's failed his exam again, but he works as a village school teacher, earns his daily bread. As for me, I was thirty when I first learned to read. My father was a serf, a real *muzhik*, made of flint stone. He instructed me in his own way. Oh, yes, I also have a daughter, Masha, in boarding school. Nothing but losses. I provided every single one of my children with an education. But all my efforts were in vain. They're idling away the time, but at whose expense? The goods get lonely without the master.

ANTON: We should ask for the samovar. I'd really like some tea.

ALEXANDER (*Undone by lust at the sight of* DUNYA): I'm his brother. His older brother. Only he has long begun to act as if I'm younger. I'm the shame of the family. They all hate me. That's because I live with my heart. I fell in love with a woman, went to live with her, messed up my whole life—because I thought about love instead of a dowry!

NIKOLAI *squints, examines* DUNYA.

NIKOLAI: It's as if the tip of your nose and your ears are made of wax. But I like it. It's expressive.

FATHER: I bet they've been lying to you, saying "father's a great tyrant." When in fact father has ruined his whole life for their sake. Couldn't make a career for myself, had to pull them up first. (*To* DUNYA.) Alexander was the best. The school principal in Taganrog was especially fond of him. Incidentally, wonderful weather today. Yes, sir. Well, why not? I respect the Jews. (*With approval.*) I had a neighbor in Taganrog, Grishka, a Yid. He squeezed the whole district dry like it was sunflower seed! Yids make good merchants! What I mean is . . . I'm ready to give you my blessing. I always carry an icon with me.

I always have the Dormition of the Mother of God from Taganrog near me. I've got it right here in the annex.

NATASHA (*Chuckles*): You mean that same icon they used to bless the oil! (*As if casting a challenge; she wants to show that she's on familiar terms with the Chekhovs.*) Evdokia Isaakovna, has Anton told you this story?

Everyone laughs.

NIKOLAI (*Choking from laughter*): A rat drowned one night in one of our oil vats. Father was so sorry to pour the oil down the drain . . . that he summoned a priest to bless it. (*Has a coughing fit.*)

FATHER: . . . Wood oil. From Odessa, ten rubles for a Smolensk barrel, and if you count the quarters, it made for a good profit.

NATASHA (*Showing off her familiarity*): You could've simply poured out the oil. . . . Now the whole town knows about it.

The Chekhovs laugh. ANTON *also laughs, against his will. Everyone laughs except* DUNYA.

FATHER (*Shaking his head*): Ten rubles a barrel! My life is one big loss as it is.

DUNYA *looks at the laughing Chekhovs. She feels like an outsider.*

DUNYA: What a sad story.

FATHER: I see, Miss, that you understand what a loss is. That's good. You see, with these sons of mine, all I have is losses. I'm like that ancient Job. With you in the picture, I might at least live to see my grandchildren. Otherwise, what a disgrace, what a crying shame—I've got five sons, a daughter, and four more underground, but you can't count on them! Barren fig trees.

ALEXANDER: Have some shame.

FATHER: . . . No little ones.

ALEXANDER: I've got two young babes. I'm ready to bring them to you even now.

Disgust on everyone's faces.

They go around in dirty linen, no one cares for them, no one looks after them, but so what? They're my dear ones. My little pups. And I love them more than my own soul. I give them my last kopecks. (*Looks at* ANTON, *falters.*) Well, that was more for effect, sister. May I call you sister? (*Catches* DUNYA *by the hand, presses it. She pulls back her hand in disgust.*) And with respect to my Kolya not speaking yet . . . he's no retard, no degenerate, as my sister Masha claims!

FATHER: Masha studies in a boarding school. The losses are enormous.

ALEXANDER: Masha's mean.

DUNYA (*Shocked*): Oh! But I'm studying together with Masha. Masha's my friend!

NIKOLAI: Oh, what difference does it make? (*Grins.*) Your Tosha doesn't speak. Your Kolya doesn't speak. And the devil with him. What good is speaking? Brother, I'd give up a lot to be an idiot like your Antosha and Nikolka. Funny that you named your idiots after your beloved brothers! Ha ha!

DUNYA: Children. Oh, yes. Children are the purpose of every marriage.

ALEXANDER: How can you say that I have no children, father?

NIKOLAI: . . . If you look at these rushes with one eye, it's just like ochre. Amazing. (*Laughs.*)

FATHER (*Stubbornly, to* ALEXANDER): . . . You don't have any children! Because illegitimate children are conceived in sin and don't inherit the kingdom of heaven. Nor do they inherit the fortune of Pavel Chekhov, merchant of the second guild. . . . Calm down! You're drunk!

Knocks with his fist on the table.

ALEXANDER: What fortune? What are you talking about? Anton's still paying off your debts. And I haven't had a drink in eight days and five hours.

ANTON (*Tries to salvage the situation*): It's time for tea. I'd really like some tea. A glass of strong sweet tea. Where's that samovar?

NATASHA: I can serve it.

ANTON (*Pushing* NATASHA *aside*): Mademoiselle Efros will serve it.

NATASHA*'s wounded right in the heart.* DUNYA *serves the tea. Everyone examines* DUNYA.

FATHER: Tea is the most tradable commodity—for those in the know.

NATASHA (*Showing off her familiarity*): Pavel Egorovich traded in used tea leaves in Taganrog. There's commerce for you. He thought it up himself. Bellboys from the hotels would bring them to him.

ALEXANDER: We'd get used tea leaves mixed in with trash brought to our shop from hotel rooms . . . it would all get dumped onto the kitchen table. (*He gets carried away—after all, these are colorful childhood memories.*) And we'd pull out loose hair, nail fragments, twigs, all sorts of rubbish . . . only to resell the tea later. (*Chuckles.*) We'd pour this tea trash into paper cones!

DUNYA *chokes on her tea from disgust.*

NIKOLAI: There's nothing more picturesque than garbage. It's extremely diverse.

ANTON (TO DUNYA): This is not the same tea, it's not from our store. This is good tea, I buy it myself.

ALEXANDER: Antosha knew how to cheat a client better than anyone! (*Chuckles.*)

FATHER: One could depend on Antosha. (*Tenderly.*) Sasha, Kolya, you should take after Antosha. God didn't give him talent. But he writes day and night. He writes for Leykin, he writes for *The Petersburg Leaflet.*

ANTON: *The Petersburg Gazette.*

FATHER: What difference does it make? He feeds his father and mother. And you, Sasha, should be ashamed! You used to give such hope.

Everyone looks at ALEXANDER. *The latter tries to bring a cup of tea to his lips. The cup rattles unbearably in* ALEXANDER*'s dancing hand. Only* NIKOLAI *is immersed in his own inner life—he squints with one eye, examines things, wriggles his fingers, picks at his leg with interest, etc.*

ANTON: What is alcoholism? It's a psychosis, same as morphine addiction, onanism, nymphomania, and others. More often than not alcoholism is passed down from the father or mother, from the grandfather or grandmother.

Unable to overcome the trembling in his hands, ALEXANDER *is forced to put the cup back on the table without taking a sip.*

FATHER: But we've never had any drunks in our family. Grandpa and father would sometimes drink too much when someone came to visit, but that didn't stop them from getting to work on time or waking up early for morning prayer.

ALEXANDER: I haven't had a drink in eight days, five hours, and ten minutes. (*Licks his lips.*)

FATHER (*Watches his favorite son with alarm but keeps droning his usual mantra*): Those who live without the law shall perish without the law.[6]

NIKOLAI *takes a small sip of tea. Has a coughing fit. Gasps for air. Spits blood.*

NIKOLAI: I shouldn't have anything hot! Not that you care. (*Crying.*) I'm afraid. It's consumption. Just like Uncle Mitrofan. Consumption will eat me alive. It will eat up my chest, my intestines. I don't want to die! Oh, how afraid I am to die and how my heart aches!

ANTON: You have an inflammation of cunning! You don't want to work—there's your illness. You don't want to finish your painting for Schechtel and Tretyakov.

NIKOLAI (*Quietly, like a child*): I'm afraid, I'm afraid. I'm dying, brother. Brother, who put a curse on us?

FATHER: All Chekhovs have iron constitutions, and they have always worked, labored, and never gotten sick. Yessir. Never gotten sick.

DUNYA *serves tea. Everyone drinks. Except* ALEXANDER. ALEXANDER*'s hands are shaking.* NIKOLAI *takes small sips, slopping loudly and impolitely.*

ALEXANDER: And what about uncle Mitrofan? And aunt Lylia? What did they die from?

FATHER (*Jumps*): Lies!

ALEXANDER (*Malevolently*): They died of consumption.

NIKOLAI *coughs. Sends his cup flying.*

NIKOLAI: I'm dying . . . it's so frightening . . . why do I forget about this? It should be the only thing one talks about.

ANTON: You're irritating your throat with alcohol. That's what's causing your so-called hemoptysis. Consumption! It's ludicrous.

ALEXANDER *finally takes a sip from the dancing cup.* FATHER *watches his son with pain.*

FATHER (*Bombastically, peevishly—the only way he can*): That's what you get for chasing after women. They'll drive a weak man out of his mind. See what he's come to. Threw himself into debauchery, drinking, and idleness. Sasha, you'd do well to dismiss Anna Ivanovna. It's time.

ALEXANDER (*Sarcastically*): Oh, I forgot. Anna's dying.

FATHER (*Calmly*): If you leave her, she'll die like a Christian and not in sin and wickedness. Your poor mother. She's eating her heart out because of you, Sasha and Kolya. And I'm eating my heart out. My achievements, my labors, the eminent Chekhov clan will turn to dust. (*To* DUNYA, *perking up.*) Evdokia Isaakovna, I'm writing a letter to his Highness. A petition to grant me a title of nobility for my accomplishments in educating my sons.

ANTON (*Quietly, with force*): Lies are so painful to the ear.

Everyone looks at ANTON, *surprised.*

ANTON (*Crying out*): I'm so tired of you. Stop lying! I'm the one who supports all of you. The hell with the fact that I can't even get hot tea. That you can't even heat up the samovar! The hell with that! But stop lying!

FATHER (*Caught off-guard, blinking*): How dare you raise your voice to your father . . .

ANTON: How dare *you*! What eminent clan? The Chekhovs are peasants, their masters used to thrash them. Your old man, our grandfather, the one who berated and beat his wife, used to get flogged with birch rods, the most insignificant clerk felt he had the right to punch him in the mug. In the mug, in the mug! Bashed in faces, flogged behinds! That's us. That's what we've inherited from you, merchant of the second guild. Slavish, rotten blood. Thank you very much.

FATHER: What are you saying, Antosha? Can't you see? You were given an education. Sasha serves in the customs office, he writes, you get published, Nikolka paints. . . . *I* gave all of this to you! No one taught me! I'm the son of a serf! And I educated you. Did all I could.

ANTON: And what was it all for? We've been bullied and beaten to death—by you. As for mother, you've chewed her up. She's afraid to cross the road by herself. She's been worn out—by you. Because of you I grow weak before scum who're immeasurably inferior to me both intellectually and morally. I'm afraid of life. Afraid of everything. It was you, papa. You've worn us out, you've been beating us to death since we were kids! (*To his brothers, who are listening to him in shock.*) Brother, Customs Pants. Don't have any more children. Who needs your idiots?

ALEXANDER: I love my little ones. Be quiet.

ANTON (*To* NIKOLAI): Slantface, Slantmug. . . . You and I shouldn't have any children. . . . Let that eminent merchant clan, the accursed Chekhov clan, die with us!

FATHER *slaps* ANTON.

FATHER: Look your father in the eye! (*Catches his breath, his voice wavering—pities himself.*) It was God's will to curse me with your kind, but I endure this trial with humility and, like Job, find solace in suffering and constant labor.

The little club disperses.

5. A DISCUSSION WITH DUNYA

DUNYA *hands a wet napkin to* ANTON. ANTON *presses it to his face.*

ANTON (*Without looking at* DUNYA): When I was little, and father would give me a beating, I had to stand up straight, hands at my sides, and look him in the eye. Now, whenever he fights, I get so embarrassed. It's as if my childhood never came to an end. . . . The funny thing is that he's old, but his muscles are still strong and it really hurts when he starts fighting.

DUNYA *is quiet. He knows he has lost her.*

ANTON: If not for the short stories that I have to write for Leykin and *The Petersburg Gazette*, the trifles with which I feed my family, I'd write a novel. About a young man, the son of a serf, a former grocer, raised on respect for rank, worshipping the ideas of others, giving thanks for every piece of bread, receiving frequent whippings . . .

DUNYA *frowns, remains silent.*

ANTON: That's right, whippings . . . making the rounds as a tutor without any galoshes, brawling, torturing animals, enjoying dinners at the houses of rich relatives, hypocritical before God and man for no other reason than his awareness of his own insignificance—about how this young man squeezes the slave out of himself drop by drop until, one day, he suddenly feels that the blood coursing through his veins is no longer the blood of a slave, but that of a real human being . . .

DUNYA: Good Lord . . .

ANTON: Isn't it vulgar of me to tell you all of this? I'm starting to pity myself like Agafopod Yedinitsyn, like Uncle Mitrofan, like the Chekhovs. These Chekhovs pity themselves so much. They're always on the verge of a meltdown. What the nobility received as a gift from nature we commoners must purchase at a high price. We must pay for it with our youth. With our love and happiness.

DUNYA *is silent.*

ANTON: Well? What do you have to say now? It's all finished between us, isn't it? It's all finished?

DUNYA (*Crying out*): Yes!!!

ANTON: That's what I thought.

DUNYA *suddenly throws herself on his neck.*

DUNYA: I give my consent. I'll convert to Russian Orthodoxy and marry you. My father will give me money. He'd never refuse me.

I'll save you. I'll take you away from here. You'll perish with them. They don't appreciate you! How can they?

They kiss.

We'll have a long life together. You'll write a novel, a long novel. Like Turgenev. Like a real writer. We'll travel to Italy. Don't you have a story in which a doctor and a princess leave for Italy? "Late-Blooming Flowers"? It's a good story.

ANTON (*To himself*): Twelve rubles. We got a pair of snow boots for mom, underwear for dad, galoshes for Kolya, although he lost them right away. (*Sniffs* NIKOLAI*'s boots in disgust.*)

DUNYA: It's a good story, but everyone in it dies of consumption. Tell me that you won't die of consumption. Tell me that you'll write a novel. Tell me . . .

ANTON: I love you.

They kiss. They embrace. ANTON *and* DUNYA *withdraw into the gazebo.*

NIKOLAI *appears. He observes their silhouettes. Draws from life.*

NATASHA *passes him another bottle.* NIKOLAI *drinks. He passes the same bottle to* ALEXANDER. ALEXANDER *looks at the bottle as if in a trance. He raises it to his lips but pushes it away and leaves.*

FATHER *is off to the side, praying.*

FATHER: Tell me, Lord, what should I do? Haven't I tried, Lord? Why are you letting my children perish? They're nothing like me, but I did so much to bring them up. Why do you punish me, Lord? Why has it started to rain even though the hay hasn't been stacked yet? It has already started to rot. What should I do, Lord? Save my sons, let them bear my name with dignity so I won't need to blush when I look down on them from the other world. (*Becomes thoughtful.*)

6. THE WRITER

ANTON *is at his desk, writing.*

ANTON (*Writing a letter, reading phrases out loud*): If I do have a gift that is worthy of respect, I have as yet failed to respect it. I have felt that I have it, but have grown used to considering myself worthless. . . . All my friends and relatives have always looked down on my work as an author . . . not a single one of them has read my work or considers me an artist. Your letter . . . struck me like lightening.

FATHER *enters.* ANTON *hides the letter.*

FATHER: What are you writing? What's this?

ANTON: How's the weather?

FATHER: It has started to rain. The hay's rotting. What's this you're writing?

ANTON: Oh, you know . . .

FATHER: Is it for *Fragments*?

FATHER *pulls the letter to himself.*

ANTON: It's personal.

FATHER: Cut it out, we don't keep secrets in our family.

Picks up an envelope lying nearby, takes out the letter. Reads out loud.

"Stop doing hack work. I don't know what means you have; if you have few, better go hungry, as we went hungry in our time, but save your impressions for work that has been pondered, polished, written in more than one sitting, written in hours of inner happiness. One such work will be judged a hundred times more worthy than a hundred wonderful stories that have been scattered here and there in our newspapers. You will instantly take the prize and distinguish yourself in the eyes of men of taste and later the entire reading public. At the heart of your stories often lies a motif of a cynical nature. Why is that?" This is not funny at all. Are you sure that you'll get paid for this? How many kopecks per line? By the way, Misha's asking for money.

ANTON: Why do all of you ask me for money? I'm not a banker, I'm a writer.

FATHER: Vanya's not asking, but it embarrasses him to go around penniless in polite company. He's about to take his exams, and it's no good for him to be a sponger among friends who can advance his career. *You* understand. One more thing, Antosha. The mail came today. . . . There was no remittance from Leykin. Today is already the second. They usually send it by the first of the month. Find out what's going on, sort it out. Debts have to be paid, after all.

FATHER *crosses himself before the icon, prays.*

ANTON: Father, I didn't send Leykin any humorous stories. I'm . . . writing a novel.

FATHER: Oh? What are they offering per line?

ANTON (*Triumphantly*): Father, dear father. I have to tell you something. I've been thinking about how to tell you. I got a letter from Grigorievich.

FATHER: Who's this Grigorievich?

ANTON: You don't know who Grigorievich is? He's a very famous writer. A noble, wonderful man. He wrote me a letter. He is holding out his hand to me. He writes that I . . . I have a great talent.

ANTON *is excited.*

FATHER: What does he want from you, this . . . Grigorievich?

ANTON *is surprised.*

FATHER: Son. These gentlemen always want something from our kind.

ANTON: He writes that I'm talented. That I must take greater care to polish my works or I'll waste my gift. That I must stop writing to order so much and should instead devote myself to something big, a novel.

FATHER: How does he know what's best for you and your family? How? Your family needs you to write for Leykin. We have to pay for the grocery store on the first of the month. I'm a positive man, a man of character. I don't forget such things. And you too should remember how many lines you need to send to Leykin. If I were as well educated as you, I'd write better than you. Eight kopecks a line.

ALEXANDER *appears.*

ALEXANDER: I met our brother Misha. He asked me for a ruble. Funny! Where would I get a ruble? (*To* ANTON.) He's too embarrassed to ask you. How did it come about that your brothers are afraid to come to you with questions about money? It's no good.

FATHER: Those who live without the law shall perish without the law.

FATHER *shakes his head and leaves.*

ALEXANDER: I'm alive and well and—the main thing—I keep myself busy. That's why I don't drink. One doesn't need to get drunk to forget oneself. Don't you want to know how I keep myself busy?

After a silence.

I'm writing a novel. (*Hesitating.*) Or a play. In any case. . . . Something big, something important. I have the feeling, on the one hand, that the subject I've chosen is too great for me; but, on the other hand, I don't want to believe it: I'm too embarrassed to admit that I can't handle it.

ANTON: You can.

ALEXANDER: Here's how I started to write. One day, at Suvorin's, they were saying that your Ivanov is a "whiner" (from the verb *to whine*) and that you portrayed him beautifully; and that there's no such play in which the hero is not, to some degree, a whiner. I decided to portray a hero *who doesn't whine*. There's the task that I set for myself.

ANTON: And what's the plot of your play?

ALEXANDER (*Taken by surprise*): The plot? The details aren't important. Suvorin said that if it comes out well, I'll leave you in the dust. So there.

ANTON: Write. Flies purify the air and plays purify the morals.

ALEXANDER: Out of everyone I know, you're the only person who doesn't whine. How's *your* novel going?

Drawing the letter to himself, reads it.

ALEXANDER: Grigorievich writes you? "You are the best writer of the new generation." That's sweet. But . . . I think the old man has lost his mind. . . . Don't you agree?

ANTON: My novel has reached the freezing point. It's not growing . . . I'm rushing to finish some trifles so as not to run out of money.

ALEXANDER: Trifles. Good thing you're so cheerful. You don't take anything too close to heart. Do you even have a heart?

Waves some sheets of newspaper.

I'd never read this to another man. But you don't give a damn. "Man Without a Spleen."[7] They write a lot about you. You know. All sorts of nasty things! Look!

ANTON: You've collected this on purpose just so you could read it to me?

ALEXANDER (*Feverishly*): Listen! "Overall, the works of Anton Chekhov present a rather sad and tragic spectacle: the suicide of a young talent. He writes too much."

"This will end with the writer turning into a squeezed lemon, and like a squeezed lemon he will live out his final days on earth in utter oblivion, under a garden fence." ". . . stubbornly repeats themes that everyone's grown tired of . . ." Oh, here's another! "Extremely long and colorless. It reminds one of a white paper ribbon pulled out of a Chinaman's mouth."

ANTON: Why a Chinaman?

ALEXANDER: And finally: "You're withering away before you've had time to flower. What a pity."

ALEXANDER *breathes heavily, as if trying to overcome some impediment, and greedily watches his brother.* ANTON *is impenetrable.*

ALEXANDER: Well? What do you have to say?

ANTON: They're right. Absolutely right.

ALEXANDER *didn't expect this reaction.*

ANTON: I've never been satisfied with myself. I don't like myself as a writer. The worst thing is that it's as if I'm in a daze and don't understand what it is that I'm writing . . . I lied so much in my childhood and youth that now I can sense falsehood without fail. I've spoken so often about the need for new forms, but now I feel that, little by little, I'm sinking into a routine myself.

ALEXANDER: Don't fall apart now.

One can see NIKOLAI *and* NATASHA, *barefoot, taking turns drinking from a bottle.* ANTON *shuts his eyes.*

ANTON: I see everything. Why do you think I'm so easily fooled?

NIKOLAI *and* NATASHA *approach. They look at* ANTON *innocently: What's he talking about? They're both hammered.*

NIKOLAI: What a perfectly lilac evening. And the shadows are lilac. Pink, even. It's funny. (*Has a coughing fit.*)

ALEXANDER (*Alarmed, in a low voice*): Antosha, you really don't believe he has consumption?

ANTON: It's daytime, not evening.

NIKOLAI: A lilac day. But if you draw it with lilac . . . they'll say . . . you've lost your mind. (*Coughs.*) You can't paint it the way it is . . . (*Coughs.*) Antosha. Brother. Give me my boots back. I'll go to Anyuta. She misses me. She's a fun little one. (*Coughs.*) I feel better. I'm recovering.

ALEXANDER (*Waves him off; he is greatly concerned for NIKOLAI but feels powerless.*): In the end, one artist more or less . . . does it make any difference?

ALEXANDER *greedily lights a cigar. Inhales. It makes abstaining from vodka easier.*

ANTON: Sasha. I no longer recognize you now that you've stopped drinking. You're always angry, irritated. (*Waves away the smoke, coughs.*) A cigar or a shot of vodka—either way, it's no longer you, but you plus a cigar. Are you afraid of being yourself?

ANTON *waves away the smoke.*

ALEXANDER: Am I inconvenient? Am I in everyone's way? Is it inconvenient for you that I don't drink? Is it because you've grown used to being the only Chekhov?

Blows smoke. NIKOLAI *coughs more strenuously from the smoke.*

NIKOLAI: I feel better, I want to live! These shadows are so expressive.

Settles into the hammock. ALEXANDER *rocks him.*

ALEXANDER: You shouldn't want to live. That's just lightheadedness speaking. All life must end—that's a law of nature.

NIKOLAI: It's just that you're healthy and don't understand. But you'll be afraid too when your time comes.

ALEXANDER: The fear of death is an animal fear. . . . One must suppress it. The only people who fear death are those who believe in eternal life, because they're afraid of their own sins. Whereas you, first of all, are not a believer . . .

NIKOLAI: That's not true. I believe. I do. I know how to pray. The way father taught us. (*Puts his hands together.* ALEXANDER *smirks.*)

NATASHA *enters. Approaches* ANTON.

NATASHA: It's all nonsense. Hopeless love exists only in novels. Trifles. One must only take care not to let oneself go and keep waiting for something, waiting for the grass to grow. . . . If love invades your heart, you have to get rid of it. I'll forget all this . . . I'll rip it out of my heart by the roots.

ANTON (*Watches her, laughs*): Your buttons aren't done up right again. Why do you look as if you're in a hurry somewhere?

NATASHA (*Through tears*): Is this funny? Do you find it funny?

ANTON *pulls her away in a familiar, comradely way, and carefully buttons up her blouse. She has tears in her eyes.*

NATASHA: You have such nice hands . . . I remember. The way you cut open an abscess under my arm. Just a moment of pain—and the pus is gone, and you're healthy again.

ANTON: My little skeleton. I remember how I used to study the ilium bone on your body. That was a long time ago. I dreamed of becoming a great doctor back then.

They stand in a gentle embrace, as friends do.

I should have married you. I should have given you peace, even if there was no love.

NATASHA: And now you're marrying for money. No. Don't deny it. How big is her dowry? You want to give this money to your family and thereby become free. But you'll never be free with her! She'll have you on a string, you'll see.

ANTON: That may be exactly what I need. She's intelligent, elegant. She's so full of life.

NATASHA (*Trembling*): No, no . . . I'm just an ordinary woman, you mustn't talk to me like this. . . . Don't torment me, Anto-chez-vous . . . I'm afraid . . .

ANTON: She's a shrew. Terribly nervous. When she comes near me, it's like an electric shock. She's strong, supple, always very hot.

NATASHA: Can it really be that I'm so uninteresting, so unattractive that you can speak to me about other women without feeling ashamed? (*Embraces and kisses him.*) I love you. There, I said it. Be more kind to me. I know how to appreciate you. You're the best, the most extraordinary.

ANTON: Someone can come in. (*Tearing himself away from her.*)

NATASHA: Let them, I'm not ashamed of my love for you. (*Kisses his hands.*) You're so talented, so smart, don't listen to anyone. They only envy you. You're greater than they are—as a man. If anyone will remember us it will only be because of you. You're the most talented of our present writers. . . . There's such sincerity, such simplicity, such freshness, such a vital sense of humor in you . . .

ANTON: The freshness is gone. Grigorievich was right—everything's written in haste, slipshod, rushed. I've got my technique all worked out, I feel at ease . . . two or three strokes and the story is ready. Off it goes. Six, even eight kopecks a line. "The neck of a broken bottle gleaming on the dam, the dark shadows of the mill wheel . . ."—and the moonlit night is all ready to go. But I passionately love this water, this sky, I have a feel for nature, it arouses my passion, the irresistible desire to write. It may well be the only thing I love. "You're withering away before you've had time to flower." Right. And how does one go about describing, without platitudes, the trembling light, the quiet shimmering of the stars, the distant sound of the piano slowly fading in the quiet aromatic air. . . . It's torture.

NATASHA: Oh, with just one stroke you can convey the main thing about a face or a landscape, your characters feel as if they are alive. Oh, one cannot read your work without feeling rapture! You think this all incense? That I'm flattering you? Look at me . . . look at me. . . . Do I look like a liar? You see, I'm the only person who knows how to appreciate you, the only person who'll tell you the truth, my dear, wonderful man. Will you really leave me? . . .

ANTON: I want to marry Dunya.

NATASHA: I don't care.

She pulls him closer, they kiss.

DUNYA *enters. She can't believe her eyes.*

DUNYA: This is so vulgar. (*Cries.*)

NATASHA (*Smothering him with kisses*): How big is her dowry? Tell me that you would have married me if I had money!

DUNYA (*Quietly*): Anton Pavlovich. Alas, my father won't give me any money if I convert.

NATASHA (*Delighted*): There's no dowry!

DUNYA: What's it got to do with you?

NATASHA: I'm Anton's friend.

DUNYA: I think you're nothing but a lost woman who's forgotten the faith of her fathers. I can't even imagine who'd ever want to marry you. Your sisters have nicknames—Sledgehammer One. Sledgehammer Two.

NATASHA: Who told you about that? Masha? That would be mean on Maria Pavlovna's part. But here's what I think—Masha's only jealous of her brothers. Especially of Anton.

DUNYA: This is simply unheard of! Why aren't you saying anything, Anton?

NATASHA (*Triumphantly*): So there won't be a dowry! There won't be a wedding!

NIKOLAI: Antosha, let me go to Anyuta.

ALEXANDER: Your Sledgehammer's playing the snitch, she's taken a police constable as her lover, and you're lying here, drunk, behind the curtain, while your Sledgehammer's screwing around with other men!

NIKOLAI: So what? It's fun over there. Anyuta's fun. When she's had a couple of drinks, her cheeks turn carmine. It's very expressive.

FATHER *appears. He's carrying an icon and singing a church song. He grabs* DUNYA *and* ANTON *by their arms. Brings them together. He's singing a psalm.* NIKOLAI *meekly sings along.*

NIKOLAI: Just like when we were kids! Holy God, Holy Strong, have mercy on us.

ANTON: What's the meaning of this buffoonery?

FATHER: Antosha. Evdokia Isaakovna. My children.

NIKOLAI (*Kisses the icon*): I have faith that it will cure me. (*Examines the icon, screws up his eyes.*) But the perspective is all wrong. And look how awkwardly they've drawn the fingers. (*Examines his own fingers.*)

FATHER (*Triumphantly*): My sons. I only ask one thing of you. Remain stalwart in your faith. (*To* DUNYA.) Evodkia Isaakovna, Antosha had a religious upbringing. Which is why he always remembers his duty. To himself and to his family. And that's as it should be!

NIKOLAI (*Strains his voice with the psalm, laughs*): I was a tenor, while Antosha was an alto.

FATHER: . . . I remember how the two of you, Antosha and Kolya, used to sing. You were so thin and small. Your voices would rise straight to heaven.

NIKOLAI (*Laughing*): . . . And if we didn't go to sing in church, then it's the birch rod, swish, swish . . . (*Laughs hard.*) My ass still burns whenever I hear church music. (*Laughs.*)

ALEXANDER: Thank you, father. At least you've turned us into atheists.

FATHER: Antosha, why don't you say something? Our choir consisted of blacksmiths. They were basses. Baritones. It wasn't pretty. But your angelic, youthful voices . . . (*Wipes his tears.*)

ANTON: What do you want me to say? When we were children, and you made us sing in the church choir, I felt like I was a little convict . . . and now I'm no longer religious. (*Shrugs.*) No wonder so many atheists came from seminaries and religious schools. We're no exception.

NIKOLAI: I have faith. . . . Although this isn't a background on this icon, but the devil knows what. It goes against all the laws of perspective.

FATHER: My children, don't blaspheme, give thanks to the Lord. Today is a day for rejoicing. Antosha has decided to marry. (*Raises the icon.*) Bless you, my children, Antony and Evdokia, may you live a long and happy life . . . (*Wipes his tears.*)

DUNYA: Pavel Egorovich. My father said that he'll put a curse upon me . . . if I convert to Christianity and marry Anton. So there you have it. There won't be a dowry!

ANTON *looks at* DUNYA. *She breaks the pencils on his desk.*

DUNYA: Will there be a wedding without a dowry?

FATHER *turns to stone with the icon.*

FATHER: Oh, these Jews! They're real merchants. They'll rob you blind, I respect them for that.

Quietly, as if unintentionally, sets down the icon.

FATHER (*Clearing his throat*): The gooseberries have ripened. Small, but sweet. Aphids have descended on our leaves, but we were able to smoke them out. I told you, Antosha. But you didn't listen to your father. (*Looks at his sons.*) My sons, my dear sons. Who needs you now? My sorrow.

NIKOLAI *falls on* ALEXANDER, *coughing up blood.*

7. A MUTE SCENE

ALEXANDER *is covered in blood, washing linen. He washes* NIKOLAI*'s blood-stained shirt, hangs up the poorly washed, yellow-and-brown-stained shirts of his children. He also hangs up an enormous women's shirt, which is full of holes. The linen keeps falling off, but* ALEXANDER *stubbornly proceeds with his work.*

8. BINGO

ANTON *and the ladies are playing bingo.*

NATASHA: Nineteen. There won't be a wedding!

DUNYA: Sixty-four. It's not up to you.

They look at ANTON. *But he is silent, eyes on the bingo.*

NATASHA: Why should he marry?

ANTON: Eleven.

NATASHA: Why should Anton marry? A writer should be above such prose.

DUNYA: He needs tenderness, comfort, family. He's surrounded by all of you, but he's all alone. Fourteen. Anton, it's your move. What are you thinking about?

NATASHA: Yes, what are you thinking about?

ANTON: I want to devote myself to science. I'm working on one little question—and plan to continue doing so in the future: the woman question. I set it on its native soil and start building: *The History of Sexual Authority*. Woman is always passive. She gives birth to cannon fodder.

NATASHA *giggles, while* DUNYA *listens with dismay. She understands that this is only the continuation of her quarrel with* ANTON.

ANTON: At no time or place is she superior to man. Buckle says that she's more deductive . . . etc. But I disagree. She makes a good doctor, a good lawyer, etc., but in the domain of *art,* she's a goose. Man is the perfect organism—he *creates,* while woman has yet to create anything at all.

NATASHA: Are you really going to marry? Twenty-seven.

ALEXANDER: Look who's here!

ALEXANDER, *drunk, appears in the garden.*

Those who've been sitting in the gazebo jump up. They are unpleasantly surprised. ALEXANDER *sees this and becomes even more brazen.*

ALEXANDER: It seems you're not pleased by my appearance. I don't give a damn.

I live my life most sadly
But never curse my fate
And though I fuck 'em badly
I fuck at any rate

I live! I live! And I like it.

(*To* DUNYA.) Sister. Allow me to kiss your hand.

Why does Antosha say that I'm an anti-Semite? Rather, I'm an archimandrite. There's a poem for you. Brother doesn't like it. You see, I used to hold more promise than him. Brother, congratulate me—I haven't written a novel either. I've come to realize that I'm incapable of writing . . . I won't leave you in the dust, and who's to blame?

ANTON (*Weary*): What am I to do with you? Two shots—and look what's become of you! Alcoholism is a hereditary disease.

But why is it that neither I nor our brother the teacher. . . . Why don't we feel the pull of alcohol, while you turn into a clown from two or three drinks?

FATHER: There haven't been any alcoholics among the Chekhovs. I don't know who he takes after. Those who live without the law shall perish without the law.

ALEXANDER: I'm a band apart, no one loves me. Sister. I'm so hungry for tenderness that I'd marry you right now even without your Jewish millions. Anna's dying. I loved her so much, I sacrificed my life for her, it's so hard to abstain! So hard! I need tenderness, the poetry of family! I have a delicate soul, I want to love!

FATHER: Alexander, my son, what's become of you?

ALEXANDER (*Examines himself*): What? My hat's turned green and my soles have come undone, I don't have clean linen . . . but I still make a first-rate match. Good all around. Here. There. (*Moves indecently.*) I live! Anton. I want to marry too. Father. I know that the Apostle Paul doesn't advise us to speak about such filth, but it's the law of life.

ANTON: But Anna's still alive.

ALEXANDER: It's the law of life. I must think about the future. Yes!

Grabs NATASHA *by the hand. Goes in for a kiss.* NATASHA *giggles.*

ALEXANDER: I want family, music, tenderness, kind words when I come home tired after a long day at work. I need the poetry of family. Tenderness. That's the main thing—tenderness.

ANTON: You're an eighty-proof hypocrite. You want to marry a free woman only to make her your nanny and nurse.

NATASHA: Maybe a free woman needs tenderness too.

ANTON: But you're strangers to each other. You see, Natasha's not so crazy, not so off her rocker, that she'd get herself tied up with you. You won't touch her with your autobiography and your runny eyes; nor with your children, for she's one thing, and your children are another. . . . All of this is just the Chekhov blood speaking. Marriage Chekhov style.

ALEXANDER: Are you saying I'm not worthy? Simple human happiness is not in my cards?

ANTON: I'm tired of you.

NATASHA (*Excited*): Anto-chez-vous, you're jealous! (*To* ALEXANDER.) I'll think it over. I don't like you, Sasha. But you have one advantage—you're his brother.

ALEXANDER *gasps for air, grabs his throat.* NIKOLAI *quietly puts on his boots and steals away. He's gone. No one pays any attention to him.*

DUNYA: Fourteen. Bingo!

NATASHA: You're lucky!

DUNYA: Well, game over. Farewell, Anton Pavlovich. *The History of Sexual Authority*? Woman always submits because she is less intelligent and less talented? But . . . to whom should I submit? For the sake of what? Despite the fact that I'm not intelligent, not talented, and lack the powers of deduction, I understand that you only wanted to marry money. And I was ready. Because I love you. You wanted to turn my money over to them in order to secure your freedom. I was ready even for that. But for whose sake are you sacrificing us? Look at them! They're monsters! You once said to me—the rotten blood of slaves. We studied it in school. It's called degeneration. Your family is in the process of degeneration. And you want to sacrifice me for *them*?

ANTON (*Sincerely*): Yes!

DUNYA *and* NATASHA *listen intently.*

ANTON: They are my family. My joy and my damnation. My warmth. I love my family. I want all of them to be happy.

DUNYA: It won't work.

ANTON: You lied to me about the dowry! Your father gives his consent!

DUNYA: Forgive me. . . . I don't want to. I . . . want to leave. Don't be upset.

DUNYA *sets off.* ANTON *follows her with his eyes.*

DUNYA (*Turning around*): Admit it, it's like a weight off your shoulders. You didn't want to get married. It's for the best.

ALEXANDER (*Not sure how to express his commiseration*): Brother, brother . . .

ANTON: . . . "Brother." You used to scare me with that word for many years. I'm ready to cast it out of my lexicon at any time.

ALEXANDER: . . . It's because you don't have a heart.

ANTON: No, it's because one has to be ready for everything in this world. (*Looks around.*) Where's Nikolai? (*Calls out.*) Nikolai! Slantface! Mr. Artist! Little Zabelin.[8] Slantmug. Has he run away?

ALEXANDER: Your nicknames are very hurtful. You cause pain with your words.

ANTON: You give me nicknames too.

ALEXANDER: You started this game. And you know what? Now I understand everything. You do it on purpose. You're depriving us of our names. So that you alone can be Chekhov.

ANTON: You're drunk.

ALEXANDER: Do you know what Suvorin said to me about my story?

ANTON: I asked, you didn't want to answer.

ALEXANDER: It's permitted to write and publish bad stories, but not to usurp another's name. That's what he said.

ANTON (*Looks around*): Where's Nikolka?

NATASHA (*Defiantly*): He's answering the call of love. What now, Anto-chez-vous? Are you forbidding your brothers to love?

FATHER: He's run away! You failed to keep an eye on him, Antosha! All that education I gave to you children! And what was the use?

ANTON: He's run off to the Sledgehammer. To drink and wallow.

NATASHA (*Shrilly*): Don't you dare call my sister Sledgehammer! You have no right! She sometimes gives her last piece of bread to your brother, seeing that you don't give him any money!

ANTON: Her last shot of vodka, you mean? *That* I'm ready to believe.

FATHER: Were all my efforts in vain? The sacrifices, three sons received an education, two more are still in school. And what for? Those who live without the law shall perish without the law.

ALEXANDER: You've really upset Nikolka. You forget that he's dying.

ANTON: Do you think I need your explanation? Which one of us is a doctor, you or me? I'm tired of you.

ALEXANDER *wants sympathy—but everyone turns away from him.* ALEXANDER *becomes thoughtful.*

ALEXANDER (*Quietly, heartfelt*): I bought a condom at the pharmacy. A cock sock, or whatever you call it. But just as I was about to put it on, it saw my bean pole and . . . burst. So it didn't work. Had to rein in the flesh again. (*Cries.*)

My life is ruined! I'm talented, smart, brave. . . . If only I lived a normal life, I could have become another Schopenhauer, Dostoevsky. . . . But look at me now! The brother of my brother! Is that fair? I got carried away! I'm losing my mind. . . . Father, I'm in despair! Father!

Falls on his father's neck.

FATHER (*Has tears in his eyes but doesn't know what to say*): Aphids eat away at the grass, rust at iron, and lies at the soul.

(*As if remembering something.*) It's no good to make your life into a novel. It won't do, Sasha.

ALEXANDER (*Suddenly cheerfully, angrily*): But you weren't able to write a novel after all, ANTON Chekhov! It's all your fault! Yours alone! You took everything from us, everything! Even our name! You exist, but we don't!

FATHER: Come now, what's this? . . . A fit. Too much education. Too much drinking. We never had . . .

ANTON *silently approaches his brother. He understands that he must say something kind, sympathetic. He remains silent.*

ALEXANDER: What is it? What do you want to tell me?

ANTON: It's nice out. Soon the gooseberries will bloom.

ALEXANDER: Nooo!

Pulls out a pistol, fires at ANTON. *Misfire.*

Realizes that the pistol won't fire. Cries.

ALEXANDER: Forgive me.

ANTON *snatches away the pistol.*

ANTON: Where did you get it?

ALEXANDER: I bought it from Levitan.

ANTON: That Yid sold you a piece of junk.

ALEXANDER: He wanted to shoot himself with it. I thought . . . I also wanted . . .

ANTON: Levitan shoots himself three times a year, at least. I think he deliberately buys the shoddiest pistols. How does it go, father? As rust eats away at iron, so lies eat away at the soul.

FATHER (*Nods meaningfully*): So lies eat away at the soul. A Chekhov doesn't lie.

ALEXANDER: I miss Annushka so much. Forgive me. . . . Forgive me. Anna. Farewell, life.

Shoots himself in the head. Falls.

■ □ ■

ANTON *stares at a blank canvas—the painting that* NIKOLAI *never produced—and describes this nonexistent painting.*

ANTON: A river. A golden afternoon. A quiet, shaded alley. A hammock. Two young ladies playing cricket. A young landowner has come out to mow the grass, barefoot. He is a Tolstoyan, but his estate has been mortgaged to the bank and will soon be used to pay off the interest. A peasant woman with a shoulder yoke is on her way to get water. Another is washing linen on the footbridge.

Maybe he wanted to paint what would soon disappear?

I got married after all. But not to Dunya. To whom? That's another story altogether. I had no children. But I'm not the only Chekhov—Alexander's son became a great actor. That's what they say.

I never wrote a single novel, but that turned out to be unimportant. The most important thing is to write. To work. And I wrote with pleasure, with joy . . .

Dunya did not stay single, of course. She married a Jewish lawyer with a long last name. As is only right and proper. And Dunya died in a German concentration camp, in Treblinka.

My brother, the artist, died a year after these events on Alexander's arms. Consumption set its fangs on him, gnawed away at his lungs, was about to set upon his kidneys. That's what always happens. (*After a pause.*) Death from consumption, our family curse. It's not very pretty.

Alexander married Natasha, they tried to live together, but it didn't work out. He wrote under the pseudonym Grayhair. Never managed to write anything of any value. Made it into the encyclopedia as the brother of Anton Chekhov. Drank himself to death. He died just like Uncle Mitrofan. Went around singing his couplets. Sometimes he'd mention his name and people would pour him a drink. Our sister Masha despised him and wouldn't let him on her porch.

The bodies of everyone I loved, everyone who loved me, have returned unto dust, and eternal matter has reduced them to stone, to water, to cloud, and their souls have melded into one. Only I remember them. . . . Only I . . . I. . . . And I remember it all, all, all, and every life that has ever lived lives once more within me.[10]

It would seem that I'm still capable of love. And I'm a writer. I can do anything. I can bring everything back with one flourish of the quill, one stroke of the pencil.

THE END

05

THE BLUE MACHINIST[1]

MIKHAIL DURNENKOV

TRANSLATED BY ANIA AIZMAN

CHARACTERS

HERO
GENNADY
RENAT
ANDREY
PETER
ZHENYA
MAGNETIC GIRL
SECURITY GUARD
FACTORY RADIO STATION

1. SHOW

HERO *stands on stage.*

Behind him, RENAT, ZHENYA, GENNADY, ANDREY, *and* PETER *are seated.*

They appear to be dressed in their best clothes.

HERO *is extremely embarrassed. He doesn't know where to start.*

HERO: I don't know where to start—Probably, I should thank—No. First: hi. I'm glad that you came. And you. And you. Hello, by the way. Hi. I want to say that my mom—She's not here, you don't need to look for her.

GENNADY: Screw your mom!

RENAT: Easy.

HERO: Mom, thank you for, you know, bringing me into this world. And you too, dad. This is such a big deal for me.

ANDREY: How are we supposed to sit? Can we, like, move around?

HERO: I'll finish in a moment, and then you can.

ANDREY: This is stupid.

GENNADY: Damn right.

HERO: I want to say a few words about the crew. No. First, I want to make a disclaimer. I constantly confuse things that I imagine with things that I don't imagine. And now that I've made my disclaimer, I can. . . . This is Gennady.

GENNADY: I want to—

HERO: This is Andrey.

ANDREY: I'm the boss. There's also the chief. These are different things. Like—for example—the difference between the main chicken in the coop and the cook. Different things, and—

HERO: This is Renat. He's not Russian, but he understands everything.

RENAT: "He understands everything." Go to hell!

PETER: I'm Peter.

HERO: He's Peter—like Heaven's gatekeeper.

PETER: Like Heaven's goalkeeper.

HERO: And here's Zhenya. Zhenya's the favorite. Not because he goes on vodka runs. Just because he's capable.

ANDREY: Capable of shit.

HERO: I'm grateful to God for this crew. Thank you, uh, God. We've gathered here to say—to talk about our lives. What's most important in life? I'm really nervous and it's, like, hard to express everything right off the bat.

ANDREY: We believe in you. Wrap it up already.

HERO: How did everything begin? Right, guys? I need to recount how everything started?

ZHENYA: Go for it.

HERO: I wasn't entirely ready at first. That is, ever. As long as I can remember myself.

GENNADY: Don't piss in the wind. You couldn't even screw a nut right. Every time: against the grain.

HERO: And now there's only the everyday world. Everything is over. Harmony. That is to say, now I understand quite well where everything is. Like, here's you, and, like, here's me, and, like, here's . . . everybody. This is a long story, which is why our show is divided into several segments. (*Turns to the workers.*) First about getting the job? Or what?

ZHENYA: Exposition.

HERO: What?

ANDREY: Talk about, like, how you lived before.

HERO: Zhenya sometimes came up with unusual expressions. Where he got them, no one knows. In a word . . .

Pause.

HERO: I want to say that if you're expecting funny stories about the manufacturing plant—do you know how mummies were made in Egypt? All a man's guts were scraped out with hooks right through the ass, and once he was all emptied out they poured the mummifying goop into him. It's not funny at all, if I start scooping out—(*Takes the deepest inhale.*) Okay. The show's started, people are here and—if I get sidetracked somewhere, that is, somewhere away from reality—

GENNADY: We're here for you.

RENAT: We'll set you straight right away.

The workers laugh, satisfied.

HERO (*Very seriously*): Thank you. Precisely for that.

ZHENYA: Now, exposition.

HERO: Okay. Exposition.

2. MAGNETIC GIRL

Only HERO *is in the room.*

HERO: Absolute boredom. Whatever you imagine, what*ever* you imagine, everything already exists. It's like a fever dream: you enter a room, cross it, enter the next one, exactly the same as the last one, cross that one, open the door, only to end up in the same room, and so on until infinity, *ad nauseam*. It's difficult to admit that the world is a better author than you are. The newspapers report, "Magnetic Girl Lives in Metro Since Age 8." Where was I with my imagination when Magnetic Girl ended up living in the metro? Or here: "Underground PlayDoh-Manufacturing Shop Discovered at Children's Sanatorium." What kind of an author am I after that? I can't even invent what already exists. "Vladivostok Man Raised By Samurai Hiding from Japanese Authorities."

Pause.

The Samurai is an immigrant. He'll marry, buy a cheap laundry machine and a refrigerator on credit, and forget all his ambitions. From dirt to dirt. "Contest Today at the Swine Cultivation Pavilion: 'Addicts Draw Jesus.'" I should forget about my scribbles, like forgetting about a nightmare. "Moldovan, Last Name Pushin, Sexually Assaulted Cat on Red Square." Forget it, just have kids and trust that's the most important thing in life. "Bolshoi Theater Ballerina Puts Fiberglass in Underwear." Some ancient sage said that the most important thing is the happiness of being. Just wake up in the morning and rejoice. Go to work, leave work, rejoice. And so on until the end, until death. "Gay Bordello at Police Department Liquidated." Let the world write instead of all the authors put together. The world is better at it. Easy and charming. "Putin to Be Laid at Lenin's Feet." At Lenin's feet. Fuck. Well, someone could invent that, at least, right? Why didn't *I* invent that? "First Iraqi Musical: Allah-Superstar." Stop, stop, stop. I've already decided, haven't I? Abandon everything and just live. Just live. Just live. To just live, you have to just sleep. And not think, about how you have to get up at five thirty. Otherwise you won't get up. "And even while sleeping / I understand I must rise at five thirty." As if— once again, poetry. Don't think. Never think again.

A knock on the door.

Come in.

MAGNETIC GIRL *enters. She is about thirty years old; her face is tired from life and pale from life in the metro.*

Have a seat. Is it alright if I offer you a drink right away? Want some? Great. Because I'd feel bad drinking alone, but I can't sleep at all. Let's drink.

He pours, for himself and her.

Listen, how did you end up in the metro?

MAGNETIC GIRL *shrugs.*

You probably came with your mother from Syzran' or some other provincial city. Your neighbor, Granny Valya, when she found out about your magnetic capabilities, said right away, "Take her to Gomel, where Nastasya the Healer lives. Let her cure that damn child." Of course, once they got there, Nastasya was nowhere to be found. But your mother met Gennady, who worked at the station in the luggage department. Right? And you spent a couple of days at the station. The travelers, with big noses and rude voices, fed you mashed potatoes, pork, and lemonade, while you amused yourself by disrupting the timetable display with your magnetic waves. After that your mother reappeared, somehow unrecognizable, with a strong, buttery shine to her eyes. She was wearing a new scarf—blue, with red phoenixes on the corners. She took you by the hand, and you went to Moscow. And there, on some metro station, she let go of your hand, took the bright scarf off her head, and dissolved in the crowd. A sad story. Do you want to drink something else? No? Then get outta here. You're of no use to me in housekeeping. Go, fight evil with your superpowers. Those like you are already gathering over there. They're waiting for you. Together with the Samurai from Vladivostok you'll fight the Moldovan and the itchy ballerina. And, of course, in the end, you will win. And later your mother will come to you, without the sparkle in her eye and without the scarf. She will tell you that she broke up with Gennady because he kept drinking with the luggage carriers at the station and beating her. And that, once she left him, she looked for you the whole time, Magnetic Girl. She looked for you everywhere. And finally she found you at a suburban metro station. You were amusing yourself by disrupting the train schedule. Grateful stray cats were rubbing against your legs.

MAGNETIC GIRL *leaves, slamming the door.*

That door slams too often because of the draft, and I drink by myself too often.

Drinks.

I need to just take everything in my life and change it. Get down to the level where there is no ambiguity. Where only that which has to happen happens.

3. CHECKPOINT

Early morning—say, six o'clock.

People are squeezed against each other as if playing "Human Knot." The factory radio station can be heard.

FACTORY RADIO STATION: "Let hearts feel wind and sorrow, let hearts beat with the rustling of thought, we are ready to grasp our tomorrow, understand how to live and to work." Alexander Varameyev, master machinist at Welding Shop 1–17, dedicates these lines of his to his beloved calibrated conductors shop, where he has worked for nearly eighteen years—

GUARD: Come over here. You and you.

RENAT *and* HERO *approach* GUARD.

GUARD: Show your bags.

RENAT: Why, hullo, Tatar.

GUARD: Why, hullo, Tatar.

RENAT (*Grumpily showing his bag*): I pass here so many times. You could just let me through.

GUARD: You'll be fine.

RENAT: What's new?

GUARD: What could be new? Well, one Boy Scout in the lathe sector made a samurai sword for himself on the sly. Wanted to smuggle it off the premises.

RENAT: And what happened?

GUARD: Nothing happened. Almost chopped up the guys at Checkpoint Six. Next.

RENAT (*Closing his bag*): Right, "nothing happened."

GUARD (*Looking inside* HERO's *bag*): What's this?

HERO: A CD player.

GUARD: CD players not allowed. Leave it here.

HERO: Why aren't they allowed?

RENAT: Don't argue.

GUARD: Because it's digital media. Pat down or metal detector?

RENAT (*Incensed*): Do you really have to ask? Pat down, of course. And for him too.

GUARD *begins to pat their clothes, slapping their pockets.*

HERO: But what's the deal here? Why does it have to be a pat down?

RENAT: After you are radiated with those detectors a couple times, you won't be able to get it up anymore. Fucking things make you impotent.

GUARD (*To* HERO): Yeah, just go on and listen to them. (*To* RENAT.) Dismissed. (RENAT *leaves.*) Fucking savages, man. . . . (*To* HERO.) Trying to get a job here?

HERO: Trying.

GUARD: Good luck. First time here?

HERO: Yeah.

GUARD: Good luck.

HERO (*Cautiously*): Thanks.

GUARD: I'm working my last days. My uncle's taking me on at the Kama Auto Plant.

HERO: Ah. . . . Got it.

GUARD: Gonna haul long distance.

HERO: Ah.

GUARD: Good luck.

Pause.

HERO: Thanks.

FACTORY RADIO STATION: Participants in the factory coat of arms design contest must turn in their proposals to the heraldic committee appointed by the trade union committee representatives of the 4–75 Paint Shop. The largest number of votes are currently going to Andrey Seizev, master machinist in the thunderclapping shop. In his design, a dragon symbolizing the natural resources of our region stands on his hind legs, rearing against a blue enamel background. His front claws rest on a yellow cogwheel with thirty-seven teeth, signifying the thirty-seven years of successful activity by our enterprise. The head of the dragon looks to the right. The proud name of our manufacturing plant is etched in Gothic letters on his collar.

4. RUSSIAN LABOR: ABSURD AND CRUEL

ANDREY *and* HERO *are in the room.*

ANDREY *is everything;* HERO *is nothing.*

ANDREY: College?

HERO: Yeah?

ANDREY: So?

HERO: What do you mean, "so?" Human resources told me that I'm a junior specialist.

ANDREY: I see that you're junior. I'm also junior.

Pause.

HERO: Er—

ANDREY: Or. Together you get "Eeyore." Seen the cartoon?

HERO: Yeah.

ANDREY: You know Eeyore?

HERO: Yeah.

ANDREY: Who else do you know?

HERO *rummages in a bag he brought with him. Looks for something in there for a long time. Straightens up sheepishly.*

HERO: I forget. I have an uncle, he gave me a name, but I forgot the note at home. Sounds like Kandinsky?

ANDREY: Kandinsky?

HERO: No?

Pause.

ANDREY *stares at* HERO*, unperturbed.*

HERO: Yes?

Pause.

ANDREY *stares at* HERO, *unperturbed.*

HERO: I think it was Kandinsky.

ANDREY: Kandinsky?

HERO: I. . . . (*Giving up.*) Okay, yes. Kandinsky. Like the painter.

Long pause.

ANDREY: Smell that?

HERO: What?

ANDREY: What. Are you deaf? It's everywhere, smell it?

HERO: I smell it.

ANDREY: What is that smell?

Pause.

HERO: Gear oil. Burned iron.

ANDREY: Right on. Right on the money.

HERO: Thank you.

ANDREY: So then. . . . If it's Kandinsky. . . . Then—

ANDREY *writes something on a scrap of paper.*

HERO: Then?

ANDREY: Thunderclapping machines.

HERO: What machines?

ANDREY: You'll find out. (*Pause. Andrey keeps writing.*) You know "Deep Purple"?

HERO (*Hurries*): Yeah, that . . . "Smoke on the water." (*Hums.*) Smoooke on the waa-ter, mm-mmm-mmm-mmm-m-mm. So is it hard to get a job at the plant?

ANDREY: Here's your note. It's called a runner here, because you have to run with it. Good luck.

HERO: You mean I can go?

ANDREY: My name is Andrey. I'm shop boss. There's also the shop chief, Gen. You'll have a chance to meet him. Try to make sure he likes you.

HERO: Who—Gen?

ANDREY (*Reluctantly tears himself away from the paperwork on the table*): What?

HERO: I have to make sure Gen likes me?

ANDREY: Do you know what a crew is?

HERO: It's when—

ANDREY: Explain it to your grandma.

HERO (*Completely flustered*): What does my grandma have to do with it?

ANDREY (*Disclosing*): Sicilian mafias, Black Brothers, Hitler Youth, Voroshilov Sharpshooters, and other gangs all started from factory crews. In Japan, for example, there are Yakuza— (*Considers* HERO.) Do you know who they are?

HERO: In Japan? (*Uncertainly.*) They're also in manufacturing?

ANDREY: You're gonna start as a machinist. There's no magic pill that can make college graduates work as engineers right away. Understand?

HERO: I . . . No . . .

ANDREY: Great. I didn't understand at first either. That's a good sign. I believe in you. Smoke on the water. I love it.

5. FIRST WARNING SIGN: THE MACHINISTS' HOKKUS

FACTORY RADIO STATION: The poetic genre of machinist hokkus developed at the same time as the conveyor belt, in Ford's factories in Detroit. At the time, many Japanese immigrants found employment at the conveyor belt and became citizens of the United States. In order to feed themselves and their large families, they worked twenty-four-hour shifts for miserable wages. These subtle Japanese poets reacted intuitively to their new surroundings. Suddenly, they had gone from working the land, observing water-drenched rice fields, and constantly admiring natural beauty to the thundering conveyor belt and the dull light of the factory floor. But for them finding beauty in every aspect of the outside world came naturally. And this is how the first lyric miniature forms appeared—*mashi*.[2] *Mashi* differed from the ancient Japanese poetic form, the tanka. They were less restrictive when it came to the number of lines and syllables, and they described other subjects. The principle, however, remained the same: the poet exercises self-restraint and gives weight to every word. In this way, he awakens the reader's creative vision.

A few of the first *mashi* have survived. The one considered most famous is called "Autumn: Sabotage," a text in which the poet admires how the pieces of a torn conveyor belt fly apart, scattering across the shop floor, while childishly asking himself:

Is it really possible that I
Misapplied the wrench?

With time the *mashi* became more strictly divided into two verses corresponding to the work shifts. It is also possible that a synthesis had occurred between the *mashi* and the memorandum.

Two different poets composed the two verses, creating a poetic dialogue of sorts. In such *mashi*, the tercet and the couplet alternated. Usually there was no unifying plot. Especially valued was the skill of creating unexpected twists. At the same time, each verse echoed its predecessors in the most complex ways. Thus a ball bearing taken out of its context is beautiful on its own, but in combination with others it acquires new, additional beauty.

The first stanza was traditionally called hokku and gradually formed as a standalone poetic form of industrial lyric.

In general, the hokku is a lyric poem in which beauty is expressed through calm, subdued colors, elegiac sadness, and harmony achieved by modest means.

Already in the nineteenth century the vast chasm between literary poetry and folk poetry began to close. Machinist hokkus quickly became popular among simple laborers.

The swarf, running in a curly stripe away from the blade, dancing and gradually fading—this image appears in hokkus as well as in folk song. The simplicity of the poems resembles the line drawn by a paintbrush across the careless space of the page. Nothing else—nothing unnecessary—occludes the true beauty of the surroundings.

Thus, for example, several skillfully chosen details give the image of a robbed warehouse. Product slips, stained with fuel oil, hang from emptied shelves. We feel the stillness of the air.

The poetic image, it seems, is barely indicated. But it possesses a wide range of meanings. It captivates and draws one away. It seems that one is looking at an unending conveyor belt. And at the same time the image is extremely concrete. The storekeeper-poet has depicted a real event at his workplace and, through it, his state of mind. He speaks not only of the loneliness of a screw left behind by thieves, but of his own loneliness.

The hokkus that gradually replaced the *mashi* gravitated toward a more laconic and minimal illustration. They were more harmonious with, and true to, the brusqueness of the workplace. For this reason, they reached wider circulation.

In Russia, the machinist hokku appeared as a genre of poetry relatively recently, basically at the time of the construction of the Volga Automobile Plant. The great master of labor hokkus, Vadim Borisovich (known to his admirers under the pseudonym Master Borisych), learned his trade at an exchange program at the Fiat Plant in the city of Turin. There he learned about the existence of machinist hokkus and was the first to bring a volume of this poetry to Togliatti.The workers are confounded by the simplicity of the hokku aesthetic, by its capacious minimalism. Thus, spontaneously, there appeared entire anthologies of hokkus. The students of Borisych publish true masterpieces: "Vacation in November" by Renat Steedov, machinist at Fleet Vehicle Services; "Night Shift Flame" by Eugene (Zhenya) Cabbagev, AutoVAZ machinist; "Paths to the Warehouse" by Gennady Vasilev, machinist at the 2–48 Thunderclapping Shop; and "The Sun of All the Grimy Windows" by second-category welder Peter Potov.

6. "THE SUN OF ALL THE GRIMY WINDOWS"

PETER POTOV, *second-category welder.*

PETER:

I carry the prepared metals to the container
They shine
Warm like bread loaves or breasts
Soft to the eye

Snow by the pipes—the photo negative
Of childhood snow
Black, but with a white dent
From a beer bottle . . .

Today the master eats
Two portions of rice
Smells of fuel oil. Lunch.

The sun of all the grimy windows
Drunk, I walk around the room
Smiling at everyone—
I won't work today!

"Waiting for our paychecks like crawling to Beijing"
The master machinist said to me
We need a new president!

After work, hung out a bit with friends
No longer welcome where I once lived
Like Alice, I'm tired of wondering . . .

7. A SEVEN-COURSE LUNCH

a. Miso Soup

GENNADY: So my wife up and died. Ran across the street, that moron. She doesn't look around. So that's it. Before dying, she'd prepared soup for the week. She always prepares it on Mondays to get the cooking over with. And it lasts until Friday. When they ran her over, I buried her and ate the soup. Then I saw that the soup isn't running out. I figured that out on maybe the third week. I was taking the pot out of the refrigerator and there was just enough for one bowl. But the next day—again, enough for just one bowl. I nearly pissed my pants. I threw out the pot. I'm eating canned beef. Then it dawns on me that she had prepared . . . all of this for me. But since then, I've learned how to make my own soup. And with that, whaddaya call it—seafood—from a can—well, all kinds of soup. But at first it always turned out disgusting, I couldn't even put it in my mouth.

b. Tori Unagi Sushi

RENAT: Damir and I went to a restaurant. Damir got a job at a little firm where they repackage cement by the kilogram. Say, if you have a hole at home, you don't need a whole bag, right? So. They were making big bucks on this. So he got his paycheck and we went to a restaurant. There was a bar on the way. And he said, let's drink some liquid courage. So we do three shots. Then after that . . . well, anyway, we get to the restaurant, and I don't remember what happened there. But anyway we spent maybe fifteen, maybe twenty dollars total. So next time, same recipe. I take my wife to the restaurant like this, then Sergei and I go. So I'm there all the time. And maybe on the fifth visit they don't let me in. That doesn't work so well with me. So I tear the place apart, basically. I'm in the cage for two weeks. And one dude in there teaches me a recipe for raw fish. I tried it at home after that—I can't, my stomach can't handle it. But my wife eats it. And nothing happens to her. I think she could probably digest a gearbox. Stomach like a horse.

c. Sake Maki Rolls

PETER: So my girl is on the way to the maternity hospital. You know, just a regular maternity hospital, Soviet era. They confiscate her phone before she goes into labor. The doctor takes it, said it's going to interfere with the equipment.

So the whole time she's giving birth, she's looking around to see that the doctor doesn't steal her cell phone. So she gave birth, made all her phone calls to say that everything is alright, and tells me she needs me to sneak underwear past the guards. All the women there get their underwear confiscated. Unclear why. That's the way they do it. So I roll up some women's underwear in a cookie box (*Demonstrates.*). And I get the old lady guard to hand it to her. So my girl is now a queen—she has underwear and the others don't. Anyway, I guess it travels through the grapevine, and the next day seven guys show up at my house to learn how to roll up underwear. And seven more the next day. So we solved the problem. And later she calls me and says, can't you, like, get me a package of cookies, for once? I never have anything for my tea.

d. Eel-Unagi Rice Bowl

ANDREY: So we went fishing. My roommate, he was down and out. So I took him with me, and he was in some shit, his girl left him because he gave her gonorrhea, he lost his job, and other stuff too. The guy needed rescuing. So we're sitting on the dam. And I look over—he's hanging his head, sniveling, staring into the water. I say, let's drink to warm up, it's cold. He says, let's. I say, can you reach that by any chance. But we're sitting right on the wall, over the water. So he turns awkwardly and *whoop*—falls. He fell for a long time, twenty-five feet straight down. And then the water spun him around and whirled him and, like, he was able to get out only 250 yards down. And I was right there with the vodka. He drank, stopped shivering, and then he says, everything fucking sucks. Well fuck, I say, yeah. Everything he says, in general, sucks, especially you. Well fuck, I say, tell me something I don't know.

And after that it was like I had a new roommate. He stopped throwing his old socks everywhere, got married, got a job at the factory. He became a man. And I really think I helped him that time, when I pushed him off the dam.

e. Sencha Tea

ZHENYA: My granddad was visiting recently. My granddad is, like, still in fighting form. He came to take care of his benefits paperwork—and right away found himself a woman. And she's from some kind of ensemble of shitty folk music, where they howl like they're at a funeral. So anyway, I come home, and they're all pissed drunk, the whole ensemble. Fifteen or so old women, I'm not shitting you. I was kicking them out until two in the morning. And my granddad is all quiet and shamed. And I'm so tired, shit, and this is after a full day of work. . . . I say, grandpa, put the kettle to boil. Then I pass out. I wake up from the smoke. The reek is so thick, you could hang an axe on it, and my granddad is gone, the door is wide open. He probably ran off, didn't even close the door. The old goat put my electric kettle on the stove and, when it melted, he poured water all over it and made off. Eventually, a package comes from the village. I open it: a tea kettle. Cast iron. I planted marijuana in it. Soon it'll be as big as a Christmas tree. (*Demonstrates.*) I'm gonna decorate it for the holidays.

f. Sake

HERO: Oleg came for a short stay. He serves in the border guard in the east. When he got the notice, he was so rasta, wore a leather jacket. . . . I shaved his head myself during the sendoff party. He was drunk, started crying. I don't want to go to the army, he was saying, they're all assholes. Well, that was back then. Now, he tells me, tons of Chinese are trying to cross the border. Over there they get the death penalty for betraying the motherland. He says, when we find a trespasser, we have to take him back, turn him over to the Chinese government, we have to use our boots and rifle butts on their heads, kick them back to the border by any means necessary, and they hold on to the ground by their hands and teeth, trying to hang on, not wanting to die. He was telling all of this to us, his old friends, and he was laughing. Lena made a face and left right away, and the others left one by one. I stayed alone with him, because I'm the only one who understands him. Then and now. We got drunk. He started crying, saying all the civilians have become such shitheads, like Lena for example. He gave me a bottle of Chinese vodka, not sake but similar. One Chinese guy tried to bribe him with it so he wouldn't turn him in.

g. Dessert

MAGNETIC GIRL: A Japanese theater visited Belarus, when I was there with my mother Veronika Simonovna Ruinina. I had sufficient free time to see the one and only show that they did there. The first shock I got was when I learned that in this theater all the female roles were performed by men. "Oh well," I said to myself sadly, "another life path that's closed off to me. You will not be a Japanese theater star. Don't plan on it." The second shock was basically the play itself. What it was about, I couldn't tell you, but I remember one scene quite clearly. In the playbill it was called "The Battle of Good and Evil in a Dark Room." Good and Evil, two allegorical figures: their eyes are closed and they dance with swords. And entirely by chance, their blades never touch each other. Slowly and beautifully. Beautifully and slowly. I watched them and cried, because it really did seem like the truth about the way my life is arranged. Too many people are waving their swords around in the dark room of my soul.

FACTORY RADIO STATION: . . . At a ratio of one to one. Altogether, one thousand two hundred and fifty-six matchboxes were used. This model of a metalworking lathe, and other such stunning pieces, can be viewed in the technology museum of the factory, ready to welcome you every day from 10 a.m. to 7 o'clock. The museum is closed for lunch from twelve to one and, for sanitary day, every penultimate day of the month. To purchase tickets and group passes for guided tours, please contact the union committee.

And now, in world culture news: the Theater of Silence continues its tour, with show dates on the twenty-third, twenty-fourth, and twenty-fifth of February, in the Electric Industry Cultural Center. The mysterious pantomime of this theater (Hamlet: valiant, sinful; Ophelia: honest and passionate) will transport you to Shakespeare's time, a time of secrets and intrigues in the Dutch royal court.

8. AN ENCOUNTER IN MACHINE SHOP 2–48

HERO *is fidgeting near the enormous Aggre-Gator, holding a small 6 by 8 wrench in his hands. This is the shop, it stretches one hundred yards to the right and four hundred to the left of* HERO. *In his new coveralls he sticks out sharply among the other workers in their greasy work clothes, like a penguin that accidentally ended up in a chicken coop.*

GENNADY *sits astride the Aggre-Gator, like a cowboy on a mustang. From time to time he pounds on it, on the Aggre-Gator, with a metal hammer. The Aggre-Gator seems to like that. Why that is is not exactly clear.*

GENNADY: First, I bought her from Troll. Seemed like everything was okay, only the oil seals were leaking. The seals were special, nonstandard. Went and bought those. Cost me half a paycheck. So here I am driving and I realize that something is knocking. Must be the valves, I think. Because Troll's assistant regulated them for me, 'cause I don't trust the natives, they'll screw anyone over. Knock, knock, knock, and then I realize, like, maybe the crankshaft. Or worse, the pistons are busted. So this is serious. I stop over in some kind of village. There's a ton of them between Moscow and Yaroslavl. Anyway, I raise the hood. And damn it to hell, there's a hole in the engine block, in the coolant passage, and the whole thingamajig sticking out. That's a major repair.

HERO: I'm sorry, but can you tell me, this new uniform they gave me, I don't understand: am I supposed to take it home after work or leave it here?

GENNADY: Guess how much? Two thousand seven hundred bucks. And what's more, I slept and drank there, and treated the mechanic to lunch too. I couldn't buy him alcohol when I saw his measuring tools. Old, slimy, with a margin of error of about two hundred. The only thing he said out loud the entire time was "all the joints and connectors need to be rubbed with a clean but unwashed rag." I'll be on my deathbed, and I won't forget that "all the joints and connectors need to be rubbed with a clean but unwashed rag."

HERO: Gennady, is it lunch soon?

GENNADY: You know what, I don't like you. So you got an engineering degree, so you think in a couple months you'll worm your way into an engineering job? Don't hold your dog breath.

HERO: I don't—

GENNADY: First work here for a couple years and then make demands. Understood?

HERO: I'm really not—

GENNADY: So listen then. We finished up, and I get in and he yells, start 'er up!—

HERO: You know, I'm also fucking tired.

- I'm fucking tired of you bringing up my college education.
- So I have an engineering degree, so what?
- Does that mean I'm not a human being, then?
- Am I worse than you all?
- Have you read even one book in your shitty life?
- Why hate people who are fucking smarter than you?
- You know what, you're an illiterate ape who doesn't know anything besides his hammers.
- My fucking books in your way, or what?
- Maybe I wanna fucking throw all the fucking books out of my head, so what now?
- So I can't work then?
- I have to sit at home then?

GENNADY: So then I realize that there is some suspicious knocking. We open the hood and look. Nothing. We closed it and drove around. Seems normal, but then this scratching again. Six times we looked. No smoke, no chips. I changed the oil, got to my destination, and only then did I figure it out. That shithead left his wrench under my hood.

The Aggre-Gator abruptly starts up.

HERO (*Yelling over the Aggre-Gator*): Asshole!

GENNADY: What I'm saying!

FACTORY RADIO STATION: Shop manager Egor Kuzmich Fingerev weighed in on these events at the last meeting. Let's read from the meeting transcript: "It is medieval barbarism, it is savagery, to think that modernization, that is, the introduction of manipulator robots in machine shops 6, 3, and 12, will take jobs away from machinists. The whole point of the technology is to reduce employee workload and to improve the work process." Nevertheless, acts of vandalism continue. Just recently, factory cooks Demyatin and Sankov fished a Robotic Welding Machine Z-60 out of a stockpot. Repairmen called to the scene judged it inoperative.

9. "PATHS TO THE WAREHOUSE"

Gennady Vasiliev, machinist at Thunderclapping Shop 2–48.

GENNADY:

"A wonderful country, the Rhineland,
Home to the sparks of myriads"
The master machinist said to me
Give me the g-rhine-der . . .

A tray with soup bowls lies on the floor.
People are quiet. Silence.
The sob of the cleaning lady—
Cry of a mockingbird in the forest.

Summer. It's hot. In the locker room,
The wind's movement
Is thick.

On the blue enamel, words scratched in:
Masturbetter CornAr
Nearby, a photo:
Julia Roberts.

At the security checkpoint,
People pressed shoulder to shoulder
The feeling of another's shoulder
Helps to get through Monday

Before the game, I climbed on the roof
To fix the antenna
Froze. In the window across: a Naked Woman.
Must mean good luck.

Smashed my head against a lifting jack.
In a flash, it'd come alive,
So I bashed it with crowbar.

10. LOCKER ROOM: ZHENYA THE FAVORITE

Straight corridors of upright lockers resembling box graves. A worker by every locker. Everyone is here: GENNARY, RENAT, ZHENYA, PETER, ANDREY. *Everyone is changing before going home.*

RENAT: . . . Fifty, he says. For a fifty I'd catch a sparrow in the field and fuck it!

ZHENYA (*Handing* RENAT*fifty rubles*): Go ahead.

Everyone laughs. HERO *laughs tensely, artificially.*

GENNADY: Do you have another fifty?

ZHENYA: No, why?

PETER (*Softly*): Fucking alcoholics . . .

ZHENYA: Oh, I get it. Beer?

GENNADY: Are you suggesting pitching in for vodka?

ANDREY (*In passing*): I didn't see anything, I didn't hear anything, and I have thirty rubles.

GENNADY: We also have a newbie, by the way.

Everyone stares at HERO. *He freezes, with his pants down.*

PETER: Let's do it on Friday. That's my birthday, we'll get together and toast.

GENNADY: You're just tryna bail.

PETER: Every damn day, though!

RENAT (*Gestures to stop him*): Enough, enough, don't whine. (*To* HERO.) So it's your first day working here, isn't it? You have to treat us.

HERO: Me?

GENNADY: I'm gonna lose my mind with this guy. Andrey, let him follow someone else around, he's a damn kid—

ANDREY (*Shrugs*): What do I have to do with it? You should train him, you have the most experience out of all of us.

GENNADY: Got yourself a scapegoat—

ZHENYA: Why are you all turning on him? See, now he's embarrassed.

He comes up to HERO *and hugs him around the shoulder. The latter stands there, still with his pants down.*

ZHENYA: Pull your pants up, you'll feel more confident. Like a man.

HERO *quickly zips his pants and straightens up.*

ZHENYA: Here's the deal. You got a job, you should try to fit in with the group. Usually fitting in happens after work on the first day. But no one is forcing you. (*To the others.*) Am I right?

GENNADY: Well, traditionally—

ZHENYA: Anyway, as you wish. But if you want to fit in, there's no better way.

HERO: I—I could—

GENNADY (*Snorts*): He could! (*Throwing his bag over his shoulder.*) Alright I'm out.

ANDREY: Wait, wait, Gen. (*To* HERO.) You have to want this, understand?

PETER: Let's drink on Friday, come on.

RENAT: Let's drink when the cows come home.

ZHENYA: Andrey is right. You should want to fit in.

Pause. Lights go out, HERO *is alone, in a spotlight.*

HERO (*Listening to himself*): I—I want to.

Lights on. The workers, already drunk, sit around HERO. HERO *sits down gingerly.*

FACTORY RADIO STATION: But let's give the birthday boy himself a word. Arkady Arkadievich, what is in your thoughts now, what do you celebrate today? After such a long and successful career, observing the vast experience you have accumulated over the years, you can look back and draw conclusions—

A HOARSE MALE VOICE: Look back where? Oh, gotcha. Well, first and foremost I'd like to say hi to the crew.

FACTORY RADIO STATION (*Interrupting*): What has been most memorable for you?

VOICE (*Interrupting*): Wait. So. Hi to all the guys, to Vasilev on the other site, to Sasha the Fatass—

FACTORY RADIO STATION (*Interrupting*): We join all of Arkady Arkadievich's friends in celebrating his retirement, and wish the birthday boy—

ZHENYA (*Drunkenly*): Turn that off.

HERO *switches the radio off.*

RENAT: *That* was a good story. And you're telling me about mushroom picking.

GENNADY (*Abruptly*): Bit by bit.

PETER: No, I mean, it's not that I don't like to fish—

ANDREY: You don't like it at all. If you liked to fish, you'd tell us.

RENAT: I just think mushroom picking is for women.

PETER: Why, why for women?

ZHENYA (*To* HERO): You smoke?

HERO: Yeah.

GENNADY (*Abruptly*): Don't pour too much.

RENAT: And for children. For the weak, in my view.

ANDREY: For passengers with children and the disabled.

PETER: I just helped a couple times, the kids do most of the picking.

GENNADY (*Abruptly*): I said, don't pour too much.

ZHENYA *and* HERO *walk downstage, smoke. They stand looking ahead, silent, swaying slightly.*

ZHENYA: Stars . . .

HERO: Yeah. It's nice.

ZHENYA: I heard you graduated college?

HERO: Yeah.

RENAT: I take mine out to the forest, and she forages out there, with a basket, while I sit by the car and smoke and wait for her.

PETER: You're not afraid that she'll get lost?

ANDREY: Like the joke, "Why do you never take your old mother to the museum?—I did once, but she returned!"

GENNADY (*Abruptly*): Hey asshole, I said don't pour too much. And what did you do?!

ZHENYA: What's it like in college? Lots of faggots, I bet.

HERO: No. Why faggots?

ZHENYA: I don't know. We don't have faggots at the plant.

HERO: Of course not, why would you?

GENNADY (*Abruptly*): Hey shithead, I'm gonna rip your throat out of your ass! What did I tell you to do?! And what did you do?!

RENAT, PETER, *and* ANDREY *finally turn to* GENNADY, *who is sleeping.*

RENAT: Maybe we should wake him up?

ANDREY: He doesn't seem to be having a nightmare. Let him sleep.

RENAT: What was I saying?

PETER: You were telling us how you take your wife to pick mushrooms.

RENAT: Nothing to tell. She's good at mushroom picking.

ZHENYA: You know what I want to say to you . . .

HERO: What?

ZHENYA: You're a good guy.

HERO: You too.

ZHENYA: Want me to suck you off?

HERO: What?

ZHENYA: Nothing.

HERO: I thought that . . .

ZHENYA: What did you think?

HERO *shakes his head.*

ZHENYA: I'm gonna kill you if you tell anyone.

HERO: I won't tell.

ZHENYA: You're not a faggot for sure?

HERO: For sure.

ZHENYA: Don't tell anyone. Okay?

HERO: I won't. Really. I have nothing against fags, they're people just like—

He doesn't finish the sentence because ZHENYA *hits him across the face.* HERO, *flailing his arms, tries to take a swipe at* ZHENYA. *The latter pays no attention; he is methodically beating him.*

PETER, RENAT, *and* ANDREY *run to intervene.* GENNADY *wakes up from the noise, gets up with great effort, and approaches them.*

ZHENYA: He called me a fag!

HERO: *Called* you? You *are* a fag!

ZHENYA (*Trying to escape* RENAT*'s bear hug*): I'm gonna fucking kill you right now!

GENNADY (*To* HERO): That's not a good start to your job here. Understand?

HERO: I understand.

GENNADY: Run and get the next bottle then.

ANDREY: Alright, now you have to, how does the song go, "shake hands and part ways for the long separation ahead . . ."

ZHENYA: He can go fuck himself!

ANDREY (*Commanding*): Gen!

GENNADY: I'm gonna have you sitting with a grinder straightening out edges all week, got it?

ZHENYA: Why the hell am I—

GENNADY: Because I said so. I'm chief. Everybody make up, right fucking now.

ZHENYA *and* HERO *reluctantly shake hands.*

ANDREY (*Cheerfully*): Now that's good teamwork.

HERO: It's hard to be a faggot in a factory.

FACTORY RADIO STATION: It's hard to be a secret agent among enemies—who might discover your identity at any moment—especially when the lives of thousands of people depend on you. But today, the descendants of the hero—all of us—can see the significance of his deed. Vasily Clampin's book *To Blow Up the Sturmbannführer* can be purchased every day during lunch break at a special low price, at B Building checkpoint 27.

And a special announcement. The HR Department is seeking a cleaner. To apply, please see Anna Gregorevna Thornina during work hours.

11. "VACATION IN NOVEMBER"

RENAT STEEDOV, *machinist in Fleet Vehicle Services.*

RENAT:

They found a screw in my pocket.
Damn rent-a-cops.
For them, it's like
The whole world exists for a screw.

All I know is:
A smoke break and the grass by the hangar,
Crushed, littered with cigarette butts,
That's all I need to be happy.

Morning. Hangover. The inky blue of the stations
In the bus the light is so bright
You'd rather take Antabuse

The welding robot dreams of night
I dream of sky beyond the hangar's vault
Of sky that will not be lit up
By fire alarms

The master plays on the koto
Even in my dreams I know
That I have to get up at five-thirty

Behind the fence, another site.
It's better, it's cleaner, it's nicer.
And there's Lena the tool setter . . .

Old man Borisych inspected the crew.
No kidding, he said.
And right then—
But we brought him back to life.

12. DREAM OF THE BLUE CHAMBER

At the table, PETER, GENNADY, RENAT, ZHENYA, *and* HERO *sit in a row on one bench. They stare silently at an ashtray full of cigarette butts.*

ANDREY *appears.*

ANDREY: Seems alright, but I'm covering for your asses one last time. Take 'er out.

Pause.

ANDREY (*To* PETER, *carefully*): Pete, we're gonna celebrate your birthday, right?

PETER (*Sadly*): Thirty years. Like hair off a dog.

Pause.

ANDREY: Something happen?

GENNADY: Damn right.

ANDREY: I don't understand.

RENAT (*Sharply*): The Korean was caught. Right at the checkpoint. Two liters he bought at the pharmacy, two pure liters.

Pause. ANDREY *sits down with the men and, with them, stares at the ashtray.*

ANDREY: How did it happen?

RENAT (*Lively at first, then apathetic and dejected*): Same way it usually happens, you know. What are we carrying? Lemonade, man. Now that's very interesting, what kind of lemonade? We would very much like to know. Peach-flavored lemonade, I just love peaches so much. Why don't you show us your peach-flavored lemonade? Sure, here it is. Open that, please. (*Pause.*) Right. . . . Here it is . . .

PETER (*Shyly*): Guys, is anybody hungry? I brought some canned food. Made the fish myself, though. I don't trust my wife, I made it myself and . . . here.

HERO (*Listlessly*): We should get someone outside of the territory and feed them.

Pause.

ZHENYA: The cherry isn't growing on my dacha. My neighbor's dacha, I look there, the cherry is blooming. I could look at it all day, it's gorgeous. And I don't have shit.

RENAT: Is the soil imported?

ANDREY: Does the manager know already?

RENAT: If he did, you woulda found out.

GENNADY: Damn right.

ZHENYA: There's just this wretched gravel. The soil was brought in afterward.

HERO: The dachas by the old factories are supposed to be cheaper. Only problem is, every time it rains, the soil gets this crusty layer. Can't break it with a crowbar.

RENAT (*Judiciously*): Well, it's for those who like order on their shop floor.

PETER: I also cooked some potatoes. If anyone is hungry, please—

ANDREY: Stop it already with the food. All of you better tell me why Huan was the one you sent to the store. The Korean is not only an alcoholic, but he *looks* like an alcoholic. It's like a ticker tape on his forehead: "I'm carrying alcohol, I'm carrying alcohol . . ."

GENNADY: Damn right.

ANDREY: And now what are we gonna do? I'm shop boss so I have to punish him, and then the manager is going to kick my ass to the curb.

RENAT: Hey, easy now—

ANDREY (*Gets up*): Easy, uneasy . . . (*Waves hopelessly, sits down.*)

Pause.

ZHENYA: Fuck it, I'm gonna uproot it and plant buckthorn instead. Looks nasty but at least it's good for tea.

HERO: It's nasty in tea too.

ZHENYA (*Melancholy*): But at least it's good for you.

ANDREY: Gen, you've been here for a long time now, you should know where we can get some now. Give us a hint and Renat will run over.

RENAT: Why me?

ANDREY: Because. What do you say, Gen?

GENNADY: Well, that's a hard one.

Pause. Everyone watches GENNADY.

GENNADY: Well, we'd have to take extreme measures . . .

ANDREY: What extreme measures? We have the money. Right, men?

HERO: I—

ZHENYA: Enough for booze.

GENNADY: Andrey, have you heard of the Blue Machinist?

ANDREY (*Wearily*): Gen, now's not a good time for fairytales. We have an important matter here.

RENAT (*Abruptly*): I saw him once! But from the side. During the third shift, when I stayed back.

ANDREY: Might as well tell me about the Golden Screw and the Killer Forklift. What other ones are there?

GENNADY: That's all bullshit about the forklift and all that. But the Blue Machinist exists. Ask anyone.

HERO: Blue Machinist. Cool.

RENAT: I think it's worth a try.

PETER: Me too. Otherwise I lugged all this food here for nothing.

ZHENYA: Blue Machinist or green—I don't care. Let him be rainbow colored. Call him over.

GENNADY: It's not so easy, men. You have to summon him.

ANDREY (*Getting up*): Well, do as you want, but I'm leaving. Summon the blue guy and tell him to show up tomorrow to work in Huan's place. Alright. Bye everybody.

ANDREY *leaves.*

RENAT: He didn't believe us.

GENNADY: He's the boss, he can't.

ZHENYA: Gen, how should we do this?

GENNADY: Just so you know, he takes a big cut.

ZHENYA: If we don't have enough, I'll pay the rest. As long as it's worth it.

HERO: I, uh, don't have any money. (*Hurriedly.*) But after I get my paycheck—

ZHENYA (*Pats him on the back*): Take it down a notch, bro. I already said, it's my treat.

HERO: Thank you. I'll get you back later.

ZHENYA: Let's do without 'em . . . college manners. Pay back—that's good. Don't pay back—screw you.

HERO (*Smiling*): Screw you.

ZHENYA (*Approvingly*): That's more like it. (*To* GENNADY.) So Gen, what are we doing?

GENNADY: Okay. Now. Does anybody have anything with alcohol in it? Cologne, acetone, something like that?

RENAT: I have this . . . foot wash. It's called "Pirouette."

Everyone stares at RENAT.

RENAT: I bought it for the Korean. We had a bet if he'd drink it. There's still half a bottle left.

GENNADY: It has to be flammable.

RENAT: It is. It's eighty proof.

GENNADY: Bring it here.

RENAT *leaves.*

ZHENYA: Gen, have you ever summoned him before?

GENNADY: Who?

ZHENYA: The Machinist, the Blue Machinist.

GENNADY: I've seen others do it.

PETER: What does he look like?

GENNADY: He looks like whoever he wants to look like.

PETER: I don't get it.

GENNADY: You'll see.

HERO: Do we have to wait a while for him, or?

GENNADY: Why are you all in such a hurry? Like damn kids.

RENAT *RETURNS.*

RENAT: Here's the foot wash. The Korean said it didn't taste good.

GENNADY: We're not gonna drink it.

RENAT: What do we do with it then?

GENNADY: Pour it in the ashtray. Good. Now, light it.

PETER: Now what?

GENNADY: Now repeat ninety-six times: Blue Machinist, come here and bring some drink.

RENAT: Why ninety-six times?

GENNADY: 'Cause it's a fucking magic number, that's why. I'm gonna smoke meanwhile. (*Lights a cigarette.*)

RENAT, ZHENYA, HERO, *and* PETER *lean over the burning ashtray and start to recite the incantation, counting on their fingers.*

GENNADY: That's probably enough.

PETER: We only said it five times.

RENAT: I said it six times.

ZHENYA: Renat said it six times.

GENNADY: I think that's enough. He's on the lookout for people like us. He just needs an excuse to appear.

PETER: I'd like to save a twenty, though, I promised the wife I'd buy eggs.

GENNADY *doesn't have time to answer because* ANDREY *appears. He's swaying and, in general, appears to be quite drunk.*

PETER (*Awed*): A master's master. Andrey, where did you manage?

ANDREY (*Trying to focus his eyes on those seated, gestures as if trying to catch something*): That's it, humans. Now I've got you. Who's boss here?

GENNADY: Me.

RENAT: Gen, Andrey, what's going on?

ANDREY: Why'd you call me? . . . Stupid question, I agree. So what's going on?

GENNADY: They caught our guy with the alcohol at the entrance. And today is this one's (*Points to* PETER.) birthday. So. We're sitting here like morons with nothing to drink.

RENAT (*Nudging* ZHENYA): No, but do you get it? That's the Blue Machinist, that's him.

ANDREY (*Swaying*): I'm observing the . . . whatchamacallit . . . discipline in your ranks . . . doesn't bode well . . .

GENNADY: Renat, shut up. So you gonna help us, Blue?

ANDREY: Help is a relative concept. Give me a cigarette.

GENNADY *gives him a cigarette,* BLUE MACHINIST *lights up.*

ANDREY: Let's evaluate the tasks at hand. Are you trying for a blackout binge or a clean slosh?

GENNADY: Blackout, of course.

ANDREY: We don't do discounts, we don't have sales. Everyone aware of the price?

GENNADY: Of course.

ANDREY: And who's the customer? Who's paying, I mean?

GENNADY: We're splitting. (*Points to* ZHENYA.) And if anything comes up, we have a volunteer sponsor.

ANDREY: Alright. So . . .

The BLUE MACHINIST *takes a pencil and a notebook out of his bathrobe and prepares to take notes.*

ANDREY: You. What's your name?

RENAT (*Standing up*): Renat.

ANDREY (*Writing*): Reeenaaaat. Your wife, Renat, is gonna leave you. She's gonna say, this life is worse than hell, and she's gonna go to her mother's, to Anna Alexandrovna's. And *she's* gonna say, I told you so, shouldn'ta tied up your life with that alcoholic. Understood?

RENAT: Let her go to hell, or wherever she wants to go. And Anna Alexandrovna, I'll see her in hell. My buddy Damir married a Tatar woman, she doesn't say a word about—

ANDREY: Enough! Now, you.

PETER: Peter.

ANDREY: Birthday boy?

PETER: Uh-huh.

ANDREY: You're gonna wake up in the ICU. That's my gift to you. Do you like it?

PETER: Makes sense.

ANDREY: And while you're wasted, the pigs are gonna steal all the money out of your wallet.

PETER: There's not much there. Are they gonna leave a twenty, at least?

ANDREY: Listen to what I'm saying—all the money.

PETER: Well, fuck it then.

ANDREY: Chief.

GENNADY: Gennady.

ANDREY (*Writing*): Gennaaadyy. So. I don't even know what to do with you. Your kind is only good for the furnace.

GENNADY: Damn right.

ANDREY: Remind me, how does it usually go for you?

GENNADY: I drink. Then I don't remember anything. Then I wake up and go to work. Maybe you can make it so I remember everything?

ANDREY: There's nothing to remember.

GENNADY: Well, then, I don't know . . .

ANDREY: Maybe. . . . Got ID on you?

GENNADY: Let me see. . . . Subway pass, factory ID, Blood Donor Legion notebook, passport.

ANDREY: You'll lose them.

GENNADY: Alright.

ANDREY: So. . . . Who's not covered yet . . . (*Squints at* HERO.) What's that on your head?

HERO (*Touching his head*): I don't know. Hair.

ZHENYA: He's a college boy, he just hasn't gone to the barber yet. Otherwise he's alright.

ANDREY: You a rocker?

HERO: Who?

ANDREY: Well that. . . . (*Hums Deep Purple off-key.*) Smoooke on the waa-ter, mm-mmm-mmm-mmm-m-mm. . . . (*Waves hand drunkenly.*) Alright, screw you. So. Next.

ZHENYA: Eugene.

ANDREY: The sponsor?

ZHENYA: Exactly.

ANDREY: So fairly basic here. But first . . . you're gonna break a hand in the doorway. Ready?

ZHENYA: Alright. Whose hand?

ANDREY: I told you: not too many options here.

ZHENYA: Okay. Got it.

ANDREY: So you agree to anything? I'm talking about the price.

ZHENYA: You mean about the hand, or?

ANDREY: I mean about your life.

ZHENYA: What do you mean?

ANDREY: Take care of yourself.

ZHENYA: That's. . . . Thank you.

ANDREY: Take your thank you and stick it you know where. And he (*Points to himself.*) he's gonna lose his bonus.

ZHENYA: What for?

ANDREY: So? We got everyone?

ZHENYA: Why the bonus, though? What's gonna happen? What are you talking about, hey?

PETER: Zhenya, my boy, come on. . . . You got yours, now relax. Don't interfere with others trying to relax.

ANDREY: I didn't forget anyone? Guys, count yourselves, I'm having some trouble.

GENNADY: Seems like you got everyone.

ANDREY: Alright, then I'm off. Ah, and . . . don't burn anything else, it stinks. I'd come anyway.

RENAT: We'll try.

ANDREY: I'm gonna grab this with me. (*Takes the bottle of foot wash.*) No one here is gonna drink this anyway.

GENNADY: Take it, of course.

ANDREY: Alright, take care. (*Starts to leave.*)

RENAT: Hey, you didn't forget anything?

ZHENYA (*Proudly*): We paid ours.

ANDREY: Ah, right. (*Snaps fingers.*) Here you go.

Darkness.

PETER: Boss, comrade, dear comrade boss, I don't give two shits about that twenty. Boss, my dear, give me back the twenty. I'm going to petition the president. Dear president comrade, I don't give two shits about that twenty. Comrade boss. Give me back the twenty. Do you give two shits about that twenty? No? Then give it back. To who? To me. I give shits about it, I give two shits about it, comrade dear president.

(*In a neutral manner.*) Police found Peter Potov sleeping at the terminal stop of the #27 "Poultry Factory" bus line. While Potov was being transferred to the ICU, he woke up and began throwing raw eggs, thirty in all, at the staff, from a carton he had stubbornly clung to up until that moment. ICU employees had no choice but to restrain the inebriated man by force. Thus, he has paid his due in full.

RENAT (*Calmly*): Get the fuck outta here. Who cares? I don't give a shit. I don't give a shit what you say. I wasted my life on you too. I shit on this kinda life. I shit on you. You shit on me? Great, then, fuck outta here. (*Mocking an invisible interlocutor.*) Youth-Shmooth. I shit on your youth. And on my youth.

(*In a neutral manner.*) In accordance with the agreement, Renat Steedov kicked his wife out of the house, so as to bring all relations with her to an end. Upon doing so, he felt the need to reiterate her mistakes to her face, but, for a variety of reasons, was unable to leave the house. He consequently threw out of the window: one ironing board, two begonias, and one cosmetic skincare set for problem skin. His due is paid in full, in accordance with his understanding of what was owed.

GENNADY: It was somewhere here. Lift up your foot, I'll take a look. It was here somewhere, or I'm a bitch. Just now it was lying here. Lift up your foot. I don't need whatever you're fucking giving me, I need mine. Your foot, I said, lift it up. No, fuck you, I don't need that, it was somewhere here. That's not mine. That's not my last name, I need my last name. Lift up your foot, somewhere here . . .

(*In a neutral manner.*) Over and above the agreed dues, Gennady Vasilev also lost his faux fur coat and his salamander shoes, size forty-two, used. Dues were paid according to his inner code of ethics.

ANDREY: You know me, Kuzmich, why write these explanatory memos? If I, for example, well, I don't know . . . I mean, everything is alright, come on. So the guys had a little party, who doesn't from time to time. But Huan I'm going to discipline. He's going to be straightening out edges all week . . .

HERO *appears.*

HERO: Andrey, wait. Er, I mean, wait. . . . Blue?

ANDREY: What? Haven't had enough? You need more?

HERO: No, I just have a few ques—

ANDREY: There you go.

HERO: No, no, I wanted—

ANDREY: Hold this too.

HERO: Enough, or, uh—

ANDREY: And more.

Pause.

ANDREY: You wanted to ask me something?

HERO: Where is the . . .

ANDREY: Where is the what?

HERO: Hhhwere is da . . .

ANDREY: O-o-o-ver there and to the right.

HERO: Riiigghhtt and fuu. . . . Thanks . . .

ANDREY: Where was I? Huan, I'll discipline him. Want me to fire him? I will. But Huan is a professional. It's a shame to let him go. But if you say I have to fire him, I will. But, I repeat, it's a shame to lose a guy like that. It's like ticker tape on his forehead: "I'm a pro, I'm a super-pro." But he's a lush. But if I have to,

I will. But the others, better not discipline them. They've already paid for it, and then some.

ZHENYA: At two o'clock in the morning Eugene Cabbagev was found by a retiree named Vasily Andreyevich Oldov at the doorway of 18 Dzerzhinsky Street. In response to the latter's attempt to help him get up, Cabbagev cruelly attacked the elderly man and chased him to his apartment. Fifteen minutes later, in an attempt to determine the root of the conflict, the son of Vasily Andreyevich damaged the radial bone in Cabbagev's right arm. Vasily Andreyevich's wife, a retired veterinarian, fixed a splint to Cabbagev's damaged arm. Cabbagev owes further payment in due time and at the earliest opportunity, in accordance with the honor code.

(*Drunkenly.*) Let go my hand. (*Pause.*) Let go my hand, bitch. (*Pause.*) Bitch, let go my hand. (*Pause.* ZHENYA *attempts to hit the person bandaging his arm.*) I said, give me back my hand, bitch. (*Again attempts a punch. Receives a slap in return, causing him to fall from his chair.*) Don't hit me, let go my hand. You bitch. (*Pause. Someone continues to bandage his arm.*) I paid, understand? And you're a bitch, not letting go my hand.

Lights dim. Only the factory radio is audible.

FACTORY RADIO STATION: Despite the expansion of the administration's efforts to prevent the transport of alcohol onto plant premises during the holidays, the work crews of machine shops 5, 18, and 22 were unable to carry out their duties due to extreme alcoholic inebriation. Shop managers are urged to reprimand employees in the aforementioned crews, as well as take away February bonuses from those who engaged in such odious disobedience of factory policies. In fact, the statistic is grim: in the first two weeks of February, the guards confiscated almost six tons of alcohol. And now, on to other news . . .

Melancholy—and, preferably, ancient—Chinese music.

13. "NIGHT SHIFT FLAME"

EUGENE CABBAGEV, *AutoVAZ machinist.*[3]

ZHENYA:

All quiet in the shops
Only somewhere, forlorn,
A sledgehammer thumps on a bumper
Third shift

All the females in Accounting
Smell like jasmine and rose
Gonna give them a sheet metal wrench
If they would only . . .

Buddy not coming to work
Probably drinking.
Dogs sniff 'round the shop.

Without cussing, the engineer explains
The work schedule
In the reflection on his eyeball
I see Jesus

A moment of insight under a KAMAZ truck
It feels like
Getting whacked with a crowbar

Seeing the beauty, the master
Shed tears on his sleeve:
Cottonwood fluff settles on diesel

A bit of frozen lip torn out with my cigarette
Dominos echo, falling from the sky
Alec, asleep, leans on the tank

14. DEATH IN VENTILATION

ZHENYA *lies on the table. Either he was carried here, or he has been lying here for a long time. Everyone else is also here.*

ANDREY: They'll come soon, I called already. I'll go take a look, see what's happening.

Leaves.

GENNADY (*Studying his hands*): Frayed wire. Product defect.

RENAT: Let me see.

GENNADY: You see, it came into contact with the metal cabinet of the air handler, here and here.

RENAT: Yeah, I see.

GENNADY: Product defect, dammit.

Throws it on the ground. HERO *picks up the bearing, looks at it.*

HERO: When we carried him, he had sunflower seeds falling out of his pockets.

GENNADY: Well, that's a matter of course.

HERO: Like in the fairytale about the brother and sister that wanted to remember the way home.

GENNADY *snatches the wire out of* HERO*'s hands and throws it on the ground.*

GENNADY (*Irritably*): Throw it out. Damn it. I told you—a defect.

Awkward pause.

PETER: Yesterday this, what's it called . . . reality TV show was on. Anyone watch it?

RENAT: When?

PETER: At nine.

RENAT: I didn't watch. I was picking my wife up from my mother-in-law's. The old hag. It's like, everybody's already kissed and made up, but she's still following us, walking behind us all the way to the station. Walking and mumbling and griping, you know. That's how much energy she has. . . . Wanna know how her husband died? Climbed into a bathtub full of boiling water and croaked. And the first one, know how he died? Fell off the balcony. That's how bad her energy is, it drives people to their death.

HERO: Whenever I imagined death, it was never like this.

PETER: Is it even imaginable? Like yesterday in that show—

GENNADY: What happened in the show?

PETER: So a Tajik left his family and came to Moscow looking for work. And he was hired . . . to play a terrorist. So his wife sees him on the TV and, like an idiot, decides that he's really become a terrorist. So she decides to rescue him. How's she gonna rescue him? She goes to real terrorists and says, like, I'm with you guys, I wanna bomb people too. She thought she might find her husband that way. The terrorists were really happy, obviously. They gave her a suicide belt and put her on the main square and blew her up. And this was all filmed, so her husband saw on the news how she was blown up and how all of it happened. Imagine that, she saw him in a movie and he saw her on the news.

GENNADY: You wouldn't get cast, you hillbilly.

RENAT: *I'd* get cast.

PETER: Yeah, you have a Tatar name, but your face. . . . Listen, Renat, if you were on a deserted island and the only thing you have for food is hunk of pork (*Demonstrates.*), what would you do?

GENNADY: Oh, you'd eat pork alright.

RENAT: I'd use the pork to catch fish in the sea.

They laugh. ANDREY *returns.*

ANDREY: They'll be here soon, they're already on site.

GENNADY: Did you hear what Pietro here figured out? If Renat was on a desert island and didn't have anything except pork, that would be the end of Islam for him.

ANDREY: Yeah, really.

RENAT (*Repeats*): I'd use the pork to catch fish in the sea.

ANDREY: You're a smartass fucking Tatar, Renat.

PETER: He knows how!

ANDREY: Alright, jokers. Let's lift 'im up?

Everyone turns to ZHENYA.

14. THE LAST CHECKPOINT

Morning. RENAT *and* HERO *are at the security checkpoint, just like at the beginning.* MAGNETIC GIRL *stands at the entry, checking IDs.*

FACTORY RADIO STATION: . . . Would like to express heartfelt gratitude to everyone who participated in the volunteer cleanup. The scrap metal gathered on site amounted to twenty-eight tons. However, as noted by chief of security Boris Vasilevich Adventov, among the collected recyclables there appears to be no nonferrous metal—a highly suspicious circumstance . . .

RENAT: Oh look, a newbie. Hey, why is it that factory women are always so ugly?

HERO: So that they think about work, not about . . . (*Notices that* MAGNETIC GIRL *is calling him over.*) Shit, gonna get scanned, looks like.

RENAT: Most important thing is, don't let them pass that thing by your zipper. You'll regret it later.

HERO: Right, I remember. Okay, see you in a bit.

RENAT *goes on, while* HERO *goes up to* MAGNETIC GIRL *and, without waiting for the request, opens up his bag to show its contents.*

HERO (*Businesslike*): That's a CD player, and that's a permission form for it from the shop manager. That's lemonade. Apricot flavored. That's an electric drill, I borrowed it to use at home and now I'm returning it. That's a permission note for it from my master machinist. Here's the date, below, today's date, you see. (*Quieter.*) How did you end up here?

MAGNETIC GIRL (*Happily*): You remembered me? I thought—

HERO: Ah, I get it, magnet superpowers. Want some lemonade? It's pure. Drink up.

MAGNETIC GIRL (*Extends her hand*): Alright, why not, to our reunion—

MAGNETIC GIRL *drinks from the lemonade, swallows quietly, and grimaces.* HERO *gives her a bite of the sandwich he takes out of his pocket.*

HERO: My wife packs me these sandwiches, because the cafeteria food tastes like it's cooked with machine oil. I'd be lost without her. Oh, I forgot, you didn't know I got married.

MAGNETIC GIRL (*Recovering her breath*): Did you? That's probably the most surprising thing I could have heard since I started working here.

HERO: Yeah, two months ago. It's a totally different life. Renat says that we'll start arguing soon but so far, everything is fine, knock on wood. How's your personal life stuff?

MAGNETIC GIRL: What personal life stuff? Look around, look closely. Well, what kind of personal life stuff can happen here?

They look around. The time is 6:05 a.m.

HERO: Hmm, yeah, I guess. You know, I can't even imagine how you got here. I forgot how to imagine, I guess.

MAGNETIC GIRL: It's tough to be a strange creature in a place where everyone is first and foremost concerned with the care of their genitalia. It's much more difficult than—for example—coming to terms with one's homosexuality in the thunderclapping shop. Everything in this world is completely accidental, and that's why an extraordinary person like me can work at a security checkpoint as a metal detector, among brutish, superstitious factory workers. Everything is accidental—even choice.

HERO: What's this all about?

MAGNETIC GIRL: I wanted to say that this is precisely why I decided to live and work as I live and work now. Those are my reasons.

HERO: No kidding. More lemonade?

MAGNETIC GIRL *shakes her head.*

HERO: Alright, look me over. Time for me to head to the site, Andrey's gonna cuss me out if I'm late. But do it by hand, not with that thing, otherwise Anya is gonna be unhappy.

MAGNETIC GIRL: As you wish. (*Grins.*) It's your choice.

MAGNETIC GIRL *pats down* HERO.

HERO: That's all? You didn't magnetize anything, did you? You sure? Alright, then I'm off.

Turns around to leave.

MAGNETIC GIRL: You're not bored? You don't get bored sometimes?

HERO: Bye.

HERO *leaves.* MAGNETIC GIRL *looks on sadly.*

15. THE END OF THE SHOW

HERO *stands on stage. Behind him, seated, are* RENAT, ZHENYA, GENNADY, ANDREY, *and* PETER.

HERO: Probably time to end. Some things turned out well, some not.

ANDREY: It turned out bullshit. Like it's about you, not about us. We wanted to make it about us.

HERO (*Agreeing*): Hm, right, that's true, that's shitty. I didn't want it to be like that.

PETER: Yeah, Andrey's laying down the truth.

ANDREY (*Gets up*): Alright, I'm off. Put this table away after this and all these, what are they called . . .

ZHENYA: Decorations.

ANDREY: Exactly. So everything's clean after you all. I'm gonna check. I'm the one who's gonna get shit from the management here, not you.

Leaves.

RENAT: It's like, just some shitheads drinking the whole time and that's all. Not doing anything else. But I have, like, an inner fucking world and everything.

HERO (*Animatedly*): Renat, but that's exactly the, that's exactly what I wanted to, shit. . . . Because they all think they're better than you, that their art is the shit, and you all are just . . . cattle. But it's not like that at all, you know? I wanted to prove that, that you're better.

ZHENYA: We're better regardless. Otherwise why the fuck did I die in your story?

GENNADY: Pete and Renat clear the table. Zhenya everything else. I'll switch the lights off.

PETER *and* RENAT *obey his instructions.*

PETER (*Picking up his side of the table*): I talked to their main guy before the show. He showed me on the meter how much electricity they're using up. It's nuts.

RENAT (*Picking up his side of the table*): It's because they're constantly boiling water for tea. They don't do anything else, just drink tea all day. The kettle eats up electricity like a pig eats swill.

RENAT *and* PETER *carry the table offstage.*

HERO: Hey, wait, dammit!

ZHENYA (*Indifferently*): Go to hell.

HERO: You go to hell.

GENNADY: Alright, calm down you all. Making a damn racket.

Everyone leaves. HERO *is alone on stage. He is looking now at the public, now after the workers who left.*

GENNADY (*Offstage*): You coming or what?

HERO: Yeah, I'm coming.

Leaves.

THE END

THE LOCKED DOOR

PAVEL PRYAZHKO

TRANSLATED BY MAKSIM HANUKAI

IN THE CENTER

A nursing home. Evening. An elderly man sits in a room reserved for games and socializing. He is singing a folk song. There is no one else in the room. Most likely he is already suffering from dementia.

■ □ ■

A shopping mall. Natasha, a person of Eurasian appearance, works at the shopping mall. In a small glass shopping booth, Natasha sells different varieties of loose leaf tea, as well as whole-bean coffee, which, if need be, she can grind on the spot. At the moment there are no customers at the kiosk. Natasha stands next to the register. She's not thinking about anything. Natasha checks her watch. It's time for her break. Natasha hangs up a sign with the words "On Break" and disappears into the depths of the shopping booth.

■ □ ■

Standing in a hallway in the service-only part of the shopping mall, Natasha lights a cigarette. Natasha is smoking a cigarette. Having finished smoking, Natasha throws the cigarette butt into the ashbin and returns to work.

■ □ ■

Natasha appears from the other side of the kiosk, as if from the far, dark side of the moon, pauses next to the cash register, and stands there, not thinking about anything. There are no customers at the kiosk.

■ □ ■

A friend of Natasha's who works in a beauty store in the same shopping mall approaches the booth. They already saw each other once today. Natasha doesn't look particularly excited about the friend's appearance.

NATASHA'S FRIEND: Let's go for a smoke.
NATASHA: Not now, I'm gonna work.
NATASHA'S FRIEND: Suit yourself.

The friend leaves. Right then a customer approaches the booth. You can't hear what he's saying. Natasha takes a paper bag, fills it with coffee beans, weighs it, then pours the beans into a grinder, grinds them, pours them back into the bag, hands the bag to the customer. The customer pays for his purchase.

■ □ ■

An apartment. Valery is visiting a friend. Not thinking about anything, Valery waits for his friend to make coffee. Valery's friend walks in with a tray holding two cups of coffee, sets down the tray, and offers a cup to Valery. Valery takes the cup. Drinks. The friend sits down on the couch holding a cup of coffee and also drinks. This does not produce any tension. Each one is preoccupied with his coffee and is not thinking about anything. A cell phone beeps. Valery's friend gets up from the couch, walks over to the phone, reads the new text message. Valery finishes his coffee and gets up from the couch.

VALERY'S FRIEND (*Without taking his eyes off the phone*):
Taking off?

Valery doesn't respond, he waits for his friend to see him out. Without taking his eyes off the phone, the friend is first to make toward the exit in order to see Valery out. Valery follows him.

■ □ ■

An apartment. Valery's at home. He turns on the TV, lies down on the couch, and flips through the channels. Having settled on something neutral—something like Euronews or a channel devoted to animals or to comedy, yes, most likely to comedy—Valery watches TV for a while. Valery doesn't laugh. This does not mean that the program isn't funny. Valery sees and understands that it is funny, but, despite this, his face remains inexpressive. This program does not force, it does not compel Valery to laugh. Valery watches the funny program, then gets up, turns off the TV, turns off the light in the room. Tomorrow's a work day.

■ □ ■

An apartment. Valery gets ready for work. Neither the radio, nor the computer, nor the TV work. Valery sits down on the couch, ties his shoelaces. Valery is well dressed, he keeps up with the latest fashions. Having tied his shoelaces, Valery leaves the apartment.

■ □ ■

A shopping mall. Valery checks his watch. He is waiting for his friend. And there's the friend walking up to Valery. The friend is holding a folder. They already saw each other once today.

VALERY'S FRIEND: My knee hurts.

Valery doesn't care about his friend's knee.

■ □ ■

Valery and his friend sit down at a vacant table near a coffee shop. There are many vacant tables, or rather, all of them are vacant, it's too early for lunch.

■ □ ■

Natasha stands at her station in the shopping booth, next to the cash register. Natasha checks her watch. It's time for her break. Natasha hangs up a sign with the words "On Break" and leaves.

■ □ ■

Sitting at the table, Valery drinks coffee and carefully examines some papers. His friend sits at the same table, also drinking coffee. He is not engaged in anything at the moment and is looking around without any particular interest.

■ □ ■

Natasha and her friend from the beauty store approach the shopping booth. Natasha hastens to enter the booth.

NATASHA: Want me to grind it?

NATASHA'S FRIEND: In a bag! (*Realizing what* NATASHA *had asked.*) No, don't.

Natasha pours the coffee beans into a paper bag, weighs them, hands the bag to her friend.

NATASHA'S FRIEND: Um-hum. (*Takes the bag and leaves.*)

Natasha sits down in a chair, takes out a nail file, and begins to file one of her fingernails, or rather to finish filing it.

■ □ ■

Valery is walking down the street with his phone pressed to his ear, waiting to be connected.

VALERY: Natasha, good evening, sorry for calling you so late, can you talk? . . . No, unfortunately I'm already turning in. Can you come to my parents' with me again?

■ □ ■

Day. Valery and Natasha get on a bus. They find empty seats and sit down next to each other. They both take out their earphones, put them on. They put on music and listen to it. They don't feel at all bored. They don't feel at all like they need to impress one another, they are completely at ease. Remembering something important, Valery touches Natasha's elbow. Natasha reacts, takes out one of her earphones.

VALERY: I've moved in with you. It's closer to work. We're planning to get a dog first.
NATASHA: Okay.

Valery assumes his initial position. Natasha puts the earphone back in her ear. They are carried forward, not thinking about anything.

■ □ ■

Valery's friend and Valery himself are making their way to their seats in a movie theater.

■ □ ■

The light in the movie theater dims, the film begins.

■ □ ■

A comedy is playing at the movie theater. The theater is almost empty. Valery and his friend are watching a film. They understand, they see that it's funny, but their emotions are not tapped in, the film does not compel them to laugh. The same old jokes, which have been repeated a million times in other films. No one in the theater is laughing. One can only hear the crunch of the popcorn and the rustle of paper bags.

■ □ ■

Valery and his friend exit the movie theater. The film is over. They walk to the parking lot. His friend retrieves his car keys and turns off the alarm. The alarm beeps—it's off.

■ □ ■

The kitchen in Valery's parents' apartment. Valery's mother is talking.

Valery peeks into the kitchen.

VALERY (*Without smiling*): Cheese fritters? I'll have some cheese fritters.

Having said this, Valery immediately leaves the kitchen.

■ □ ■

Valery's mother, Valery's father, Valery, and Natasha are sitting at the table, eating. No one is talking. The silence is making Valery's parents a little anxious, or rather, they are a little surprised by it. Both Valery and Natasha are perfectly at ease.

■ □ ■

A room in Valery's parents' apartment. Valery enters, turns on the TV, sits down on the couch, watches TV. On the coffee table next to him there is a glass of water out of which Valery periodically drinks. Valery's mother appears in the doorway. She watches him for some time. She sees that she has a good son, who doesn't drink and who's always well dressed. But something is bothering her. Valery knows that his mother is there but doesn't pay any attention to her. In the years that he has lived away from home, Valery has gotten used to living alone and does not feel compelled to speak right now. Valery gets up, turns off the TV, walks over to his mom, kisses her cheek.

VALERY: Goodnight mom.

Valery turns off the lights, lies down on the couch.

■ □ ■

A nursing home. Evening. Elderly men and women are sitting in a room reserved for games and socializing, singing a merry folk song. Most likely they are all already suffering from dementia.

■ □ ■

Valery's parents' apartment. Valery's parents and Natasha sit in a room. They're having a conversation. To Valery's parents, both Valery and Natasha may as well be aliens. They can see that Natasha is a good girl. She doesn't drink. It's true that she smokes, but she dresses well and she's neat. Nevertheless, something bothers Valery's parents, especially his mother.

NATASHA: I'm interested in all things Arabic.
MOTHER: Are you planning to study anywhere?
NATASHA: No. I've found myself.

■ □ ■

A shopping mall. Natasha makes her way to her shopping booth, enters it. She stands next to the cash register and doesn't think about anything. She's perfectly at ease, and she's not troubled by any vain thoughts. A customer comes over after a while. You can't hear what he's asking. Natasha opens a container with tea, pours some into a paper bag, weighs it, and hands it to the customer. The customer pays for his purchase.

■ □ ■

The service hallway of a shopping mall. Natasha's friend is smoking. Natasha appears.

NATASHA: You're smoking already.

Lights a cigarette, not requiring a response. Nor did her friend have any intention of responding to this rhetorical question. She takes a step toward the ashbin, puts out the cigarette.

NATASHA: How did you like that tea?
NATASHA'S FRIEND: Well . . .

Nods, as if to say, you know, it was so-so, that is, that she has ambivalent feelings about this tea. The friend intends to wait for Natasha to finish smoking. Natasha guesses her friend's wish, hurries to finish smoking.

■ □ ■

A shopping mall. Valery looks at his phone, which he is holding in his hand. Natasha hurries over to him. Natasha's break is about to end, she has to do everything very quickly.

VALERY: We've gotten into a fight. You call to say that, overall, I'm a very good person. If only I didn't have to get up so early.
NATASHA: Why did we get into a fight?

VALERY: . . . walking the dog. That's why we decided to give it away. Also, I'm afraid of responsibility. (*Dials a number, hangs up.*) No. Tell them that you were upset when I didn't walk you home that time, but that we've already made up.

Having dialed the number, Valery hands the phone to Natasha. The call is connected. Natasha speaks in a polite, pleasant tone, just as if she was speaking to her future mother-in-law.

NATASHA: Elena Yegorovna, good afternoon, this is Angelina. . . . My voice? Don't worry, it's nothing. You know. Just a little argument.

■ □ ■

Valery is processing a cash withdrawal at his work station in a bank. He is attending to a client. Having done everything he needed to do, Valery passes the cash and receipt to the client. The client leaves. Valery checks his watch. It's time for his break. Valery hangs up a sign with the words "On Break," lightly stretches on his chair, turns this way and that, then gets up and leaves his work station.

■ □ ■

A shopping mall. Valery and his friend examine the cell phones in a display window, which are being sold in the same kind of glass booth as the one in which Natasha works. Valery leans over to his friend, whispers something. Without taking his eyes off the display, his friend nods, smiles. Valery again turns his attention to the display, to examining the phones. Examining the phones, Valery's friend and Valery himself begin to move along the periphery of the kiosk.

■ □ ■

Valery is in a shoe store in the same shopping mall, trying on a pair of shoes. His friend is standing nearby, sizing up how the shoes fit. Valery is interested in this pair of shoes, but something is bothering him, he needs confirmation from a second party. Valery shifts his gaze toward his friend. His friend gestures with his wrist, screws up his face, as if to say they're so-so, definitely not a masterpiece. Valery again looks at the reflection in the mirror. Having failed to ascertain the quality of this pair of shoes, Valery sits back down, takes the shoes off. His friend sweeps the store with his eyes. He's not thinking about anything at this moment.

■ □ ■

An apartment. Valery has just walked into the apartment. Walks in, sits down on the couch. He can't get the shoes from the store out of his mind. Valery gets up from the couch and exits decisively, leaving the apartment.

■ □ ■

A shopping mall. A shoe store. Holding a box with the same pair of shoes, Valery walks over to an empty seat to try them on. Valery is trying on the shoes, looking at the reflection in the mirror, at how the shoes fit. He still can't come to any final decision.

■ □ ■

An apartment. Valery walks in, turns on the TV, sits down on the couch. He watches TV, but is thinking about that pair of shoes, which he still hasn't bought. This weighs over Valery, this uncertainty troubles him. Thinking about the shoes, Valery gets up, turns off the TV, turns off the lights, and lies down on the couch.

■ □ ■

A shopping mall. A shoe store. Holding a purse and a cell phone, Natasha examines the shoes. She's on break. A pair of shoes catches her eye. Natasha takes the shoes into her hands, examines them, decides to try them on, walks over to a seat, tries on the shoes. She tries them on for no particular reason, she has no intention of buying them. Looks at the reflection in the mirror. Then she takes the shoes off, puts them back in their place, and exits the store.

■ □ ■

In a hallway in the shopping mall, Natasha waits for Valery. They have agreed to meet. Natasha came here from the shoe store. She is holding a purse and a cell phone. Valery approaches, hands her a paper bag with coffee.

VALERY: Thanks, Natasha.
NATASHA (*Smiles, takes the bag*): You're welcome.
VALERY: I hope I can continue using your services in the future. Do you work somewhere here?
NATASHA: Yes. I sell coffee.

Valery rolls his eyes, slaps his forehead. He understands that he has made an inappropriate gift.

■ □ ■

Natasha's apartment. The TV is on. Natasha enters. She has just taken a shower. She's wearing a bathrobe, her hair is wrapped in a towel. Natasha grabs the remote, flips through the channels, looks for a channel with Arabic music, finds a clip with an Arab singer on one of the music channels, sets aside the remote. Watching the clip, she applies cream to her cheeks, forehead, neck. Her face doesn't express anything. Her reaction to the music clip is unclear. It would seem she's just watching it while she's rubbing cream on her face. Natasha has finished applying the mask, gets up, and begins to perform a belly dance. This time her face does express something. Evidently she did need the music for something. Evidently, while she dances, Natasha imagines she is an Arab woman.

ON THE OUTSKIRTS

The rather small office of a company that trades in building materials. Olga sits at her desk, looking over consignment bills and other papers. A customer stands in front of her.

OLGA: Christ, what do you have. Moldings. I forgot.
CUSTOMER: Five kilometers of glass moldings.

It's the middle of the work day and Olga's already feeling a bit tired. Enter Dima, a coworker at the office. Having turned around to see who just walked in, the customer once again turns to face Olga. Dima is wearing a sweater and jeans. Dima was in the bathroom, washing a mug. He sets the mug down in the right place on his desk. Sits down at his desk. Olga finishes filling out the consignment bills. There's another coworker in the office, Slava, a lanky and permanently tired young man. Slava doesn't at all like working in the office. He doesn't think it is the right place for him. But there's one big advantage: the internet. One can keep a diary and download music. Right now, Slava is doing something on his computer, and so is Dima. Only Dima is clearly deriving pleasure from it. He's looking at something interesting, while Slava looks tense. Extending his neck, bringing his face right up to the computer screen, Slava downloads music. Having finished filling out the consignment bills, Olga holds them out to the customer and says.

OLGA: This one's the consignment bill.
CUSTOMER: Uh-huh.
OLGA: This one's for the warehouse.

The customer takes the next piece of paper.

OLGA: This one's for the guard or, Christ, what's his name, at the gate.
CUSTOMER: I know. The watchman.

Olga doesn't let go of the paper, doesn't give it to the customer.

OLGA: No. We don't call him a watchman. We have a fancier name for him. Anyway, the guy in the booth.

Only now does Olga let go of the paper. The customer laughs, takes the paper.

OLGA: Where do they find these people.

Neither Slava nor Dima react to Olga's statement. They are minding their own business. Dima is looking at something amusing, smiles. The customer folds away the papers. Olga takes hold of a pen, begins to play with it, waits for the customer to leave. Her work is done.

CUSTOMER: For storage.

Deliberately exaggerating for comical effect, because such is the character of this young woman, Olga listens to the customer.

The customer has no choice but to respond to such conduct with a smile.

CUSTOMER (*Smiling*): I'll keep this one, this one's for that worker at the gate.

OLGA: That's right, something like that.

Winking, Olga lowers her head to signal consent.

CUSTOMER: I'll come back later today for the paint.

OLGA: Only, I beg you!

CUSTOMER: I know, you close at five.

OLGA: . . . 'cause someone came from your office once!

CUSTOMER: I always come . . .

OLGA: Not you. I'm not talking about you!

CUSTOMER: Who then?

OLGA: This one guy . . .

CUSTOMER: White sneakers?

OLGA: Christ, like I have nothing better to do than look at his sneakers.

CUSTOMER: Vitaly?

OLGA: I don't know. I didn't ask his name.

CUSTOMER: Vitaly's the only one who can come instead of me.

OLGA: Then it must've been Vitaly.

CUSTOMER: Blue jacket?

OLGA: I don't remember. I didn't look at his jacket! I didn't raise my head from and until six thirty!

DIMA: When was this?

OLGA: Friday. Someone came from JSC "Kaliyda" at ten to five, can you believe it? Write up an order for us!

DIMA: Should've told him off.

CUSTOMER: I'll talk to him.

OLGA: That's right! Please tell your Vitaly that because of him I was late to my friend's birthday party.

CUSTOMER: Alright. I'll tell him.

OLGA: Tell him that he can go to hell.

CUSTOMER: Thank you.

OLGA: You remember what's what? Christ, you're not even the first one today!

CUSTOMER (*Smiling*): See you soon.

OLGA: I hope.

CUSTOMER: Have you hung up the towel?

OLGA: After one of you dunked it in the toilet?

The customer knows this story, smiles. Tearing himself away from his computer, Slava suddenly takes an interest.

SLAVA: Someone lowered a towel into the toilet?

OLGA: This happened before your time. This guy came . . . in a Peugeot. Was it a Peugeot, Dima?

DIMA (*Without tearing himself away from the computer screen, still looking at it*): Yes.

CUSTOMER (*Smiling*): Have I ever run into him? I don't know.

OLGA: Don't know! As if I know whether you've run into him or not?!

CUSTOMER (*Smiling*): What kind of Peugeot?

OLGA: Christ! Think I remember! Just a Peugeot! A coupe! And he was pushing stuff into it! We were standing there watching, waiting for his car to burst! Dima, what kind of Peugeot was it?

CUSTOMER (*Turning to* DIMA): A white one?

DIMA: No. Sand colored.

Slava waits for the rest of the story. The customer also stands there, smiling. He wouldn't mind hearing it himself.

OLGA: Someone had given him bad service!

DIMA (*Without taking his eyes off the computer screen*): Sveta.

Everyone turns to face Dima. Dima presses the pause button. He'll listen too.

OLGA: She'd mixed up the delivery slip or had given him another one or something like that, in any case, this, how should I put it, (*Smirking.*) bad man, thaaaat's it, had to make another trip. And this man in his sand-colored Peugeot dunked our towel, the one I always ask my mom to starch, in the toilet. Gave it a rinse.

SLAVA: Gross. (*Again stares at the computer screen, checking to see if it's done or not.*)

OLGA (*To the* CUSTOMER): It was revenge, you see.

Smiling bitterly, the customer nods, because what can one say after that.

OLGA: I mean, what can one say after that.

CUSTOMER: Right!

OLGA: And after that we no longer trust anyone.

The customer wants to leave already, but for some reason he thinks that he needs to endure a pause, to not leave right away.

DIMA: In the final analysis it's . . .

Everyone except Slava turns toward Dima.

DIMA: To make excuses in this case is . . .

OLGA: No! You see, Dima, you don't understand! It has nothing to do with making excuses. The fact of the matter is that we're dealing with ordinary scum.

Glancing at Dima, Olga waits for an answer.

CUSTOMER: Right!

OLGA: You see his royal highness was forced to make another trip!

CUSTOMER: Right! . . . You guys are alright! I should go.

The customer leaves. No one pays any attention to him. Olga waits for Dima to answer. Dima smiles absent-mindedly. He has nothing to say, starts to rock in his chair. Olga can't let it go.

OLGA: Truth be told, we should've called management. Should've turned up the pressure on him to make him fish out the towel.

DIMA: But he's . . .

OLGA: Our management!

DIMA: Oh, you mean ours.

Dima really wants to go back to looking at what he was looking at before.

OLGA: Our management! I mean our management. Or be a man and kick the (*Whispering, but very expressively.*) shit out of him!

DIMA (*Smiling*): Sorry, Olga, I wasn't working here at the time.

OLGA: I know you weren't.

Dima turns whatever he was watching before back on. Olga calms down. Without taking his eyes off the computer screen, Dima says.

DIMA: Slava, you'll eat up all the bandwidth again!

Slava doesn't respond. He needs to move a file he has downloaded into another folder and that's what he's doing. Dima laughs, pressing his fist to his mouth. He's able to pull this off. He's also touching his nose with his index finger.

OLGA: Whatcha got there?

Dima is talking to Olga while staring at the computer screen.

DIMA: The Office.
OLGA: I've seen it.

Dima laughs again.

OLGA: Have you seen *KVN*?[1]
DIMA: No.
OLGA: It was hilarious. That Dvinyatin. I don't get it, is he gay or is that just how he is?
DIMA: What do you care?
OLGA: I don't. Couldn't care less.

Dima presses the pause button, starts to rock in his chair, and tells a story.

DIMA: I have a cousin who's an idiot. A third cousin. Works at a police station or something like that, I don't remember.

Anyway, it's not important. He put on a colonel's uniform and went to the village to impress the girls. Twenty-three years old, a colonel's uniform, told them he'd fought in Karabakh, Chechnya, in three other campaigns.

Slava suddenly puts on some music. Some sort of freak folk with singing in a high male voice. Slava involuntarily smiles.

OLGA (*Upset*): Christ, turn it off!

Slava turns the music off.

DIMA (*Smiling*): Olga likes everything to be beautiful.
OLGA: So what?! (*To* SLAVA.) What did you upload for me? Travis? Cold Play? What was that you played for me yesterday?

Slava mumbles something unintelligible. Olga didn't catch what he just said either, but she thinks it's the name of the band whose music Slava played yesterday.

OLGA: Yes! Can you put it on, please?
SLAVA: I deleted it.
OLGA: I can't wait for vacation.
DIMA (*Smiling*): I know!
OLGA: What do you know, you had yours two weeks ago!
DIMA (*Smiling*): Feels like ages!
OLGA: It's been ages since I've taken a shuttle bus.
DIMA: What do you usually . . . take?
OLGA (*Ignoring the question*): I could drink something.
DIMA (*Gets up. He's ready for tea.*): There's tea in the kettle!

OLGA: Again?

DIMA (*Smiling*): Will you be so good as to spare me some tea?

Olga makes a funny face, as if to say yes, you screwed up. Dima checks the kettle. There's water in it. He turns it on. Then, still in the same spot, says.

DIMA (*Smiling*): First of all, it wasn't tea, but coffee. Wanna smell the mug?

OLGA: Sure you won't burst from all that liquid?

DIMA: Not if you don't jinx me.

Dima exits the office for some reason.

OLGA: Where ya going?

Dima, turning around with a smile, says.

DIMA: Can I go take a leak. Or am I not allowed to do that either anymore?

Olga smiles, Dima exits. Olga shifts her gaze to Slava. Slava is busy doing something on the computer. Olga knows that Slava is not a diligent worker. Olga gets up, approaches Slava.

OLGA: Show me how you format tables.

SLAVA (*Stops what he's doing*): Well, in Excel, yeh you can format them.

OLGA: No. Formatting a document. Can you . . .

SLAVA: What does formatting mean, it mea . . .

OLGA: It means working with columns in Word.

SLAVA: To insert for example.

OLGA: To delete a row.

SLAVA (*Thinking*): What else can you do with a table.

OLGA: What?

SLAVA: Depends on where you're working?

The kettle is about to boil. Olga looks at the kettle, Slava stops talking. Olga is again ready to listen to Slava.

SLAVA: Well, honestly, I don't know if what I'm saying makes any sense, I don't know, after all, accountants have their own software. I don't know how to use it, they have their own application system, 1C:AccountingSuite, but I don't know how to use it. For example, in Excel there's you can set up geometric sequencing. You enter some, you can select parameter A one C six, there's a row like that, for instance a column, you can enter a formula . . .

Done boiling, the kettle switches off. Neither Olga nor Slava pays the kettle any attention. Olga attentively listens to Slava.

SLAVA: You can set up a sequence of years, months, temperatures.

Enter Dima. Olga's done listening to Slava.

DIMA: It's cold today!

OLGA (*Walking to her desk*): Where'd you run off to?

DIMA (*Turning on the kettle again*): To the tinsmiths'. My mother wants a barrel for our dacha. Tea, Slava?

SLAVA: No, thanks.

Done boiling again, the kettle switches off. Slava doesn't drink tea or have lunch with his coworkers on principle. He gets up, gets ready to leave. Dima walks over to the tea and coffee and takes a tea bag.

OLGA: Where you going?
SLAVA: To get some fresh air. (*Leaves.*)

Dima returns, places the tea bag in the mug.

DIMA (*Raises the kettle, says with contentment*): My little kettle.

Pours boiled water into the mug. Olga patiently watches Dima from her desk.

DIMA: Okay! (*Having filled his mug, he looks for the sugar.*) Ah, there it is.

Dima sets down the kettle, takes a few steps toward the sugar bowl, grabs it, returns to his work station, pours sugar into his tea.

DIMA: One spoon, two spoons, three spoons.

Dima stirs in the sugar and only now notices that Olga is not making tea for herself. Smiling (in fact, Dima often smiles), he says.

DIMA: What's going on? Why aren't you making tea for yourself? Or maybe you're waiting for me to make it for you?

Olga doesn't say anything, smiles, looking at Dima.

DIMA (*Smiling*): Don't bother waiting. (*Looks around.*) Right, and where do we keep the. The cookies.
OLGA: There! That's what I was waiting for!
DIMA (*Smiling*): Didn't anyone buy some?

OLGA: Dima, you should be ashamed of yourself! (*Taking her mug, gets up from her chair.*)

DIMA (*Smiling*): Was it my turn?

OLGA (*Makes a face*): Poppy seed cookies are so yummy. (*Takes a tea bag.*)

DIMA: Wait!

Dima is sure that it wasn't his turn to buy cookies. Smiling, Olga stays where she is.

DIMA (*Trying to remember what he bought*): Remember we had those gingerbread cookies with blue with cherry . . .

OLGA: With bluecherry.

While Dima is speaking, Olga smiles.

DIMA (*Ignoring* OLGA*'s dig*): Filling. Those roll waffles. (*Remembering that it's his turn to buy cookies, he immediately trains his eyes on* OLGA. *Smiling, he says resentfully*) I said that?

Olga walks over to the kettle.

DIMA (*Smiling*): I said yummy?! (*Meaning, he's not even capable of pronouncing such words.*)

OLGA (*Smiling, knowing that* DIMA *would never use such words*): Well it wasn't me.

Olga fills her mug with tea.

DIMA: Yummy! You're probably confusing me with Valery Dmitrievich.

Olga, smiling, sets down the kettle.

DIMA: C'mon, Olga!

Abruptly raises her head.

OLGA: You know what! (*Smiling, looks at* DIMA *as if to challenge him, jerks her head.*)

DIMA (*Smiling*): Fine. Not a word.

Smiling, now more calmly, Olga turns away, picks up a teaspoon, uses it to press the tea bag to the wall of the mug, squeezing out the tea. Dima settles into his desk chair, takes his mug, the hot tea. Dima takes a sip.

OLGA (*Without looking at* DIMA, *continues squeezing out the tea from the tea bag*): Don't slurp!

DIMA (*Smiling*): Olga, what do you mean don't slurp!

OLGA (*Smiling, looking at her mug*): I mean don't slurp.

DIMA: You also slurp.

OLGA (*Looking at* DIMA): When?!

DIMA: I heard you. You just don't notice it when you do it.

OLGA (*Looking at her mug*): Sure! (*Uses the teaspoon to fish the tea bag out of the mug.*)

DIMA (*Smiling*): Sure. As if you don't.

Smiling, Olga uses the teaspoon to carry the tea bag to the trash bin.

OLGA: Right!

DIMA: Well then let's listen and see.

Smiling, Olga throws the used tea bag into the trash. Dima watches her. Olga does not look at Dima. She returns for her mug, takes it. Watching Olga, Dima carefully takes a sip of tea.

OLGA (*Smiling, without looking at* DIMA): Guess you're capable of it after all. (*Walks over to her desk.*)
DIMA: Who said I wasn't.

Dima watches as Olga sets her mug down on her desk, settles into her desk chair, takes the mug in her hands, gets ready to drink, and only now, having brought the mug to her lips, notices that Dima is watching her.

OLGA (*Smiling*): Zamirovsky what's going on?!
DIMA (*Smiling*): What, I can't look at you now?
OLGA: Wanna lose your bonus?
DIMA (*Smiling*): No.
OLGA: Then be quiet! (*Looks at her mug.*) . . . What an asswad. (*Takes a sip of tea.*)
DIMA: Look who's talking.
OLGA (*Again looking at* DIMA): Zamirovsky!! . . . You're about to get it! (*Takes a sip of tea.*)
DIMA: Poppy seed cookies . . . so delicious . . . those cookies . . . can't buy 'em anywhere.
OLGA (*Smiling, drinks her tea without looking at* DIMA): Moron.

Dima begins to rock in his chair. Sipping his tea, says.

DIMA: So this fly has a scientist . . .

Slava enters with a sandwich wrapped in plastic.

DIMA: Slava it has meat?!

Slava, making his way to his desk, says.

SLAVA: I eat meat sometimes.

DIMA: You have it all planned out in your calendar?

SLAVA: No.

Slava sits down at his desk. It's as if he has the habit of hiding behind his computer. Slava begins to make noise with the plastic while he unwraps his sandwich. Olga turns away from Slava, looks at Dima in disbelief.

DIMA (*Smiling*): Anyway, this fly has a scientist. Who makes a note of everything he says.

OLGA: Um-hum. (*Drinks her tea, listening to* DIMA.)

DIMA: He conducts an experiment. Tears off two of the fly's legs and commands it to crawl. It crawls. He makes a note.

OLGA: Um-hum.

DIMA: Tears off two more legs. Crawl! It crawls.

OLGA: Um-hum.

DIMA: Makes a note. Tears off its last two legs. Crawl! Crawl! I command you to crawl! The fly refuses to crawl.
Makes a note: after I tore off its last two legs, the fly lost its hearing.

Slava suddenly gets up from his chair. Chewing his sandwich, holding the plastic wrapping from this sandwich in his hand, he rushes out of the office. Slava slouches as he walks, which makes him look extremely helpless. Olga follows Slava with her eyes. Slava has gone out.

OLGA (*Referring to* SLAVA): Imagine the lucky girl. (*To* DIMA.) Dima, do you have a tattoo?

DIMA (*Smiles at the question*): God forbid! Do I look like the sort of person who'd have a tattoo?

Olga frowns, as if to say that Dima's no macho man.

DIMA (*Smiling*): I do push-ups. Want me to show you?

OLGA (*Smiling*): You don't say.

DIMA (*Smiling, but seriously now*): Though one shouldn't after tea.

Dima thinks that it's not good to do push-ups after tea.

OLGA: I'm waiting.

DIMA: Thirty reps!

Olga nods. Dima sets down his mug, takes off his sweater, leaving on his clean but old and washed out t-shirt. This last detail doesn't escape Olga.

DIMA: Count!

Dima gets into the plank position and, performing push-ups, counts.

DIMA: One, two, three, four, five, six, seven, eight, nine, ten . . . (*Until he reaches thirty.*)

Olga involuntarily starts to smile.

DIMA: Thirty! (*Gets up.*)

OLGA (*Smiling*): Fine you're a macho man.

Dima grabs his sweater. Catching his breath, he turns the sleeves inside out and says.

DIMA: Although it's bad for you after tea.

Dima puts on his sweater. Straightening it out on himself, says.

DIMA: I was in Gdansk.

OLGA (*Upset, she has no use for this city.*): No! Don't even!

DIMA: What?

Dima doesn't wait for an answer. He grabs his mug, stretches out his hand so that Olga would give him hers. Olga rushes to finish her tea.

DIMA: Are you counting the days?

OLGA: It's you who's counting instead of me! (*Hands him her empty mug.*)

DIMA (*Takes the mug*): Yeh, I'm counting, can't wait.

Dima makes for the exit with the mugs.

OLGA (*Takes a deep breath*): Like little boys!

DIMA (*On the go, without turning his head*): You think everyone can be replaced?

Dima exits the office. Olga is alone, grabs a pen, props her chin up on her wrist, and plays with the pen. Enter Dima. He has washed the mugs. First he stretches a clean mug out to Olga.

DIMA: Here.

Olga listlessly takes the mug, sets it down on her desk.

DIMA (*Walking over to his desk*): Set up the solitaire board.

OLGA: I don't wanna.

Dima sets his mug down on his desk.

OLGA: It's starting to get a little boring.

DIMA: No! Don't jinx it!

Dima settles into his chair, gets ready to work on his computer.

OLGA: Where are your croutons?

DIMA (*Looking at the computer screen*): Really you want my croutons?

OLGA: Let me nibble on one.

DIMA (*Quits the application*): My croutons are no more, Olga.

OLGA: Ugh. Meany. I'm dying for a crouton.

DIMA: (*Gets up, looking at the computer screen.*) Want a crouton? (*There's nothing wrong with the computer. He walks to the cabinet.*) You'll have one if I can find it. (*Opens the ceiling cabinet, peeks in.*) You know, when I was still working at Coca-Cola . . . (*Falls silent, looking for a crouton.*)

OLGA: Enough! I can't take it anymore!

DIMA (*Smiling, turns to* OLGA. *He sees that* OLGA *needs something sweet.*): What?

OLGA (*Grabs her bag*): I'm gonna go buy something.

Olga rummages in her bag. She's looking for her purse. Dima stands by the cabinet, watching her. Olga found her purse, takes it out of the bag. At that very moment, Dima's phone rings on his desk. Dima walks to his phone. Olga decides to wait, not to leave yet. She may need to stay in the office. Dima picks up the receiver.

DIMA: Really? . . . Grreat! . . . Thanks! . . . Fine! In fifteen minutes. . . . (*Smirking.*) Fine, I'm waiting. (*Puts down the receiver.*) The barrel's ready.
OLGA: Already?

Gets up from her chair. Everything's okay, she can go buy dessert.

DIMA (*Shuffling papers on his desk*): Well . . . I'll need a consignment bill to take it out.

Olga walks up to Dima, leans over his desk. Helping him sort out his papers.

OLGA: It's right in front of you! (*Points to a piece of paper.*)
DIMA: You're right! (*Takes the consignment bill.*)

Olga stands up straight, rests her butt on Dima's desk.

DIMA (*Looking at the consignment bill, in reference to* OLGA*'s perfume*): Did he buy it?
OLGA: To hell with him!!

Dima did not expect such a reaction to his question. He raises his head. Looking at Olga, smiling, says.

DIMA: Got into a fight?
OLGA (*Smiling*): What do you care? (*Pinches* DIMA*'s nose.*)
DIMA (*Drops the papers*): It hurts, you idiot!

Olga lets go of Dima's nose.

DIMA (*Smiling, touches his nose*): You broke my nose. God forbid it'll leave a mark.

OLGA (*Smiling*): So you won't stick it where it doesn't belong.

DIMA (*Touching his nose with his fingers, looking at* OLGA): What do you mean, Olga, you were so in love.

OLGA: Zamirovsky!! . . . I'll kill you one of these days!

DIMA (*Smiling, turns away, takes the consignment bill*): What would be the point of killing me?

OLGA: And your stupid jokes!

Dima sets aside the consignment bill, touches his nose, and says.

DIMA: God forbid it'll leave a mark.

OLGA: What, your eleven-year-old girlfriends will fall out of love with you?

Touching Olga's thighs with his hands, Dima says.

DIMA: Be so kind as to take these away, please.

OLGA (*Smiling, not rushing to step back from the desk*): Incidentally, I have pretty thighs.

DIMA (*Gently squeezing* OLGA*'s thighs*): Take them away anyway.

Olga steps back from Dima's desk, tilts her head forward and, no longer smiling, starts to press down with her fingers on the upper part of her eye socket, near the nose. Dima doesn't pay any attention to this, he's filling out the consignment bill. Olga, still pressing, waits for Dima to finish filling it out. Seeing that Dima has finished filling it out, says, while continuing to press.

OLGA: I have knots here . . . little beads.

Dima notices Olga pressing down on her eye socket. He starts to smile, dumbfounded, as if to say, what's all this nonsense about little beads. Olga stops pressing down on her eye socket, makes as if she's going to press down on Dima's. Dima tenses up but doesn't pull back from Olga's fingers.

OLGA (*About to press down on* DIMA'*s*): Don't worry.
DIMA (*Without stepping back*): Olga, what are you trying to do, first you leave a mark . . .

Olga, all business, presses down on Dima's eye socket.

DIMA: Careful! You'll poke out my eye! (*Steps back.*) What's gotten into you today? Wanna turn me into a cripple?
OLGA: You don't have them. Yours is straight.
DIMA: Of course it's straight! You want to make it crooked?!
OLGA: Touch here! (*Tilting her head, invites him to touch her eye socket.*)
DIMA (*Smiling*): Oh, it's my turn to touch now. Get ready.

Dima starts to touch Olga's eye socket.

OLGA: Feel it?

Dima touches it, silent.

OLGA: Can you feel it?
DIMA: I can't feel a thing.
OLGA: What do you mean you can't feel it! (*Steps back.*) Touch yours!

Dima touches his.

OLGA: Can you feel that yours is straight?
DIMA (*Touching*): I guess, yeh.
OLGA (*Takes his hand*): Now touch mine again!

Olga brings Dima's hand up to her eyes. Smiling, Dima presses down on Olga's eye socket.

DIMA: Feels like grooves.

Olga steps back. Dima takes away his hand.

DIMA: Sinus infection.
OLGA: No.
DIMA (*Rushes to correct himself*): Whatchamacallit, tonsi . . .
OLGA: No. It's because I have bad vision. Sodium. My doctor said that I should massage it when it hurts.

Enter Slava. He has a bottle of drinking water in his hand. Slouching, Slava rushes to reach his desk as quickly as possible, reaches it, and settles into his chair. Dima and Olga watch him. Slava doesn't see what he needs on his desk, gets up from his chair, and looks around.

DIMA (*Smiling*): Coming to the cafeteria with us or staying?
SLAVA (*Without looking at anyone*): No, thanks, I don't need anything. (*As if he's discovered a way out of this situation.*) Oh! Awesome!

Slava sits back down. You can't see him behind the computer. Smiling, Dima and Olga leave the office. You can't see Slava behind the computer, his water bottle is on his desk. Slava is doing something, one can feel something stirring. Olga enters in haste, followed by the same customer who was there earlier to pick up the glass molding. Walking over to her computer, Olga says.

OLGA: Let's go to the warehouse first.

The customer pauses, Olga takes the papers she needs from her desk. The customer pays no attention to Slava, who is stirring, hiding behind his computer. Olga is ready to go.

OLGA: One sec.

Olga picks up the receiver from her desk, dials a short internal number, speaks.

OLGA: Are you there? . . . I'm gonna come by with someone in a minute. (*Hangs up.*) Let's go. (*Approaches the customer.*) Yasha's there too. (*Without stopping, walks past the customer, makes toward the exit.*)

The customer follows Olga. Olga exits the office first, the customer follows, closes the door behind him. Slava stops stirring, music comes on. Slava has turned on one of the last albums by the rock band Civil Defense.[2] Dima enters with a bag of cookies in his hands. Hearing the music, Dima smiles, walks over to his desk.

DIMA: Rocking out?

Slava nods in agreement, without looking at Dima, doing something with his hands, as if he is twisting a cable. He is facing the other way and we can't see what exactly he is doing. For some reason, Dima's words made Slava sad. Dima was not even waiting for a response. He puts the cookies away in one of his desk drawers, grabs the consignment bill for the conveyance of the tin barrel from the desk, and leaves. Slava gets up from his chair, flustered, says.

SLAVA: So then (*Immediately reconsidering.*) anyway . . . (*Takes out his cell phone, dials a number, speaks.*) Alyona, please, tell me, what kind of water did you buy that time? . . . And what if I just bought. . . . (*Takes the water bottle from the table, looks to see what it's called.*) . . . Oh! I bought the same one! Is it alright to drink it? . . . Listen, you remember today's the anniversary of Yegor Letov's. . . . You remember? Alright, I just wanted to. . . . Sausage. Sausage from the Meatmart. . . . Alright. (*Turning off his cell phone, ending the call.*) Right away, then, that's good.

Slava puts the phone in his pocket, settles into his chair, opens his diary on his computer and, all worked up, begins to type. One can hear how quick he is at the keyboard. Dima opens the door. Standing in the doorway, holding the door handle, Dima says.

DIMA: Slava, you're not busy now are you?
SLAVA (*Still typing*): Well not really, what's up?
DIMA: Can you help me lift the barrel. Onto the car. It's not heavy, eighty kilos.

Slava doesn't react at all to this request. Dima waits. Slava stops working, gets up from his chair.

SLAVA: One sec. (*Turns off the music.*)
DIMA (*Smiling*): Rocking out while Olga isn't here.

Slava is ready to help Dima. He knows that one should help people even when one doesn't want to.

DIMA: Let's go. (*Exits the office.*)
SLAVA (*Walking to the door*): Where to?
DIMA (*Holding the door open, from the hallway*): To the tinsmiths'.

Slava exits, Dima closes the door. No more than a few seconds later, Dima opens the door, enters the office. He forgot his cell phone. Dima walks over to his desk, grabs the phone. At that moment another cell phone rings on Olga's desk. Dima walks over to it, answers the call for Olga.

DIMA: Zoya, she went to the warehouse . . . probably forgot it, I forgot mine too, had to come back . . . nothing, my mom asked for a barrel for our dacha, Slava and I are going to load it into the truck . . . the tinsmiths' . . . it's not very big . . . that you don't know the job rates! . . . Okay, I'll tell her, bye.

Ending the call, Dima puts the cell phone back on the desk, gets ready to leave.

DIMA: Got the consignment bill, got that.

Dima hastens to leave the office, bumps into Olga in the doorway. The customer wants to enter after Olga. Olga is holding consignment bills.

DIMA (*Surprised*): Is it raining?
OLGA (*Also surprised that it's raining*): Can you believe it.
CUSTOMER: They said it would!
DIMA: Slava's going to get wet. Alright! Call Zoya. (*Leaves.*)

Turning around, Olga asks Dima, who's already in the hallway.

OLGA: What did she want?

The customer, also turning around, also addressing Dima.

CUSTOMER: Supposed to snow already next week!

Dima has no time to stop or to respond to them. He hurries out. Olga walks over to her work station, about to settle into her chair.

OLGA: Ugh, can you close . . .

The customer hastens to close the office door, which was left open.

OLGA: Um-hum.

Olga settles into her chair, she is working on her computer. The customer enters the office, stops.

CUSTOMER: Yasha's the cross-eyed one?

OLGA (*Working on her computer*): The cross-eyed one is Zhenya.

CUSTOMER: Oh! Now I know. Yasha's the one with the bandana . . . sturdy fellas.

OLGA (*Without tearing away from the computer*): Um-hum.

CUSTOMER: . . . Won't come again today, don't want to disturb you. (*Turns around, looks at the window sill.*) Nice garden you have there.

OLGA: Sveta's. (*Stops working on her computer, takes a rubber stamp from the desk.*) A bequest. (*Stamps the consignment bills.*)

The customer gets ready to take the papers. Olga hands him the papers, one by one, saying.

OLGA: This one you know. And this one. And this one.

CUSTOMER: Um-hum. (*Takes all the papers, puts them away.*)

OLGA: You don't have an . . .

CUSTOMER: He's already there!

OLGA: Wait. (*Gets up from her chair, about to put on a warm jacket hanging on the back of the chair.*)

CUSTOMER: Don't worry, Olga! Don't worry! For God's sake!

Olga looks at the customer questioningly. Does he know what she wants to do.

CUSTOMER: I'll fill out the permit myself. At the gate.

OLGA: Suit yourself. (*Sits back down, gets ready to work on her computer.*)

The customer puts away the consignment bills into his bag, takes out a towel. At that moment Olga notices the customer, sees the towel in his hands, starts to smile.

OLGA: You got it for us?

CUSTOMER (*Smiling*): Yes. Because you're orphans.

OLGA: Oh, thanks. (*Takes the towel.*)

CUSTOMER (*Smiling*): There's no one to pity you.

OLGA (*No longer smiling, looks around to see where she can put the towel. The present lost its charm very quickly.*): Right, no one. You're right about that.

CUSTOMER: Orphans. So I brought it for you orphans.

OLGA: Thanks so much.

CUSTOMER: So that someday without waiting in line you'll let me.

OLGA: Thanks, yes . . . great, now we have. (*Puts the towel on the desk, walks over to the* CUSTOMER.)

CUSTOMER: You orphans. (*Turns to leave.*)

OLGA: Oh, you said it.

Olga follows the customer to the door.

CUSTOMER: You sit there all sad all day.

OLGA: That's the job.

CUSTOMER (*Meaning when he'll be in his car*): I'll turn the radio on.

OLGA: Yes. (*Opens the door.*)

CUSTOMER: Bye.

OLGA: Bye.

Olga closes the door behind the customer, walks over to her desk, grabs her phone, walks to the door, pushing some buttons on her phone as she's walking. Olga leaves the office. A few seconds later, she returns, says from the threshold.

OLGA: You should be more.

Olga enters the office, the customer follows her. Olga is holding her cell phone, a lighter, and a pack of cigarettes.

CUSTOMER (*Looking around*): Don't know where I put it myself!

OLGA (*Doubting that it's in the office*): Go ahead and look, but . . .

CUSTOMER: Right (*Sees that the thing he needs isn't there.*) . . . (*Remembers.*) What an idiot! The cap's in the car!

Olga smiles. Waving his hand as if to say I've completely lost it, the customer leaves the office. Smiling, Olga lets him pass. The customer makes toward the exit, followed by Olga.

OLGA (*Closing the door*): Nail it down next time.

There's no one in the office. A few seconds later, Olga returns. For some reason she wasn't able to smoke. Olga walks over to her desk, puts her phone down on her desk and the cigarettes and lighter in her bag, which is hanging on the back of the chair. Slava enters, followed by Dima. Slava is wet, he looks upset, tries to hide the fact that he is upset. He helped out, but the rain came down hard on him. Slouching, as always, Slava hurries to his desk. Dima walks over to his own desk.

DIMA: The barrel's ready.
OLGA (*Trying to zip up her bag*): Did you load it?
DIMA (*Tells her about it while standing by his desk*): With Slava, then Yasha helped too.
SLAVA (*Without looking at them*): It's alright, everything's fine.
DIMA: Their lead engineer is coming!
OLGA: He's okay.

Feeling bad about what happened to Slava, after all it was his fault that Slava got wet, Dima turns around, looks to see what Slava is doing. Olga has already managed to zip up her bag. She stands there, resting her knee on the chair, also looking at Slava, holding her keys in her hand. Water drips from Slava's head, not a lot, but still. Suddenly stirring, as if he's just remembered something, Slava gets up, looks around. He needs the clock that's hanging on the office wall.

He knows perfectly well where it's hanging, but for some reason he keeps searching for it. Turning his head, says.

SLAVA: What time is it . . . (*Found the clock.*) Right! Great! (*Takes the water bottle in his hand.*)

OLGA: Take a towel, it's dripping from your head.

SLAVA (*Without looking at* OLGA. *In fact, he tries to never look his coworkers in the eye.*): Everything's fine, everything's fine. (*Twisting the cap off the bottle.*)

DIMA (*Smiling*): You seem flustered today, Slava.

SLAVA (*Having twisted the cap off*): Right! Twisting and turning. (*In reference to the time.*) Half past! Great. (*Gets ready to drink the water, brings the bottle up to his mouth.*)

OLGA: Are you on a diet, Slava?

Slava freezes, he was prevented from drinking the water.

SLAVA: No. Just because.

Slava is willing to answer their questions before they finally let him take a sip of water.

DIMA: C'mon, tell us. Don't play dumb. See how concerned Olga has become all of a sudden.

SLAVA: No. Just because. It's without gas.

DIMA: We can see that.

SLAVA: No, just because. I'm drinking. . . . Just the way it is.

Slava waits. Olga and Dima look at him.

OLGA: Are you on a diet?

SLAVA (*Smiling*): No.

OLGA: Come on, I see you have it all planned out by the hour.
SLAVA: Christ, it's just water. (*Glancing at* OLGA.) Isn't it strange? (*Immediately hastens to shift his gaze.*)
OLGA: What's strange?

Smiling, Slava remains silent, not looking at anyone. Olga is dumbfounded, she settles into her chair. She's a little hurt, it's like she feels stupid all of a sudden. Slava can feel the mounting tension, he feels embarrassed himself because of it. Slava starts to drink the water. Still standing there, smiling, Dima says.

DIMA: Come on, tell the collective, don't play dumb.

Not responding, Slava continues to drink the water. Dima exchanges glances with Olga. Dima smiles. Olga is dumbfounded, which is rather clear from her face. Slava has finished almost half the bottle, stops drinking, twists the cap back on the bottle. Dima walks to the kettle, picks it up.

DIMA: There's a soccer match today! (*Holding the kettle in his hands and looking at* SLAVA.) Slava, wanna go to the soccer match with us today?

Slava stops twisting on the cap, frowns, he's not a fan and knows how to say no.

DIMA: We play in the rain too.
SLAVA: No. Thanks.

Slava sets the bottle on the table, settles into his chair. Having exchanged glances with Olga, Dima leaves with the kettle to get water. Olga grabs a pen. Propping her chin up on her fist, she plays with the pen, looking out the window. Slava looks at his desk, smiling faintly, as one smiles sometimes when one feels guilty.

SLAVA: Please forgive me, Olga, I'm a strange guy. (*Faintly smiling, takes a breath.*)

Olga doesn't change her pose or facial expression but looking at her it becomes clear that she's no longer upset.

SLAVA (*Still looking at his desk*): About the water. Two, two and a half liters a day. Usually two.

OLGA (*Turning to* SLAVA, *propping her chin up on her fist*): Do you drink anything else? What about coffee or tea?

SLAVA: No, I used to drink it. It made me feel bad. I had headaches. (*More animated.*) By the way. (*Leaning forward to his computer.*) I also have (*Doing something on his computer.*) Emilíana Torrini. You might like it.

Slava turns on the music. The song "Jungle Drum" by Emilíana Torrini comes on.

SLAVA (*Looking at the screen*): Here's another one. (*Stretching his neck out as far as possible, as always, starts to quickly type something on his keyboard.*)

OLGA: Is that her?

SLAVA (*Without reducing the speed with which he is typing, looking at the computer screen*): Um-hum.

Olga doesn't pay too much attention to the song, she's not into music. Dima enters with the kettle in his hands. He has filled it with water. Dima has immediately taken stock of the situation. He knows that Olga's not into music. Smiling, he walks to the place where they keep the kettle. Olga understands why Dima's smiling, addresses Slava, not without a challenge in her voice.

OLGA: These aren't your stupid . . .?
SLAVA (*Without taking his eyes off the computer screen, smiling*): No.

Dima sets the kettle down on the stand. At that moment, Slava, like an Aspie, having forgotten he's not alone, looking at the computer screen, begins to sing along just as heartily as the singer, saying.

SLAVA: tatatamtamtamtamtam . . .

Dima switches on the kettle, the situation amuses him. This time Olga addresses her challenge to Dima.

OLGA: What's going?!

Dima smiles. Not looking at Olga, standing next to the boiling kettle, says, referring to the possibility that Olga will develop an interest in music.

DIMA: Nothing. God willing.
OLGA (*To* SLAVA): Fine, I get it!

Slava slaps the keyboard a little too recklessly, which is meant to say, that's it, I'm done, leans back in his chair but doesn't take his eyes off the computer screen, then immediately leans forward again to the computer screen and again begins to pound on his keyboard.

SLAVA: Want me to turn it off?
OLGA: Yes.

Dima leans back against the table with his butt, still by the kettle.

SLAVA (*Stops pounding on his keyboard, leans back from the computer*): Give me your flash drive, I'll upload it for you.

Slava raises his eyes from the computer screen, Olga finds her flash drive on her desk.

OLGA: Catch.

SLAVA (*Smiling, afraid he won't catch it*): Oh, I don't know. (*Raises himself a little from the chair, holds out his hands in order to catch the flash drive.*)

Olga tosses the flash drive to Slava.

SLAVA (*Having caught it*): Got it!

Dima smiles at Slava's exclamation. Slava starts to fidget, he really likes sharing music with others. To upload music onto another person's flash drive is a far more important matter to him than helping load a tin barrel into a truck.

SLAVA (*Inserting the flash drive into his computer*): Flashy drive. . . . Hold on. . . . (*Inserts the flash drive, looking at the computer screen to see if the flash drive has been recognized.*) We'll up-and-load it.

Slava performs the necessary operations for uploading music onto a flash drive.

OLGA (*To* DIMA): Will you tell her how much the barrel cost?!

DIMA (*Without changing his pose, smiling*): I will. See how popular you are, everyone's getting in line to upload something onto your drive.

SLAVA (*Ejecting the flash drive from his computer*): There. Done.

Slava raises himself a little from the chair, wants to throw Olga the flash drive. Still sitting, Olga holds out her hand, she's sure that she'll catch it. Smiling, Slava is worried, he really wants to throw the flash drive in such a way that it will land right in Olga's hand. Done boiling, the kettle switches off. At that moment, Slava throws the flash drive. The flash drive does not reach Olga's hand. It falls down near her desk.

Without looking at them, Dima walks over to his desk with the kettle.

SLAVA: Damn.

OLGA: No worries.

SLAVA: Sorry.

DIMA (*Smiling*): What an idiot.

Suddenly afraid that this was about him, Slava turns to face Dima.

DIMA (*To* OLGA, *holding the kettle*): I got the kettle but forgot to put the tea bag into the mug.

Smiling, Olga holds the flash drive in her hand. She no longer wants tea.

SLAVA: There's a new store in our neighborhood called Meatmart, they sell sausage without soy.

Ignoring Slava's announcement, Dima addresses Olga.

DIMA: Why don't you want any?

Olga crinkles her nose, as if to say, I've changed my mind. Slava notices that his announcement has been completely ignored. Faith in others has once again abandoned him.

DIMA: Well, you're no fun.

Dima walks over to where they keep the kettle. Slava assumes his usual position at his desk, hiding behind the computer.

DIMA (*As he's walking*): Why drink alone. I refuse to drink alone. (*Places the kettle back in its place.*) We were gonna drink tea.
OLGA: Chill out! (*Grabs her bag from the back of her chair.*)
DIMA (*Glancing at the windowsill*): When's the last time we watered the garden?

Dima walks over to the windowsill. Olga checks to see if she's got everything in her bag. Packs what she needs from the desk. Dima has reached the windowsill, looks at the miniature garden on top of it. It's a large box with cacti. There's a miniature rock garden with small animal figures in the sand. Dima touches the soil of this curious large flower pot with his finger.

DIMA: The soil's wet. That means it's been watered recently. Slava, who watered the garden? Was it you?
SLAVA: I don't know.
DIMA: Olga, who watered the garden?
OLGA (*Packing her bag without looking at* DIMA): Like I've got nothing better to do, Zamirovsky.

DIMA (*Smiling*): What's on your mind?

OLGA (*Zipping up her bag*): The engineer from Parade might give me a lift.

DIMA: That's fantastic, Olga. I'm not saying anything.

Dima walks over to his desk, begins to put his papers in order.

DIMA: The usual, you said it yourself.

Smiling, Olga begins to sort out the papers on her desk. Dima leans forward, opens his desk drawer. There's a rustle from a bag of cookies.

OLGA (*Smiling*): Let go of the cookies . . . Zamirovsky! Let go of the cookies!

Putting the cookies down, he closes the desk drawer.

OLGA (*Smiling*): On Monday!

DIMA (*Smiling*): Maybe I won't survive 'til Monday.

OLGA: For Christ's sake, what do you think will happen to you? God's little angel!

Dima smiles at Olga. Smiling, Olga leans forward to her computer, quits her applications.

DIMA: So should I upload the new Office for you or what?

OLGA (*Shutting down her computer*): No.

DIMA (*Also bending forward to the computer on his desk*): Suit yourself. (*Shuts down the computer.*)

Olga gets up, walks over to the closet, takes her jacket off the hanger, puts it on. Without zipping it up, she walks over to her bag, takes the bag, glances at her reflection in the little mirror on her desk.

OLGA: Bye everyone.

Olga makes for the exit.

DIMA: Bye. See you Monday.

Trying to open the door, Olga becomes agitated. The door is locked. Dima gets up, walks to the door.

DIMA (*Smiling*): Won't open?
OLGA: Why the hell do you lock it?
DIMA (*Smiling*): No reason. (*Unlocks the door with his key.*) What, against the rules?
OLGA (*Throwing open the door*): Bye Slava!
SLAVA: Bye!
DIMA (*Smiling, to* OLGA*'s back*): Off you go! (*Smiling, closes the door.*)
SLAVA: That's it, I'm off!

Slava jumps up, puts on his jacket, which was hanging on the back of his chair. Smiling at his own thoughts, Dima walks over to the closet, opens it, takes his jacket, puts it on. Dima and Slava are not paying each other any attention.

IN THE CENTER

Valery's parents' apartment. Valery's parents, Valery, and Natasha sit in a room, watching TV. Natasha's stomach has become noticeably round. Valery's parents exchange glances. They are concerned about Natasha, they think that someone in her condition should not watch so much TV. Looking at the TV, Natasha and Valery feel perfectly at ease. Natasha gets up from the couch.

MOTHER: Leaving already?
VALERY: Yes, mom. We have to go. (*Gets up from the couch.*)

Valery's mother and father get up from the couch in order to walk Natasha and Valery out. Everyone exits the room.

■ □ ■

Natasha and Valery are riding a bus. Both of them are wearing earphones. They are listening to music. Having thrown back her head, Natasha has closed her eyes. She's sleeping. Valery is looking straight in front of him. He is not thinking about anything.

■ □ ■

Natasha's apartment. Natasha enters. She has just come home. She takes off her windbreaker, leaves it on the couch, lifts up her blouse, unfastens the fake pregnancy belly. Having taken off the fake pregnancy belly, Natasha carries it out of the room, not forgetting to turn off the lights.

■ □ ■

Valery and Natasha are sitting in a movie theater, watching a movie. It's unclear whether they like the movie or not. Natasha's phone rings in her bag. Natasha takes the phone out of her bag. Valery shifts his gaze to Natasha, reflexively reacting to the call. He doesn't care who's calling Natasha. Plugging one ear, Natasha answers the call. Valery turns away, watches the movie.

NATASHA: Hello? . . . I'm at the movie theater. (*Turns off the phone, puts it in her bag, resumes watching the movie.*)

It's unclear whether Natasha likes the movie or not. Most likely she has already seen films like this a million times.

■ □ ■

The service hallway of a shopping mall. Valery, having just brought Natasha here, hands her a new fake belly, which he has taken out of a plastic bag.

VALERY: Try it on, please.
NATASHA (A *bit at a loss*): Here? I'll try it on at home.
VALERY (*Upset*): I want to see it. We may need to make adjustments.

Natasha agrees. She takes the fake belly, tries to fasten it on. It's not very comfortable, her blouse is getting in the way. Natasha is frustrated. She is nervous. Valery starts to help Natasha. They don't have any sexual desire for one another. Natasha may be a little tense because Valery might touch her. Valery has managed to fasten the belly.

NATASHA: Is that all?

Straightens her blouse. Valery looks Natasha over.

NATASHA: What next?

Valery doesn't respond, he is appraising Natasha's belly.

■ □ ■

A shopping mall. A bank. Valery is at his work station, checks his watch. That's it. It's the end of the work day. Valery cleans up his desk and, grabbing his cell phone, leaves.

■ □ ■

Valery's parents' apartment. Valery is sitting in the room by himself, on the couch. Valery's mother peeks into the room.

MOTHER: Want a meat patty? It's hot off the pan.
VALERY (A *little annoyed*): No, mom. Thanks, I'm full. Maybe later.

Valery's mother watches him for some time. Valery doesn't pay any attention to his mother, he is looking straight in front of him and not thinking about anything.

MOTHER: Aren't you bored, Valery?
VALERY: No. I like it when it's quiet.

Valery's mother would be happy to ask more questions, but knows that there's no point to it. She leaves. Valery continues to sit there as before. He then picks up a glass of water from the table and takes a few sips.

■ □ ■

A shopping mall. A bank. Valery is processing a cash withdrawal, passes the cash and receipt to a client. The client leaves. Valery hangs up a sign with the words "On Break" and leaves.

■ □ ■

A shopping mall. Valery and his friend exit a coffee shop with coffee cups, sit down at a table near the coffee shop, drink their coffees. They are at ease. The fact that they are not engaging in verbal communication does not make them tense. A few moments later, Valery finishes the coffee with one decisive sip.

VALERY: Sorry.

Valery gets up from the table. Walking away, he takes out his cell phone, dials a number, pauses by a wall in a quiet, uncrowded spot, and waits to be connected.

VALERY (*Talking on the phone*): Natasha, I'm sorry, can you talk? . . . Here's what's next. You accidentally picked up something really heavy while cleaning the apartment. (*Listening to what* NATASHA*'s saying.*) A table, let's say.

Listening to Natasha, Valery is walking around the shopping mall.

■ □ ■

Valery's friend gets up from the table, takes out some money, getting ready to pay the bill. Valery hastens toward him.

VALERY: I'm sorry, have you already paid?
VALERY'S FRIEND: Not yet.

Valery mechanically glances at the bill. He has had coffee here a million times already. He then pulls out his wallet, takes out some cash from the wallet. His friend has already left what he owes, waits for Valery. Valery leaves some cash. The friend looks around in search of the waitress.

VALERY: Let's go.

Valery and his friend leave.

■ □ ■

Natasha's apartment. Natasha enters in her underwear, bra, and the fake belly strapped onto her. Natasha looks at the fake belly, then, humming some abracadabra from fragments of Arabic words that she has heard, begins to dance. Natasha is singing and trying to dance in a way that could be considered erotic.

■ □ ■

Valery's parents' apartment. Valery's father and Valery's mother anxiously wait for the end of Valery's story.

VALERY: That's all, there's nothing more to tell.
VALERY'S FATHER (*Glumly, dejectedly*): Right.

Everyone is silent. A few moments later, Valery gets up from the couch, his mother and father turn to him. They don't know what he is going to do now.

■ □ ■

A shopping mall. Natasha is standing next to the cash register at work. Checks her watch, it's time for her break. Natasha hangs up a sign with the words "On Break" and leaves.

■ □ ■

The service hallway of a shopping mall. Valery is following Natasha. Natasha stops, gets ready to light a cigarette.

VALERY: Where's the belly?

NATASHA: One sec.

Natasha exits into one of the back rooms. Valery is left by himself, looks around the hallway. He is rarely in this part of the shopping mall. Natasha returns holding a plastic bag with the fake belly, gives it to Valery.

VALERY: Um-hum.

Valery takes the plastic bag, looks to see if everything's okay with the belly. Natasha gets ready to smoke, pulls out a cigarette.

NATASHA: Now what?

Valery doesn't respond. Natasha sees the bag of coffee in Valery's outstretched hand. Dumbfounded, Natasha glances at Valery. Valery slaps his forehead, as if to say, fuck, I messed up again. Natasha is dumbfounded.

VALERY: Go on, look inside.

Natasha takes the coffee bag, looks inside. Her face is transformed. She takes out an expensive bottle of perfume from the bag, smiles.

NATASHA: Thanks.

All of a sudden, Natasha has the desire to give Valery a kiss on the cheek. Valery and Natasha, touching each other's shoulders with their hands, touch each other with their cheeks. This touch comes in place of a kiss.

NATASHA: Of course, they were really surprised when I said I plan to sell coffee the rest of my life.

VALERY: They don't get it. They don't get it. For instance, I've also found myself. (*Again referring to his parents' inability to understand him.*) . . . How is it possible not to drink vodka, tea, not to fuck. (*Meaning he doesn't drink vodka or fuck, while his parents don't get it.*)

NATASHA (*Approvingly*): Right.

VALERY: You can't imagine how many problems I've had.

NATASHA (*Smiling*): I can. (*Lights a cigarette.*)

VALERY: You're either a fucking homo or.

NATASHA (*Smiling*): Right.

Natasha *gets* Valery.

VALERY (*Smiling*): When they saw me with the raw carrot.

Natasha chuckles, she gets him.

VALERY: I like it when it's quiet. I don't need any of that. I like it when my brain is at rest.

NATASHA: Yes. Exactly.

Natasha puts out her cigarette.

■ □ ■

A nursing home. An elderly man who loves to sing both by himself and with others sits alone in a room reserved for games and socializing. He is falling asleep, his eyes slowly begin to close, his head falls back, and he starts to snore. Loudly, with a whistle.

■ □ ■

A shopping mall. Natasha is standing in her glass booth. There are no customers. Natasha is not thinking about anything. A few moments later, she checks her watch. It's time for lunch. Natasha hangs up the sign with the words "On Break" and leaves the kiosk.

■ □ ■

A shopping mall. A shoe store. Enter Valery with his friend. Valery is looking for the same pair of shoes that filled him with so many doubts. His friend has come along for the company. Valery finds the shoes, takes them from the shelf together with the box, and walks over to the register. He has decided to buy them.

■ □ ■

Valery's parents' apartment. Valery is alone in the room, sitting on the couch, takes the new pair of shoes out of the box, and puts them on. Valery's mother enters, pauses in the doorway. Valery's already wearing the new shoes, gets up from the couch, smiling, turns to his mother.

VALERY: What do you think? I came to show you. (*Looks at the reflection in the mirror to see how the shoes fit him.*)

Valery's mother watches Valery. A few moments later, she says.

VALERY'S MOTHER: So what happened with Angelina?

VALERY (*Satisfied with his shoes, examines his reflection*): She's gone away.

VALERY'S MOTHER: Where to?

VALERY: I don't know. (*Starts to roll from heel to toe, heel to toe.*) These shoes are really snug and comfortable.

■ □ ■

A shopping mall. A shoe store. Natasha enters, holding her cell phone and purse in her hands. In no hurry, Natasha walks around the store, examining the shoes. She again spots the same pair of shoes, studies it for some time, then picks up a shoe from the display, turns around, searching for the salesman, finds him, says.

NATASHA: Excuse me, do you have these in a 37? . . . Oh!

Natasha notices that she's in fact holding a 37. She makes her way to an empty seat and tries on the pair that she likes.

THE END

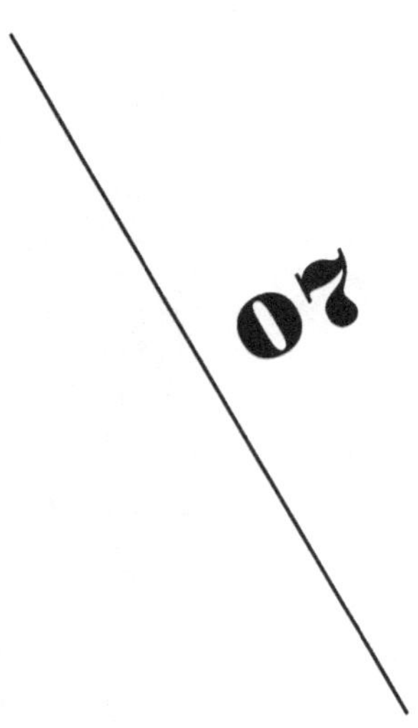

THE SOLDIER

PAVEL PRYAZHKO

TRANSLATED BY MAKSIM HANUKAI

The soldier came home on leave. When it was time to return to the army, he did not go back to the army.

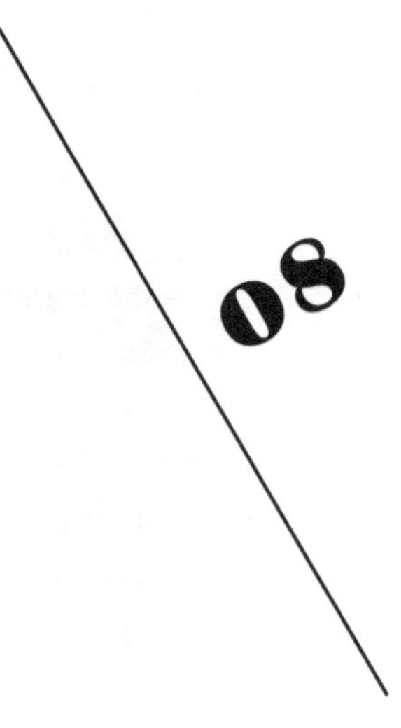

SUMMER WASPS STING IN NOVEMBER, TOO

A Comedy in One Act

IVAN VYRYPAEV

TRANSLATED BY MAKSIM HANUKAI

—Why do you weep?
—Because I'm alone.
—Are you truly alone?
—I feel and live as if I were alone.

▸ Ingmar Bern, *The Dialogues of Solitary Men,* Stockholm, 1986

CHARACTERS

ELENA—thirty-five to fifty years old
MARK—sixty to seventy years old
JOSEPH—sixty to seventy years old

On stage are MARK, ELENA, *and* JOSEPH. *A long pause. Everyone remains silent for a while.*

MARK: You know, Sarah, Marcus could not have been at your place last Monday, because last Monday he was at Donald's place.

JOSEPH: Yes, that's true, last Monday Marcus was at my place, he came to our place late Sunday evening, and he left early in the morning on Tuesday to catch the eleven o'clock train to Stockholm.

ELENA: Are you saying that I'm lying, Robert?

MARK: I would prefer not to use such sharp language, but you must agree that you need to explain to me what strange man was at our house last Monday.

ELENA: Marcus was at our place last Monday.

MARK: Donald?

JOSEPH: Marcus stayed at my place all of last Monday, and I beg you, let's finally put an end to this strange conversation.

MARK: But I have to straighten this out, dammit! I have the right to know who visited my wife in my absence and why you're lying to me Sarah?!

ELENA: I'm not lying to you, Robert, it was your brother Marcus who stayed at our place last Monday.

MARK: Sarah, I beg you to stop, you hear?! Out of respect for me, for our marriage, I beg you to stop immediately!

JOSEPH: Robert, I think we should all put an end to this conversation, given that things have gone this far and there's no sensible solution to this question . . .

ELENA: There is a sensible solution to this question.

ELENA *takes a cell phone out of her pocket.*

ELENA: We'll call Marcus and find out.

MARK: For God's sake, don't be crazy, Sarah. Why this circus? Why drag poor Marcus into this business? Enough, I beg you?!

ELENA *is talking on the phone.*

ELENA: Hello? Hi, Marcus. It's Sarah, your brother Robert is next to me, I think he wants to ask you something, I'm giving him the phone. . . . What? No, no, your mother's fine, Robert will explain everything to you in a minute.

ELENA *passes the phone to* MARK.

MARK: Hello? Hi, Marcus. Ha, ha. Seems summer wasps sting in November, too. How's life, old man? What? Oh! No, no. We just don't know what to do with ourselves here. No, we're not at home, and Donald's with us, it's the three of us here, and, to be honest, we're losing our minds, and, it seems, now we want to make you lose *your* mind. Mom? I spoke to her in the morning and she said that she doesn't want to come back yet, so I'm planning to pick her up next week, why, has she said anything to you about it? Ah, Seylent! Oh, that Seylent. Listen, Marcus, it hasn't even been two years since father died but our mother's spending more and more time with this Seylent. I'm certain that her wish to stay at the rest home until the end of November is connected precisely with this. By the way, Marcus, were you at our place last Monday when it just so happened that I was visiting mother? Aha. Really?! No, what do you mean? What do you mean? She told me about it, it's just that . . . ? Hmm. Then you really were at our place last Monday? No, everything's fine, I just wanted to make sure because. . . . Well, of course, Sarah told me . . . it's just that. . . . Well, listen. . . . No, no, nothing. . . . Too bad we didn't get to see each other, I hope you'll come visit us again this Monday, alright? What? Oh, this Monday you're planning to visit Donald? Aha. He has invited you. But weren't you at his place last Monday, Marcus? What?! Oh, for God's sake, of course! I'm sorry, I'm not making fun of you, it's just that I'm really not able to think straight today. No, I'm not sick, Marcus. Everything's fine. It was good to hear your voice, my dear, and see you on Monday. Oh, right! Right, I forgot that you're going to see Donald. I'm sorry, to be honest, we smoked a bit of, well, you know what. I can't talk about it over the phone . . . well, you know, well, when someone smokes this stuff . . .

well . . . well, they're not ordinary cigarettes but you know what I mean, anyway, we can't discuss this over the phone . . . well, I think you know what I . . . it also makes you laugh real hard. . . . Ha, ha . . .

MARK *starts to laugh. He laughs as if he really is stoned.*

MARK (*Laughing*): I'm sorry, Marcus . . . it's hard for me to speak right now because I'm laughing. . . . I'm passing the phone to Sarah . . . she'll explain everything to you . . .

MARK *passes the phone to* ELENA *and slowly calms down.*

ELENA: Yes, Marcus. Well, of course, everything's fine. We're just goofing around, that's all. Yes, yes, I mean it, everything's great. You know your brother, he never loses his head completely. We love you, it was nice to hear your voice. See you Marcus. And Donald says hi too, he's waving to you as we speak. I'll be sure to pass it on. Bye Marcus.

ELENA *puts the phone in her pocket.*

ELENA: Marcus says hi, Donald.

Pause. ELENA *and* MARK *look at* JOSEPH.

MARK: What's going on, Donald?

JOSEPH: I don't know.

MARK: What do you mean you don't know?

JOSEPH: I don't know what to tell you.

MARK: But don't you want to explain to us why you thought all of this was necessary?

JOSEPH: What was necessary, Robert?

MARK: All of this, Donald. This whole game about Marcus and his mythical presence in your house on Monday. I mean, this isn't some joke, Donald. Because of you, Sarah and I almost got into a fight . . .

ELENA: We did get into a fight, Robert.

MARK: What?

ELENA: You just said, "We almost got into a fight," but I want to clarify that we did get into a fight, Robert.

MARK: Well then, all the more so.

Pause. Everyone remains silent for a while.

MARK: Well, why are you silent, Donald?

JOSEPH: Summer wasps sting in November, too.

MARK: Damn it, Donald! Have you taken into your head to make fun of us today?! Donald?!

Pause. MARK *calms down and looks at* JOSEPH *with compassion.*

MARK: Maybe you're not feeling well, Donald? Tell us about it.

Pause.

JOSEPH: You see, I'm tired. I don't even know how to explain it to you. I'm really tired from everything that surrounds me. From everything, literally everything, that I see. I'm tired of these trees, of the street outside my window. I'm tired of my window, of the blinds on my window. Of the view from my window. I'm tired of the birds flying in the sky and from their songs in the mornings and evenings. I'm tired of breakfast, lunch, and dinner. Tired of words, of my dog, of my wife, of the fact that day always replaces night and vice versa. I'm tired of newspapers, of information, tired of the smell of soap in our bathroom, of our neighbors' smiles, of the color of the walls in my house. Tired of the words that I need to pronounce every day. Tired of the water that I need to drink in order not to die of thirst. I'm tired of everything, you understand? Of everything that surrounds me, and even of everything that's inside me. I'm tired of my heart, of my lungs, and all of my blood, which flows through my veins. But most of all I'm tired of myself, you understand? I don't even know how to explain this. You see, I'm always alone with myself, wherever I may be, I'm always there. And there's not a second when I could be without myself, even for a little. And even when I sleep, I still feel my own presence. I'm always alone with myself, and I've grown so tired of myself all these years that I can no longer stand my own presence, but sadly there's nothing to be done, and I don't know how to get rid of myself. I've thought about suicide, but I don't have the courage, and then I hate the thought of resembling those stupid poets and rock musicians, whom I can't stand, like that fucking Jim Morrison.

ELENA: Jim Morrison didn't commit suicide, Donald, he died young, but he died of natural causes.

JOSEPH: What does that have to do with anything? You know perfectly well what I mean!

Pause.

MARK: When was the last time you saw your therapist, Donald?

JOSEPH: I don't have and never had a therapist, I'm not one of those people.

MARK: What people, Donald?

JOSEPH: The sort of people that go to a therapist.

MARK: And what's wrong with seeing a therapist once in a while? I think, Donald, that if you saw a therapist once in a while, you wouldn't be experiencing the problems that you're experiencing right now. Because a good therapist can always give you advice about what to do so as not to grow tired of the song of birds outside your window. Do you catch my drift?

JOSEPH: I'm not sick, Robert. I know perfectly well that I'm not sick.

MARK: Fine, but does anyone know about this except yourself?

JOSEPH: Of course. My wife knows that I'm not sick. My neighbors know that I'm not sick. Your brother Marcus knows that I'm not sick.

MARK: Speaking of Marcus. Why did you come up with that whole story about Marcus, Donald?

JOSEPH: I don't know, Robert. I'm really tired, aren't you listening to what I'm saying to you?

Pause. Everyone remains silent for a while.

MARK: Seems you really should talk to a good therapist, Donald. I can recommend a very good therapist to you, Donald. Really, a very, very good one.

Pause.

JOSEPH: Robert, I want to tell you that Marcus wasn't at your place last Monday, because he was at my place. He really was at my place, Robert.

MARK: That's enough, Donald. I'm not at all angry with you, I can see that you really aren't feeling very well and I want to help you. Why don't I call my therapist friend right now and you'll set up an appointment?

JOSEPH: Oh, Robert, Robert! I really don't want to drag my wife into this business, but it seems I have no choice.

JOSEPH *takes a cell phone out of his pocket and presses the call button.*

MARK: What are you doing, Donald?

JOSEPH: I'm calling my wife, I'm calling Martha. I hope you'll believe her at least.

MARK: That's enough, Donald, why drag Martha into this?

JOSEPH: But there's no other way to prove it to you. Hello, Martha? Listen, I have Robert here with me and he's got some important question that he wants to ask you. I'm passing the phone to him, darling.

JOSEPH *passes the phone to* MARK.

MARK: Hello. Hi, Martha. How's it going, how's your leg? No, I have another question for you, but I'm asking about your leg because I'm worried about your leg, although I have another question for you altogether. But first, tell me about your leg. Are you still going to rehab? Aha. And what does the doctor say, how long will it take? Another six months? Why that long? Oh, stop it, you're not old, it's just that you had a compound fracture, seems you just need to have patience. Well, alright, I'll be sure to come visit you soon. I hope so. Things have been very busy at my bank lately. Oh, and my mother doesn't want to come back from the rest home, so I have to visit her every week. Marcus and I take turns, as if we're on watch duty, one week it's him, and the next week it's me. By the way, Donald says that you guys had a nice time with Marcus last Monday? Donald says that Marcus stayed two nights and one day at your place? What? Oh, you really did have a nice time? I'm sorry, are you trying to say that you spent this time with Marcus? That means he was at your place on Monday?! Are you sure about this, Martha? That is, what I meant to say was, are you sure it was Marcus, that is, what I meant to say was, are you sure it was last Monday and not . . . say, Monday two weeks ago? What? No, Martha, of course, nothing has happened. Oh, no, don't pay any attention to me, I'm only joking. I said I'm joking, it's a joke, Martha, everything's fine. Where's the joke? Well, it would seem, in the fact that Marcus was at your place last Monday, I guess that's the joke, Martha. Ha, ha. To be honest, we had a bit to smoke here . . . but not cigarettes . . . we smoked . . . well, you know what . . . the same stuff that we smoked once on my birthday about six years ago, do you remember? We all had a bit to smoke then . . . you too, Martha, remember? We were laughing all night, remember, Martha? Well, there you go, we decided to do it again. . . . What do you mean, who's we? Me, Sarah, and your husband Donald. Yes, Donald too. I'm sorry, we would've invited you, but you have that thing with your leg, you could have tripped, lost your balance, and harmed your leg. What do you mean, why did we do it? What do you mean why, Martha, what a strange question? So we could have a laugh, of course. Ha, ha, ha. I'm sorry, I can't talk anymore, I'm simply dying of laughter. Get well, darling, and see you soon.

MARK *passes the phone to* JOSEPH. JOSEPH *puts the phone in his pocket.* MARK *watches* ELENA *intently.*

MARK: Sarah?

ELENA: Yes, Robert.

MARK: What do you mean "yes," Sarah? What does this "yes" of yours mean, Sarah?

ELENA: That I'm listening to you, Robert.

MARK: No, Sarah, my dear, it's I who am listening to you!

ELENA: I don't know what to tell you, Robert.

MARK: What's going on, Sarah?

ELENA: I don't know, Robert.

MARK: You don't know? What the hell you do you mean, you don't know?! Why the hell are you saying that you don't know? Then who does, Sarah?! And Marcus?! That means he lied to me?! Marcus! Who would've thought, our Marcus! Ten minutes ago, on the phone, he lied to me?! My own brother lied to me? I want to know why you're doing this? I want to know what you're doing this for?! Sarah, I want to know, tell me, what reason do you have to do this, you and Marcus?

ELENA: What are we doing, Robert?

MARK: This. These lies, these phone calls. I want to know what's going on, Sarah? And I don't want to hear you say that you don't know. You hear? I don't want to hear you say that you don't know?! You hear? Do you hear me, Sarah? I don't want to hear you say that you can't hear me, Sarah?

ELENA: I hear you, Robert, calm down.

MARK: Then explain it to me, goddammit!

Pause.

ELENA: It's not so easy to explain, Robert.

MARK: I don't want to hear anything about what's easy and what's difficult, I demand an explanation, no matter how difficult it may be! I demand an explanation, and as soon as possible. Or better yet, I'll call Marcus, let him explain it to me.

MARK *takes out his phone and presses the call button.*

ELENA: You don't need to call him, Robert.

MARK: Why not?! After all, he's my own brother. . . . Damn! He's unavailable. He's turned off his phone. Well, of course, he doesn't want to explain himself, I get it!

MARK *puts the phone in his pocket.*

ELENA: Marcus is at mass right now, today's Sunday.

MARK: Marcus is at mass! I wonder how he'll find the strength to approach the Blessed Sacrament after all this lying?!

JOSEPH: Let me explain something to you, Robert.

MARK: What do you have to do with this, Donald? I want to hear an explanation from my wife.

JOSEPH: Because I'm your friend, Robert. I'm a family friend. I love both of you, you and Sarah, and I want everything to be alright between you, and I think I understand what's happening here, and I think I can explain it. Sarah, Robert, allow me to speak to you frankly. I'm your friend, and no one except me will say to you what needs to be said, say it to your face, you understand? Even your therapist, Robert, won't say everything to you because he's too dependent on that enormous fee that you pay him. No one will say this to you, but I will. Just hear me out. I really do want to help you.

MARK *shrugs his shoulders. Pause.*

ELENA: Well, if you really have something to say . . .

JOSEPH: I do have something to say, Sarah. I do have something to say to you, Robert.

A short pause. JOSEPH *collects his thoughts.*

JOSEPH: Once upon a time a small herd of wild deer was wading across a mountain stream. The stream wasn't very deep, but the current was strong. So strong that all of the deer were having a hard time holding their balance against the current. And so these deer just weren't able to cross the stream. But they really needed to cross it because here, on this side of the stream, was a desert, rocks, cliffs, and rare trees, while there, beyond the stream: beautiful fields with green grass, magnificent shrubs with their favorite nettles, and, moreover, all around there grew that . . . um, what's it called, that round, red berry that grows on those special large shrubs, the one that wolves die from.

ELENA: Wolfberry.

JOSEPH: No! What are you talking about? It's the other way around, wolfberry makes wolves live longer, that's why it's called "wolfberry." But I'm talking about a kind of berry that deer really love, but that frightens away wolves. Which is why the deer try to get close to this berry. First of all, it's really tasty, and second, it frightens away the wolves.

MARK: Have you lost your mind, Donald?

JOSEPH: Just wait, Robert, don't interrupt me. Now then, a powerful, rapid stream, and none of the deer can wade across it. None. And all this paradise, all this beauty, all this yumminess that we, the deer, love more than anything in the world—it's all over there, on the other side. While we are here. So there you have it, my dear Robert, there you have it.

Pause.

MARK: I must be missing something. Have you really lost your mind, Donald?! What the hell are you talking about?

JOSEPH: If you have an objection for me, then please be so kind as to tell me.

MARK: An objection?! An objection to what, Donald?

JOSEPH: To what I just said, Robert?

MARK: To what you just said, Donald? Only a qualified therapist can give you an objection to what you just said, although, in this case, what may be needed is a qualified psychiatrist.

ELENA: But why, Robert? I, for one, do have something to say to Donald in response, although I'm not a psychiatrist. The thing is, Donald, that if you follow the stream long enough you're bound to hit upon a bridge.

JOSEPH: Wha-at?! What bridge, Sarah, I beg you, where would it, this bridge of yours, come from, who will build it, this bridge of yours?

ELENA: God will build it, Donald. God.

JOSEPH: Stop it, Sarah, we're all adults here.

MARK: What the hell is going on here?! What are you talking about?!

ELENA: I'm sorry, Robert, but I can't keep from responding to him. You see, Donald, there's something in your heart that you don't want to notice. And do you know why you don't want to notice it, my dear?

MARK: Sarah, I beg you to stop this immediately.

JOSEPH: But why, Robert? Let her continue, I'm very interested in hearing what she has to say.

ELENA: Actually, there's very little to say here, Donald. You don't want to notice in yourself that responsibility that each of us has for this world. You are responsible for your own life, Donald, but you don't want to admit it because it's easier to live without responsibility, and that's all there is to it.

JOSEPH: Then who's responsible for all those dead children in Libya, in Afghanistan, in Iraq, in Vietnam, in Hiroshima, and in Nagasaki? Am I responsible for them too?

ELENA: Yes, Donald. That's the thing, my dear, precisely you.

JOSEPH: I'm responsible?

ELENA: All of us, Donald. I'm responsible, and Robert, and you, and your wife Martha.

MARK: I think I'm starting to understand what's going on here! Is all of this just a way of steering the conversation to another subject? Really, do you think I'm an idiot? Do you think that I don't see what's going on?

ELENA: There's no reason to get angry, dear. Donald has brought up a very sensitive and thorny subject. Don't you have anything to say about it?

MARK: I demand that you immediately put an end to all of this! Out of respect for me, for our friendship, I ask you to immediately put an end to all of this!

JOSEPH: Why are you getting so emotional, Robert, can't we disagree for the sake of establishing the truth, and not for the sake of affirming one's own ego?

ELENA: Just look at the words he's using now, Robert!

MARK: I demand that both of you immediately shut up! Shut up! I demand that you put an end to all of this. What's going on here? I demand that both of you explain it to me?!

Pause. MARK *calms down a bit.*

MARK: I repeat my question, what's going on here right now?

JOSEPH *doesn't respond.*

MARK: Why are you silent? Sarah?

ELENA: It's impossible to shut up and respond to questions at the same time.

MARK (*Beside himself, yelling*): What?! Have you . . . ?! I'll . . . ! You . . . ! Goddammit . . . ! I don't even want to see the two of your after all of this. I don't want to see you!!!!! I don't want to see you, Sarah! I don't want to see you!!!

MARK *is angry. Exits.*

Pause.

JOSEPH: I'm not a child murderer, Sarah. I didn't vote for the people who're in power right now, and I don't work for any government enterprise. I don't even wear shoes made of natural leather, and, as you know, Martha and I have been vegetarians for many years now, therefore I take no part not only in the murder of human children, but even in the murder of the children of cows.

ELENA: You mean calves?

JOSEPH: What?

ELENA: The children of cows are called calves, I just wanted to clarify.

JOSEPH: Why pick on words, Sarah?

ELENA: Because when your wife Martha was young and had an abortion, you not only knew about it, Donald, but even, to some degree, insisted upon it, at least that's what Martha told me. That's why I pick on words, my dear.

Pause.

JOSEPH: Oh, that Martha! You women really can't keep your mouths shut.

ELENA: I hope you're not going to tell me that abortion is not the same as child murder?

Pause.

ELENA: Abortion is child murder, Donald?

JOSEPH: Well, of course, Sarah. Of course.

Pause.

ELENA: Well then, Donald? Why don't you say something, Donald?

JOSEPH: I'm sorry, Sarah, I don't want to talk about this. Let's not continue this conversation. Let's switch to another topic. Let's talk about you, for instance.

ELENA: Oh, Donald! I'm afraid I'm not the most interesting topic for conversation.

JOSEPH: Nevertheless, I'd be very interested to know who it was that came to your place last Monday, who was the man whose visit you tried to conceal from your husband?

ELENA: If you don't want to talk about Martha's abortion, why should I tell you about my personal life? Friendship is built on trust, Donald? If you trust me, then I trust you. If you don't trust me, then I don't trust you. Trust in exchange for trust.

Pause.

JOSEPH: Yes, many years ago I insisted that Martha get an abortion because I don't like children, Sarah. I haven't liked children since I was a child, and I would've become a bad father. And I always knew that. And I never wanted to have children. And that's why Martha and I have always been extra careful when it comes to birth control. But it so happened that, one day, my condom broke, and my damned spermatozoid got into her unfortunate ovum. However, being sensible people, Martha and I came to the conclusion that it would be better for a new person not to come into this world at all than to become the son of a bad father who doesn't love him. That was the decision I made. And Martha agreed with my decision.

ELENA: That was the decision you made, Donald? And who are you to decide who should or should not come into this world? Do you think you're God? Haven't you bitten off more than you can chew, Donald?

JOSEPH: Not really, Sarah. I've bitten off exactly the right amount. Especially since I don't believe in God and think that no one makes any conscious decisions on this planet besides us people. We are the ones who make all the damned decisions. End of story. And now it's your turn, Sarah. Tell me, who was at your place last Monday? Trust in exchange for trust.

ELENA: Alright, Donald. Trust in exchange for trust. It's been several years now that I've been seeing another man. I love another man. I'm happy and miserable at the same time.

JOSEPH: And you see him in your husband's house? But how did you manage to convince Marcus to confirm your lie? I mean, to my knowledge, Marcus never lies.

ELENA: That's very strange of you to say this, Donald. Since you know perfectly well that, last Monday, Marcus really was at my place. And he didn't need to lie.

JOSEPH: That's enough, Sarah. Last Monday, Marcus was at my place, and you know this perfectly well. Why keep up this charade when Robert isn't here with us?

ELENA: Exactly, Donald, why keep up this charade when Robert isn't here, since you know that Marcus wasn't and couldn't possibly have been at your place last Monday. However, I was struck by the ease with which Martha's able to tell lies. I must confess, I never thought she was capable of that.

JOSEPH: Oh yeah?

ELENA: Oh yeah.

Pause.

ELENA: My goodness?! Who would've thought that Martha was capable of that!

JOSEPH: Yes, Martha's capable of a great deal, a very great deal, Sarah. It even turns out that she's capable of eating her own finger.

ELENA: What sort of strange metaphor is that, Donald?

JOSEPH: It's not a metaphor, Sarah. It's an experience that Martha and I once shared. Hasn't she ever told you about how we ate her finger?

ELENA: Wha-at?

JOSEPH: But you know perfectly well that Martha's missing a finger on her right hand. She's missing her index finger.

She lost it when she was young. It was the result of an unfortunate incident at her work . . .

ELENA: I've heard this story, Donald.

JOSEPH: You've heard the story about how we ate her finger?

ELENA: Oh, for God's sake, of course not! I've heard the story about how Martha lost her finger.

ELENA *watches* JOSEPH *intently.*

ELENA: What are you saying, Donald?!!

JOSEPH: You see, when this unfortunate incident occurred, Martha was taken to the hospital, and they amputated her finger. Well, Martha asked the surgeons to give her the amputated finger. I don't know why she did this, probably because she was in shock? So she came home from the hospital with her amputated finger. Not knowing yet what she wanted to do with it, Martha put it in the fridge. Which is where I discovered it. And, you know, when I saw this finger lying there, two thoughts came to me. The first thought was that this was an ordinary piece of meat, and it's lying there next to another piece of meat, we weren't yet vegetarians then, and lying right next to the finger in the fridge was a frozen piece of beef. Well, so I thought, here's a piece of meat from a cow, and here's a piece of human meat. Meat is meat. And then a second thought entered my mind, namely that I'll live out my whole life without ever tasting human meat. I mean, how would I get the opportunity? Where would I obtain human meat? I'm not a murderer. And then this comes along. It's right there. And no one had to give up their life, no sins have been committed. And so I got the idea of tasting a human being, since the opportunity presented itself in the shape of a finger. And so I told Martha about it, and, to my surprise, she immediately agreed. And so we boiled this finger then and there, after which, having separated the meat from the bones, we ate it. Each of us got only a bite-sized piece, I mean, what do you expect, a woman's finger, especially since, at that time, Martha was a slender girl and not the baggy pillow she's become today. So that's what we did, and by the way, right afterward we decided to become vegetarians, and ever since then we've stopped eating not only meat, but fish too, so there you have it.

ELENA *looks at* JOSEPH *in horror.*

ELENA: Why did you do that, Donald?!

JOSEPH: To gain experience. Have you ever eaten a human being, Sarah?

ELENA: Of course not.

JOSEPH: Well, I have.

ELENA: But what about God, Donald? What about God?!

JOSEPH: There is no God, Sarah. And besides, you'll have to forgive me, but eating your own finger isn't much of a sin compared to a certain someone I know cheating on her husband in his own house . . .

ELENA: First of all, we don't meet in our house, but in a hotel. And second, it's love, Donald. Don't you see the difference between sin and love? This man and I love each other, do you understand? However, I forgot, you don't know what love is.

JOSEPH: Why do you feel the need to insult me, Sarah? I'm much older than you and don't deserve such treatment. I love my wife, and we've been together almost forty years, while you and Robert have lived together less than ten and there are already cracks in your marriage. Therefore, which of us knows better what love is, my dear?

ELENA: I do! Because I love this man, but you don't love your wife, Donald.

JOSEPH: How do you know that, Sarah? I love Martha.

ELENA: Martha told me. She told me how, on your wedding night, you confessed to her that you don't love her and that you only married her for her father's money.

Pause.

JOSEPH: Which, by the way, we never got, because her father, that ninety-year-old bag of garden fertilizer, is still smoking his stinking cigars on the veranda of his magnificent villa. And I think he'll outlive all of us.

ELENA: Martha told me that you even refused to make love to her on your wedding night because you didn't have condoms. And that when she started crying, you didn't even try to calm her down, but simply went to the other room and calmly fell asleep there. Not that she was complaining to me, Donald, it's just that sometimes Martha feels very lonely and she wants to talk to someone about her difficult life.

JOSEPH: Oh, that Martha. I guess it's true what they say, summer wasps sting in November, too.

MARK *enters.*

MARK: I've spoken to Marcus. I went to his place. I went straight to him. Mass had just ended and Marcus was coming out of church. We had a serious talk, face to face. And naturally, all of my doubts have vanished. Marcus really was at our place last Monday. He was with Sarah. You don't need to explain anything to me, Donald. I don't want to know why you did this and why your wife, Martha, took part in it. I still love you both. And I repeat: if you want, Donald, I can put you in touch with a very, very decent therapist.

Pause.

MARK: Sarah, I beg you to forgive me, I got too worked up. I really did behave very badly, forgive me.

ELENA: Never mind, Robert. Everything's fine. Kiss me.

MARK *kisses* ELENA *on the cheek.* ELENA *puts her arms around* MARK*'s head and pulls it to herself.* MARK *puts his arms around* ELENA*'s waist. They stand holding each other tight.*

JOSEPH: Life never ceases to amaze me. Just a moment ago this woman was telling me about her lover, about how much she loves him, about how it's the real thing, and now, just a few minutes later, she's melting from joy in the embrace of her hubby, who doesn't even suspect that he's a cuckold.

MARK *approaches* JOSEPH.

MARK: What did you say, Donald?

JOSEPH: Ask your wife about it, Robert. By God, direct all of your questions to her, my friend, and not to me.

MARK: What is he saying, Sarah?

ELENA: I don't know what he's saying, Robert. Can't you see, our Donald isn't feeling well.

JOSEPH: But you told me yourself about your lover. About him being at your place this Monday.

ELENA: Marcus was at my place this Monday, Donald, and I think our conversation is no longer funny.

MARK: It was never funny to *me*. Donald, my friend, what's wrong with you? How are you feeling, my dear?

JOSEPH: I'm feeling worse by the minute. I'm in utter despair. I'm really tired from this whole world that surrounds me. I'm tired of the desert in which my soul dwells. I live without love, without God, without hope for salvation. And without understanding, Robert. Without any understanding from anyone whatsoever. I'm alone in a lonely world.

MARK: Donald, my dear. My dear boy, Donald.

MARK *gives* JOSEPH *a hug, holds him tight.*

MARK: You're not alone, old friend. Aren't we here with you, pal? We're your faithful friends—me, Sarah, Martha, and

Marcus, we all love you. Believe me. We love you, our dear Donald. And we'll help you, we'll cure you, we'll enlist the help of the best doctors, the best therapists, the best psychiatrists.

Pause.

JOSEPH: Robert, your brother Marcus was at our place last Monday.

MARK: Alright, alright, calm down, my dear, it'll pass, believe me, it'll pass.

JOSEPH: But listen, Sarah, you just told me yourself that you have a lover, trust in exchange for trust, Sarah.

ELENA: I'm here, Donald, I'm here. Robert and I will do everything in our power to cure you, you just have to trust us and everything will be well. Trust us, Donald, trust in exchange for trust, my dear.

JOSEPH: I know who can prove it to you! Mrs. Gertrude, our neighbor. It just so happened that she stopped by to see Martha last Monday, to get a recipe for goulash, and she not only saw Marcus, but they even had a conversation about the essence of Christian confession. I'll call her. I'm sure I have her number.

JOSEPH *takes out his phone and searches for Mrs. Gertrude's phone number in his address book.*

MARK: Come on, Donald. Cut it out, you hear?

JOSEPH: You won't suspect Mrs. Gertrude of lying, will you?

JOSEPH *presses the call button.*

MARK: Donald, for God's sake, cut it out, there's no need to disturb a poor woman.

JOSEPH: She's not poor, Robert. Hello? Good afternoon, Mrs. Gertrude! This is your neighbor, Donald.

MARK: Good Lord, I didn't think it was this serious, I'll call my friend today, he's a psychiatry professor in Copenhagen.

JOSEPH: Forgive me for calling you on a weekend, but I have my old friend, Mr. Robert Joachim, next to me, and he has a question for you. No, no, he's not a member of our congregation. But he is my best friend. What's that? No, I don't know why he's not a member of our congregation. Yes, he's a Catholic. Yes, despite his last name. Of course, he goes to church. You know his younger brother very well . . . but it would be better for you to speak to Mr. Joachim directly, I'm passing the phone to him. Have a wonderful Sunday, Mrs. Gertrude.

JOSEPH *passes the phone to* MARK.

MARK: I won't talk to her, Donald. Please excuse yourself right away and tell her that we'll call her back later.

JOSEPH: The woman is waiting, Robert. Talk to her, she's an ardent Catholic, the president of our Catholic congregation, you can count on her to speak only the truth, talk to her. It's not nice to keep the woman waiting, Robert.

MARK *takes the phone.*

MARK: Hello? Good afternoon, Mrs. Gertrude. My name is Robert Joachim, as my friend Donald has already informed you. You see. . . . What's that? No, I don't belong to any congregation, I just attend a Catholic church on Sundays. What? Um-hum. Well, alright, I'll consider your proposal. You see, my brother. . . . What's that? Oh, you know me? What's that? You know my brother? Of course, that's not surprising, he sometimes visits Martha and Donald. What's that? Oh, you spoke to him last Monday? Wha-at?! Which Monday was it that you spoke to him, Mrs. Gertrude? Are you sure? Are you sure it was last Monday? And are you sure it was my brother? What did you speak to him about? Oh, about the essence of confession, um-hum. How old are you, Mrs. Gertrude? Oh, forgive me! It just slipped out. Oh, I didn't mean to ask about your age, it just slipped out. I'm not sure how it happened.

Please forgive me, Mrs. Gertrude, I want you to know that I didn't mean to ask you about your age, it's just that I'm a bit out of it, I, well, I had a bit to smoke, though not cigarettes, Mrs. Gertrude, but, you know, different sorts of cigarettes altogether. What's that? You don't know what I'm talking about? Well, of course you don't know what I'm talking about, because you most certainly don't smoke "different sorts of cigarettes." What's that? Oh, you don't smoke at all? And that's for the best, Mrs. Gertrude. What? Why am I calling? I don't know, Mrs. Gertrude, lately I feel like I no longer understanding anything at all. Good day!

MARK *hangs up and passes the phone to* JOSEPH.

MARK: I really don't understand anything. Sarah, can you explain it to me?

ELENA: I don't know, Robert.

MARK: How about you, Donald, do you know?

JOSEPH: Summer wasps sting in November, too, Robert.

MARK: Maybe you're all just messing with me? Maybe you're all in on it: Marcus, Martha, and even Mrs. Gertrude.

ELENA: You're a bastard, Donald.

JOSEPH: I'm just tired, Sarah, that's all.

Pause.

MARK: Why is life such a pathetic joke? Why is it so worthless? Why is there so much lying, hypocrisy, and filth? So much filth all around us. So much filth all around us. So much filth all around us. A filthy, mutilated world. What's it all for? Why did God create a world that is so monstrously cruel? Why did he send his son into the world only for the world to crucify Him? He sent his son into the world only for the world to crucify Him, but, I'm afraid, it didn't help the world in any way. This sacrifice didn't save the world, no matter what we think.

ELENA: What are you saying, Robert? Come to your senses!

MARK: This sacrifice was in vain, the world is still mired in lies and sin, and every day it only gets worse and worse.

ELENA: Don't say such things, Robert. Don't take on yourself such an awful sin as blasphemy.

JOSEPH: Say whatever you want, buddy, and don't be afraid of anyone. The world is a filthy puddle of shit, there's no God, and there's no one to punish us for all the horrible things that we do here. And there's no one to save us from ourselves either, for that matter. We're all doomed.

MARK: Filth under our fingernails, filth in our souls, filth in our families, filth in our churches. Filth, filth, filth, only filth all around us.

ELENA: Get a grip on yourself, Robert, Marcus wouldn't have appreciated what you just said.

MARK: Marcus?! And who is this Marcus? Isn't he the same man who lied to his own brother twice in one day?

ELENA: Marcus didn't lie to you, Robert. He really was at our place last Monday. Don't listen to Donald, don't you see, he's not himself.

JOSEPH: But Robert isn't listening to me, Sarah, but to Mrs. Gertrude. Or will you say that she's lost her mind too, like I did?

ELENA: I don't know, Donald. I can't explain yet how you've managed to turn all of this around. I don't know why these two perfectly nice women—your wife. Martha. and your neighbor Gertrude—why they have agreed to encourage your sick fantasy, but I won't let this matter drop and will see it through to the end. I'll do it for the sake of family, for the sake of love, for the sake of faith. And for the sake of the Holy Sacrifice that was delivered for all of us. Marcus was at our place last Monday, Robert, because Marcus and I love each other. Two weeks ago, Marcus and I began an affair. We couldn't find the strength to tell you, we tried to break up several times, so as not to sin, but we couldn't hold back our feelings. We genuinely love each other, and we've decided that love will redeem our sin. Because love redeems all. We love each other, Robert. I know it's probably hard for you to hear all of this. But it had to happen sooner or later. I'm not at all trying to justify myself, but let our feelings be the only justification for me and Marcus. Love redeems all if it is love. And it *is* love, Robert. And forgive me for informing you about it only now, forgive me.

Pause.

JOSEPH: But that doesn't prove that Marcus was at your place last Monday?

ELENA: What else is there to say, Donald? It's perfectly clear.

MARK: But it's impossible, Sarah?

JOSEPH: It's perfectly possible, Robert. But I continue to insist that Marcus was at my place.

ELENA: I was with Marcus last Monday, Robert. I was with him in our bed.

MARK: But it's impossible, Sarah?

JOSEPH: It's perfectly possible, Robert, any day except last Monday.

MARK: Sarah?!

ELENA: Forgive me, Robert.

MARK: Donald?!

JOSEPH: I'm sorry, old friend.

MARK, *in despair, looks at* JOSEPH, *then at* ELENA, *then suddenly turns around and walks out very quickly.*

Pause.

JOSEPH: I don't understand, Sarah. If Marcus is your lover, then who was at your place last Monday?

ELENA: Marcus was at my place last Monday, Donald.

JOSEPH: But Marcus was at my place last Monday, Sarah.

ELENA: You know perfectly well where Marcus was last Monday, Donald.

JOSEPH: He was at my place.

ELENA: You know perfectly well where he was.

JOSEPH: He was at my place.

JOSEPH *and* ELENA *stare at each other. More than a minute passes while they intently look each other in the eye.*

JOSEPH: What do you believe in, Sarah?

ELENA: In salvation, Donald.

JOSEPH: Who will save you, Sarah?

ELENA: God will save me, Donald.

JOSEPH: You believe in God?

ELENA: Yes.

JOSEPH: And who will save me, Sarah?

ELENA: God will save you, Donald, if you ask Him to.

JOSEPH: But I don't believe in God, Sarah, so what should I do?

ELENA: Ask God to give you faith.

JOSEPH: I can't ask God for anything, Sarah.

ELENA: Why's that, Donald?

JOSEPH: Because you can't ask anything of someone in whom you don't believe.

ELENA: Why's that, Donald?

JOSEPH: What do you mean why's that?

ELENA: Why can't you ask of someone in whom you don't believe? After all, what you're asking Him is precisely for His help in making you believe.

JOSEPH: Well, alright, and can I count on salvation without God?

ELENA: And what do you mean by "salvation," Donald?

Pause. JOSEPH *reflects.*

JOSEPH: When it stops raining.

ELENA: What? Forgive me, I don't understand?

JOSEPH: Haven't you noticed that, for the third day in a row now, it's raining?

ELENA: Are you joking, Donald?

JOSEPH: No, Sarah, I'm not joking at all. It's just that I can't stand this damned rain any longer. All these drops that fall to the ground. Millions upon millions of drops fall to the ground, fall on our rooftops, fall on our heads, fall on our children's heads.

ELENA: Well, and so what, Donald?

JOSEPH: It's just that I hate all of them. All of these drops collectively and each drop individually. I hate the flight of the drop from the sky and the sound of it splattering on the asphalt, or on the roof tiles in my house, or, even worse, on my metallic window ledge. Splat, splat, splat.

Pause.

JOSEPH: Splat, splat, splat.

ELENA: Well, in that case, maybe you really do need to see a therapist.

JOSEPH: But the problem is that I believe in therapy even less than I believe in God.

ELENA: And is there anything in which you do believe, Donald, even a little?

JOSEPH: Yes, Sarah. I believe in the fact that Marcus was at my place last Monday.

MARK *enters.*

MARK: I've spoken to Mrs. Gertrude. Or rather, I tried to speak to Mrs. Gertrude. I drove to your house, Donald, to speak to your neighbor face to face. But, it turns out, you don't have a neighbor by the name of Mrs. Gertrude. To your right lives Mr. Helmut, an old bachelor, to the left, a young family, but there's no Mrs. Gertrude, not on your street, not even in your settlement. Just as there's no Catholic congregation to which you supposedly belong, Donald. I don't know who that poor woman was to whom I spoke on the phone, or how you even managed to organize this whole spectacle, and more importantly—why? What for, Donald?

JOSEPH: Yes, it would seem that summer wasps really do sting in November, too, Robert.

MARK: Indeed.

ELENA: And did it by any chance enter into your head to drop in on Martha?

MARK: Of course, it did. But the problem is that Martha didn't open the gate for me. I stood by the gate and rang her, but she didn't open it for me. Even though she was at home, because her car stood in the yard and there was smoke coming out of the chimney pipe. I'm 100 percent certain that she was at home. I mean, of course, I understand her, in a way, after all, it was hard for her to look me in the eye. But I'm not angry with her, I know that it was Donald who made her lie to me. I mean, we both know how much she fears her husband.

ELENA: And is it true, Donald, that you once spent several hours straight forcing Martha to fall out of love with you?

MARK: What for, Donald?!

ELENA: Martha told me that he was pressing her to stop loving him, that he wanted Martha to find him repulsive and to admit that she no longer loves him. In this manner he wanted to prove to her that love is something that passes. But it ended with poor Martha losing consciousness, not having admitted a thing.

MARK: How awful. Poor Martha!

JOSEPH: Oh, that Martha.

MARK: I'm sorry, Donald, but I have no choice but to report everything to the local psychiatric hospital. Forgive me, but your behavior is becoming unsafe for those around you.

Pause.

JOSEPH: Summer wasps sting in November, too.

MARK: Yes, summer wasps sting in November, too.

ELENA: Indeed.

Pause.

MARK: Once, when I was a little boy, my father made a little ship for me out of tree bark and attached a paper sail to it. It was so pretty, I was simply overjoyed. I ran with this little ship to the river. And, dying of joy, I lowered the little ship into the water. I still remember every second of that day. I remember with what joy I ran along the trail to the forest, how I wanted to get to the river faster and how I got to the river. And how I lowered the little ship into the water with hands trembling from joy.

Pause.

ELENA: Well, and what then, Robert? What happened to the little ship?

MARK: It sailed away.

ELENA: Robert?

MARK (*Yelling at* ELENA): Why are you looking at me as if I'm mad?! It sailed away, get it, it sailed away? The most valuable things we have, the most beautiful things we have, they all leave us. They sail out of our hands. I stood there, by the river, and I begged it to return, but it sailed away, further and further down the river. And I stood there weeping. And I begged your God, Sarah, to return that little ship to me. But the river took it forever. God doesn't have the power to change the direction of the river. And if God doesn't have the power to change the direction of the river, then what need do I have of such a God? I wanted this ship to sail on the water, but I didn't want it to sail away from me forever. And I understood, then and there, that everything that sails will one day sail away from you. And everything that flies will fly away from you. And everyone who's able to walk will sooner or later walk away from you. And everyone who loves you will sooner or later fall out of love with you. While we, we always remain standing by the river. We always watch our love and our joy sail away from us down the river.

Pause.

MARK: I didn't go to see Mrs. Gertrude, Sarah. I didn't go anywhere. I just sat there and sat there on a bench and tried not to think about anything. Forgive me, Donald, I believe you that Marcus was at your place last Monday. It's just that I'm afraid of facing the truth. I'm afraid to live. That's all. My therapist isn't helping me. And I'm just as tired as you are, Donald. And I'm still standing there, by the river, just as I did when I was little, watching my little ship sail away from me further and further. And I know that God can't stop the river from flowing. Forgive me, Donald.

Pause.

ELENA: Robert, it's been three years since I started seeing another man. But, of course, it's not Marcus, Robert. I couldn't find the strength to tell you.

MARK: I didn't think it was Marcus, Sarah. To be honest, I haven't thought about it at all.

ELENA: And what *have* you been thinking about, Robert?

MARK: I don't know. Probably about the fact that summer wasps sting in November, too.

JOSEPH: And what does that mean, Robert?

MARK: I don't know.

ELENA: Forgive me, I feel so guilty.

MARK: Do you love this man, Sarah?

ELENA: I don't know, Robert. I don't think I even know what that word means.

MARK: Why were you silent these three whole years?

ELENA: Because I kept waiting for it to end. After each of our meetings, I thought it was the last meeting. Every time he left me, I was sure that he wouldn't call again. And just yesterday we had a serious conversation, and we decided to end our relationship. That is our final decision. I've thought it over thoroughly and cannot go back to the way things were, and he won't come back either, he has chosen his family, because he's married and has children. And so he's decided to go back to his family. And that's the end of it. I don't know if you'll be able to forgive me or not? Most likely you won't and our marriage is over. But, either way, I ask you to forgive me for everything, and believe me, I've always been very fond of you, I've always respected you as a man. Did I love you? In a way, I did. Did I love you the way a wife should love her husband? Probably not, Robert. Although, I don't know. I don't know anything anymore.

Pause.

ELENA: But I swear, Robert, it was Marcus, and not this man, who was at our place last Monday. I had asked Marcus to come because I wanted to tell him about my relationship with this man. I needed to tell someone, I needed advice about what I should do. And Marcus and I spoke until late at night. And when he was leaving, he advised me to tell you everything, Robert, because one shouldn't live a lie. Marcus said that even if you won't be able to forgive me, you'd still understand. One can't live a lie. Forgive me, Robert, I've been living a lie, I lied to you, I acted cruelly toward you. But now you know everything, Robert. Now you know the whole truth about everything. About my lover, about us breaking up, and about the reason for Marcus coming to see me last Monday.

JOSEPH: Then how do you explain Mrs. Gertrude, who spoke to Marcus about the essence of confession last Monday?

And how do you explain my wife Martha, who also confirms everything.

ELENA: Donald was very clever in setting it all up, Robert. I'm certain that he has put these two poor women up to it, and maybe even threatened them, after all, he's capable of such things. Marcus was at our place last Monday, I swear, Robert, I've already told you everything, I mean, think about it, what reason do I have to lie?

Pause.

MARK: Yes, that's true, no reason at all.

JOSEPH: And what reason do I have to lie, Robert?

MARK: Also true.

Pause.

MARK: There's no reason to any of this. This whole world completely lacks reason. That's all there is to it.

Pause.

ELENA: Woman must submit to man—this is her only salvation, this is her only purpose. Woman must belong to another. She must not have freedom of choice. In the past, for example, a woman would be married off against her will, and then she'd spend her whole life serving her husband. Even now these customs are preserved in some countries. But things have long been otherwise in our civilization. It's as if we women have choice, it's as if we're free. But, in fact, this freedom that has been granted to us is not true freedom, because the essence of woman, her purpose, is to belong to another, to give her freedom to her man. It doesn't matter if we want it or not, if we agree with it or not, but our female being is constituted in such a way that we must give ourselves. Woman gives, man takes. God has created woman out of man's rib and commanded her to listen to him and revere him as her master. And maybe I would've consented to this, but the thing is,

I'd like to belong to and serve a man who's worthy of ruling over me. And that's the problem with contemporary society, and that's the problem with our so-called democratic society. We've decided that we can choose what's best for us. And as soon as we decided that we can choose, from that very second, we lost the capacity to choose. We choose what's best for us—and that's our problem. Because it's God who must decide what's best for us. That's our whole problem, do you understand? And that's why as soon as woman decided that she'll choose her man herself, from that very second, she began searching for the right man, she began searching for the man whom she'd be willing to serve. But such men don't exist. Such men don't exist. It's very hard to find a man whom I'd be willing to serve. It's very hard, in our day and age, to find a man before whom I could bow my head in submission. I've searched far and wide and still haven't found him. I haven't found a single man to whom I'd be willing to give myself with my whole being and to whom I'd want to belong. And that's the problem. I mean, men must've been even worse in the past than they are today, but women didn't choose then, they loved the one that God gave them. But today I want to choose, and that's why I'm not able to find my master. I'm not able, because I know what he must be like. And that stands in my way. I know what he must be like. And it's the same with God. I know what He must be like, and that's why I can't find the right God for myself, a God whom I could serve. Because I'm choosing him myself. And what sort of servant is it who chooses her own master? And that's why there's no happiness for women in this world. Because we've decided to search for our men ourselves. It's no longer God who gives us the one we deserve, but we ourselves who search for the one deserving of us. But if no one would bother to ask us, like before, if we'd be married off against our will, if we'd revere and serve any man who became our husband, if looking at our husband's face we'd see our Lord, see the image of our Creator, then a woman's happiness would be possible and we women would be chaste, wise, and modest like before. That's all.

Pause.

JOSEPH: Are you serious?

ELENA: Absolutely.

MARK: And doesn't the real issue consist in the fact that the world is a monster that devours its own children, and that's all?

ELENA: The issue is that we have no one but ourselves in this world, we live by ourselves, we're alone with ourselves. We're alone. That's the problem.

JOSEPH: You seriously think so?

ELENA: Absolutely.

MARK: But we're intelligent, and there's nothing to be done about that. I know a few things about this world that prevent me from believing in and agreeing with what you've just said here. And therefore if we're going to speak about the main problem, then it consists precisely in the fact that we're intelligent. Not everyone, but many of us. And he who's intelligent is unhappy. But I'm not to blame for the fact that I'm intelligent.

ELENA: Who's to blame, then?

MARK: Well, if it's come down to this, then it's you women. Eve is to blame, that same Eve who persuaded Adam to eat the apple of knowledge. We ate the apple. And now we're intelligent. And we know that everything you've just said here isn't really true. Or not true at all. And that's why we suffer, because we know everything, and if there's something we don't know, we have a hunch about it. That's all.

JOSEPH: And isn't there any way for us to become stupid again?

MARK: I don't think there is, because I can't unknow what I already know.

ELENA: And what do you know?

MARK: I know everything. That's my main problem—the problem is that I know everything. I know everything, and that's why knowledge is closed off to me, I can't learn anything new, because I already know everything. And that, I think, is the cause of that catastrophe that has befallen the world. We know everything.

ELENA: And do you know everything too, Donald?

JOSEPH: Unfortunately, I do.

ELENA: That means you know where Marcus was last Monday?

JOSEPH: Of course, I know. Marcus was at my place last Monday.

ELENA: But that's not true, Donald. And you know it's not true. And you know that Marcus was at my place last Monday.

JOSEPH: Marcus was at my place, Robert, believe me.

ELENA: He was in our house, dear, so believe me.

Pause.

JOSEPH: It's best if you believed me, Robert.

ELENA: No, it's best if you believed me, my dear.

MARK: Oh, why is this world such a monster? A monster that devours its own children? Why is this hideous world so bloodthirsty, why does it bite off the heads of its own children? What have we done to deserve this, how have we sinned? What is it all for? What is it all for? What for?

JOSEPH: Didn't you vote for the current president, Robert? Of course, you did. And doesn't your current president express his support for the bombing campaign in Iraq, didn't he support the president of the United States who ordered his pilots to bomb cities with peaceful Iraqi civilians, and much more. And didn't someone's children die from these bombs? And didn't the mothers of these children, running outside with dead children in their hands, cry, "What is it all for? What have we done to deserve this?" Don't they think the world is a monster that bites off the heads of their children, Robert? Who's to blame for it? The ones to blame are: the pilots who dropped these bombs, the U.S. president, who gave the order, your president, who supported this bombing campaign, and you, who voted for your president.

MARK: And is that why my wife is cheating on me with another man in my own bed? What is this, God's punishment for participating in the elections?

ELENA: I never slept with this man in our bed, Robert, we always met in a hotel.

MARK: Fine, then I'll rephrase my question: Is there anything sacred in this world? Is there anything sacred in this world or not?

Pause.

MARK: Donald?

JOSEPH: I don't think there's anything sacred, old friend.

MARK: And what about you, Sarah, what do you think?

JOSEPH: Just wait, she's going to say: God.

Pause. ELENA *shuts her eyes.*

MARK: Sarah?

ELENA *opens her eyes and looks at* MARK.

ELENA: For this rain to stop.

MARK: Are you serious, Sarah?

ELENA: Of course I'm serious, Robert.

MARK: Then you believe that the main cause behind the tragedy of our life is this rain, which has been falling for three days now and can't seem to stop?

ELENA: Yes, I think the problem consists precisely in this, Robert. And Donald thinks so too, he recently told me himself.

JOSEPH: I see the problem precisely in this rain, Robert. The rain has been falling for three days already and doesn't pause for a minute. These drops! They keep falling on my roof and on my window ledge, and I can't reconcile myself to it, I can't accept it, Robert. Splat, splat, splat.

MARK: Then you're serious? Then I'm not the only one who thinks so?!

ELENA: Wha-at? You think so too, Robert?

MARK: Well, of course. It's just that I was afraid to admit it, afraid to admit it not only to you but also to myself. When this rain started falling three days ago, I thought, it can't be for long, I mean, after all, it's the end of November, and it's high time for snow to fall in our northern regions. But when I woke up this morning and saw that it was still pouring in buckets, I felt that something cracked inside me, something snapped inside me, somewhere very, very deep inside, in my innermost depths, something snapped or, rather, shattered to pieces because of this rain. There, inside me, something irreversible happened today, it was as if there, inside me, a very expensive vase fell from a cabinet and shattered to pieces. Something shattered inside me because of this relentless rain, because of all these drops, which, as Donald has rightly observed, keep pounding and pounding on my window ledge. I felt hundreds of tiny fragments scatter all over my soul, all over my heart, and it was as if I too became cracked and warped. And then I thought that this damned rain is to blame for everything that's happening to me, that it's probably because of this rain that my whole life has gone sideways. But then I thought it was scarcely possible that a whole life can shatter to pieces because of ordinary rain, it's highly unlikely, or maybe I'm failing to grasp something? Maybe I'm failing to grasp something about this life? And then I decided that, no doubt, there's something else going on here, that maybe there are more profound causes for all of this than this rain? And I started to look for these causes. But I couldn't find them. The causes of my tragedy turned out to be hidden from me. I couldn't locate them. And so the causes of my tragedy remain unknown to me.

JOSEPH: It's that damned rain, Robert.

MARK: Yes, now I finally understand, Donald.

JOSEPH: Well, I'm very happy that you understand, dear friend.

MARK: Yes, now I understand 100 percent. And it's all thanks to Sarah.

ELENA: It's all thanks to Donald, Robert. He was the first to speak openly about it.

MARK: Thank you, Donald.

JOSEPH: Not at all! It's not even worth talking about. Deep down, we all knew it.

ELENA: As for me, already three days ago, as soon as the first drops started falling from the sky, I immediately thought, my life's about to get a little more complicated, and that's exactly what happened.

JOSEPH: It's a good thing we're all friends and can support each other in this difficult situation.

MARK: Yes, yes, it's so important to be with each other, to argue with each other, to disagree, to challenge, but to still love each other. I love you so much, my friends. Sarah! Donald!

JOSEPH: Robert, Sarah.

MARK, ELENA, *and* JOSEPH *embrace each other. They stand, embracing, like three school fellows.*

ELENA: God, it's so nice to have friends who are older and wiser than you, who can teach you something, who can pass on to you their life experience, who can teach you wisdom. Robert, Donald, I love you so much.

JOSEPH: Something inside me is tickling me like a sparrow, something there, inside me, tickling and twittering like a little bird and trying to break out, some bird flying hither and tither inside me, in my heart, rushing about like a sparrow, but unable to break out. What is it that I feel inside me, so wonderful, but so restless, eh?!

MARK: Oh, and there's something scratching at me too, from the inside, as if a cat has climbed into my stomach and now scratches its paws there. What is that scratching there inside me, what is that burst of joy there inside me, eh?! Eh!?

ELENA: It's as if someone inside me is washing the floor and tickling me with his mop, and singing, to boot.

MARK: Oh! You don't say! Singing his lungs out! Who's that suddenly singing his lungs out inside me?

ELENA: And even dancing whole dances inside me!

JOSEPH: Birds, whole flocks of birds flying inside me and tickling me with their wings. Oh! Come now, you birds! Come now, stop tickling me this instant or I'll . . . ! I'll . . . ! Oh, I'll . . . ! Oh, you birds! Oh!

MARK: Singing inside me in such a way that my heart is dancing and, any minute now, will burst out. Still, my heart, still, it's only a joke, it's only, oh, a joke, it's a joke, oh, oh!

ELENA: Oh, don't tickle me. Aw!

MARK: I can't do anything about it, my hands are reaching for your hips on their own accord, in order to tickle them.

ELENA: Oh, what are you doing, it tickles, stop. Aw! Aw! Aw!

JOSEPH: Tickle me too, please tickle me too.

MARK: Look out!

JOSEPH: Aw, it tickles, Oh! Stop, I beg you, sto-o-op! Aw!

MARK: Didn't you ask me to tickle me yourself, old friend?!

JOSEPH: Oh, I'm only saying "stop" because that's what you're supposed to say, but actually sting me, old chap, as soon as you can.

MARK: These summer wasps sting in November.

ELENA: Aw! A-a-aw!

JOSEPH: Summer wasps, aw! A-a-aw! Oh now you look out, old chap. Summer wasps are moving on you.

MARK: Wow! A-a-aw! It tickles!

ELENA: And here are my summer wasps coming to his aid!

MARK: Oh! It tickles! Oh, oh, oh! Stop it, there are two of you, it's not fair!

JOSEPH: Summer wasps sting in November, too. Bzzz, bzzz, bzzz.

MARK: Oh that's how it is! In that case, both of you look out. Here are the sacred summer bees falling upon you, beware!

ELENA: Oh how painfully they prick!

MARK: That's because these aren't ordinary bees, but sacred summer bees! That's what's truly sacred in this world—sacred summer bees. Which sting in November, too!

JOSEPH: Oh! Oh, it really does hurt! So that's how it is! In that case, sacred summer bees are moving on you! Help me with your wasps, we'll move on him together!

MARK: Ouch, that hurts!

JOSEPH: Well, what did you expect, they're sacred bees?!!

MARK: You think I'm afraid. Well, look out!

ELENA: A-a-aw! Aw!

JOSEPH: Ow, o-o-ow!

MARK: Aw! Aw! Aw!

MARK, ELENA, *and* JOSEPH *tickle each other and laugh.*

THE END

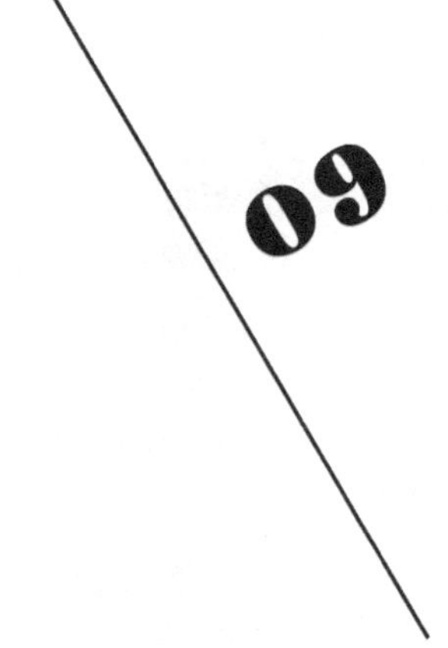

SOMNAMBULISM

YAROSLAVA PULINOVICH
TRANSLATED BY KIRA ALEXANDRA ROSE

CHARACTERS

SLAVA—thirty-nine years old
ALLA—thirty-five years old
MAXIM—fifteen years old
DIMA—forty years old
BORIS—forty-five years old
YOUNG WOMAN—twenty-five years old

1

SLAVA *climbs the stairs of a Khrushchev-style apartment building. He climbs, hearing and seeing nothing. He climbs because he's got to go somewhere. Right now, his mind is entirely cloudy, as if wrapped in some kind of haze or fog. And if you ask him for a smoke . . . or if you ask him what day it is . . . he likely won't answer, or he'll mumble something incomprehensible and keep going, because he's got to get somewhere. Right now, it's absolutely vital that* SLAVA *get somewhere where there's life, where they'll ask him a question and his answer can be irrelevant. Where something usually happens. Something having to do with the established rhythms of life. And so our thirty-nine-year-old hero* SLAVA *goes up to the fifth floor, where he rings a doorbell. And his long-time friend* DIMA *opens the door. Now that* SLAVA*'s thirty-nine, it's fair to say that* DIMA*'s more like an old acquaintance, rather than a friend. But really, they've known each other for so long that, at least for now, he seems like a friend: one who's never done him a bad turn, harmed him in any way, or ever overstepped his limits. Their friendship is, at least on some level, sincere, but already frayed by life. Not like when they were third-year college students. But where can you find "those" kinds of relations anyway, I ask you? As though something can really stay that same "something" when a certain number of years go by. And so it is that* DIMA*, dressed in an old t-shirt and slippers, answers the door. But he's still in good shape. He still strolls around the house in worn jeans. That means that he's still got it together and can answer when someone comes calling just like that, out of a need to end up somewhere.* SLAVA *is quiet. And* DIMA*, seeing that the number of demons swarming in* SLAVA*'s head has surpassed all human limits, silently lets him into the apartment.* SLAVA *goes into the kitchen without taking off his coat, sits down in a chair, and stares ahead, fixing the space around him with a vacant, unfocused gaze.* DIMA *follows him into the kitchen and, already understanding why* SLAVA *came over, takes out an almost full bottle of vodka. This gesture gives us a better understanding of* DIMA. *He's not a big drinker or an alcoholic; after all, he can easily keep a full bottle of vodka in the fridge. Just in case.* DIMA *pours two shots and hands one to* SLAVA. *After signaling a toast,* SLAVA *downs it.*

They don't talk for some time.

DIMA: That bad?

SLAVA: Yeh . . .

DIMA: I just don't know, Slava. I don't know what to say. I know what *they* say—you've got to bear up until it's over.

SLAVA: I don't know . . .

DIMA: They say the first six months are total hell, and then everything's less . . .

SLAVA: Uh-huh.

DIMA: Were you even at work today? I didn't see you . . .

SLAVA: Yeh. Seems I was . . .

DIMA: Another shot?

SLAVA: Uh-huh.

DIMA *pours two shots.*

DIMA: May she rest in peace.

SLAVA: Yeh . . .

They drink.

SLAVA: I thought . . . that whole time, I thought. . . . I acted like such an idiot, after all . . . after all, I . . . (*He stammers.*)

DIMA: Say it. If you've got something to say, then say it . . .

SLAVA: But you already know everything . . . it's so stupid, if you think about it. It's like fate, or someone else . . . yes, that's it, someone else, up there, played some kind of joke on me. Just played a joke. I never thought about *where* it'll come from. I've already known for a while that it would come down on me. That even if you don't expect it, it'll come without a doubt. I sensed it at the edge of my conscious being. But I never even considered it could be . . . didn't expect it quite like this. Exactly like this. And of course, you know that when they called, I was stuck in a traffic jam. This gigantic fucking traffic jam. And where, Dima? What? Where? Should I ditch my car? Should I run? Scream? I'm in the middle lane! Where can someone really go in such a jam? What can I do? I'm crying, I'm screaming, my blood pressure spikes. Meanwhile, I'm still in a traffic jam. And I'm waiting, waiting, waiting . . . and my eyes only make out flashing green specks ahead . . .

DIMA: But Slava . . . no one's safe from this kind of thing, after all.

SLAVA: That's exactly it . . . no one's safe. No one's safe from lies. No one. From betrayal. From death. No one *has* to tell you the truth. No one *has* to live for your sake. That's just something you made up. That's just you being too full of yourself.

DIMA: Well, be that as it may, you and Renata . . .

SLAVA: What about us?

DIMA: You managed to do a lot together. Look at how well you've raised Max. Now you've got to live for him, Slava . . . you must.

SLAVA: What for? Max is an adult now.

DIMA: Really, at fifteen, an adult? He's still a kid, Slava! His mother just died. You're the only one he's got left. You feel like crap. How do you think he feels? Try to remember yourself at fifteen—whether *you* were an adult then.

SLAVA: He'll get over it. He's not a child.

DIMA: Slava, what's gotten into you? How is he going to get over it? Pull yourself together. You've got to keep going. If not for yourself, then for him.

SLAVA: Look, I get it. I feel bad for him. He's no stranger to me either . . .

DIMA: He's now the only flesh and blood you've got in this world. And you're his. You're bound by blood. Neither of you has anyone closer. . . . Listen, what am I doing explaining this to you, as though I'm some Dr. Phil?[1] After all, you yourself . . .

SLAVA: I know. I get it. Pour.

DIMA *pours two shots. They drink.*

DIMA: You'd better go see a psychologist, Slava. . . . There's no need to be ashamed of it. It's been standard practice for ages now.

SLAVA: Go see a psychologist yourself! Can he bring my wife back?

DIMA: No, of course not, but . . .

SLAVA: What is it with you bastards and your psychologists? With all your advice? I know everything without your help—you've got to hold on, you've got to get it together, you've got to tell yourself that it's a test, and God doesn't give out tests for no reason. Right? Is that it? The thing is, you're all afraid. You're afraid of me because you've got it good! In fact, you're happy that it happened to me and not to you. That I got the bullet and you dodged it. That I'm the one writhing and that it passed you by. All of yours are alive and healthy. You're all doing well! You're all safe, hunky-dory! Well, today it's me, tomorrow it'll be you! And so that I don't remind you of this, you quite rightly send me off to a psychologist, to a psycho ward, a loony bin! So that those who've been knocked off their course, like me, won't ruin your mood!

DIMA: Slava, I understand, but seriously, one more word and you'll get it!

SLAVA: Go on! One word, two words! Here's ten words at once!

DIMA: Don't shout!!! I've got a child sleeping in the next room!

SLAVA: Oh, I totally forgot!! It's so important for you people that everything stays quiet! I totally forgot the law of the land, so sorry! After all, you've got kids and flowers!

DIMA *takes a watering can from the windowsill and pours it out on* SLAVA*'s head.*

SLAVA: What the hell?

DIMA: Nothing. Sober up, my sweet flower, and get on home.

SLAVA: Of course, of course. No problem. Why come late knowing full well that you're late? What an idiot!

DIMA: Slava, buddy . . . it's none of my business, of course. I truly feel for you. And I wouldn't dream of avoiding you. If I were in your position, I don't know how I'd behave . . .

SLAVA: Rejoice. You're not me.

DIMA: Let me talk! Slava, listen, I get everything. But you've completely let yourself go. I'll tell you something in secret, but it's just between us, okay?

SLAVA: Well?

DIMA: Boris hinted to Zhdanova that she can prepare the order . . .

SLAVA: What do you mean by that?

DIMA: Take it as you will. I said nothing. You just can't behave this way with people. Everyone gets it, but you just can't. . . . You're grieving. Everyone knows that, but you can't . . .

SLAVA: Whatever. Let them fire me. You can all go to hell. . . . Pour me another.

DIMA: I won't.

SLAVA: Pour it or I'll go find some myself.

DIMA: Go to hell, if you want. I've got no desire to help you get wasted.

SLAVA: Who's helping me . . . ?

DIMA: I told you. I won't pour it. Period.

SLAVA: You're a dick!

Pause.

DIMA: The only reason I didn't kick you out right now is because you're drunk and not yourself. But seriously—go home, Slava. Max is waiting for you.

SLAVA: He's already asleep . . .

DIMA: He calls my son as late as one a.m. sometimes. Wakes him up. Valya has school at eight in the morning, I'll have you know. Max, by the way, hasn't been to school for a month. Were you even aware of that?

SLAVA: Who cares if he's been to school or not? What's it to you?

DIMA: Nothing. I'm worried that Valya's exams are coming up. And Maxim's too, by the way. Has he decided to graduate after the ninth grade or maybe get a certificate?[2]

SLAVA: Listen, are you a prosecutor? The school principal? A juvenile justice?

DIMA: Fine then. It's useless talking to you. You refuse to see your own son . . .

SLAVA: He's not my son.

DIMA: Slava, that's enough. Stop your nonsense . . .

SLAVA: He's not my son. I'm not his father.

DIMA: Have you gone completely off your rocker?

SLAVA: He's not my son. There are documents. I'll show them to you if you want.

DIMA: Listen, calm down . . .

SLAVA *rummages in his coat pockets and takes out a piece of paper. He extends it to* DIMA.

SLAVA: Here. Read . . .

DIMA *reads it.*

DIMA: Right . . .

SLAVA: There you have it. Do you smoke in here?

DIMA: No, Lyuba and I quit. Right, but . . . but why did you decide all of a sudden? What for?

SLAVA: Can I light up?

DIMA: Go for it. Here, blow into the vent . . .

SLAVA *lights up.*

SLAVA: After Renata died, I decided to delete her inbox. Well, before deleting everything, I glanced at her history, from the very beginning. That's how I stumbled upon their correspondence. Read it all. Edward. What a name! There were photos attached too. Of them together. Turns out she got with him three years after we were married. . . . Well, so I looked closely at his photos. A shitty thought crept up on me. Let's calculate, I thought. And it stacked up. . . . In that last letter, he writes come back, why'd you leave me, what happened, and all that crap. It makes me sick to even recall it. . . . So it turns out she ditched him while she was four months pregnant with Max. At first, I sort of decided not to dwell on it. But then, the more time went on, the more, well, you know. Until it became ridiculous. I printed a photo of the bastard. Would lie in bed at night comparing it to my son's. I'd stare and stare 'til my head would hammer with rage. To make a long story short, I thought, to hell with him. . . . Better to learn the truth than keep torturing myself. Had the genetic test done. Should have kept tormenting myself. Turns out, I paid dearly for my own verdict.

DIMA: Slavka. . . . That's awful, of course. But listen. . . . Max is still your son regardless. I mean, you're still the one who raised him. I mean, he's still yours . . .

SLAVA: Sure, of course that's true. Am I denying it? But what happened? One more deception revealed. I'm used to it. But who can I ask now? Death? God? They won't answer.

SLAVA *extinguishes his cigarette in the sink.*

SLAVA: I should head out . . .

DIMA: I promise, this will stay between us.

SLAVA: What does it matter? Let the whole city know, for all I care. What do I care?

DIMA: Maybe you don't, but what about Max? I'd keep it to myself. How will you guys live with it if he finds out?

SLAVA: How do we live with it now?

SLAVA *gets up and leaves without saying goodbye, having left his pack of cigarettes on the table. After thinking a moment, DIMA takes a cigarette from the pack. Lights up.*

2

A car. SLAVA *and* ALLA *sit inside it.* ALLA *is wearing some sort of hat from which unkempt locks of hair peek out.* SLAVA *had woken her up.*

ALLA: Well?

SLAVA: What?

ALLA: Well, they're gonna fire you?

SLAVA: So?

ALLA: How will you get by?

SLAVA: What can I do—I'll drown or hang myself. . . . You know that people don't live long after losing their job. Two days after being let go, the mark of "outcast" appears on a person's brow. Friends and acquaintances turn their backs on him. Everywhere on the streets, he's turned out like a leper. After that, you know how it goes—alcohol, death, the abyss . . .

ALLA: Stop it. You've got to solve problems, to the extent that you can, before they hit you. You haven't lost your job yet.

SLAVA: Did you say I haven't lost my life yet?

ALLA: You haven't lost your job. Now, with respect to your son . . .

SLAVA: Enough. Your place?

ALLA: I can't.

SLAVA: What do you mean, you can't? Let's go, I'll be quiet. I won't snore. I won't fall sleep anyway . . .

ALLA: Don't you get it? Vika's sleeping.

SLAVA: So what? She's sleeping.

ALLA: I can't bring a man home with my grownup daughter there . . .

SLAVA: Why not?

ALLA: Well. . . . Not under these circumstances. Although, we can talk about it. Since we *are* together, and now, with this particular turn of events, we can also try living together, getting to know each other better. That's what I wanted to say. That I've got nothing against your son. We can try to. . . . Slavka, we're grownups after all. We need to . . . make decisions, somehow.

SLAVA: You don't want your daughter growing up to be easy. That's why you don't bring men home, hide your phone, aren't friends with her on Facebook. You want her to believe that you're what you want *her* to be. You're lying to her. I bet she's lying to you too. All's as it should be.

ALLA: How am I lying to her? Come out with it. You wanted to say that I'm lying to her because I'm a slut myself and I'm hiding that from her? Is that it? Is that right?

SLAVA: No.

ALLA: Bullshit. I have it right. Let's not play games, dear. You've decided to open my eyes? Fine, then don't back out. So? Why am I a slut? Because I threw away four years of my life on you? Because I'm raising my daughter alone? Any other complaints?

SLAVA: I have no right to complain to you. I deceived my wife, told her I loved her, but kept seeing you. I deceived you, told you we'd get married, all the while telling my wife I'd never leave her. My wife deceived me, told me she loved me, but had someone else's son and pretended he was mine. And now, I'm left with no son and no wife. I've got no one left to lie to. You said you loved me, but now it's clear that you didn't spend four years of your life with me, but merely wasted them on me . . .

ALLA: God knows I understand how bad things are for you right now. God, it must be really bad, Slavka. . . . Forgive me, I lost my cool. I do love you. Come on, let's calm down . . .

SLAVA: And I wanted to live forever . . .

ALLA: What are you talking about, Slava?

SLAVA: That was back then, remember? You grew up there too, in that same courtyard. Studied at that same school, sat on those same benches, went to those same universities . . . and remember, beer kegs, bottles of "Royal,"[3] those all-night gatherings. Dimka and I pasted almost a thousand leaflets one night. We wanted freedom. . . . We'd talk and talk. Butusov was famous already, Bashlachev still unknown.[4] . . . We craved justice. Freedom and justice. Am I wrong? Did you really forget? Or did I make it all up? And then . . . family, a son. Life became better, then worse again. Status became more important than truth, career more important than family. Before we knew it, we started to lie. And then, as time goes on—you think it's love, and you take a closer look and it's—lies, lies. . . . And then, you again. I dreamed about buying a car, and bought one. My wife died, I was stuck in traffic. Never mind—that's life. Of course, that's life. Only, how can it be? So unexpectedly, so quietly: one moment, it's there—and then it's gone.

ALLA: Come on, Slava, sober up. . . . It's hard for me too. You think I'm happy about the way things turned out? When you called, I was at work bawling my eyes out. . . . I went and lit a candle for Renata. Paid the priest to say a prayer. A prayer for the dead.

Pause.

SLAVA: You know, Alla . . . here's what I've decided. We'd better stop seeing each other.

ALLA: What do you mean?

SLAVA: What I said. I'm sick of lying. Seems like nothing's stopping us anymore. And still . . . I deceived her.
And now her soul hovers over us and sees everything. . . .
I don't want that.

ALLA: Then you're leaving me?

SLAVA: Yes.

ALLA: Fine then. Is that your final decision?

SLAVA: Yes.

ALLA: Fine. Promise me just one thing . . .

SLAVA: Yes?

ALLA: Tomorrow, you'll come to your senses and call me. Promise.

SLAVA: No. I can't promise that.

ALLA: Please. . . . Let's at least talk about all of this tomorrow. If you've decided, fine . . . fine. We're adults. If that's your decision, then I'll accept it. But you can't do it just like that. . . . Four years—what did they mean? Yes, we behaved badly toward Renata. We're guilty. But it's not our fault that. . . . Slava, you know I'm ready to raise Maxim. I'll try to be the best stepmother in the world. I've thought this through, you know. Not because I was happy that Renata died. It's just that it's obviously crossed my mind. That's not a bad thing, I think. I was just thinking about our future. I was searching for a way out. I was worried about you. Slava . . . please . . . talking is really hard for me right now. Let's call each other tomorrow. Let's meet. . . . Just. . . . Well, we just can't do it like this. Four years and, all of a sudden, see ya . . .

SLAVA: I can't lie anymore.

ALLA: But hold on, she lied to you too . . .

SLAVA: She lied. But I can't anymore. I was very happy with you, Alla. . . . I think I'm even in love with you. Or at least, I've gotten really used to . . .

SLAVA *gets out of the car.* ALLA *watches as* SLAVA *staggers away across the dark courtyard. A blizzard rages. No one else is out. Dark windows. Bare, bristly trees.*

3

SLAVA enters his apartment. The standard two-bedroom apartment of an ordinary inhabitant of a big city. SLAVA's son MAXIM, a chubby fifteen year old, sits at a computer in the living room, wearing headphones. SLAVA takes his coat off and enters the room. He has a paper bag in his hand. From it, he takes out a bottle of vodka and plastic cups.

SLAVA: Max . . . Max! Maxim!

MAXIM takes off his headphones and turns to look at his father.

MAXIM: Hey . . .

SLAVA: Why aren't you in bed?

MAXIM: Because . . .

SLAVA: Oh. . . . Okay . . .

Pause.

SLAVA: Drink with me?

MAXIM: No.

SLAVA: Why not?

MAXIM: I don't drink.

SLAVA: Oh-h. You drank at the funeral.

MAXIM: Yeh, that was at the funeral . . .

SLAVA: So otherwise you don't drink?

MAXIM: Otherwise I don't.

SLAVA: But, in theory, you'll start drinking eventually?

MAXIM: Dunno. For now, I don't intend to.

SLAVA: Got it.

MAXIM: Okay, can I go now?

SLAVA: Wait up. What's that you're playing there?

MAXIM: A computer game.

SLAVA: Which one?

MAXIM: You won't know it anyway.

SLAVA: Well, is it interesting, at least?

MAXIM: It's interesting.

SLAVA: So what are the rules?

MAXIM: Well, you know. . . . You have to kill.

SLAVA: And who do you kill?

MAXIM: Enemies.

SLAVA: And how do you know they're enemies?

MAXIM: That's what it says.

SLAVA: And if it said that I was the enemy—would you kill me too?

MAXIM: It's just a game. . . . Can I go now?

SLAVA: Wait. Sit with me a bit. You spend all day in front of the computer and can't spend five minutes with me?

MAXIM: What do you mean? I can.

SLAVA *pours some vodka into his cup and drinks.*

SLAVA: So what did you do today?

MAXIM: Nothing.

SLAVA: What do you mean nothing?

MAXIM: I don't know. . . . I played on the computer, ate . . .

SLAVA: Played on the computer, ate . . . (*Pause.*) Maxim, you know—you're fat. You *do* know that, right?

MAXIM: Well, yeh . . . I know. . . . But no, I'm not fat, there's another kid in my class who's even fatter.

SLAVA: What do I care about the other kid! *You're* fat. Your mom didn't think so. She never mentioned it and forbade me to mention it too. You know we fought over it, right?

MAXIM: No.

SLAVA: I told her to do something about it. Put you on a diet or something. . . . Told her that it wasn't okay. I was already telling her that when you started putting on weight in first grade. Because it's just not normal, somehow. I'd tell her, okay, maybe if we were fatsos ourselves, or at least one of us was. But your mom and I are thin. I'm thin, and mom is thin. *Was* thin.

MAXIM: And so what . . .

SLAVA: What do you mean so what? Remember I gave you weights for your birthday?

MAXIM: I remember.

SLAVA: So where are they?

MAXIM: Dunno. Under my bed probably . . .

SLAVA: Mom didn't let me tell you, but you are fat. And that's unacceptable. It's unacceptable for *you*, in the first place.

MAXIM: I've accepted it.

SLAVA: What do you mean you've accepted it? What if you fall for a girl? Do you really think she'll be into you?

MAXIM: Well, I don't want to fall for anyone.

SLAVA: And what if you do anyway?

MAXIM: Nah. I'm not interested in that.

SLAVA: Listen, Maxim. . . . What do you think about—in general?

MAXIM: In general?

SLAVA: Well, yeh, in general.

MAXIM: Oh, nothing really.

SLAVA: How's that, nothing?

MAXIM: Well, in general, I don't think about anything. And specifically—I dunno. It depends.

SLAVA: Hold on, let's say you're playing on the computer—what do you think about?

MAXIM: It depends. How to jump in time, or not lose one of my lives. . . . Or kill someone with the right weapon . . .

SLAVA: Alright. Say you want to eat. What do you think about?

MAXIM: Well, nothing. I see what there is in the fridge. Or I make sure the dumplings don't overcook.

SLAVA: Well, what about when you call Valya? What do you guys talk about?

MAXIM: I dunno. We talk about YouTube videos, and about school too . . .

SLAVA: And what about school?

MAXIM: Well, you know. . . . Sometimes I ask him about h-work . . .

SLAVA: What's that?

MAXIM: Homework.

SLAVA: Do you do your homework?

MAXIM: Well, it's like . . . the teacher told him to pass it on to me . . .

SLAVA: And why don't you go to school?

MAXIM: Oh, well I can't yet.

SLAVA: Why?

MAXIM: Because of mom.

SLAVA: Why are you lying right now?! You lie without so much as blushing! You sit at that computer all day! Have you even once visited her grave in all this time? Have you picked up her photograph even once?

MAXIM: Well, I just . . .

SLAVA: Just what!? Just using mom's death as an excuse not to go to school! That's low, Maxim, you hear me? That's very low. Only hypocrites act like this. Are you a hypocrite?

MAXIM: Well I . . .

SLAVA: Answer my question! Are you a hypocrite?

MAXIM: No.

SLAVA: Well, it seems you are. And then you'll ask for pity! You've grown a belly that practically goes down to your knees, spent the month playing computer games, and then you'll show up saying—pity me, I'm so poor, so miserable, my mom died! Is that right?

MAXIM: No.

SLAVA: What then?

MAXIM: Can I go now?

SLAVA: Sit.

SLAVA *drinks some vodka.*

SLAVA: Tell me, Maxim, what gets you excited in life?

MAXIM: Well, you know . . . I'm studying.

SLAVA: As we've concluded, you haven't gone to school in a month.

MAXIM: But I'll make up all the homework . . .

SLAVA: What excites you? What troubles you in life?

MAXIM: I don't know . . .

SLAVA: Alright, so your mother passed away. Have you even stopped to think after that happened?

MAXIM: Well, yeh . . .

SLAVA: About what?

MAXIM: Well, just . . .

SLAVA: Just what?

MAXIM: Well, I thought about . . . how we'll live afterward.

SLAVA: Well, that's at least something. But have you thought deeply about anything? About death, for example? About God? Fate? I don't know . . .

MAXIM *is silent and tries not to look at his dad.*

SLAVA: I was a hippy at your age. You know what hippies are?

MAXIM: I've heard about them . . .

SLAVA: What have you heard?

MAXIM: Well, they did drugs.

SLAVA: They fought for freedom. Every kind of freedom. Freedom of spirit and thought in the first place! They fought for love! Do you know what freedom is?

MAXIM: Yes . . .

SLAVA: What is it?

MAXIM: Well . . . it's . . .

MAXIM *is silent.*

SLAVA: Well, say something . . .

MAXIM: I don't know.

SLAVA: Come on! Repeat it loudly! I don't know what freedom is! Come on, repeat it! Why are you quiet? Come on!

MAXIM: I don't know what. . . . Dad, I'm tired.

SLAVA: You'll catch up on sleep tomorrow! After all, as I understand it, you don't intend to go to school!

MAXIM: Come on, can I tell you what freedom is tomorrow?

SLAVA: You'll Google it?

MAXIM (*Softly*): At least I don't drink and smoke.

SLAVA: What did you say?

MAXIM: At least I don't drink and smoke.

SLAVA: Funny! When I grew my hair out, my dad told me: "At your age, I did sports and didn't stuff my head with all kinds of nonsense!" Get it? He was against me thinking so much! But I'm telling you—drink if you want, smoke, grow your hair out, but think, read books, listen to music, only be a human being for God's sake! Whatever you do, just be your own person. Learn to love, to suffer, to worry! Not drinking or smoking doesn't make you good or bad. A healthy lifestyle doesn't say anything about your integrity, your decency. Maxim, what country do you live in?

MAXIM: Russia.

SLAVA: And what kind of country do you think it is? Have you read its history?

MAXIM: Well, yeh. . . . In school, we . . .

SLAVA: Let's leave your school out of it for a moment! Now, off the top of your head, name three Russian poets?

MAXIM: Pushkin.

SLAVA: Another?

MAXIM: Lermontov.

SLAVA: Good. Another.

MAXIM: Well, and . . .

SLAVA: Well?

MAXIM: Yesenin.

SLAVA: Well done. Do you remember at least one poem?

MAXIM: Only, we haven't covered Yesenin yet . . .

SLAVA: Go with Pushkin.

Pause.

MAXIM: Dad, I don't remember right now . . . can I tell it to you tomorrow?

Pause. SLAVA *drinks vodka.*

SLAVA: You know, we're nothing alike, Maxim. We've lived together so many years—yet we've got nothing in common.

MAXIM *silently stares at the floor.*

SLAVA: Well, say something . . .

MAXIM: I get it.

SLAVA: What do you get?

MAXIM: Nothing, I just get it.

SLAVA: Well, so tell me what it is that you get. You don't know what freedom means, you don't know your own culture, you don't think about or get excited about anything, but at least you don't drink or smoke. What can I say? It's very commendable. Being healthy and stupid—that's very good indeed. People like you don't ask questions. That's valued in our time. That's always been valued. . . . So why are you quiet?

MAXIM *soundlessly cries. His thick shoulders shake from his sobbing.*

SLAVA: Well, what are you crying for? If it's because I insulted you—then no big deal. It's what you need, my boy. And if it's because something hurts inside—you'll thank me later. . . . Why are you crying? Maxim! Can you answer me?

MAXIM (*Between sobs*): Leave me alone!

MAXIM *gets up abruptly and rushes to his room. He locks his door.* SLAVA *pours vodka into his plastic cup. He drinks. It's quiet. Semi-dark. The window reflects the computer monitor's faint light. Beyond the windows—night's black void.*

SLAVA *gets up and approaches* MAXIM*'s door. He knocks.*

SLAVA: Max! Open up! Open up, I said! (*He knocks roughly.*) Either open up, or I'll break down the door!

MAXIM *opens the door.*

SLAVA: Were you scared?

MAXIM: No . . .

SLAVA: Well, forgive me . . . Max . . .

MAXIM *tries to shut the door.* SLAVA *blocks it with his hand.*

SLAVA: Hold on . . . Max . . .

MAXIM: Let go.

SLAVA: Wait. Let's talk.

MAXIM: I don't want to.

SLAVA: But you don't even know what I want to talk about. And already—I don't want to.

MAXIM: Let me go.

SLAVA: You don't want to talk?

MAXIM: I don't.

SLAVA: I wanted to talk to you. About what we should do next. What should we do next, Max? After all, we can't keep living the way we are now.

MAXIM: I'm living just fine.

SLAVA: What do you mean just fine? You eat and sleep, eat and sleep, practically like an animal . . . a vegetable! Oh, yeh, you also play computer games!

MAXIM: Dad . . . leave me alone. I want to go to bed.

SLAVA: Wait. (*Pause.*) I'm sorry. I don't want to hurt your feelings, you know. Forgive me. I want to be open with you, that's why all these things spill out . . .

MAXIM: Let go, I want to close the door . . .

SLAVA: Why do you keep saying let go, let go? Max! You're my son. Mine, right? Mine! I raised you. I love you. That's what I wanted to say. Just that I'm your only father, and you're my only son. That I'll always hear you out. . . . No matter what happens, you come to me first!

MAXIM: Okay.

SLAVA: Okay what?

MAXIM: Nothing.

SLAVA: Max. . . . Are you actually normal or are you mentally challenged? Can you give me a normal answer?

MAXIM: I can.

SLAVA: What's your answer then? Answer!

MAXIM *pushes his dad.*

MAXIM: Let go of the door! I want to go to sleep!

MAXIM *slams the door and locks it from the inside.*

SLAVA: Let me in! I'm not done talking to you!

SLAVA *bangs on the door and then returns to the table. He drinks vodka. Having downed some, he goes back to the door.*

SLAVA: Maxim! I've decided to tell you. You're not my son. There it is—the truth. I thought I'd lose my mind if I told you. And now there it is—it's so easy. Nothing special. Here's what I've decided, Maxim. I've decided I shouldn't lie. I had a genetic test done, Maxim. Took a hair of yours from your pillow. Like a thief. You left, and I went for it: tweezers and envelope. You're not my son. Your mom cheated on me. But I'm not angry at her, you know. I cheated on her too. I'm the more guilty party. I promised to marry another woman, Maxim.

I was cheating on your mom with her for four years. And so—your mom lied to me, but I also lied to her! We're even! So that's how things stand. That's how things stand. . . . How's it going over there? Shall I tell you how things stand, all the news of our small city? Jacob quit drinking, his wife gave birth yesterday, and as for me, all's okay for now! You know that song?[5] Well? Well, Max? Max, can you hear me? (SLAVA *bangs on the door and shouts.*) You hear me, Maxim, don't you?! You alive in there? Can you hear me? Say something! Answer, will you—I told you the truth! Max!!! You're still my son, Max! Hear me?!

Silence. Night. The clock on the wall keeps ticking.

4

Morning. SLAVA *sits in the kitchen drinking mineral water. He still has his clothes on from the day before and looks hungover and bedraggled. We hear footsteps from the living room.* SLAVA *walks into the living room and bumps into* MAXIM. *The latter is wearing a backpack and trying to soundlessly creep into the corridor. But because* MAXIM *is fat and bulky, he's not able to reach the corridor without making noise.*

SLAVA: Good morning . . .

MAXIM *has stopped. He's silent.*

SLAVA: Good morning, Maxim . . .

Pause.

SLAVA: Are you capable of saying hi?

MAXIM: Good morning . . . (*After a pause.*) Vyacheslav Anatolyevich.

SLAVA: So that's how it is now? Thanks a lot, sonny.

MAXIM: Can I go now?

SLAVA: Where do you think you're off to?

MAXIM: School.

SLAVA: Why are you lying?

MAXIM: I'm not lying.

SLAVA: With a hiking backpack?

MAXIM: Yes.

SLAVA: You're lying! Where do you think you're going? Decided to leave home?

MAXIM: Yeh . . .

SLAVA: I won't let you. Where will you go?

MAXIM: Don't know . . .

SLAVA: To your dear friend Valya's? Since you don't have any other friends. And you think Valya wants you around?

MAXIM: Can I go now?

SLAVA: No. (*Pause.*) Although you know what . . . I left home at sixteen. Went to a hippy commune. Left home for a girl, or chick, as we'd say then. She lived there. She was older and thought of me as a kid, a boy scout. So I ran away to her. I wanted to prove. . . . I even fought with my parents. To the point of hysterics. I lived there for half a year. And it was fine—I finished school, got into university. It was in spring that we'd leave home. A time when we'd be leaving home for good. You know what? Go, Max. I can't keep you here anyway. Call if you need anything. I'll always be here to help you.

MAXIM *stands silently, without budging.*

SLAVA: Well, what's gotten into you?

MAXIM: The . . . the utility bill came—we need to pay it.

SLAVA: Alright.

MAXIM: It's there on my table.

SLAVA: Fine.

MAXIM *isn't leaving. Pause.*

SLAVA: Maybe you want some breakfast first?

MAXIM: Well, I could, as a matter of . . .

SLAVA: Well, then put down your bag, since as a matter of . . .

MAXIM *puts down his backpack and he and* SLAVA *go to the kitchen.* SLAVA *gets milk out of the fridge and cereal from the cabinet. He pours milk into the cereal and puts the bowl in front of* MAXIM.

SLAVA: Well, that's a start . . . I can make an omelet.

MAXIM: No, this is fine . . .

SLAVA: Omelet seems healthy. It's good for you.

MAXIM: It's fine . . . won't you have anything?

SLAVA: I don't ever eat with a hangover.

MAXIM: Oh-h-h.

MAXIM *digs in. He eats slowly and slurps noisily from his spoon.*

SLAVA: So you've definitely decided?

MAXIM: What?

SLAVA: To leave home?

MAXIM: Well, maybe . . . not sure yet . . .

SLAVA: Well, you call me. I'm proud of you, you know. Just as it should be . . . a normal teenager has to run away from home at least once. Otherwise, what sort of person will he become? Get it?

MAXIM *looks at his dad sadly.* SLAVA*'s cell phone rings. He answers.*

SLAVA: Yes, hello? Well, I think half past nine. Ten fifteen? I think the clock is off. It's lying. Clocks lie like everyone lies. Got it, Dima. . . . Okay, I'm coming. No, I didn't sleep through it. I'm dealing with some issues right now. Got it. Okay. (*Hanging up,* SLAVA *says to* MAXIM.) Can you believe it, I'm late. What should I do? To hell with them, or should I hustle?

MAXIM: I dunno . . .

SLAVA: Alright, I'll go . . .

SLAVA *gets ready at army speed—he changes, washes up, and brushes his hair. Ready to go and briefcase in hand, he reappears in the kitchen. He puts some money in front of* MAXIM.

SLAVA: This is to keep you going for now, Max. Call me and keep me informed about everything. And by no means am I kicking you out. . . . Come back as soon as you're sick of it. To be honest, I never expected . . .

MAXIM (*Nodding*): Thank you . . .

SLAVA *gives* MAXIM *an awkward slap on the back and leaves. The door slams.* MAXIM *sits in the kitchen staring into his bowl. Then he gets up and pours the remainder of his breakfast into the sink. He puts the bowl on the table. Takes the money. Goes to the living room. Returns to the kitchen. Washes the bowl after himself. He then goes to the living room again. He very slowly ties his shoelaces. He puts on his jacket just as slowly. He unzips his backpack and takes out a few CDs with computer games. Picks up his backpack and leaves the house.*

5

SLAVA *hurriedly climbs the stairs to the fifth floor. That's where his office is. In the staff smoking room, by the stairwell between the fourth and fifth floors,* SLAVA *runs into* DIMA. DIMA *is smoking.*

DIMA: Had a bit too much last night?

SLAVA: Nah.

DIMA: Wherefore so late then?

SLAVA: Tram broke down.

DIMA: Right. Some aspirin? Mineral water?

SLAVA: Nah, I'm fine.

DIMA: Can you work?

SLAVA: Yeh.

DIMA: Listen, we've got a laugh fest over here. . . . I want it for the front page.

SLAVA: What is it?

DIMA *grabs some sheets of paper from the windowsill and starts reading.*

DIMA: "Good afternoon. My name is Vera and I'm twenty-five years old. I'm a totally ordinary person, except for one thing. I've been suffering from somnambulism for about five years. I'm a human somnambulist. For those of you who don't know, somnambulism is sleepwalking, a medical condition where those afflicted carry out certain actions while asleep. The behavior of someone in this state looks purposeful and normal. But, in fact, they're acting unintentionally or in response to whatever they're dreaming at that moment. Sleepwalking usually happens when someone hasn't fully emerged from the deep sleep phase; at this point, the brain is half-asleep and half-conscious. The eyes of a somnambulist are usually open. He or she can move in a variety of ways, sidestep obstacles, sometimes complete difficult tasks, and answer simple questions. Yet these actions aren't conscious, and the person doesn't remember them upon waking. This is taken from Wikipedia and describes me almost exactly . . . my sleepwalking episodes can last for hours. The worst of it is that, the next day, I can't remember a thing. In this state, I can go outside, call someone on the phone, or surf the Net and even comment on friends' posts. Only it's not me doing it, but my other 'sleeping' self."

SLAVA: What *is* this?

DIMA: Hold on, let me finish . . . there are some absolute gems here. (*He reads.*) "Otherwise, in everyday life, I'm not very physically active. I'm overweight, I'm frequently sleepy, and, in general, it's as if I'm sleeping through life. And if I do something unusual—post clever comments online, or abruptly answer the phone, or even greet unfamiliar people in the street—I do it all while I'm sleepwalking. Unfortunately, my condition has gotten to the point where the somnambulism happens almost every night. Although, I think I'm even happy about this. Sometimes I don't even know who I am anymore—a somnambulist or a human being. For several years, I was treated at various institutions, but the doctors can't help me at all. I'd really like for your newspaper to write about this condition and ask those with a similar diagnosis to come forward. I've never met anyone like me. Even though I'd really like to talk to people like me about this. Afterword: As I'm writing these lines, I can feel myself starting to nod off, but to be honest—I'm not sure if I'm writing this to you as a human being or as a somnambulist. So I'll just sign as 'human somnambulist Vera.' " (DIMA *says to* SLAVA.) Cool, huh?

SLAVA: What's cool?

DIMA: The topic! Somnambulism! Want the story? You'll have to go see this girl and get an interview.

SLAVA: I think she's mentally ill.

DIMA: I already talked to her on the phone this morning. You know, I've got to say—she's alright. But she talks slow as hell. Seems like she really *is* asleep all the time.

SLAVA: She's not the only one.

DIMA: Meaning?

SLAVA: At least half the people I know fit her description.

DIMA: Slava, you're exaggerating.

SLAVA: But it's true, Dima. Most people I know . . . they're simply asleep.

DIMA: What about me?

SLAVA: And you too.

DIMA: Here come the accusations. Alright, what else have you got? We're bad, you're good. We're bourgeois, you're a poet. We're yuppies, you're a hippy. Long live puberty! Slava, get a grip. Aren't you just the same?

SLAVA: Sure I am. Only I've made up my mind.

DIMA: To do what?

SLAVA: To wake up.

DIMA: How's that? I don't see it. You've got such a look that . . .

SLAVA: That what?

DIMA: That you woke up for nothing. You've got to get more sleep. Well? Will you take the somnambulist story? Or should I go myself?

SLAVA: I don't know. Why the sleepwalker? Aren't there other topics? No news in the city?

DIMA: Nada. "All Quiet on the Western . . ." as they say . . .

SLAVA: Timelessness.

DIMA: What?

SLAVA: It's as though time has stopped. Don't you think?

DIMA: I don't know, seems to be moving. And why not? After all, why do we necessarily have to write either horror stories or triumphant reports? Why shouldn't we cover an ordinary, relatable topic like sleepwalking? Why, it's awesome, Slava! The girl will find herself new friends. Look, you said it yourself—we're no different than she is, we're the same. We're—human somnambulists. A generation afflicted with somnambulism. Only she's sick, and we're not. Super! Let's use that angle. Let's look at somnambulism broadly, as a mass phenomenon. Stop by the loony bin, interview a few doctors. . . . Reflect on our age, on the fact that it's the twenty-first century . . . a century of somnambulists and advanced technologies . . . that we may be great in number, but weak in spirit! Oh yeh, I wonder. . . . How do they reproduce? Also in their sleep? By the way, that's an awesome topic. Maybe Vera will tell us about her personal life . . .

SLAVA: Oh, go to hell with your somnambulists!

DIMA *stops talking and looks at* SLAVA. *Then he suddenly slaps him in the face.*

DIMA: That's for yesterday too.

SLAVA *wobbles. He rubs his jaw.* BORIS *Yevgenyevich, the chief editor and* SLAVA *and* DIMA*'s boss, comes down to the smoking room.*

BORIS: You'd better crack the window—it's impossible to breathe in here. (*He notices* SLAVA.) Slava? Something happen?

SLAVA: Nothing, everything's fine.

BORIS: What happened?

SLAVA: I hit myself.

BORIS: How?

SLAVA: On the door post, I suppose? Well, I mean . . . I mean . . . that's not the truth, but I won't tell the truth, so let's say on the door post.

BORIS: (*He lights up.*) Understood. Well then, my friends, have we decided who's covering what today?

DIMA: I'm definitely taking the athletics meeting, and housing.

BORIS: And the fire?

DIMA: I was gonna give that one to Slava, but we got stuck on somnambulism . . .

BORIS: Oh, the human somnambulist. Funny stuff. Yes, let's put that one in the issue too.

SLAVA *grins kind of strangely, almost painfully.*

BORIS: Slava, are you alright?

SLAVA: Yeh. All good.

BORIS: You look like you . . .

SLAVA: Need more sleep? I got enough, thank you.

BORIS: No, I didn't mean. . . . Well, if all's well, then full speed ahead, lads . . .

SLAVA: Boris Yevgenyevich?

BORIS: Yes?

SLAVA: I wanted to confess to something.

BORIS: What?

SLAVA: I wanted to apologize.

BORIS: What for? I hope it wasn't you who put that dead mouse in the first-grade teacher's desk?!

SLAVA: I, Vyacheslav Gorinov, admit to stealing the Canon reflex camera last winter from the editorial office. I had gone to shoot a rock concert on assignment. If you recall, I said that someone in the crowd shattered the camera. You wrote it off. In fact, it really was damaged, but not as badly as I said. Once you had written it off, I stole it, got it fixed, and kept it. My late wife really wanted that fuckin' Canon to teach herself professional photography. She even managed to get a couple of good shots before she got bored with it. When I decided to steal the camera, I thought that everyone steals, and I'm no worse. I thought that, for us, stealing has become a national pastime, that it's no big deal and no one would lose anything by it. But now I feel rotten. And also, I think my job is total crap, but I don't think anyone's to blame for that but me.

SLAVA *takes the camera out of his briefcase and places it on the windowsill.*

SLAVA: Here it is. So long, Boris Yevgenyevich. (*To* DIMA.) And as for you, we're no longer on speaking terms, so I've got no parting words.

BORIS: Slava . . . Slava, wait. I don't know what to say. Slava, hold on. . . . You're shaking all over. . . . Are you drunk?

SLAVA: No. Just a bit hungover.

BORIS: Slava, buddy, don't rush.

SLAVA: Do I look like I'm rushing?

BORIS: Not so fast. I mean, to hell with this camera! So you stole it. Yeh, that's bad. . . . But so what? The paper didn't go broke. Slava, you know I've got a tender spot in my heart for you. Come on, Slava dear, calm down . . .

SLAVA: I *am* calm.

BORIS: Come on, take the camera and let's get to work . . .

SLAVA: Well, I actually brought it for *you.*

BORIS: What do I need that camera for? I've already got one, thanks.

SLAVA: Give it back to the editorial office.

BORIS: If you recall, we wrote it off. Enough, Slava. Calm down. We saw nothing and we know nothing.

SLAVA: No, you did see it. You saw it because I told you. And right now, it seems to you like it's no big deal, that everything's as it was before, that I've just lost it a bit. Because you're still in shock. But later on, you'll understand that everything isn't at all like it was before. And then we'll no longer look each other in the eye. . . . But I'm still glad this happened, I'm still . . .

DIMA: Slava, have you lost your fuckin' mind?

SLAVA: Yes, I have.

DIMA: I noticed.

SLAVA: I'm so glad.

SLAVA *heads down the stairs.* BORIS *Yevgenyevich thoughtfully watches him go.*

BORIS: So what are we gonna do with him?

DIMA: What *can* you do with him? Do you see what state he's in?

BORIS: Has he been drinking long?

DIMA: Well, since Renata . . .

BORIS: Right. So what were you saying back there? Which clinic?

DIMA: "Pine Forest." They say that it's an elite mental asylum. Do you think he's lost it?

BORIS: Well, I'm no doctor. I think there are problems. Why don't you stop by his place this evening, okay?

DIMA: I'm definitely not going to his place.

BORIS: Too bad. . . . Did you guys have a fight?

DIMA: That's our business.

BORIS: Got it. Alright, we'll think of something.

DIMA: It's just that, this is unacceptable, I think. He's already acting like a complete swine.

BORIS: And what if it happened to you . . . ?

DIMA: I don't know. God forbid. But this is total crap.

BORIS: Yeh. . . . Everyone's so worked up these days. You can't escape.

DIMA: I mean, I kinda get where he's coming from, of course. He's definitely right about some things . . .

BORIS: Like what?

DIMA: Well, I mean, in general, about the general attitude. . . . What I mean is that his condition right now is so . . .

BORIS: Never mind, let's get to work. (*He notices the camera lying on the windowsill.*) Take it.

DIMA: Me? Why?

BORIS: I dunno. Have it.

DIMA: Me? (*He hesitates.*) Well alright . . .

DIMA *takes the camera.*

BORIS: Yes, Slavka. . . . Your heroic deed has gone unnoticed.

DIMA: What do you mean? I can give it back if you want . . .

BORIS: Right.

BORIS *Yevgenyevich goes up the stairs and enters his office.* DIMA *leaves after him.*

6

SLAVA *climbs the stairs to the sixth floor. The elevator is broken. He rings a doorbell.* ALLA *opens the door.*

ALLA: Come in.

SLAVA *walks into* ALLA*'s apartment. He takes off his jacket.* ALLA *is walking around the apartment in her workout clothes.*

ALLA: Couldn't you have called?

SLAVA: I couldn't have.

ALLA: Why's that?

SLAVA: I was afraid you'd tell me to go to hell.

ALLA: So you were afraid after all, were you? You were right to be. And what if Veronica was home?

SLAVA: So what? Veronica's grown up. Why are you so worried about her?

ALLA: She can't forgive me for leaving Karasev. She thinks that I'm the one who divorced him and that his second family only came afterward.

SLAVA: You should tell her the truth.

ALLA: I can't. That bastard Karasev also happens to be a perfect father. Why traumatize the child? It's me who's the bad mom, she thinks. I don't want what happened with you to be added into the bargain.

ALLA *lights up.*

SLAVA: I didn't want to come here, you know.

ALLA: Then why did you?

SLAVA: Because. I left my job. And as soon as I walked out of the office, I felt miserable. So I decided to stop by your place uninvited, thinking you weren't home anyway. But here you are.

ALLA: What do you mean you left?

SLAVA: What it sounds like. For good.

ALLA: Were you fired?

SLAVA: No. I quit.

ALLA: What happened?

SLAVA: Nothing. I just left.

ALLA: For God's sake, Slava. . . . You poor thing . . .

ALLA tries to hug SLAVA. He distances himself.

SLAVA: Don't . . .

Pause.

ALLA: Well, I took the day off from work. After what happened yesterday, I decided I couldn't. . . . I'm afraid I'd break down in front of the clients.

SLAVA: You mean you're upset?

ALLA: Of course I'm upset! It's you who takes things so lightly, but I'm actually in pain! This isn't what I was counting on during those four long years!

SLAVA: I know. You wanted me to divorce Renata.

ALLA: Yes. And so what? I never wished Renata any ill, you know. But she was a stranger to me. I didn't know anything about her. Whereas you're like family to me, understand? And if I had had to choose between Renata's happiness and my own, I would of course have chosen mine. And what's so bad about that? Can you explain it to me?

SLAVA: Nothing. It's a normal thing to want, I get it . . .

ALLA: You don't get anything! In fact, you egged me on yourself! You told me yourself, just a little longer and we'll get married! I didn't force you! Why are you looking at me like an innocent lamb? You'd like to say that you're not the one responsible for this mess? No? What's so bad about the fact that, at thirty-five years old, I'd like a normal, fulfilling family life? I'm an idiot. I fell for you—you were so brash. But don't you dare blame me right now, you hear?! Another woman in my place would have called Renata ten times by now and told her everything, and you would have already left her ten times! But note that I didn't do that. I waited patiently.

SLAVA: Though you also contemplated it as a possible scenario for how our relationship would develop . . .

ALLA: Of course I contemplated it! Yes, I contemplated it. I wanted to call your wife. Many times. And don't look at me like that. You, my dear, are also no chocolate-covered strawberry! . . . I'll never forget that time we met. Remember, at the supermarket? You've probably already forgotten . . . but I'll never forget. How Veronica and I are standing there, choosing shampoo, and you and Renata turn the corner and your cart collides with ours. Later, I even thought—my God, a city of millions, and we just *had* to run into each other at that damn supermarket! And I'm standing there, and I get that I should say something. And you're standing there, and you get that too. And Renata senses that something's up, and even Veronica somehow looks nervous. But I stand there and can't force out a single word. And you say "Hey. Renata, this is Alla." And Renata gives a kind of strained nod and the two of you leave with your cart. Meanwhile, I'm standing surrounded by these piles of shampoo and pads and thinking—God, what humiliation and loneliness, to run into you like that, in this consumer's paradise. . . . Veronica tugs on my sleeve, demanding I buy her something or other, and all that's going around in my head is—it can't go on like this, it can't go on like. . . . And then we get together and it's as though it never happened. Do you remember?

SLAVA: Yes. But I'm pretty sure we've already talked about this.

ALLA: We have. But still, I'll never forget it. Never, you hear?

SLAVA: And what do you want now? For me to repent in front of you? Ask for forgiveness? Tell Renata that two years ago, at the supermarket, we ran into my mistress? Well, Renata's not here anymore.

ALLA: I want you to understand.

SLAVA: What?

ALLA: That I'm hurting! That your antics are causing me pain! That these four years have been painful for me, and this last month, I'm simply living in hell!

SLAVA: Forgive me.

ALLA: Of course, I can forgive you. But some decisions need to be made, Slava. . . . Either we part for good or we start from scratch, move in together . . .

SLAVA: That would be betrayal.

ALLA: Betrayal was cheating on Renata while she was alive. And now she's gone. It's horrible, it's awful, but she died. And you can't betray her anymore now that she's dead . . .

SLAVA: It doesn't matter. I'd be betraying myself.

ALLA: Strange that you somehow didn't think about that those four years . . .

SLAVA: Quiet!

ALLA: What, has your conscience suddenly piped up?

SLAVA: I'm just like her, get it? She's a traitor, but I'm even worse . . .

ALLA: Calm down, Slava . . . I can't bear to watch you tear yourself apart. Everyone lives like this. Absolutely everyone. Karasev cheated on me. Out of anger, I cheated on Karasev. I wanted to get back at him for everything. Everyone has skeletons in their closet, so calm down.

SLAVA: Then there's no way out?

ALLA: You and I have one option—start over and try not to keep repeating past mistakes. We're no longer twenty, after all.

SLAVA: I've thought about this, you know. I thought about it that very morning. I thought—how do I tell her? And also—do I need that? You're my friend, Alla. Don't get offended but, first and foremost, you're a true friend. But Renata—she was that erratic her whole life, always wearing her huge heels, always picking fights with me twenty times a day over the most trivial things. I loved her one minute and hated her the next. With you, I was somehow at peace. But I also couldn't do without Renata. I know why it turned out the way it did. . . . She never could stop for long enough at traffic lights. She'd go through red lights, always rushing somewhere. . . . That morning, I was driving and thinking—should I tell her or not? And if I do tell her—then how? Then I decided, better not. Because we have a family, and if we're lying to each other, then that's just what everyone wants. But then they called . . . and that traffic jam. It was like God had punished me for those thoughts. It hurt so much that I thought I'd die, that my heart couldn't bear it. But no—I'm alive, walking around, making a mess of everything . . .

ALLA: There—you've figured it out yourself. You just need to stop messing around and that's it.

SLAVA: But how? What can I do if it hurts?

ALLA: Nothing. Find a job. Work, work hard, raise Max.

SLAVA: And look at him every day and see . . . ?

ALLA: Cool it! Genetic tests aren't 100 percent accurate. Maybe 99.99, but that's not 100! Thousands of fathers raise someone else's children, and it's fine. Many of them love these adopted children even more than their own!

SLAVA: But she . . .

ALLA: You just don't want to look for a way out! You're more comfortable being miserable, moaning and whining. It's easier for you to blame the rest of the world, while shielding yourself with your wife's death!

SLAVA: What?!!

ALLA: You heard me! He who looks for a way out finds it!

ALLA's phone rings. ALLA *answers.*

ALLA: Hi, honey? Okay. Can you get some bread on your way? Well, what did you do with it? But I gave you two hundred rubles. Alright. Well, alright, see you soon. (*To* SLAVA.) Vika will be home in five minutes.

SLAVA: And?

ALLA: And nothing. Either she comes, I introduce you, and announce that we'll live together, or you leave before she gets here.

SLAVA: Understood.

SLAVA *lights up.*

ALLA: Clock's ticking.

SLAVA: Okay.

Pause.

ALLA: So have you decided?

SLAVA: No.

SLAVA *gets up and goes to the corridor.*

ALLA: Leaving?

SLAVA: No, going to wash my face.

SLAVA *goes into the bathroom. We hear the sound of running water.* SLAVA *comes back to the room.* ALLA *is pacing and smoking.*

ALLA: Okay, we need to crack the window . . . or the kid will come and the place will be full of smoke.

ALLA *opens the window.*

ALLA: She's just at that disagreeable age now. . . . Everything I do—is wrong. I try not to smoke in front of her . . .

SLAVA *sits down on the floor. Silence.*

ALLA: Hey, we probably shouldn't tell her the minute she hits the doorstep. . . . But we still need to explain somehow. Too bad I didn't cook anything. . . . Otherwise, we'd sit down, have dinner like a normal family. . . . Wine. . . . Want some wine? I have some. Of course, we'll have to lie a bit, tell her we met recently. She won't remember you from the supermarket, she's bad at remembering faces. . . . She's a good girl. Difficult, but good. . . . I'll bring the wine. Would you open it? I still can't figure out how to use the corkscrew. You'd think that a single woman would know how. . . . I'm breaking stereotypes . . .

ALLA *goes to the kitchen.* SLAVA *gets up and walks to the corridor. The door slams.*

7

The cemetery. SLAVA *is walking down a path. He reaches Renata's grave. There are fresh, bright flowers on it. A wooden cross. A large photograph of a beautiful, black-haired woman. They still haven't put up the fence and tombstone. They'll put them up once the soil settles.* SLAVA *sits down on the frozen spring earth. He pulls a bottle out of his coat and opens it. He drinks vodka straight out of the bottle.*

SLAVA: Well, hello, Renata. . . . (*Pause.*) You're a traitor, my darling. . . . How could you keep quiet? All these years? After all, you knew. I know that you knew everything. When I found out, I thought I'd bring you back from the afterlife and break your face. . . . But then I realized. I'm the same. Completely. . . . I'm no different than . . .

He drinks vodka.

SLAVA: I'm just as much a traitor as you. You and I are no different. We're a perfect pair. We're traitors. . . . Why did we renew our vows on our tenth anniversary? Why did we repeat those vows after the priest? Why? It was so stupid. A life lived, yet so impetuously, for nothing. My poor darling. . . . Renata, can you hear me? We deceived each other. We're two good for nothings who've been lied to. I've been lied to. They lied to me, get it? Lied to me. Promised to get me ice skates as a child. Lied. Promised that, if I got good grades, I'd become a boss. Lied. Said I've got to live by Lenin's Testament,[6] but didn't do that themselves. They promised democracy in the nineties. Lied. Bought shares of MMM.[7] Lied. Promised they'd soon invent eternal life. They didn't. Lied. Promised smooth roads and world peace. . . . Promised good medical care that would save everyone. Promised to wipe out terrorism. Lied, lied, lied. The president lied, my wife lied, my son lies, the newspapers lie . . . I myself lie. I'm a lie, and the world around me is a lie. (*Pause.*) When did it all start, Renata? When? You know I wasn't like this before. I wasn't. . . . After all, you remember me when I was a long-haired fool. And so I don't get it Renata. . . . Did I start lying because the world lied to me, or is the world lying to me because I'm the one who's the cheat? How can you live and not lie when you walk down the street and understand that everyone is like that? Some look for someone to fuck over, and everyone else has already been fucked over! So how do I, personally, survive when I'm surrounded by all of this? (*Pause.*) Max left home. For good. Everything else is the same.

A young woman of about twenty-five in black slowly approaches SLAVA. *She looks like she has the chills.* SLAVA *only notices her when he raises his head and sees the stranger a few meters away from him.* SLAVA *gives a start.*

SLAVA: Shit! I practically had a heart attack! Where in God's name did you come from, black angel?

YOUNG WOMAN: Got any vodka?

SLAVA: Yeh. Have a seat.

The YOUNG WOMAN *sits down on the ground next to* SLAVA. *He extends the bottle. She drinks from it.*

YOUNG WOMAN (*Nods toward the photograph*): Your wife?

SLAVA: The one and only . . .

YOUNG WOMAN: Right.

Silence.

SLAVA: And what are you doing here?

YOUNG WOMAN: My man died. The funeral's on the other side.

SLAVA: Oh-h-h . . .

Silence.

YOUNG WOMAN: His relatives are there and all that . . .

SLAVA: And you?

YOUNG WOMAN: And what about me? I'm no one to him. His wife and kid are over there . . . everyone's bawling. And I just came to stand in the crowd. He and I were, how do I put it? . . . Well, you get it, right?

SLAVA: I get it. You're shaking all over.

YOUNG WOMAN: It's nothing. I'll live.

SLAVA *unzips his coat, covers her with it, and presses her to him for warmth.*

YOUNG WOMAN: I feel so shitty. Even at his funeral, I didn't say a proper goodbye. You know what the scariest thing is? That very morning, he wanted to tell his wife everything. We'd already been together a long time, and he'd wanted to tell her for a while. And had he gotten up the courage . . . if only . . .

Pause.

SLAVA: So what happened?

YOUNG WOMAN: Who knows? He was in a traffic jam. Heart attack—his heart just stopped.

Pause. The YOUNG WOMAN *drinks vodka.*

YOUNG WOMAN: I feel so shitty . . . (*Pause.*) Would you kiss me?

SLAVA: What for?

YOUNG WOMAN: It would make me feel better. Kiss me?

SLAVA: You'd better go home now . . .

YOUNG WOMAN: I'll get there fine, don't worry. Kiss me? Why don't we both close our eyes and imagine the person we want . . .

The YOUNG WOMAN *closes her eyes.* SLAVA *closes his eyes as well. They lean in toward each other and kiss. Afterward, they both open their eyes.*

YOUNG WOMAN: Did you imagine her?

SLAVA: I did.

YOUNG WOMAN: I imagined him too.

Pause.

SLAVA: I'm sorry . . . I'm going home.

YOUNG WOMAN: I'll go too. In a bit.

SLAVA: Well, bye then. . . . Farewell?

YOUNG WOMAN: And don't you get too lonely either.

SLAVA *extends the open bottle to the* YOUNG WOMAN. *He gets up and leaves.*

8

SLAVA *is walking through some construction site. The skeleton of an unfinished house protrudes like a dark mass.* SLAVA *hears youthful voices. He strains his ears.* ALLA, BORIS, *and* DIMA *sit ten meters away from him.* DIMA *holds a guitar.* BORIS *and* DIMA *wear jeans, or are dressed "in jean," as they used to say, and leather jackets.* ALLA *has on a stretched-out top and a long skirt with Indian patterns.*

BORIS: On "I'm," stop on "I'm." . . . Then Help! Ta-da-ta-da! Help! Ta-da-Ta-da! Help! And then "I'm"! Help me if you can . . .

DIMA: Okay, I got it . . .

ALLA: Guys, let's do Tsoi . . .[8]

BORIS: Hold up with your Tsoi . . .

DIMA: There, look, like this?

DIMA *strums "Help" by The Beatles.*

BORIS: Yes, yes, like that! Cool, man! Straight up awesome!

ALLA: That's it, just wait, Paul will call you up in a few days and put you in his band!

DIMA: What's the deal with the port?

ALLA: It's on the march . . .

BORIS (*Hugging* ALLA): The Pioneers never gave up marching on the fortress![9]

ALLA: Is someone over there, or am I imagining things?

BORIS: Where?

ALLA: Right over there, in the dark . . .

DIMA: Who's there? Come out, child of night!

SLAVA *emerges from the darkness.*

ALLA: Slavka!

BORIS: Slavka, so you're finally here!

DIMA: Come here, the port's on its way with the masses!

ALLA: Slavka, what happened to you?

BORIS: Have you decided to join the Communist Party? What's with the trench coat?

DIMA: Slavka, when did you start carrying a briefcase? Look at you!

ALLA: Slavka, you probably also wear ties now, to go with the rest of your costume!

BORIS: Look, Slavka, you've got gray in your hair!

DIMA: Look, Slavka, you've got love handles!

ALLA: Slavka, why do you have such a depleted look?

DIMA: Slavka, your eye's twitching. Is it nerves, eh?

BORIS: Slavka, you've got bags under your eyes!

ALLA: Slavka, why've you gotten so old?

BORIS: They say you've accomplished nothing in your life, Slavka.

DIMA: They say you've started lying a lot.

ALLA: You know, they say you're basically a failure and an alcoholic.

BORIS: Slavka, come here!

ALLA: Slavka, will ya drink with us?

DIMA: Slavka, let's sing that hip song of ours, remember?

DIMA, BORIS, *and* ALLA *all start yelling at* SLAVA *to come join them.* SLAVA *peers into his friends' faces, illuminated by a single flashlight.*

SLAVA: The masses . . . ?

As though in a dream, SLAVA *walks through the construction site toward his friends. A few meters before he reaches them, he falls into a construction pit. Pealing youthful laughter. Darkness.*

9

Hospital. SLAVA *is lying in a hospital bed. Both of his legs and his right hand are in casts. His face is severely damaged, his head is wrapped in bandages, and he wears a neck brace.* SLAVA *looks out the window. He can't move.* ALLA *enters the hospital room.*

ALLA: My God, Slava!

ALLA *sits down on a chair next to* SLAVA*'s bed.*

ALLA: Had enough to drink, my dear? Never mind, you don't need to say anything. I understand. My, what we have lived through. Max was at home alone for three days.

SLAVA: But . . .

ALLA: Shhh, don't speak! Don't worry, he's at my place. You're okay with him living with me for now, aren't you? And you can thank me for not holding any grudges. The very next day,

I couldn't keep myself from calling you. Your phone's disconnected. I thought you'd lost your marbles. But on Saturday, I went to your place. It was then that Max told me you hadn't been back for four days already. The kid's been eating God knows what for three days. My God, Slava, how could you have neglected your home and son like this? No, I completely get it, but your kid hasn't been to school in a month. Were you even aware of that? Never mind, quiet, don't say anything. We're taking care of that now. I've arranged things. He can't take his exams this year, he's fallen too far behind. He'll go into ninth grade next year with Veronica. To our school. It's a good school with special programs. Slavka, you have no idea how hard it's been. . . . The only god I *didn't* pray to was probably Huitzilopochtli. The rest I covered. While calling the hospitals. Praying you were still alive. You hear me? I love you, you crazy fool. Just don't worry. Everything's fine. Max settled in. He and Veronica are friends. I even think that Veronica has an eye for him. Although she's hard to figure out. But in front of Max, she's become all proper and polite—mommy, let me help, mommy this, mommy that. I wanted to tell her: "Vika, what's this circus? You haven't called me mommy since the day you were born." But I keep mum, I let it be. . . . Or maybe she just took a look at Max and realized how easy it is to lose your mom. It's all nonsense, of course. They don't really understand anything at this age. More importantly, how are you feeling? They called this morning to say that you'd regained consciousness. . . . It's a good hospital—we made sure. Main thing is, just stay quiet. No need to speak. Everything'll be fine. Doctor says you'll be back on your feet in six months. If all goes well, definitely in half a year . . .

SLAVA: Alla . . .

ALLA: Hush, don't speak!

SLAVA: Alla . . .

ALLA: What, my darling?

SLAVA: So this is what hell is like?

Pause.

ALLA: You know what I'd like to tell you. . . . Accept things, Slava. Accept things. You don't want to accept what's been given to you, but that's life. And also—Slavka, you should know . . . I'm always here for you. (*Pause.*) Okay, I'll call Max over now. You need to tell him that. . . . Well, you know yourself. He's your son, after all. He's a good boy. He's just at that age, and the circumstances are such that . . .

ALLA *leaves the hospital room.* MAXIM *enters the room. He sits in* ALLA*'s place.*

MAXIM: Hey . . .

SLAVA: Hey. How're you holding up?

MAXIM: Good. I'm staying with Auntie Alla now.

SLAVA: And how do you like it there?

MAXIM: Well, it's good. Only I don't like steamed vegetables, but Auntie Alla says I need to eat them. Well, I guess they're okay with ketchup.

SLAVA: How were your adventures? Why'd you come back home?

MAXIM: Oh, well, like . . . I left and went to the train station. I wanted to get a ticket to grandma's and go live with her. And I did go up to the ticket counter. . . . But then—well, I dunno, I somehow felt. . . . Well, I just ended up turning around and going back. Home.

Pause.

SLAVA: You know, I wanted to say that. . . . You and I are very similar. I'm just like you.

MAXIM: Oh-h-h . . .

SLAVA: I told you a bunch of drunken nonsense the other day. Forgive me, will you? You're my son. And I drank like a brute and spewed a ton of nonsense.

MAXIM: I knew that . . .

SLAVA: So what do you think of Auntie Alla?

MAXIM: She's alright. And Veronica lets me play on her computer.

SLAVA: Do you know who she is?

MAXIM: Veronica?

SLAVA: No, Alla.

MAXIM: Oh-h-h, that. Well, she's your lover, right? I know. We'll all live together now.

Pause.

SLAVA: And how do you feel about that?

MAXIM: Well, it's fine. I like her, in general. Also, she's sending me and Veronica to summer camp.

SLAVA: Well, that's good.

MAXIM: Well yeh . . .

Silence.

MAXIM: Dad, I wanna tell you something. Well, I . . . you said then that. . . . And then I kinda . . . I kept thinking about it all this time. I'm gonna lose weight. Auntie Alla cooks everything for me especially, and I'll start doing sports. That's what I wanted to say. I'll lose weight. I already lost some. There. Yeh. That's it.

Pause.

SLAVA: I love you just as you are.

MAXIM: Oh-h-h, well. . . . Well, I'm still gonna lose weight, and then I'll do sports. There, I wanted you to know. . . . What's most important is that you get well. And don't do that to yourself again. Better drink at home, if that's what you wanna do, but don't go to construction sites. Auntie Alla and I took a walk to that foundation pit. The bars are so thick it's a wonder you fell through . . .

SLAVA: That's for sure. It's a miracle.

MAXIM: Auntie Alla and I cried together. There.

Pause.

MAXIM: Want to hear something funny?

SLAVA: Go on.

MAXIM: A girl somnambulist is over in the next room. Your newspaper wrote about her. The nurse told me.

SLAVA: What happened to her?

MAXIM: Well, they say she fell off a roof. . . . It's just that you shouldn't wake somnambulists up while they're asleep, or something bad might happen. But someone woke her up.

Silence.

MAXIM: So should I tell them to come in?

SLAVA: Who?

MAXIM: You'll see. It's kind of a present . . .

MAXIM *gets up and goes to the door. He peeks out into the corridor and makes some kind of signal with his hand.* ALLA, BORIS, *and* DIMA *come in with balloons, flowers, and a cake. Together, they sing "Happy Birthday."*

ALLA: Admit it, Slavka, you thought I forgot?

BORIS: He didn't remember himself what day it is!

DIMA: Happy Birthday, buddy! May you grow up to be big and clever!

BORIS: How much more clever does he need to get? He's already too clever for his own good—all woe from wit![10]

The guests put the flowers on SLAVA*'s bed.*

BORIS: Slavka! It's too bad, of course, that we have to congratulate you here! But I want to tell you that you're very dear to me. Get well soon and come back to work!

DIMA: Yeh, Slava, you scared us good! I miss you, old chap, that's the truth. Happy Birthday! Happy fortieth!

ALLA: And now the big moment . . . forty candles, right on cue!

ALLA *brings the cake with burning candles up to* SLAVA*'s mouth.* SLAVA *looks around like a trapped animal. The guests emphatically cheer "Happy Birthday! Happy Birthday!"* SLAVA *tries to turn his head away from the blurry cake in front of him, but he can't—the neck brace keeps his neck firmly in place. And* SLAVA*'s left with no option but to blow out the candles.*

DIMA: Hey, well done! All in one go!

BORIS: Now where's that good ol' cognac?

DIMA: Why of course!

DIMA *pulls a bottle of cognac from his front pocket.* ALLA *takes out plastic cups from her purse.* DIMA *quickly pours a round of cognac.*

ALLA: As for you Slava—for your bad behavior, you get to lie there in silent envy.

BORIS: Oh, pour him a tiny bit.

ALLA: Are you serious? The doctor expressly forbade it. . . . This alcoholic practically got written up for narcotics, and you want to give him a tiny bit.

BORIS: That's it, I take it back! Sorry, Slavka, but your lady won't allow it. . . . I can't go against her wishes.

DIMA: Alright, Slavka, let's drink to you! To our mutual foolish youth and our twenty-five-year friendship. God willing, may we have another fifty years as friends!

BORIS: And to your charming rescuer!

ALLA: Save that for another toast!

BORIS: No, I insist. You belong in this one.

ALLA: Nah, that doesn't seem right. What, don't we have enough cognac? The next one's for me. Slavka, I love you very much, you know. I want to drink to your new, happy life!

ALLA, BORIS, and DIMA clink cups and drink. MAXIM lets go of the balloons and they float up to the ceiling. The bell rings in the church across from the hospital.

9

Darkness. Thick, impenetrable, and absolute. Two voices call out—RENATA's and SLAVA's.

SLAVA: Renata . . . Renata . . .

RENATA: I'm here . . .

Pause.

SLAVA: Renata, Renata, save me, will you? Why did things turn out this way?

RENATA: I don't know . . .

SLAVA: I thought there was more life ahead. . . . But it turns out—it's all in the past.

RENATA: I thought so too.

Pause.

SLAVA: You know I love you . . .

RENATA: And I love you.

SLAVA: I didn't want to deceive you. I don't know how things turned out like this . . .

RENATA: And I didn't want to either. (*Pause.*) Shall we go?

SLAVA: There's no way out.

RENATA: I know a way from the roof . . .

THE END

10

PROJECT "SWAN"

ANDREY RODIONOV AND EKATERINA TROEPOLSKAYA
TRANSLATED BY THOMAS CAMPBELL

CHARACTERS

CLAUDIA "KLAVA" PETROVNA—thirty years old, Commissar of the Poetic Tribunal

VYACHESLAV "SLAVA" HOMELAND—thirty-five years old, poet and poetry teacher

ELENA NECHAEVNA and MARINA ALEXANDROVNA—members of the Poetic Tribunal and officers of the Federal Migration Service (FMS); they also appear as new FMS employees in act 5

GOLDEN ANGEL—officer of the Orthodox Police

OCTAVIA, MOLDAKUL, and UZBEK SAID SHAH—immigrants applying for Russian citizenship; they also appear as SLAVA's party guests in act 3

PROLOGUE

THE GOLDEN ANGEL'S INTRODUCTORY SONG

In the distant, mighty future of the Russian Federation,
A law was passed regarding poetic speech.
Introducing universal rhymification,
The law was a burden to apparatchiks.

Russian syllabotonic verse
Was made the idiom of the mandarin caste.
Poetry replaced bureaucratic discourse,
And civil servants commenced to poetaste.

In the galaxy's first poetic nation,
A person applying for citizenship
Has to pass a test on versification
And show their grasp of rhymesmanship.

■ □ ■

SLAVA *and a migrant worker appear onstage.*

SLAVA:

Sign up now for the School of Versification!

It's just the ticket for passing the Federal Migration Service's exam.

In a month, you'll be able to fill out questionnaires, applications, and other documents in verse and answer the Poetic Tribunal's questions in rhyme.

MIGRANT WORKER:

It's better to pay them off.

SLAVA:

We have an original curriculum featuring traditional oriental musical instruments.

MIGRANT WORKER:

You're shameless.

Suddenly, the GOLDEN ANGEL *addresses the* MIGRANT WORKER.

GOLDEN ANGEL:

You are in the Russian Federation unlawfully.

MIGRANT WORKER (*Frightened*):

Why do you bother me? I only have to take the exam. You gave me permission.

GOLDEN ANGEL:

Don't worry. We just wanted to remind you that you are unlawfully—

MIGRANT WORKER (*Interrupting him*):

Stop it! Don't hassle me. You gave me permission to take the exam in a week.

GOLDEN ANGEL:

Farewell!

The GOLDEN ANGEL *disappears.*

ACT 1

ELENA NECHAEVNA, MARINA ALEXANDROVNA, *and* CLAUDIA PETROVNA *in a local FMS office.*

MARINA ALEXANDROVNA (M.A.):

Elena Nechaevna, did you bring something sweet?

I asked you to bring elephant ears.

ELENA NECHAEVNA (E.N.):

Marina Alexandrovna, I despaired of meeting
You in the office here.

M.A.:

Claudia Petrovna, you are my witness.
The elephant ears were for my daughter.

E.N.:

Marina Alexandrova, did you chip in?
Your money's still sitting in your wallet.

M.A.:

As soon as you came, I'd have paid you back.

E.N.:

I took the exact amount along, without any change.

M.A.:

You, Elena Nechaevna, are nothing but a cad.

E.N.:

Claudia Petrovna, do you hear how she complains?
And why, Marina Alexandrovna, are you still in the office?

M.A.:

What, have you been tracking my whereabouts?

E.N. (*Mimicking her*):

It was you who said, "Well, I'm off now!
I have a versification test to vouch."

M.A.:

We've overdone it. I'll hit the road mañana.
The people I need are free in the morning.
(*Grumbling.*)
I ask for sweets, and she brings me nada.

E.N.:

Claudia Petrovna, did you hear that snarling?

M.A.:

She's working, not listening to our tiff.
Why don't you tell us properly
How a bore like yourself
Was demoted so suddenly?

E.N.:

Claudia Petrovna knows poetry like an ace.
She was hired to strengthen our team.
You can see her mind is like a blade.
Nowadays, knowledge is a vital meme.

M.A.:

How's that? She was canned for incompetence.
She worked in the defense industry.
It's not like here. In return for arrogance,
You lose your head, not just your salary.
Testing Tajiks on their ABCs
At the Federal Migration Service
Does not require self-esteem
Or, for that matter, tons of class.
Elena Nechaevna, do you have any cookies
To munch on with our tea?

E.N.:

Marina Alexandrovna, turn on the kettle!

M.A.:

Elena Nechaevna, as you please.

A VISITOR *enters the office.*

VISITOR:

Hello. May I?

M.A.:

This isn't a Caucasian aul.[1]

VISITOR:

I want to take the test on time.
My name, if you recall, is Moldakul.

E.N.:

Close the door! We'll call you in.

The VISITOR *leaves.* CLAUDIA PETROVNA *gives her colleagues a curious look.*

M.A.:

Claudia Petrovna, don't be a wimp.
It's not as if I've offended the man.

E.N.:

If you're not strict, they get the whiff,
Like wolves smelling a lamb.

M.A.:

This is Office No. 22, not a paddock.
We have to be a single unit.

E.N.:

You work for Project Swan, where ugly ducks
Are turned into civic cygnets.

KLAVA'S SONG

For words uttered inopportune
My military career went awry.
Now I'm employed at Project Swan.
The cosmos says what lies in store for me.

My astrologer sent me a horoscope
To help me track down my soulmate.
Here's the Cinderella Gateway, but it's eclipsed
By the shadow of Jupiter in retrograde.

The Milky Way murmurs and shines.
How can I pay back my karmic debt?
But Lilith the fake black moon
Leads us into darkness and clouds our steps.

M.A.:

Well, come in.

MOLDAKUL *enters.*

MOLDAKUL:

Moldakul is my name.
I want to sign up for the test.
I want to be a Russian national
And in Russian poetry score the best.

E.N.:

Give us the papers for your application.
Here's the list. We need everything on it.

MOLDAKUL:

Marina Alexandrovna, here is my certificate.
And here, Elena Nechaevna, is my bank statement.
It shows how much I made this year,
And how much in my account is left.
Moldakul, what a stupid hajji you are!
And I did all my medical tests.

MOLDAKUL *hands* MARINA ALEXANDROVNA *a plastic bag. We hear the sound of bottles clinking.*

MOLDAKUL:

Look in the bag at your leisure.
It's a seal from my registered address,
An ID tag given me by my super.
Let me take the poetical test.

M.A.:

Elena Nechaevna, is everything in order?

E.N. (*Peering into the bag filled with bottles*):

Marina Alexandrovna, everything is swell.

M.A.:

Claudia Petrovna, o righteous lady,
Say something at last. Well?

KLAVA (CLAUDIA PETROVNA):

Mr. Moldakul, take a chair.
You say you want to become Russian?
I've had a look at your name, sir,
And it has left me in sad confusion.
I found ten Moldakuls in our archives.
The first Moldakul is listed as a poacher.
The second was a show business shark.
The third, an opium pusher,
The fourth, a producer of contemporary art,
Or a performance artist, to put it plainly.
And you know, each one had a medical chart
About which we had no complaints.
The fifth was a pimp.
The sixth illegally downloaded films.
The seventh took a dump on Red Square.
The eighth spied for a foreign firm.
The ninth and tenth were tuberculosis carriers.
You know, Moldakul, there's a question I'd like you to hear.
What need does our country have for such slippery men?
How many needless, bitter tears
Shall the Motherland shed again? How many?

ELENA NECHAEVNA *and* MARINA ALEXANDROVNA *exchange admiring glances.* SLAVA *enters bearing flowers.*

SLAVA:

The color of the Kremlin's *étoiles,*
Ruby peonies salute ye,
O lassies who spend your days toiling
In the factory of migrant worker dreams.
Marina Alexandrovna, my lady!
Elena Nechaevna, my fair!
Quick, fill your beautiful vases
With tears of migrant worker despair.

M.A.:

Slava!

E.N.:

Vyacheslav, you are a poet, and that's that.

SLAVA:

Take it up a notch: a teacher of harmony.

INDIAN SONG FOR SLAVA AND THE PROJECT "SWAN" STAFF

SLAVA:

Who's so drunk? Who so flustered?
It is I, Vyacheslav.
Oh, speak what words you can muster,
Ye fair ladies of Project Swan.

Bring me the most utterly bitter,
Littlest lemon you can find.
In the shadow of your glitter
It shall taste like sweetest wine.

Damsels, you are in my prayers,
And I see you in my dreams.
Who's your poet? Your knight in armor?
It's Vyacheslav, it's me.

E.N. & M.A.:

Slava, Slava
Slava, Slava

E.N.:

Oh, your flowers smell so fine.

SLAVA:

In Latin, they're called Paeonia.
There's an allegory in this bouquet.
The doctor who healed the gods was Paean.
May you beautiful gals find a remedy
To your daily weariness, your federal peonage.

E.N. (*Pointing to* CLAUDIA PETROVNA):

Please meet Claudia Petrovna,
Commissar of our examination tribunal.

SLAVA:

So it was you who put Moldakul in a coma?
He is my best pupil.

KLAVA:

Sorry, I didn't know.

SLAVA:

Vyacheslav Homeland. I tutor foreigners
To answer the questions on the poetry test.
Please take pity on my deplorables,
Future citizens of our dear Swan's Nest.

KLAVA:

So you are the one who taught these unfortunates?
As Pushkin wrote, "He created us. He nurtured our flames."

SLAVA:

I earn good money.

KLAVA:

But not often.

For you're obliged to refund those who don't pass the exams.

SLAVA:

Oh yes, you're the source of my vexation.

KLAVA:

Because you and I have different aims.
You teach them childish notions,
While our exam is for graduates of lycées.

M.A.:

Get out of here!

E.N.:

In two hours, the exam commences.

KLAVA:

Fine, Vyacheslav, I'll give you a chance.
Run fetch Moldakul. Let him come to his senses
And report to the exam room with the other applicants.

M.A.:

Well, she has set her sights on Vyacheslav.

SLAVA:

Claudia Petrovna, you rule!

E.N.:

Of course, he's a first-class lad.
And the fact he has no money is even cool.

ACT 2

ELENA NECHAEVNA, MARINA ALEXANDROVNA, CLAUDIA PETROVNA, *and* MIGRANT WORKERS *in the exam room.*

E.N.:

Future citizens, come in, take your places.
In five minutes, the exam begins.

M.A.:

Remove all your electronic devices.

E.N.:

Claudia Petrovna, please come in.
MOLDAKUL (*Repeating aloud*):
Cherries are berries, ivy is jivey . . .

E.N.:

Moldakul, be quiet. That's harsh.

MOLDAKUL:

Excuse me, I'm paying my dues and catching a vibe.

M.A.:

No need to pay your dues; the test's free of charge.
The road to citizenship is elusive and long.
It's easier to pass through the eye of a needle.
Every ugly duckling, each client of Project Swan,
Can take the test and become a swan for real.

SAID SHAH (*Coming into foreground*):

I'm Said Shah, by the name of Uzbek,
Same as the famous dude I want to name check.
I was born on the Lena, my dad was in the air force.
The northern rivers were the place I was born.
I was sent to the desert by a sad twist of fate.
I'll be herding camels 'til the end of days.

The northern rivers are where I feel at home.
My dreams call me back to Russia like a telephone.

E.N.:

Dear Said Shah, what was your mom?
Tell us a bit about her in verse.

SAID SHAH:

Mom was a builder. Dad jumped in a fighter.
We returned to the desert. He vanished without a trace.

E.N.:

What is your trade, profession, or craft, Uzbek?
Why should we give you citizenship?

SAID SHAH:

By trade, I'm a house painter and plasterer,
A bit of an artist, a bit of a poet.
Here's a little sample.
I was born by the ocean
In a little white hovel,
Its walls made of porcelain.
I came outside, and what did I see?
My porcelain hovel was rubble.
I lived in the desert, not by the sea.
I headed for Moscow, farther from trouble.

M.A.:

Your house wasn't made of porcelain.
It was probably made of clay, right?

SAID SHAH:

That's right: clay.

M.A.:

And of dung too?

SAID SHAH:

That's right, dung too.

KLAVA:

And how do you like the Russian outdoors?
Do you like the Russian woods?

SAID SHAH:

I mowed dandelions for two years
At the FMS in Podolsk.

KLAVA:

Have a seat and wait for your score.

SAID SHAH:

I'm really worried.

KLAVA:

Take it easy.
Next!

MOLDAKUL:

I'm Moldakul Amalatov.
I've been living in Podolsk ten years.
I was born in the Pamir. War rages apace
While my people live for the dream of peace.
No more destruction: I want to create!
I want to build people decent houses.

KLAVA:

Moldakul, recite us a nature verse.
Compare your native saxaul to the local birch.

MOLDAKUL:

Birch trunks are dope, our saxauls are bent.
The desert wind gnarled them so fierce.

E.N.:

Talk about your family.

MOLDAKUL:

My dad's a geologist.

E.N.:

What does your mom do?

MOLDAKUL:

My mom's a cosmetologist.

E.N.:

Does she earn well?

MOLDAKUL:

They are migrant workers.
They also want to stay here awhile.

KLAVA:

Fine, Moldakul. Wait for your score.

A ROMANI WOMAN *gets up.*

KLAVA:

Ma'am, come sit here.

M.A.:

You're from Moldova?

ROMANI WOMAN:

I am the blind Octavia.

SLAVA:

I wasn't her teacher.

ROMANI WOMAN:

I taught myself.
My father was a great Romani bard.
He wrote poems and taught me in the cradle
To write to the howl of incessant February blizzards
And the loud chant of the cicadas.
I earn my keep by seeing the outcome
Of each person in time and in space.
A poet and seer of storms to come,
I offer my help in exchange for a place.
In an anxious time, the enemy at the gate,
I dream of serving as Russia's sibyl.
Mr. President, sacred Russian nation,
I want to light you up with paths celestial.

KLAVA:

Why are we letting in crazy people?

E.N.:

Because she was the only one with an invitation.

KLAVA:

From what institution?

E.N.:

From counterintelligence.

KLAVA:

You checked?

E.N.:

We checked, Claudia Petrovna.

KLAVA:

Octavia, tell me—

E.N.:

Claudia Petrovna, don't tempt destiny.

KLAVA (*Insistent*):

Octavia, could you make a prophecy?

M.A.:

It's a state secret.

KLAVA:

About me personally.

And please tell me in verse, dear blind Octavia.

ROMANI WOMAN:

Soon you'll be a homeland,
But first you shall find out
The name of your betrothed, and that
Death picks life like currants from the bough.
You shall be a homeland to many,
The only one to a prince you shall.
But if you do not marry, paranoia
Will undo your mind and you shall kill.

ELENA NECHAEVNA *suddenly grabs a razor and kills* OCTAVIA. *Everyone rushes toward her. In the ensuing struggle,* ELENA NECHAEVNA *kills everyone except* KLAVA *and* SLAVA. *The* GOLDEN ANGEL *suddenly appears, apprehends* ELENA NECHAEVNA *with a golden net, and takes her away.*

SLAVA:

The thing is my surname's Homeland.

KLAVA:

Is that important now, Homeland?

The GOLDEN ANGEL *returns.* SAID SHAH *is on his last legs. He lifts his head.*

SAID SHAH:

When I worked on Povarskaya,
I saw a dead tree, black and dry.
It was an elm from Pushkin's day.
But it was still pleasing to the eye.

He dies.

GOLDEN ANGEL (*Addressing* KLAVA):

Where were you?

KLAVA:

In this chair at this desk
In the thick of it.
(*Turning to* SLAVA.)
Slava, do you think about existence?
Or, as a poet, do you ignore it?

SLAVA:

I love life and see it as a source of inspiration.

GOLDEN ANGEL:

You sat in this chair, you confess?
We discovered traces of perspiration
On the seat and your dress.

KLAVA:

I also sat in this chair
While I was waiting for the exam to begin.
(*Addressing* SLAVA.)
Slava, loving life is quite a dare
For a poet, foe of everything mundane.

GOLDEN ANGEL:

You got up and moved to that chair?
And didn't again make a switch?

SLAVA:

Indeed, the daily grind doesn't get in my hair.

GOLDEN ANGEL:

In other chairs you had no occasion to sit?

KLAVA:

I did not.
(*Addressing* SLAVA.)
You know, Slava,
Don't call me Claudia Petrovna henceforward.
You can call me Klava.
I beg you: it is much more informal.

GOLDEN ANGEL:

You didn't move this chair by chance?

KLAVA:

I moved it slightly to one side.

SLAVA:

Permit me to call you Klava behind the curtains,
As it were, in the absence of outsiders.

GOLDEN ANGEL:

Claudia Petrovna, don't get off track.
Otherwise, our conversation won't gel.
Can you recall whether you put your jacket
On this chair from the hall?

KLAVA:

My jacket? Of course, I left it.

GOLDEN ANGEL:

And your purse? What's in your purse?

Klava (*Addressing* SLAVA):

Slava, tell me, what have you been gifted
By the art of verse?

SLAVA:

Nothing.

KLAVA:

Nothing!

GOLDEN ANGEL:

You have nothing in your bag?

KLAVA:

I have shitloads of junk!

GOLDEN ANGEL:

Claudia Petrovna, please don't be a wag.

KLAVA:

I'm not. I'm in a funk.
(*To* SLAVA.)
Slava, your answers are nonsense.

SLAVA:

Klava, I'm rather upset.

KLAVA:

I understand: blood, shouting, curses,
Pity for the innocent heroes, struck dead.

SLAVA:

Klava, for them I am truly sorry.
They came to me. I taught them tricks.
That stupid rhyme "mourning"
Or terrible prosody that sucks.
They prayed and worked hard,

They studied and raised children,
So Elena Nechaevna could spill their blood
During an exam in a faraway land.

KLAVA:

It's true, she flunked them to death!

SLAVA:

You treated them like dirt.
The Ivan Susanins at the FMS
Only show you the way to death.[2]

SLAVA *leaves.*

KLAVA (*Addressing the* GOLDEN ANGEL):

Well, now will you explain to me
What this is all about?

GOLDEN ANGEL:

In your profession, woefully,
Such cases abound.
Acute outbursts of gratuitous cruelty
Have plagued Project Swan staff.
They have come undone one by one,
Assaulting applicants during exams,
Stabbing, shooting, and strangling some.

KLAVA:

There's something nasty about the work.

GOLDEN ANGEL:

Perhaps poetry short-circuits their wires.

KLAVA:

Really? You think that verse
Will get the best of me before I retire?

ACT 3

A year has passed. The setting is SLAVA*'s house. The furnishings are not homey, suggesting the place is a barn or warehouse.* SLAVA *drinks with three guests.*

SLAVA (*Making a toast*):

Saints Peter and Fevronia Day[3] is today.
In the company of friends and with no strangers among us,
We celebrate the day of love, we mark this family holiday
With vodka flowing from our cups.
We can live out the day without meeting
A single Fevronia or a single Peter.

GUEST 1 (OCTAVIA):

Who is pictured in that portrait?

SLAVA:

The one whom it is time I should forget.

GUEST 2 (MOLDAKUL):

On a day like this we can drink to her memory.

OCTAVIA:

Leave it be. You see it's hard for him. It's better not to remember misfortunes.

SLAVA:

Shall we not make a sacrifice to memory's god? Friends, may I ask you (only don't think me mad) to resurrect my students today? (*Addressing guests.*) You'll be Said Shah, and you Moldakul.

GUEST 3 (SAID SHAH):

The guy has the shakes.

OCTAVIA:

And I'll be the beautiful Issykul.

SLAVA:

No, you shall have a different name: Octavia.

OCTAVIA (*Pointing at the portrait*):

That was your broad's name?

SLAVA:

No, Octavia was Romani.

OCTAVIA:

Fine. I'm Octavia.

SAID SHAH:

Who did you say I was?

SLAVA:

Uzbek.

SAID SHAH:

That's my ethnicity?

SLAVA:

No, it was your name when you were alive.

OCTAVIA:

Mister Uzbek!

MOLDAKUL:

Moldakul. . . . You surprise me, Slava. Fine, I'll be Moldakul, and the vodka will be koumiss.

They take a drink.

SLAVA:

Let's divide up the roles and start the exam.

MOLDAKUL:

Who's the examiner?

SLAVA:

This portrait.

OCTAVIA:

Oh, how much pain in that voice.

(*Mimicking* SLAVA.)

This portrait, this portrait . . .

SLAVA:

Moldakul, introduce yourself first.

MOLDAKUL:

Well, I'm Moldakul.

(*Pausing to think.*)

Who the heck am I?

OCTAVIA:

How much have you drunk?

SLAVA:

Quiet, Octavia.

(*Addressing* MOLDAKUL.)

You'll be asked a question, for example—

CLAUDIA PETROVNA *enters.*

KLAVA:

Moldakul, recite us a nature verse.

Compare your native saxaul to the local birch.

SLAVA:

Claudia Petrovna!

MOLDAKUL:

The gal in the painting!

SAID SHAH:

A portrait from life!

KLAVA:

As I live and breathe.

Slava, I've been looking for you for ages.

Where have you been?

SLAVA:

Klava, I went on a drinking spree.

KLAVA:

You live in such a very odd place.

What is it? Is it a garage or warehouse?

And why does poetry resound in every phrase?
In Russia, only officials speak in verse.

SLAVA:

You'll gradually learn the whole story.
We're having a séance of a kind.
This warehouse is Ethiopian territory.

SAID SHAH:

Here you're abroad and in Russia at the same time.

KLAVA:

Yes, I had to show a pass.
Were you invited here?

SLAVA:

Not here, but to Ethiopia, abroad.
My great-grandmother worked in the Russian embassy
In faraway Ethiopia,
And my great-grandfather was a prince.

MOLDAKUL:

Now you're the prince of Podolsk and Mytishchi.

KLAVA:

Oh, Slava, you told me so hilariously in anapest
About your Ethiopian parents
Right in the middle of a test at the FMS.

SLAVA:

Why have you come, Klava?

KLAVA:

Would you agree to take me as your spouse?

SLAVA:

Good Lord, of course I won't!
Why would you want me, a louse?
A country where poetry rules needs no poets.

KLAVA:

You can do it formally.
I've got money aplenty.
I can help you financially.

SAID SHAH:

Were I not an Uzbek, this would be a party.
On Peter and Fevronia's official feast
A serious woman has come to offer her hand
To a quiet drunk from the mean streets.
I'll be damned! I'll be damned!

Everyone drinks. SLAVA *is clearly drunk.*

SLAVA:

If you want my riddles to unwind,
Klava, then come and play our game.
Give the test to these titans,
Or Titanics, rather. You're an officer of the state.

KLAVA:

Does one of you want Russian papers?

SAID SHAH:

It gives us Ethiopians no end of misery.

KLAVA:

It's best to live in a superpower.

SAID SHAH:

It's best to live in a remote province by the sea.

MOLDAKUL:

Our province is particularly remote.
Although there is no sea in Ethiopia, I'd wager.

OCTAVIA:

So tell her: paradise doesn't float our boat!
Give Ethiopians their Ethiopian dinner.

KLAVA:

Slava, I won't be able to do anything with them.

SLAVA:

You had no such problems at the last exam.

KLAVA:

But those people wanted to be citizens.

SLAVA:

You're learning . . .
Other morals prevailed on that test.
This is a very important fact.
We're playing a game: luck rules the roost.
Maybe, Klava, you'll luck out.
Try again!

KLAVA:

Octavia, do you have children?
Your kids will want an education.

OCTAVIA:

Your education put my daughter in incarceration.

SLAVA:

Don't slip out of character!

OCTAVIA:

Why shouldn't I slip?
When my daughter gets out of the clinker
Then we can talk citizenship.

KLAVA:

Okay, I'll help her. Soon there's a general pardon.

SAID SHAH:

And I have no desire to fight for oil.

OCTAVIA:

And rake leaves in yards.

KLAVA:

My dear Octavia, do nothing against your will.

SLAVA:

Be a little stricter, Klava. Russia isn't made of rubber.

OCTAVIA:

Why are you turning your nose up at us?

MOLDAKUL:

When you're used to dealing with unskilled labor,
You forget how to talk with the educated class.

SLAVA:

You noticed how smoothly he raps?
It's not for nothing. A tycoon's
Paying him a tidy sum to teach him the knack
Of speaking poetically in the Duma.
These cats are also from the poetry cluster.

KLAVA:

So all of you are poets!

SLAVA:

Trust me, the taste of these folks is swish.
They don't teach poetry to furniture dusters,
But to the wives of moneybags who can dish.

MOLDAKUL:

Slava is a romantic, turning slaves into rhymers.
Here, the two of us are the only poets.
Poetry is like a comet in the sky.
Your citizenship has nothing on it.

SLAVA:

Do you still remember the feeling of compassion?
Poets call us to be merciful to the slain.
Moldakul and Uzbek, now part of the Russian
Soil, would have pitied you or, rather, what remains.

KLAVA:

You don't feel sorry for me?

SLAVA:

Tell me, whatever for?
Yes, I feel as sorry for you as I would for a pet cat
Who jumps from the tenth floor
And, sadly, is smashed pancake flat.
So I believe the poetic word
Improves and refines anyone.
It's now less at home among the empowered
Than among Tajiks and Uzbeks with brooms.

MOLDAKUL:

He's on a sentimental trip. He'll now recall
How his students were remarkable.
But they are the ones who sell
Anything but their brains on the market.
They enjoy all the benefits
Only language can vouchsafe,
While Russia, since they are citizens,
Will have to triple their pay.
What's the profit in that?

KLAVA:

None at all.

SAID SHAH:

I am still entirely befuddled
Who is cajoling whom: we her or she us?
As for telling me about work, don't take the trouble.
You'd better explain where you're asking us to go.

MOLDAKUL:

How's the weather?

SAID SHAH:

How much are potatoes?

MOLDAKUL:

How much is whiskey?

SAID SHAH:

Tell me about the scenery,
For I'm uneducated and frisky.

KLAVA:

Amid white flax and black oil
The peoples of Russia live amicably as one.
Serving them faithfully and loyally
Are the gray wolf and white swan.
Cornflowers blossom in their wheat,
And, hard on the heels of vegetal joy,
The basilisks blaze and flash with heat
In their fields of natural gas and oil.

SLAVA:

Marry me, Klava!

ACT 4

KLAVA *and* SLAVA *outside the registry office.*

KLAVA:

I've been doing the paperwork. I've been all over the place.
The housing authority and the Bureau of Poetic Translation—
I cannot stop, I'm speaking in verse—
Everywhere you're a problem, a source of consternation.
The housing authority didn't want to give their blessing,
Because I didn't have your baptism certificate copy,
And you're registered in nonresidential premises
Belonging to the Embassy of Ethiopia.
The Bureau of Poetic Translation
Translated your birth certificate from trochees to dactyls.
Our freedom will soon suffer termination,
And we'll start living as married adults.

SLAVA:

Can you imagine? I ran into Moldakul’s son.

KLAVA:

The son of your pupil?

SLAVA:

Yes. They’re deporting him to Tajikistan.
I think for now I’ll register him at my domicile.

KLAVA:

Slava, that is a noble thing to do.
Who’s last in line for Office Twenty-Three?
We’re after you. Oh, how I hate red-taped hullabaloo,
The quibbles and tricks of uniformed banshees,
Their repulsive rhymes. It’s gotten better at work.
Hatred no longer eclipses rationality.
But the poems of Russian female state clerks
Make me mad and furious immediately.
Excuse me, may we come in?

FEMALE REGISTRY OFFICE CLERK (OCTAVIA):

Come in, friends.
Filing an application? Our server is down.
Can you come back tomorrow?

KLAVA:

No, tomorrow won’t do.

OCTAVIA:

Oh, I see you’re in a rush. So many papers.

KLAVA:

Yes, thirty references from the consulate and the embassy.

OCTAVIA:

Then which of you is the foreigner?

SLAVA:

I am the prisoner of Russian hospitality.
My parents were diplomatic workers.

I was born in one land, registered in another.
Later, they were convicted as wreckers.[4]
Now paperwork is a perennial bother.
I was raised by an Ethiopian, my first cousin once removed.
What are you looking at? I've chosen the right game.
Swan's Nest has forced its intellectuals to go on the move,
But diplomacy and poetry are in my veins.

OCTAVIA:

But you chose the latter, perchance.
Claudia Petrovna, are we marrying a bard?
For love? It looks like a mésalliance.
As a foreigner, he should tone it down a tad.
And you will have to—

SLAVA:

What's wrong with me?

OCTAVIA:

And you will have to—

SLAVA:

As if I've had previous convictions!

OCTAVIA:

And you will have to—

SLAVA:

There is no such decree!

OCTAVIA:

—take the poetic compatibility examination.
I'm initiating the procedure without further ado.
Recite poems about the Russian woods, the ancient oak groves,
About the great Russian outdoors,
And the birch, our white Russian betrothed.

KLAVA (*Screams*):

Ughghgh!

SLAVA:

Klava, get a grip on yourself.
Let's try and do this together, okay?
(*He begins to recite.*)
Motley woodpeckers took to tapping
In the evenings in the grove.

KLAVA:

The crowns of trees were crimson and gold.

SLAVA:

Autumn had arrived, obviously.
While in winter white, giant crows
Cawed on the black boughs plaintively.

KLAVA:

The sky and snowbanks took on a bluish tone.

SLAVA:

Brooks dashed amid the roots of trees.
Let the sap of birches touch the soul.

KLAVA:

Nightingales warbled in the breeze.

SLAVA AND KLAVA'S DUET

KLAVA:

Slava, do your words have a simple meaning?
You love and want to marry me, you say.
For simplicity is worse than stealing.
Simplicity is, therefore, a lie.

SLAVA:

Klava, my words are complicated,
So terribly complicated they are.
But if they are articulated,
The heart freezes, it slows to a crawl.

KLAVA:

The road winds amid the fields,
Among the woods and leas.
Poetry thrives only among people.
Love lives between you and me.

SLAVA:

Among the woods and lakes
The road winds: drive quickly.
This time you're not mistaken.
My Homeland you shall be.

ACT 5

CLAUDIA PETROVNA *and* TWO NEW FEMALE EMPLOYEES *(played by the same actresses as in acts 1 and 2) in the FMS office.*

ELENA VALERYEVNA:

Ekaterina Vasilyevna, have you brought something sweet?

EKATERINA VASILYEVNA (KATYA):

Yes, on the corner there were fresh biscuits.

ELENA VALERYEVNA:

One geezer left me a box of treats.
I signed him up for the test.

EKATERINA VASILYEVNA (KATYA):

Elena Valeryevna, put on the kettle.
Claudia Petrovna, will you take tea with us?

KLAVA:

Definitely, ladies, it's been put to the test.
Tea does worlds of good for the FMS.

MOLDAKUL'S SON, *also named* MOLDAKUL, *enters, carrying flowers.*

MOLDAKUL:

Comrade Homeland, my respects.

KLAVA:

Oh, Moldakul, welcome. To what do we owe the honor?
You got citizenship for your poetic text.

MOLDAKUL:

I'm here unofficially, on a personal matter.
I'm here to see Katya. (*Gives her flowers.*) Hello, Katya.
Are you ready to go for a hike?

EKATERINA VASILYEVNA (KATYA):

I'll just have a cuppa.

MOLDAKUL:

I shall wait outside.

EKATERINA VASILYEVNA (KATYA):

Claudia Petrovna, may Moldakul stay?

KLAVA:

Stay, Moldakul, and have some tea.

MOLDAKUL:

Tea? Gladly.

FINAL TEATIME SONG

CLAUDIA PETROVNA:

How does Russia resemble sunlight?

EKATERINA VASILYEVNA:

I think I can make a conjecture.

ELENA VALERYEVNA:

You mean you can get the answer right?

EKATERINA VASILYEVNA:

I mean the years in light years.

CLAUDIA PETROVNA:

It's not the same thing, Katyusha.

NOTES

INTRODUCTION

1. Konstantin Stanislavski, *My Life in Art*, trans. Jean Benedetti (New York: Routledge, 2008), 166.
2. Qtd. in Jean Benedetti, *Stanislavski: An Introduction* (New York: Routledge, 1982), 17. As Benedetti explains, in his later years, Stanislavski drew a distinction between realism and mere naturalism: whereas naturalism implied an indiscriminate reproduction of the surface of life, realism, for Stanislavski, was increasingly concerned with "the relationships and tendencies lying under the surface," the revelation of which makes possible greater truth in scenic action (p. 17).
3. The first two quotes are from Mikhail Ugarov, "Krasota pogubit mir! Manifest 'novoi dramy,'" *Iskusstvo kino*, no. 2 (2004), http://old.kinoart.ru/archive/2004/02/n2-article15; the second two are from a proposed manifesto for the documentary theater Teatr.doc, qtd. in Il'mira Bolotian, "'Dok' and 'Dogma': Teoriia i praktika," *Teatr*, no. 19 (2015): 131. The last statement is Teatr.doc's motto, which may also be translated as "a theater where no one plays games [*ne igraiut*]."
4. For *chernukha* as a distinct mode of "noir" writing in the post-Soviet period, see Eliot Borenstein, *Overkill: Sex and Violence in Contemporary Russia* (Ithaca, NY: Cornell University Press, 2007).
5. Andrei Zhdanov, "Soviet Literature: The Richest in Ideas, the Most Advanced Literature," in *Problems of Soviet Literature: Reports and Speeches at the First Soviet Writers' Congress*, ed. H. F. Scott (New York: International Publishers, 1935), 22.

6. See, for example, John Freedman, "Contemporary Russian Drama: The Journey from Stagnation to a Golden Age," *Theatre Journal* 62, no. 3 (October 2010): 389–420. Freedman edited the first and, at the time of writing, only other anthology of New Drama in English, titled *Real and Phantom Pains: An Anthology of New Russian Drama* (Washington, DC: New Academia Publishing, 2014).
7. John Freedman, "Russian Theater in the Twenty-First Century: A Critic's Journal," *Theater* 36, no. 1 (2006): 5.
8. Birgit Beumers and Mark Lipovetsky, *Performing Violence: Literary and Theatrical Experiments of New Russian Drama* (Bristol and Chicago: Intellect Ltd., 2009), 28.
9. *Chitki*, often followed by discussion, were first popularized at the Lyubimovka festival as a practical and cost-effective format for introducing new plays. They have since become an important theatrical genre, giving rise to a kind of "*chitka* aesthetic" that conveys a powerful sense of immediacy and rawness, while forcing actors to take a more distanced position vis-à-vis their characters.
10. We borrow the term "postdocumentary" from Zara Abdullaeva's study *Postdok: igrovoe/neigrovoe* (Moscow: NLO, 2011).
11. Pryazhko is one of several playwrights from the former Soviet republics whose works have been central to New Drama. Other notable figures include Ukrainian playwrights Anna Yablonaskaya and Natalia Vorozhbit. Although we follow earlier translators and critics in referring to the movement as New Russian Drama, we want to stress that the word *Russian* here denotes linguistic rather than strictly national ties. In Russian, the movement is usually simply called *novaia drama* (new drama).
12. Pavel Rudnev, *Drama pamiati: ocherki rossiiskoi dramaturgii. 1950–2010-e* (Moscow: NLO, 2018), 412.
13. As the Fomenko Workshop Theater's uproarious production showed, directors will be well advised to take seriously the play's subtitle "A Comedy in One Act."
14. On postdramatic theater, see Hans-Thies Lehmann, *Postdramatic Theatre*, trans. Karen Jürs-Munby (New York: Routledge, 2006). A Russian translation was published in 2013, prompting heated debate among Russian theater makers and critics.
15. Russian film especially has been rejuvenated by the works of playwrights like the Presnyakov Brothers, Ivan Vyrypaev, and Vassily Sigarev, but New Drama's influence also extends to poetry and even graphic art. See, for instance, Andrei Rodionov's poetry collection *Novaia dramaturgiia* (Moscow: NLO, 2010) and Viktoria Lomasko's recently translated collection of guerrilla journalism *Other Russias* (New York: n+1 Books, 2017).
16. Rudnev, *Drama pamiati*, 257.
17. This figure is cited by Nika Parkhomovskaia in "Prolog: 2008–2012: teatral'nye innovatsii v deistviia," *Teatr*, no. 32 (December 2017): 20. Only five years earlier, in 2009, the number of such productions had been 17 percent; see *Rasporiazhenie Pravitel'stva Rossiiskoi Federatsii ot 10.06.2011 N 1019-r* ("O kontseptsii razvitiia teatral'nogo dela v Rossiiskoi Federatsii na period do 2020 goda"), http://rulaws.ru/goverment/Rasporyazhenie-Pravitelstva-RF-ot-10.06.2011-N-1019-r . These statistics only cover Russian state theaters.

18. Qtd. in Rudnev, *Drama pamiati*, 232.
19. Kirill Kobrin, *Postsovetskii mavzolei proshlogo* (Moscow: NLO, 2017), 18.

PLASTICINE

1. Adapted for American audiences by Maksim Hanukai and Susanna Weygandt.
2. Several characters who appear or are mentioned in the play have meaningful nicknames: Sedoy means "gray haired," Dlinny means "long," Bulka means "bread bun," and Bogatka derives from the word *bogatyi* or "rich."

PLAYING THE VICTIM

1. Adapted for American audiences by Maksim Hanukai and Susanna Weygandt.

SEPTEMBER.DOC

1. On September 1, 2004, hundreds of children and parents were attending the first day of school in Beslan, Russia, when a group of armed militants, mostly Islamist Ingush and Chechen fighters, attacked the school, taking over 1,100 people hostage. On the third day of the siege, Russian forces stormed the building and, firing at random while rockets flew into the school, killed many hostages attempting to escape, leading to the deaths of hundreds. The official and unofficial accounts of the Beslan events differ widely and remain highly controversial. Independent and state-sponsored investigations continue to this day. For this play, playwrights Elena Gremina and Mikhail Ugarov compiled comments posted in internet blogs, chat rooms, and forums in the weeks following the Beslan school siege. The present translation is based on the script used for the June 23, 2005 premiere of the play and published in Teatr.doc's 2016 anthology *P'esy: Sbornik vazhnykh dlia nas tekstov za vse 14 let teatra*.
2. "Martyr."
3. "Satan."
4. Plaza in Grozny.
5. The pose of prostration in prayer.
6. "God willing."
7. A special police unit within the National Guard of Russia, somewhat comparable to U.S. SWAT units. The OMON played a key role in the Chechen Wars in the 1990s and 2000s.
8. "God is perfect."
9. "Faith."

10. "Creed."
11. "Jihadist martyr."
12. Movsar Baraev was a key figure in the Second Chechen War. In 2002, he was among the leaders of the siege at the Dubrovka Theater in Moscow (an event also known as the Nord-Ost siege).
13. Mosque or congregation.
14. Originally *khach*, a derogatory term for North Caucasus people that stems from the common Armenian first name Khachik.
15. Possibly implying that the writer is part of an organization—religious or paramilitary.
16. "I seek protection (within God)."
17. Translation of a hadith from Ibn Asaakir.
18. *Churka* literally means "block of wood"; it is a derogatory term for people from the Caucasus or Central Asia.
19. A Russian special forces unit under the command of the FSB.

THE BROTHERS CH.

1. This play draws on letters by Anton and Alexander Chekhov, the memoirs of Alexander and Mikhail Chekhov, and the diary of Pavel Egorovich Chekhov. It also makes use of motifs from Anton Chekhov's *Ivanov, Uncle Vanya, The Seagull, Three Years, My Life,* "A Joke," *The Duel,* and other works. [*Author.*]
2. A popular humor magazine published by Nikolai Leykin to which Chekhov contributed more than 250 stories in the 1880s.
3. Fyodor Osipovich Schechtel (1859–1926) was a Russian architect, graphic artist, and stage designer; Pavel Mikhailovich Tretyakov (1832–1898) was a Russian businessman, art patron, collector, and philanthropist who, together with his brother Sergei Mikhailovich Tretyakov, co-founded the Tretyakov Gallery in Moscow.
4. A reference to *The Firefighter,* a journal dedicated to firefighting in Russia that Alexander Chekhov edited in 1892.
5. One of Alexander's pen names.
6. A paraphrase of Romans 2:12.
7. One of the many pen names that Chekhov used in the 1880s.
8. Zabelin was the last name of a landowner from Zvenigorod—a town in the Moscow region—who was known to be an alcoholic. Chekhov briefly worked in a hospital in Zvenigorod and visited the town often thereafter.
9. In the original, Gremina writes *v sebe samoi*—an unexpected shift to the feminine gender. The line is taken verbatim from Act One of *The Seagull.*

THE BLUE MACHINIST

1. The Russian title, *Sinii slesar'*, plays on the double meaning of *sinii*, which means "blue," but is also a slang term for "drunk."
2. This is a neologism meant to evoke the word *machine*.
3. AutoVAZ is an automobile manufacturer based in Tolyatti, Russia, best known for producing Soviet cars such as the Zhiguli and today manufacturing the Lada car brand.

THE LOCKED DOOR

1. *KVN*, which stands for *Klub vesiolykh i nakhodchivykh* (or "Club of the Funny and Inventive People"), is a long-running Russian TV show in which teams compete by giving funny answers to questions and coming up with comedy sketches. One such team was led by Feodor Dvinyatin, who is mentioned shortly.
2. *Grazhdanskaia oborona*, a Russian psychedelic and punk rock band that existed from 1987 until the death of its band leader Yegor Letov in 2008.

SOMNAMBULISM

1. Russian television personality Andrey Malakhov in the original. Malakhov hosts a show, *Let Them Talk*, on which guests broach personal and social issues.
2. Prior to 2007, high school students in Russia could choose to leave with a certificate after the ninth grade, which allowed them to enter a vocational school and not a regular college. In 2007, eleven-year secondary education in Russia became compulsory.
3. "Royal" was a popular brand of strong alcohol sold in the 1990s in post-Soviet countries.
4. Vyacheslav Butusov (b. 1961) used to be the lead singer for the Russian rock group Nautilus Pompilius; Alexander Bashlachev (1960–1988) was a Soviet poet, songwriter, and rock musician.
5. Slava is alluding to a song by Russian rock band Chizh & Co.
6. Lenin's Testament refers to a document either written or dictated by an ailing Lenin that outlines proposed changes to Soviet governance. It suggests that Stalin be removed from his position as General Secretary of the Russian Communist Party's Central Committee. The document was made available to the party after Lenin's death in 1924 and its distribution was limited. Stalin consolidated his position as leader of the Communist Party and Soviet Union regardless. Under his leadership, referring to Lenin's Testament was punishable as anti-Soviet agitation.

7. MMM was a Russian company that led one of the largest Ponzi schemes of all time in the 1990s.
8. Viktor Tsoi (1962–1990) was the lead singer of the popular late Soviet rock band Kino.
9. The Young Pioneers (1922–1991) was a mass youth organization in the former USSR. It provided children from nine to fifteen years of age with social cooperation skills and included publicly funded summer camps. The Young Pioneer motto was "Always Ready!"
10. This is a reference to Alexander Griboyedov's (1795–1829) play *Woe from Wit*, written in 1823 and published in full in 1861. It was compulsory reading in Soviet schools and the title remains a catchphrase.

PROJECT "SWAN"

1. Pronounced "ah-OOL," a type of fortified mountain village found throughout the Caucasus region.
2. Ivan Susanin was a serf who became a Russian national hero. In the winter of 1613, he tricked a regiment of Polish soldiers to follow him in the opposite direction from the hideout of the young tsar Mikhail Romanov. After sending a messenger to warn the tsar of looming danger, he led the soldiers to a nearby marsh, at which point he was found out, tortured, and killed.
3. Peter and Fevronia are the Russian Orthodox patron saints of marriage. A holiday in their honor, also known as the Day of Family, Love, and Faithfulness, was adopted in 2008 as an alternative to Valentine's Day, which has become popular in post-Soviet Russia. Saints Peter and Fevronia Day is celebrated on July 8 but is entirely ignored by the vast majority of Russians.
4. So-called wreckers (*vrediteli*) were a special category of loosely defined saboteurs and underminers, as defined by Soviet criminal law during the Stalin era. They were often sentenced to death and shot.

ABOUT THE AUTHORS

Vassily Sigarev (b. 1977) grew up in Upper Salda, a small industrial town 100 miles north of Yekaterinburg. In 1997 he enrolled at the Yekaterinburg Theater Institute, where he studied playwriting under Nikolai Kolyada. Three years later he received the Debut Prize for *Plasticine,* which premiered at the Lyubimovka festival in a rowdy production directed by Kirill Serebrennikov. The play became Sigarev's calling card. Within a few years, it was translated into several languages and staged in a number of European theaters, including the Royal Court Theatre in London. Sigarev further solidified his reputation with plays like *Phantom Pains* (2001) and *Ladybird* (2003), but turned to screenwriting and directing with *Wolfy* (2009), which was soon followed by *Living* (2012) and *The Land of Oz* (2015). All three films won major awards in Russia and abroad. Sigarev lives in Yekaterinburg with his wife, the actress Yana Troyanova.

Oleg and Vladimir Presnyakov (b. 1969 and 1974), also known as the Presnyakov Brothers, hail from Yekaterinburg. Both brothers received doctoral degrees from Ural State University—Oleg specialized in Russian literature, Vladimir in pedagogy—and held teaching positions at their alma mater before devoting themselves more fully to writing. Wide acclaim came with *Playing the Victim* (2001) and *Terrorism* (2002), both of which were staged by Kirill Serebrennikov at the Moscow Art Theater. *Playing the Victim* exists in two different versions: the original version published in the journal *Sovremennaia dramaturgiia* (2002) and a revised version first published in the Presnyakovs' collection *The Best* (2005). Although in our view the 2002 version is actually "better"—among other things, it contains a number of plot elements linking the play to *Hamlet*—for reasons of copyright and convenience we are here reprinting Sasha Dugdale's translation of the more recent version, which was originally commissioned for the Royal Court Theatre and which we have adapted for an American audience. *Playing the Victim* exists in two additional versions: as a film and a novel.

Elena Gremina (1956–2018) and **Mikhail Ugarov** (1956–2018) were towering figures on the Russian theater scene when they passed away, less than two months apart, in the spring of 2018. Both had been involved in promoting contemporary playwriting from the early 1990s, organizing myriad workshops, laboratories, and festivals and, most importantly, founding Teatr.doc—a small independent theater specializing in documentary plays. Among the documentary plays staged at Teatr.doc were Gremina's *One Hour, Eighteen Minutes* (2005), about the death of the whistleblower Sergei Magnitsky, and *Akyn-Opera* (2012), a show about migrant workers from Central Asia. However, the theater also stages more traditional "literary" plays, as well as experimental postdramatic works, making it one of the best venues for learning about the latest trends in Russian theater and playwriting. The two plays featured here showcase the artistic versatility of these two artists. *September.doc* deals with the aftermath of a horrific terrorist act in the North Ossetian town of Beslan and is made entirely out of posts culled from internet chat rooms, blogs, and forums; it premiered in 2005 at Teatr.doc (dir. Mikhail Ugarov and Ruslan Malikov). Although partly documentary in nature, *The Brothers Ch.* is a more conventional family drama about the Chekhov family; it premiered in 2010 at the Stanislavski Drama Theater (dir. Alexander Galibin) as part of celebrations marking Chekhov's 150-year anniversary.

Mikhail Durnenkov (b. 1976) grew up in the Russian Far East before moving, as a teenager, to the industrial town of Tolyatti. He was working as an engineer in a car factory upon graduating from the Tolyatti Polytechnic Institute when, "out of boredom," he decided to join Vadim Levanov's Golosova-20 theater as an actor and student in his "guild of playwrights." On Levanov's suggestion, he co-wrote a play about Tolyatti with his brother, the playwright Vyacheslav Durnenkov. The play was featured at Lyubimovka. Since then, Durnenkov has become a mainstay of the New Drama movement thanks to his prolific work as a playwright, screenwriter, teacher, and co-organizer of Lyubimovka. His plays, including *Trash* (2009) and *The War Has Not Yet Started* (2016), have been translated into multiple languages and staged in a number of theaters in Russia and abroad. *The Blue Machinist* emerged from a series of "machinist haikus" about Durnenkov's experience working in a car factory. It premiered at Teatr.doc in 2007 (dir. Mikhail Ugarov and Ruslan Malikov).

Pavel Pryazhko (b. 1975) is the Belarusian author of more than twenty plays (or, as he prefers to call them, "texts"), the radically experimental nature of which has earned him as many admirers as critics. It is often said that language is the main hero of his plays, and indeed Pryazhko has an uncanny ability to record the way Russian is spoken in everyday, seemingly undramatic circumstances. Just as important, however, is Pryazhko's pursuit of new *theatrical* languages, which sometimes leads him to sacrifice words, the traditional building blocks of drama, for other forms of communication. He pares down a full-length play to just over a dozen words, allows dialogue to be swallowed up by stage directions, replaces words with photos or music. The resulting works are not simply postdramatic; they are, at times, postverbal, requiring very particular directorial and acting talents to realize them on stage. Fortunately, Pryazhko has found a more than capable collaborator in the St. Petersburg director Dmitry Volkostrelov. *The Locked Door* was staged by Volkostrelov in 2011 during the "ON.TEATR" directing laboratory in St. Petersburg; *The Soldier* also premiered in 2011, at Teatr.doc, in a production that lasted only five minutes. Pryazhko lives in his hometown of Minsk, Belarus, and largely avoids public appearances.

Ivan Vyrypaev (b. 1974) is perhaps New Drama's most internationally recognized playwright. Originally from Irkutsk, where in 1998 he founded his own theater studio, Play Space, he later became a founding member of Teatr.doc, making an immediate splash in 2002 with his "modern gospel" play *Oxygen*. To date, he has written seventeen plays, among them *July* (2006), *Delhi Dance* (2009), *Illusions* (2011), and *DREAMWORKS* (2011). His plays are regularly staged at the Moscow Art Theater, the Tovstonogov Bolshoi Drama Theater, the Meyerhold Center, and Praktika. Many of them have also been translated and staged around the world at venues such as the Baryshnikov Art Center in New York and the Avignon Theater Festival in France. Vyrypaev is also one of Russia's most important and controversial film directors. He has adapted several of his plays for film, winning awards at the Venice Film Festival for *Euphoria* and the Kinotavr festival for *Oxygen*. From 2013 to 2016 he was the artistic director of the Praktika Theater in Moscow. In 2015 he published an article in *Izvestiia* newspaper blasting the Russian culture minister's call for more patriotism in publicly funded art. Shortly thereafter, Vyrypaev moved to Warsaw, where he now lives with his wife, the Polish actress Karolina Gruszka. *Summer Wasps Sting in November, Too* premiered at the Pyotr Fomenko Workshop Theater in Moscow in 2013 (dir. Sigrid Strøm Reibo).

Yaroslava Pulinovich (b. 1987) is a prolific young playwright from Omsk, southwest Siberia, who studied in Yekaterinburg under Nikolai Kolyada. She won initial notice for *The Carnival of Cherished Desires* (2005) and *The Chemistry Teacher* (2006), but true recognition came with the twin plays *Natasha's Dream* (2008) and *I Won* (2009), which have been staged in several theaters in Russia and abroad. Both plays are included in John Freedman's anthology *Real and Phantom Pains*. Pulinovich also writes screenplays: *I Won't Come Back* (2014), directed by Ilmar Raag, received a special jury mention at the Tribeca Film Festival and won the Mirror Award at the Andrei Tarkovsky International Film Festival. *Somnambulism* premiered in Romanian translation at the B-Critic Cultural Center in Bucharest in 2016 (dir. Alexandru Mâzgăreanu); the Russian premiere took place in 2018 at the Chekhov Theater in Yekaterinburg (dir. Yulia Baturina).

Andrei Rodionov (b. 1971) is a leading Russian poet and organizer of slam- and video-poetry festivals who is best known for his "rap ballads" that document the lives of marginal individuals and social groups. He is the author of several collections of poetry, including *Toys for the Outskirts*, *People with Hopelessly Antiquated Professions*, and *Bestial Style*, and has won major literary awards, including the Andrei Bely Prize and the Triumph Prize. In recent years, Rodionov has begun to collaborate with his wife **Ekaterina Troepolskaya** (b. 1982), a festival curator and journalist who currently serves as the director of the Dmitry Brusnikin Theater Workshop. Together the couple has already written several satirical verse plays, a screenplay, and a libretto, which were collected in the ironically titled volume *Optimism: Poetic Plays* (*Optimizm: poeticheskie p'esy*, 2017). *Project "Swan"* premiered under the title *SWAN* at the Meyerhold Center in 2015 (dir. Yury Kvyatovsky).

R

RUSSIAN LIBRARY

Between Dog and Wolf by Sasha Sokolov, translated by Alexander Boguslawski

Strolls with Pushkin by Andrei Sinyavsky, translated by Catharine Theimer Nepomnyashchy and Slava I. Yastremski

Fourteen Little Red Huts and Other Plays by Andrei Platonov, translated by Robert Chandler, Jesse Irwin, and Susan Larsen

Rapture: A Novel by Iliazd, translated by Thomas J. Kitson

City Folk and Country Folk by Sofia Khvoshchinskaya, translated by Nora Seligman Favorov

Writings from the Golden Age of Russian Poetry by Konstantin Batyushkov, presented and translated by Peter France

Found Life: Poems, Stories, Comics, a Play, and an Interview by Linor Goralik, edited by Ainsley Morse, Maria Vassileva, and Maya Vinokur

Sisters of the Cross by Alexei Remizov, translated by Roger John Keys and Brian Murphy

Sentimental Tales by Mikhail Zoshchenko, translated by Boris Dralyuk

Redemption by Friedrich Gorenstein, translated by Andrew Bromfield

The Man Who Couldn't Die: The Tale of an Authentic Human Being by Olga Slavnikova, translated by Marian Schwartz

Necropolis by Vladislav Khodasevich, translated by Sarah Vitali

Nikolai Nikolaevich and Camouflage: Two Novellas by Yuz Aleshkovsky, translated by Duffield White, edited by Susanne Fusso

A Double Life by Karolina Pavlova, translated and with an introduction by Barbara Heldt

Klotsvog by Margarita Khemlin, translated by Lisa Hayden

If you say, "He's a Russian, thus a poet,"
It's not the same as "He's a poet, thus a Russian."
Do you understand the difference or not?

EKATERINA VASILYEVNA:

Claudia Petrovna, here's what I've divined.
Yesterday, I had a visit from a village elder.
I tested him on his poetry lines.
I invited him to drink tea after.
I offered him sugar. The old man grew serious.
"I must refuse it, but there's sweetness aplenty,
For the FMS is like molasses,
For the FMS is like honey."

MOLDAKUL:

I've understood something about my new country.
Katya and I were recently traveling by car one evening,
And this was what I felt, Comrade Homeland.

We were driving in the forest's gloomy shade.
You looked at me, I looked out the window.
Hungover and espying a little lane in the glade,
I sighed and whispered, "A Russian road."

"All you Russians are that way," you said sadly.
"What is the enigma of your strange instinct?
Why not say it quietly and plainly?
Why is that lane of yours so Russian and distinct?

"In English gardens, the Congo's jungles
Brazil's rainforests, and the Australian bush,
No one would ever think to smuggle
In a residence permit, even were he sloshed.

"What made you decide the path was Russian?
Was it really 'cause it was chockablock
With your Russian shit? With bags of rubbish,
Crumpled cups, and broken bottles?"

I sadly held my tongue. No, you don't comprehend,
Stupid foreign woman—this is the Russian wood—
Because I have turned down the path to heaven,
While you languish and despair in the world.

I turned off, vanishing with a quiet, cheerful air.
But come looking for me if you're so dull.
The joy on my path is weird,
But the sweet path leads straight to hell.

The black forest fell silent, like lovers in the trance
That ensues after their commotion.
Black colonels stand guard at the entrance.
No offense, but they too are Russian.

THE END